Art:
Asahiro Kakashi
Original Story:
Okina Baba
Character Design:
Tsukasa Kiryu

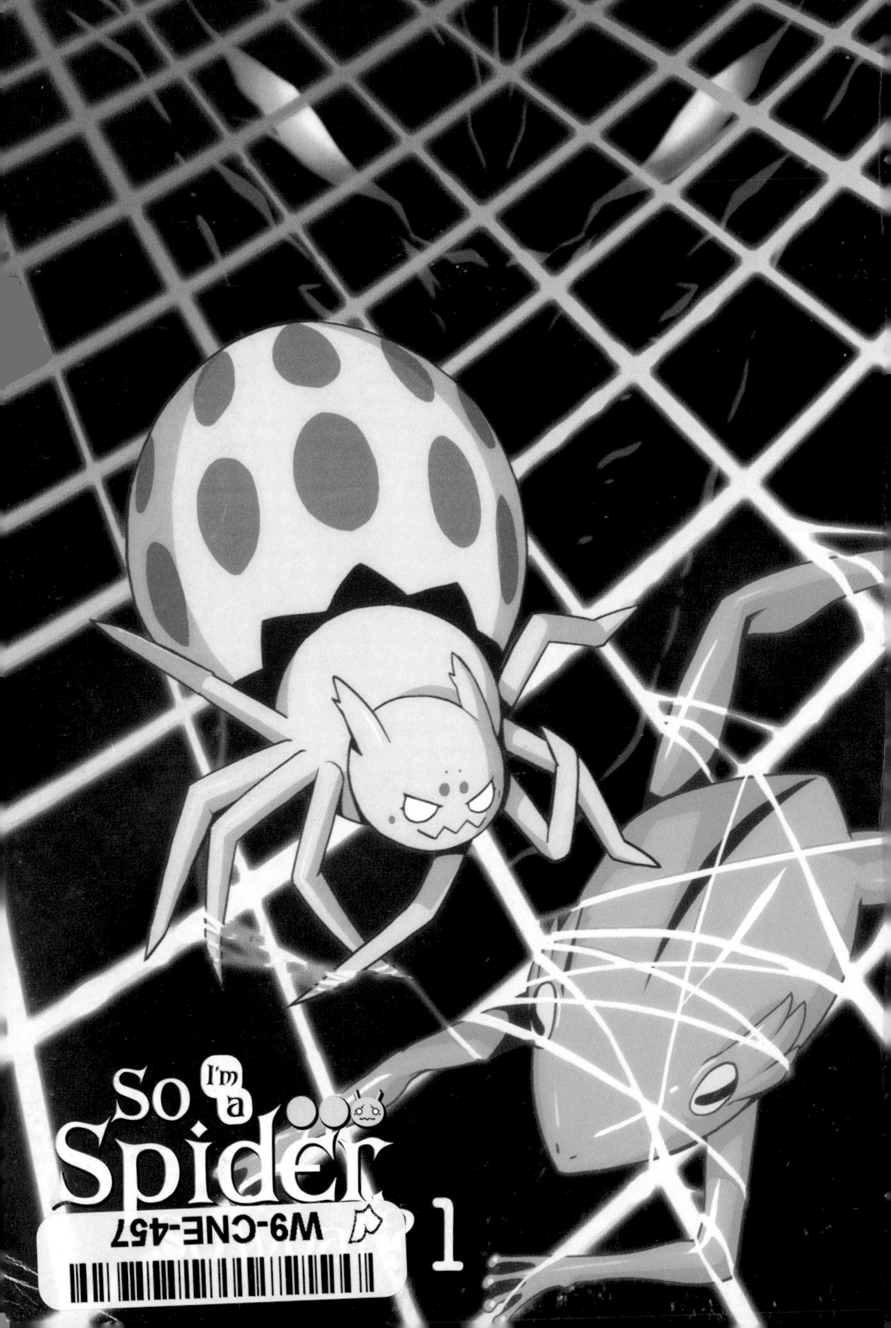
So I'm a Spider, So What?
1

So I'm a Spider, So What?

CONTENTS

So I'm a Spider, So What?

0

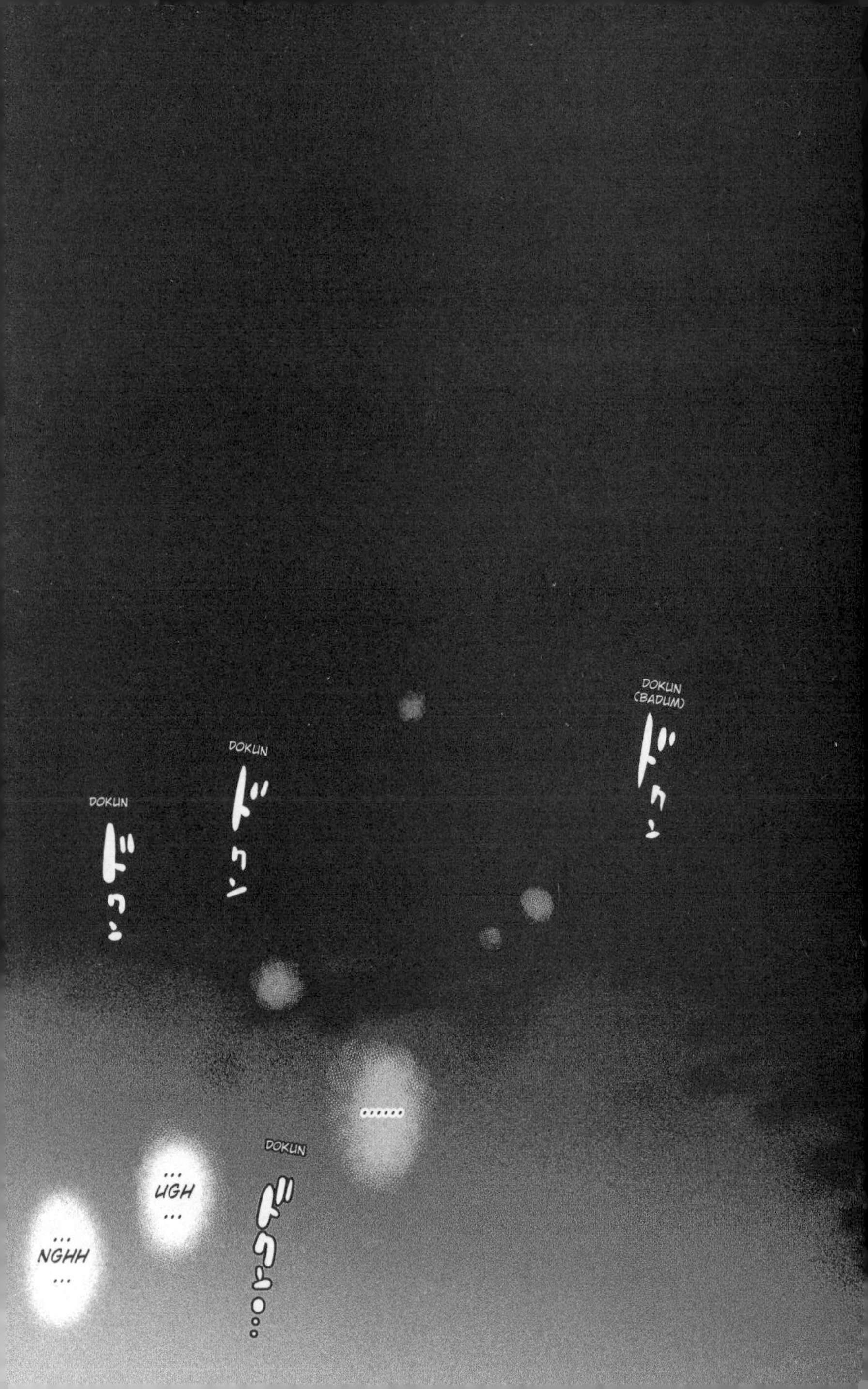
DOKUN (BADUM)
ドクン
DOKUN
ドクン
DOKUN
ドクン
......
DOKUN
ドクン...
...UGH...
...NGHH...

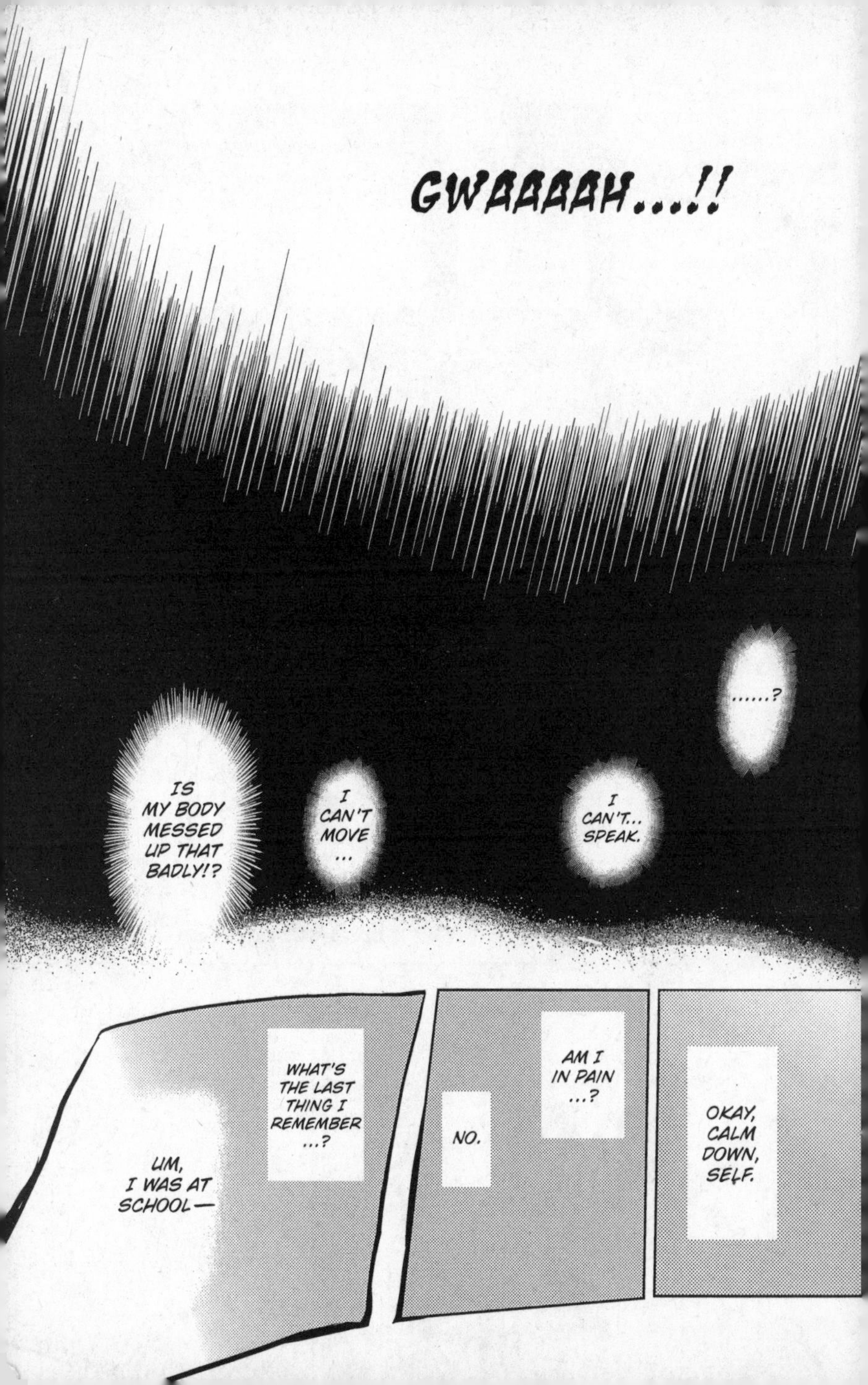
GWAAAAH...!!
......?
I CAN'T... SPEAK.
I CAN'T MOVE ...
IS MY BODY MESSED UP THAT BADLY!?
OKAY, CALM DOWN, SELF.
AM I IN PAIN ...?
NO.
WHAT'S THE LAST THING I REMEMBER ...?
UM, I WAS AT SCHOOL—

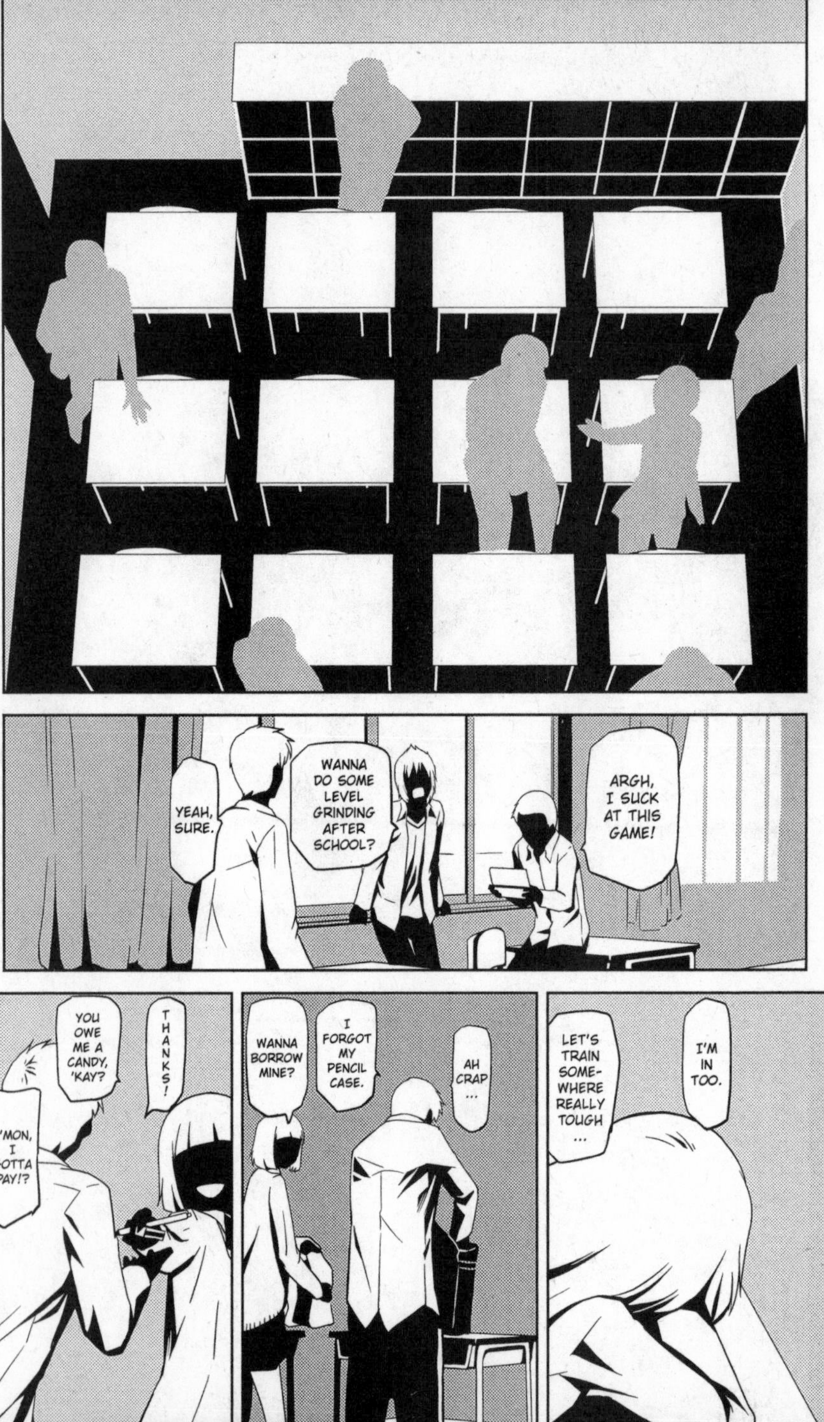
ARGH, I SUCK AT THIS GAME!
WANNA DO SOME LEVEL GRINDING AFTER SCHOOL?
YEAH, SURE.
I'M IN TOO.
LET'S TRAIN SOME-WHERE REALLY TOUGH ...
AH CRAP ...
I FORGOT MY PENCIL CASE.
WANNA BORROW MINE?
THANKS!
YOU OWE ME A CANDY, 'KAY?
C'MON, I GOTTA PAY!?

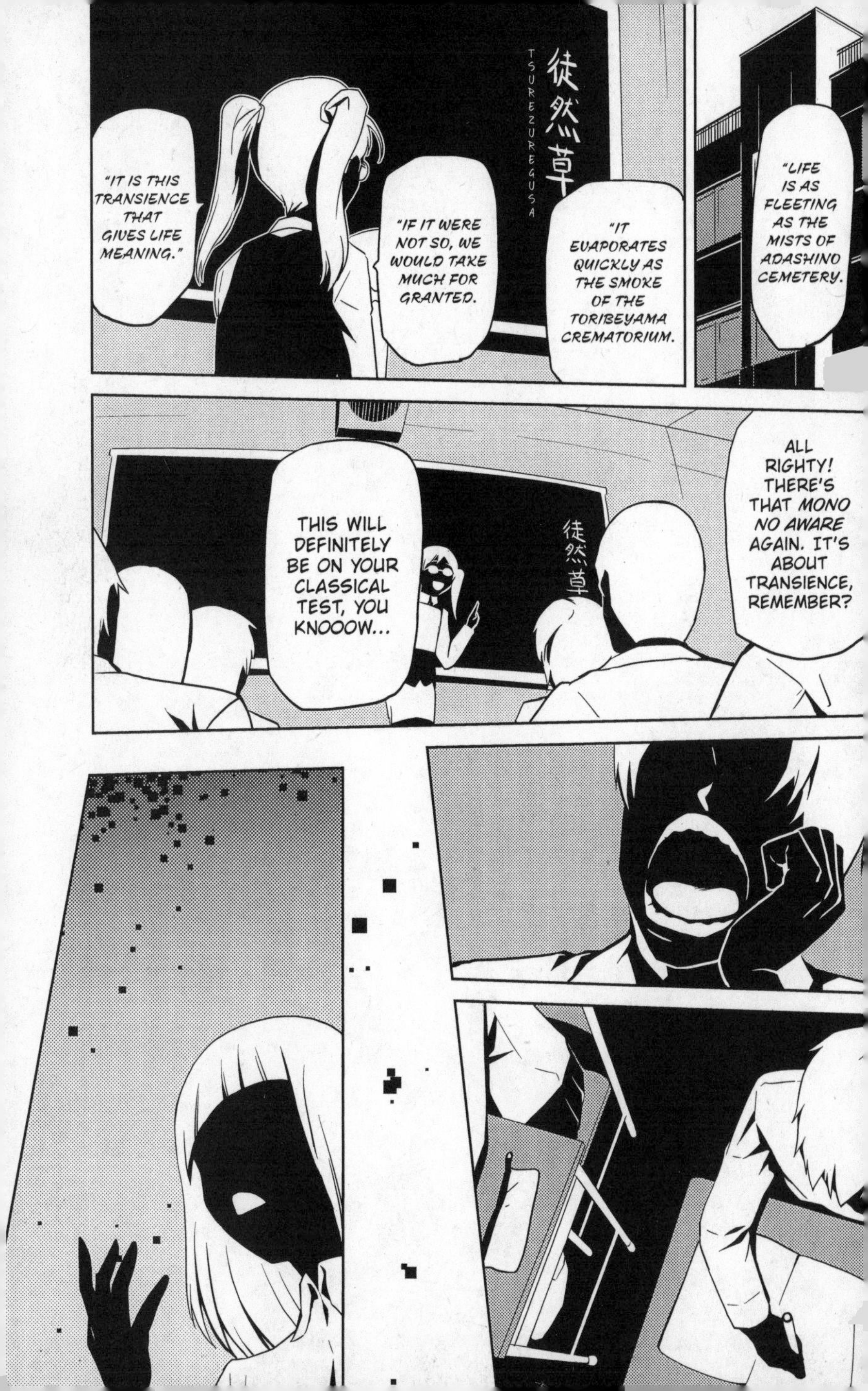
"LIFE IS AS FLEETING AS THE MISTS OF ADASHINO CEMETERY.
徒然草
TSUREZUREGUSA
"IT EVAPORATES QUICKLY AS THE SMOKE OF THE TORIBEYAMA CREMATORIUM.
"IF IT WERE NOT SO, WE WOULD TAKE MUCH FOR GRANTED.
"IT IS THIS TRANSIENCE THAT GIVES LIFE MEANING."
ALL RIGHTY! THERE'S THAT *MONO NO AWARE* AGAIN. IT'S ABOUT TRANSIENCE, REMEMBER?
徒然草
THIS WILL DEFINITELY BE ON YOUR CLASSICAL TEST, YOU KNOOOW...

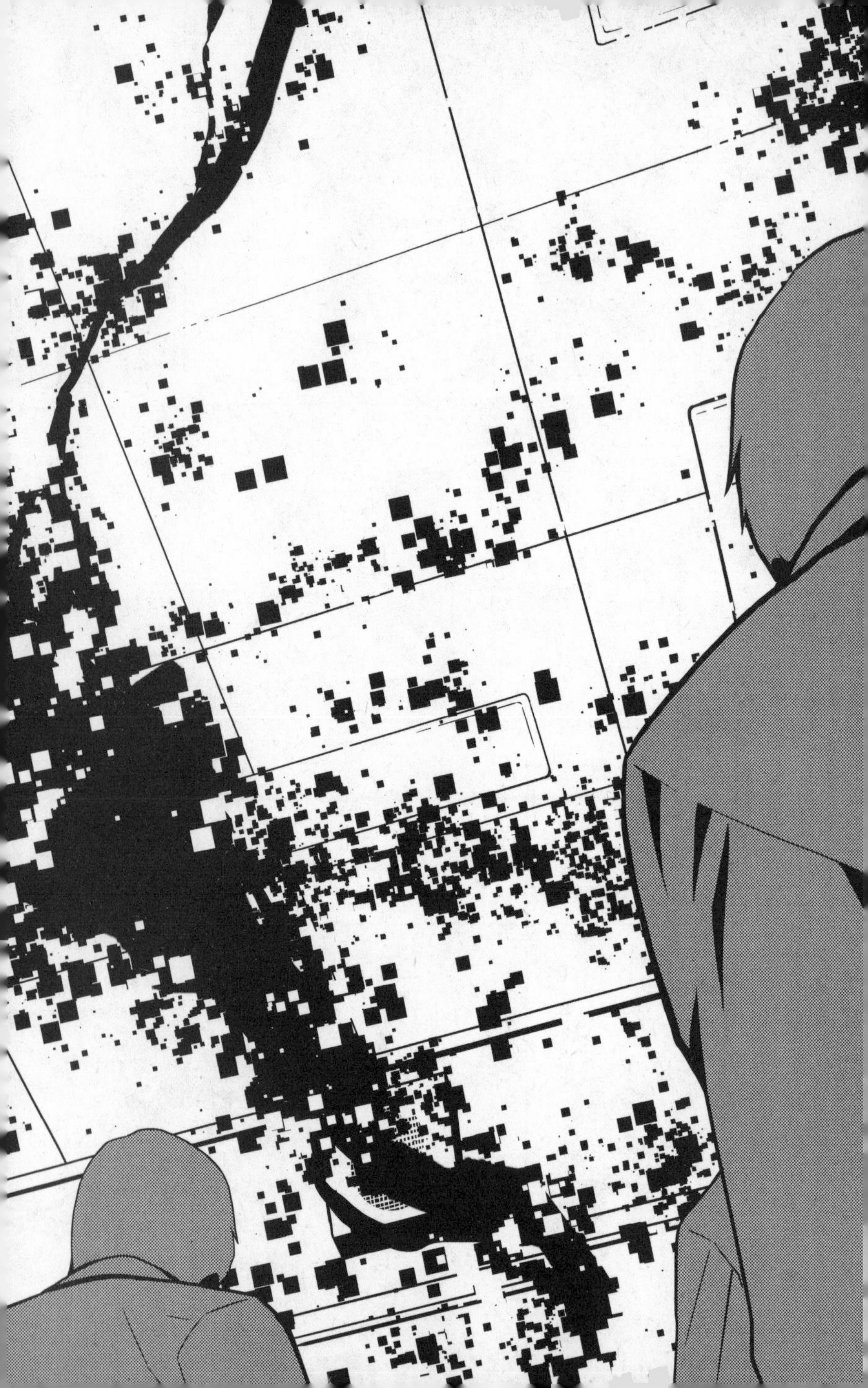

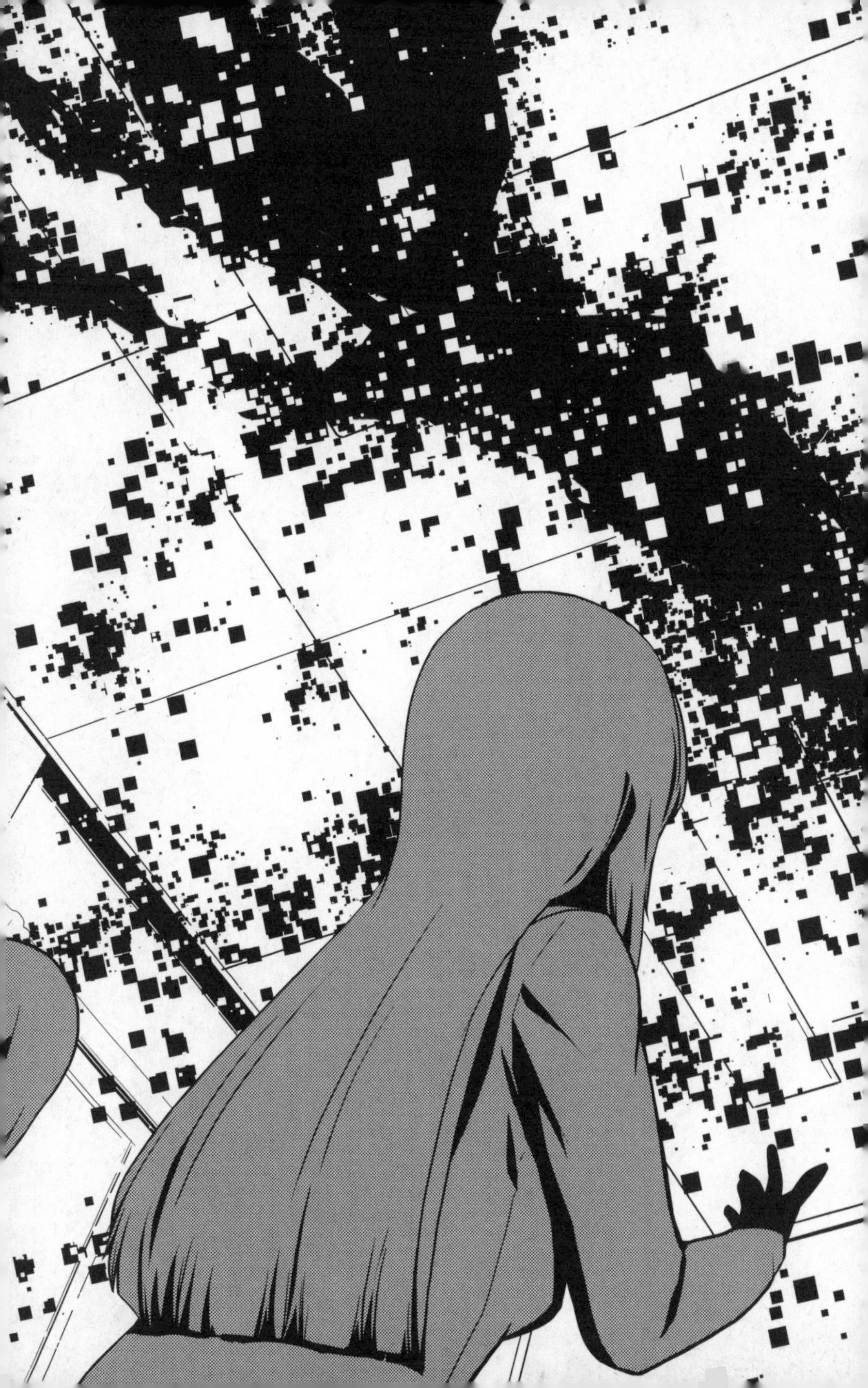

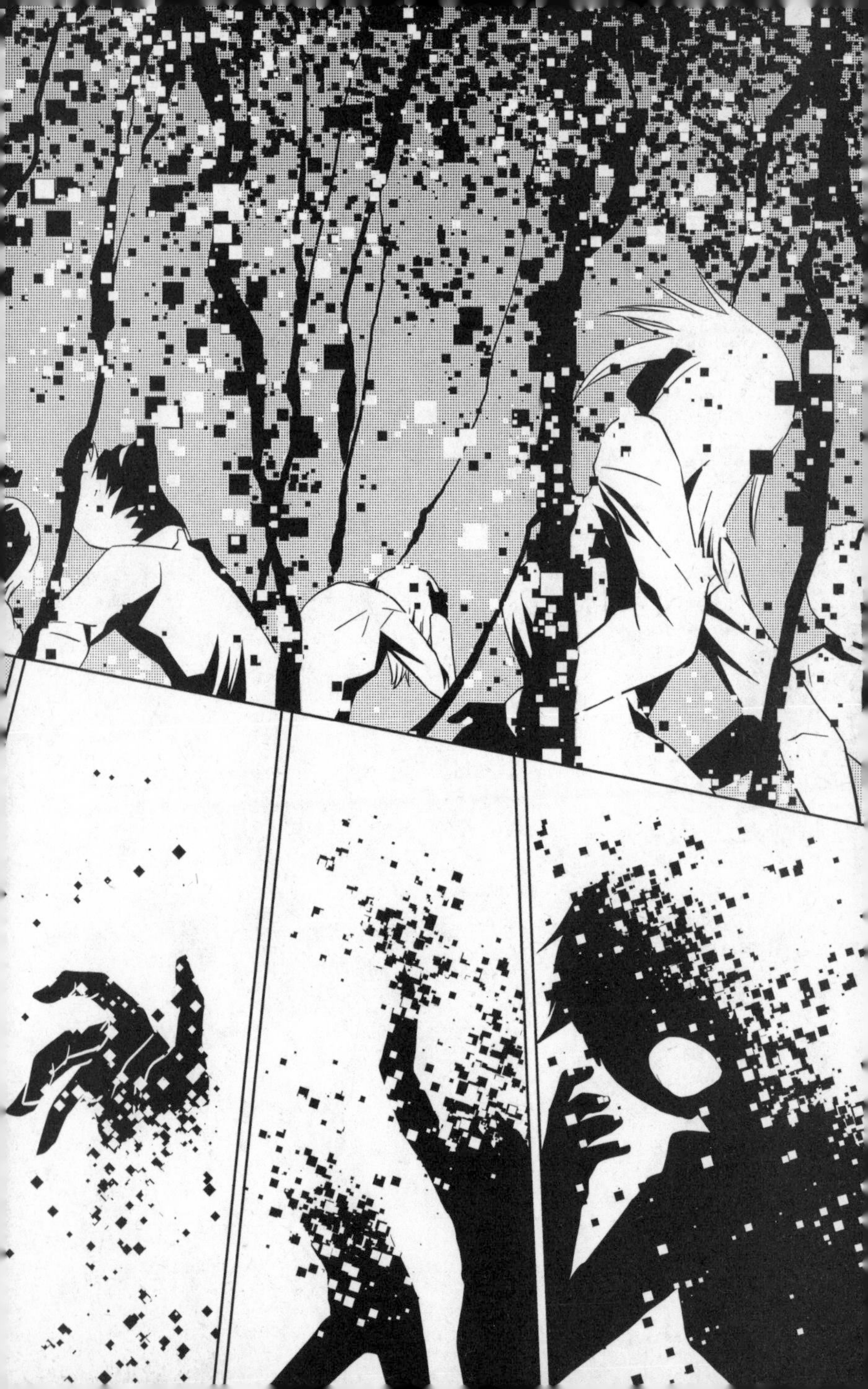

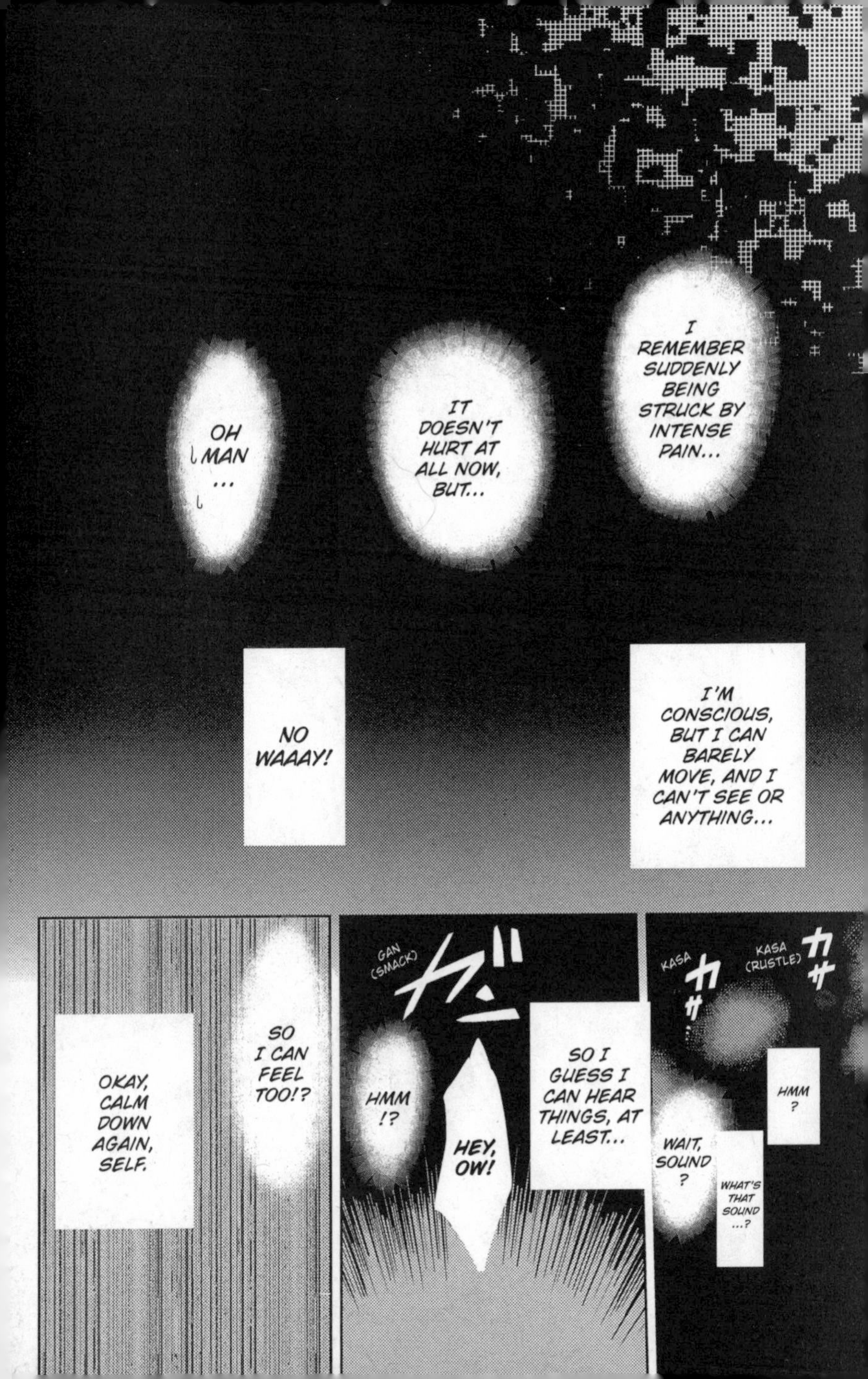
I REMEMBER SUDDENLY BEING STRUCK BY INTENSE PAIN...
IT DOESN'T HURT AT ALL NOW, BUT...
OH MAN...
I'M CONSCIOUS, BUT I CAN BARELY MOVE, AND I CAN'T SEE OR ANYTHING...
NO WAAAY!
KASA (RUSTLE)
カサ
KASA
カサ
HMM?
WAIT, SOUND?
WHAT'S THAT SOUND...?
SO I GUESS I CAN HEAR THINGS, AT LEAST...
GAN (SMACK)
ガン
HMM!?
HEY, OW!
SO I CAN FEEL TOO!?
OKAY, CALM DOWN AGAIN, SELF.

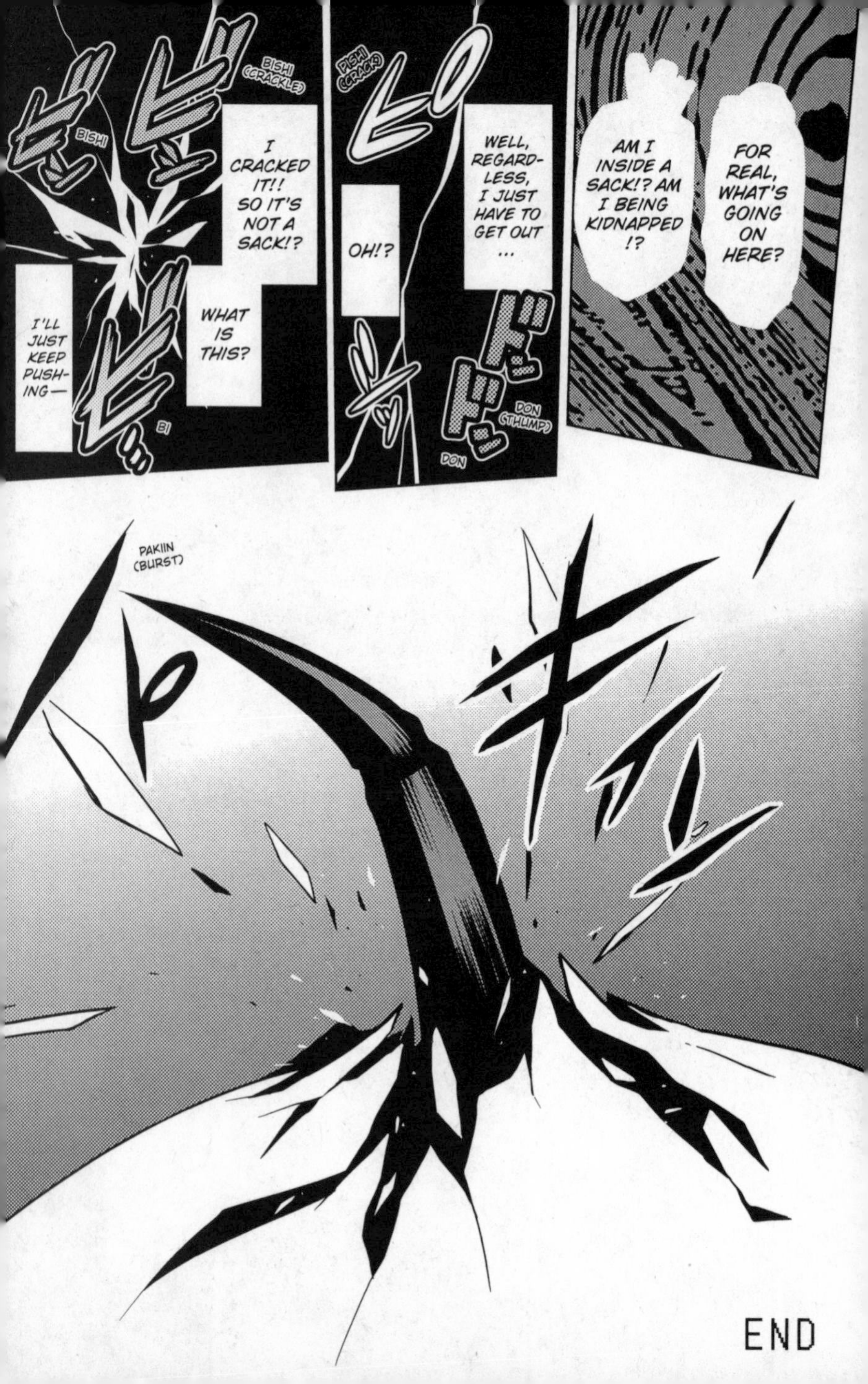
FOR REAL, WHAT'S GOING ON HERE?
AM I INSIDE A SACK!? AM I BEING KIDNAPPED!?
WELL, REGARDLESS, I JUST HAVE TO GET OUT ...
PISHI (CRACK)
OH!?
DON (THUMP)
DON
BISHI (CRACKLE)
I CRACKED IT!! SO IT'S NOT A SACK!?
BISHI
WHAT IS THIS?
I'LL JUST KEEP PUSHING—
BI
PAKIIN (BURST)
END

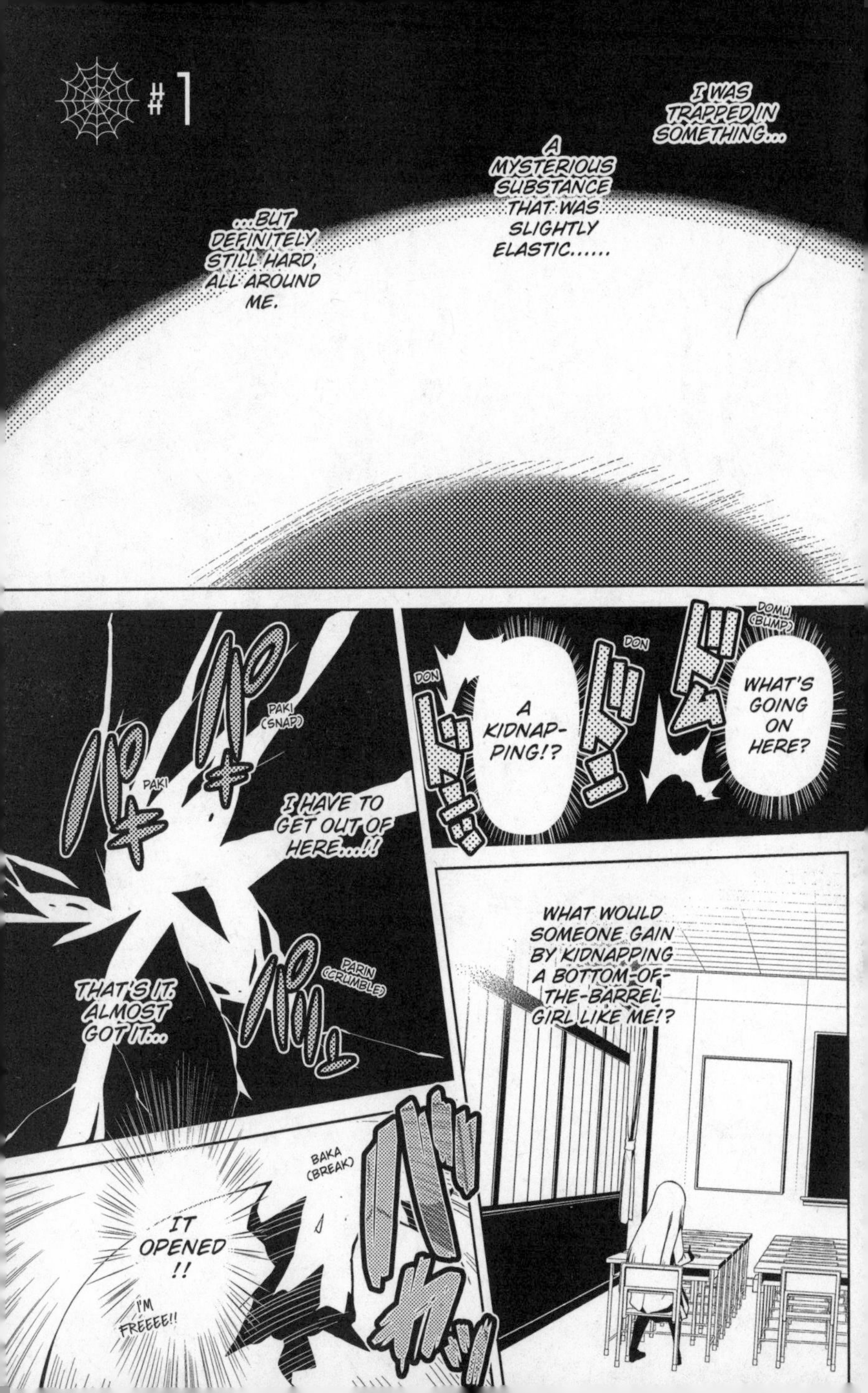
#1
I WAS TRAPPED IN SOMETHING...
A MYSTERIOUS SUBSTANCE THAT WAS SLIGHTLY ELASTIC......
...BUT DEFINITELY STILL HARD, ALL AROUND ME.
DOMU (BUMP)
WHAT'S GOING ON HERE?
DON
A KIDNAP-PING!?
DON
WHAT WOULD SOMEONE GAIN BY KIDNAPPING A BOTTOM-OF-THE-BARREL GIRL LIKE ME!?
PAKI (SNAP)
PAKI
I HAVE TO GET OUT OF HERE...!!
PARIN (CRUMBLE)
THAT'S IT. ALMOST GOT IT...
BAKA (BREAK)
IT OPENED!!
I'M FREEEEE!!

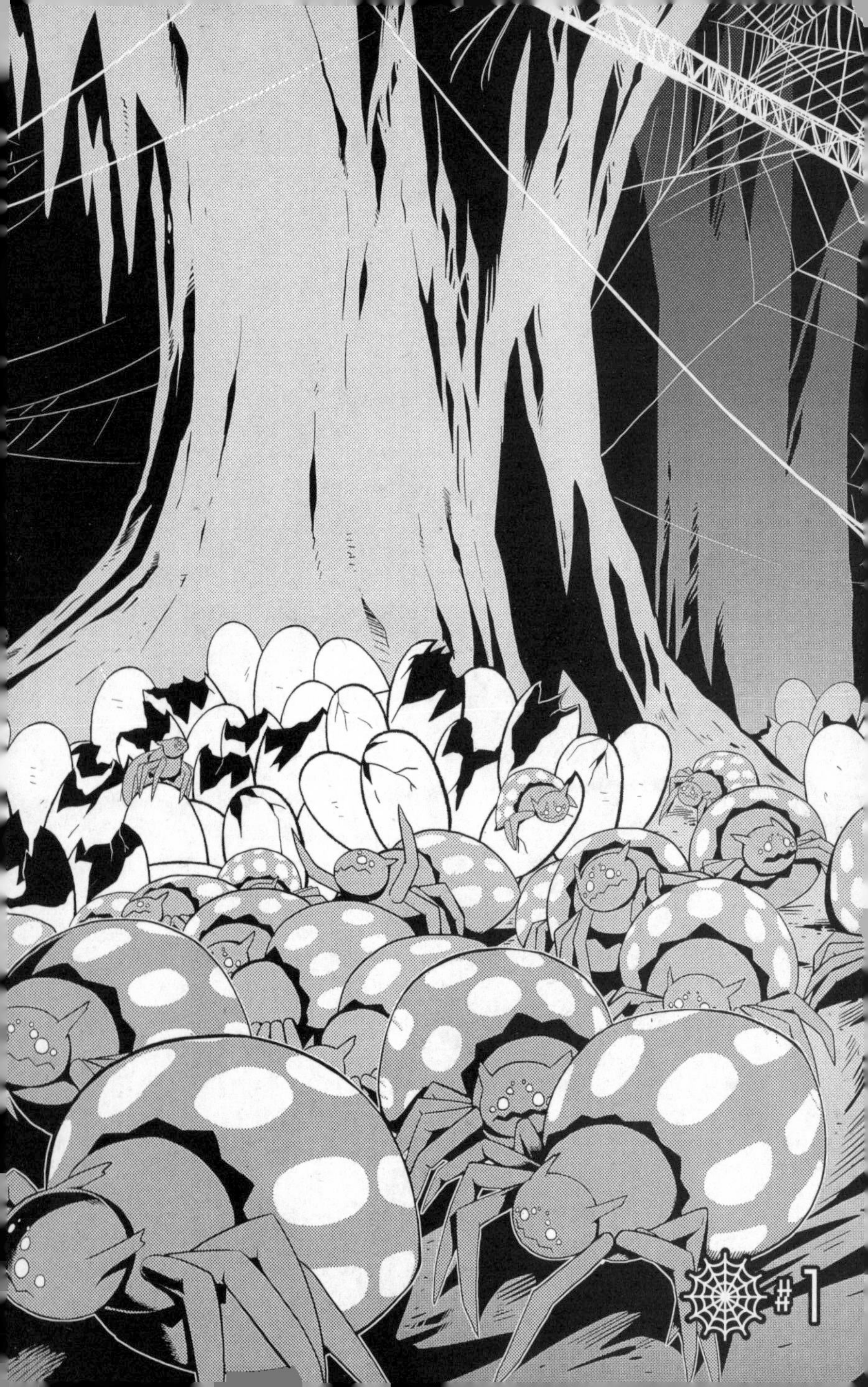
#1

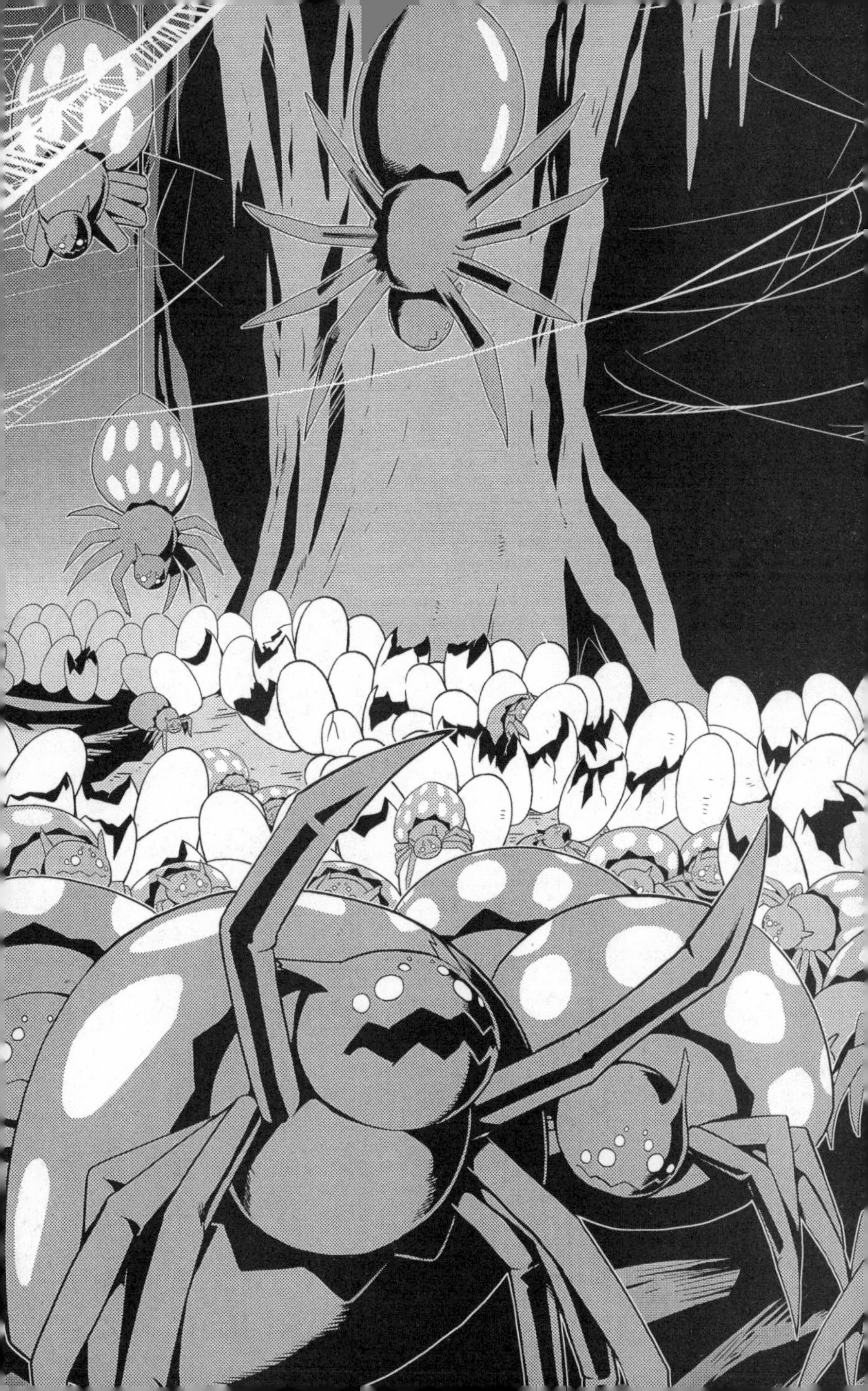

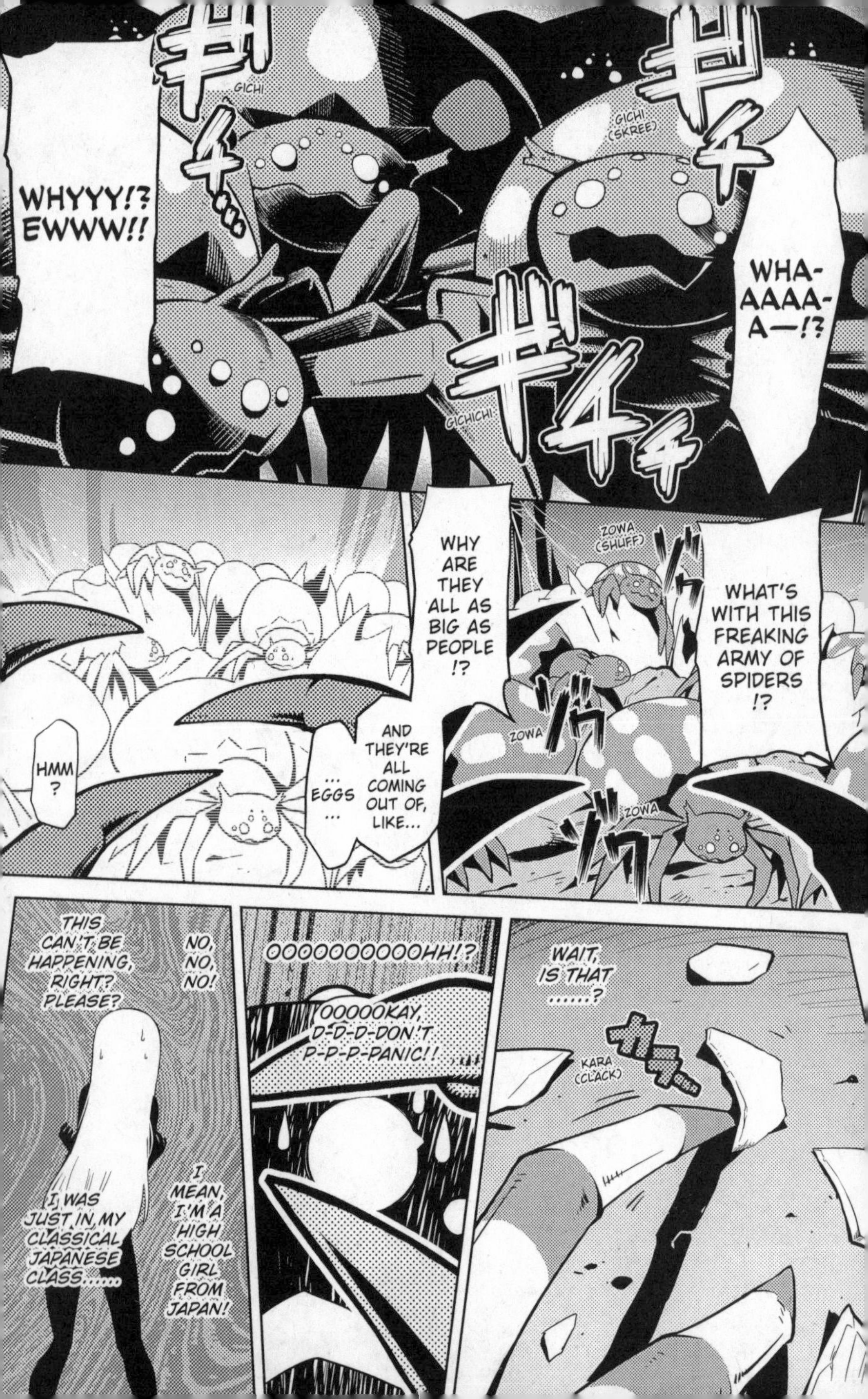
WHA-AAAA-A—!?
GICHI (SKREE)
GICHICHI
GICHI
WHYYY!? EWWW!!
WHAT'S WITH THIS FREAKING ARMY OF SPIDERS!?
ZOWA (SHUFF)
ZOWA
ZOWA
WHY ARE THEY ALL AS BIG AS PEOPLE!?
AND THEY'RE ALL COMING OUT OF, LIKE...
...EGGS...
HMM?
WAIT, IS THAT ......?
KARA (CLACK)
OOOOOOOOOOHH!?
OOOOOKAY, D-D-D-DON'T P-P-P-PANIC!!
NO, NO, NO!
THIS CAN'T BE HAPPENING, RIGHT? PLEASE?
I MEAN, I'M A HIGH SCHOOL GIRL FROM JAPAN!
I WAS JUST IN MY CLASSICAL JAPANESE CLASS......

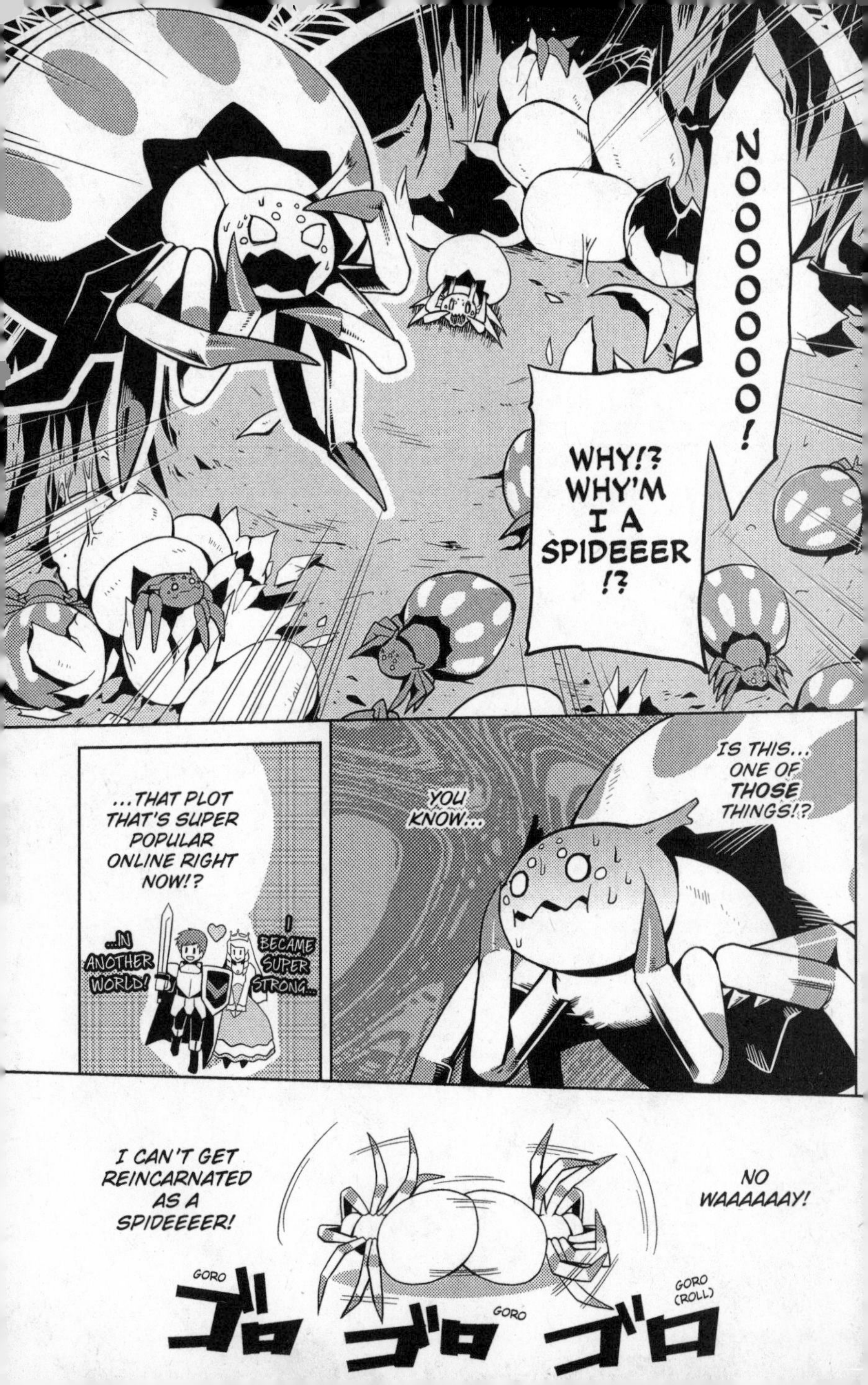
NOOOOOOO!
WHY!? WHY'M I A SPIDEEEER!?
IS THIS... ONE OF THOSE THINGS!?
YOU KNOW...
...THAT PLOT THAT'S SUPER POPULAR ONLINE RIGHT NOW!?
I BECAME SUPER STRONG...
...IN ANOTHER WORLD!
NO WAAAAAAY!
I CAN'T GET REINCARNATED AS A SPIDEEEER!
ゴロ
GORO (ROLL)
ゴロ
GORO
ゴロ
GORO

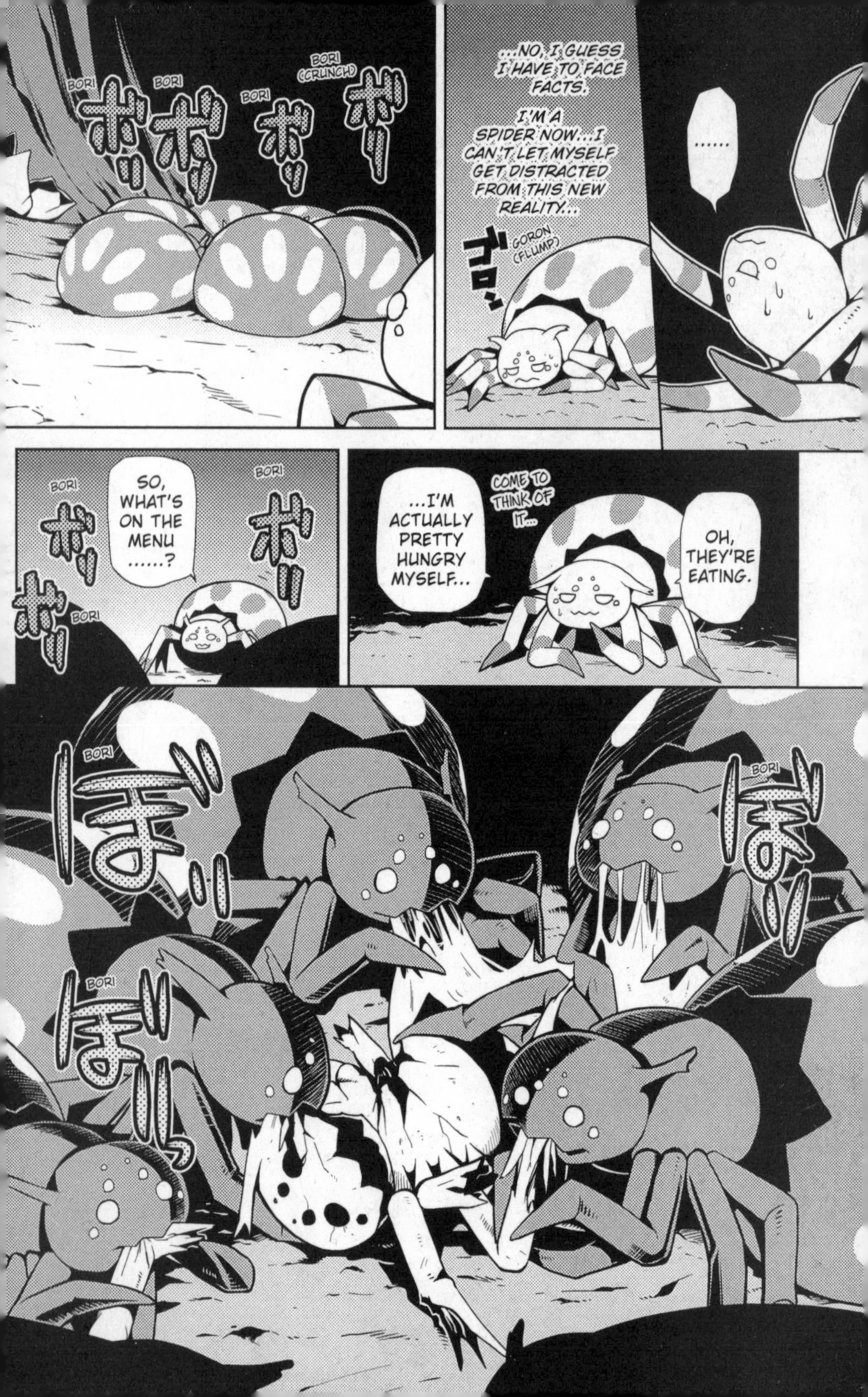
......
...NO, I GUESS I HAVE TO FACE FACTS.
I'M A SPIDER NOW... I CAN'T LET MYSELF GET DISTRACTED FROM THIS NEW REALITY...
GORON (FLUMP)
BORI (CRUNCH)
BORI
BORI
BORI
OH, THEY'RE EATING.
COME TO THINK OF IT...
...I'M ACTUALLY PRETTY HUNGRY MYSELF...
BORI
SO, WHAT'S ON THE MENU ......?
BORI
BORI
BORI
BORI
BORI

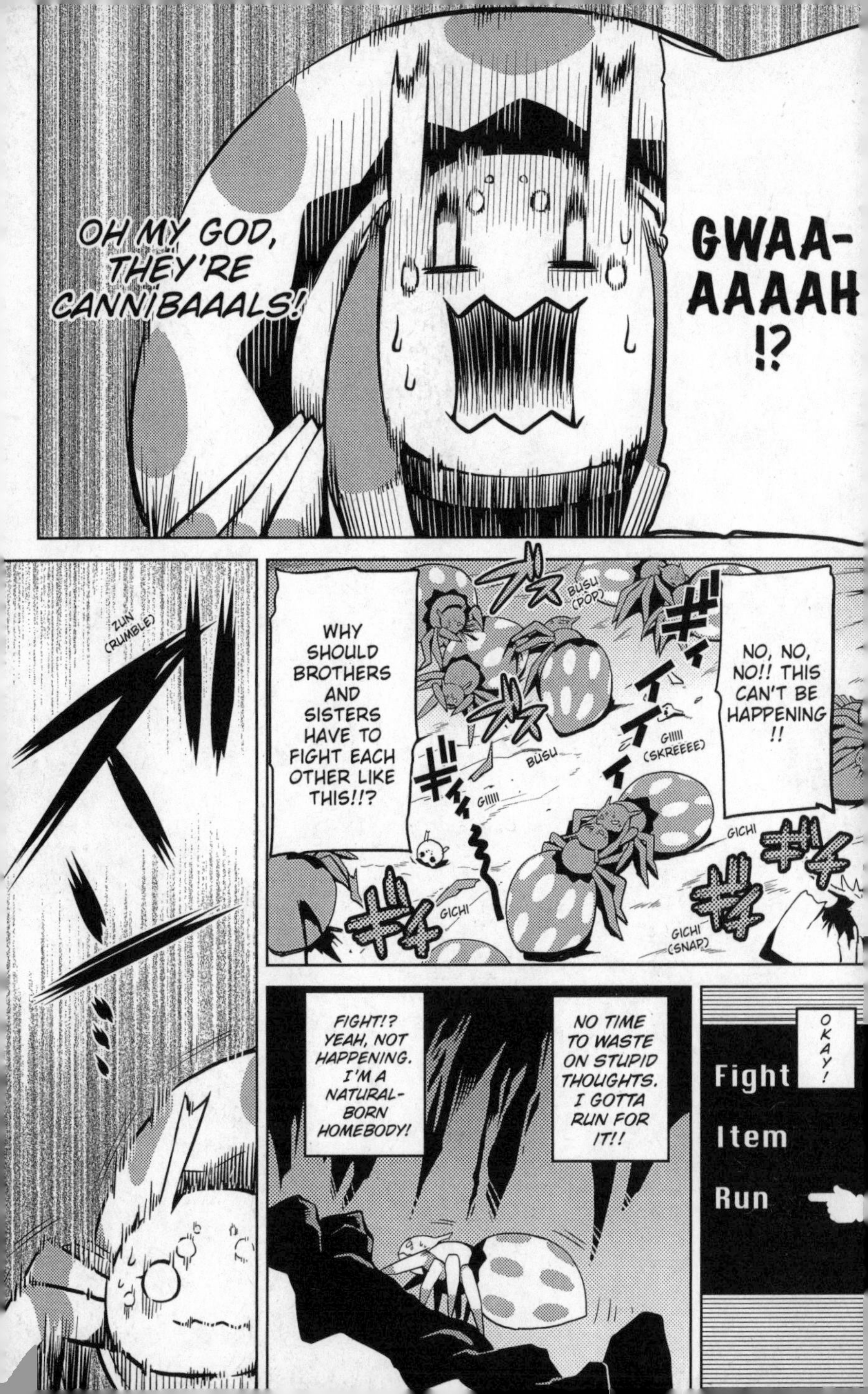
GWAA-AAAAH!?
OH MY GOD, THEY'RE CANNIBAAALS!
NO, NO, NO!! THIS CAN'T BE HAPPENING!!
BUSU (POP)
GIIII (SKREEEE)
WHY SHOULD BROTHERS AND SISTERS HAVE TO FIGHT EACH OTHER LIKE THIS!!?
BUSU
GIIII
GICHI
GICHI (SNAP)
GICHI
OKAY!
Fight
Item
Run
NO TIME TO WASTE ON STUPID THOUGHTS. I GOTTA RUN FOR IT!!
FIGHT!? YEAH, NOT HAPPENING. I'M A NATURAL-BORN HOMEBODY!
ZUN (RUMBLE)

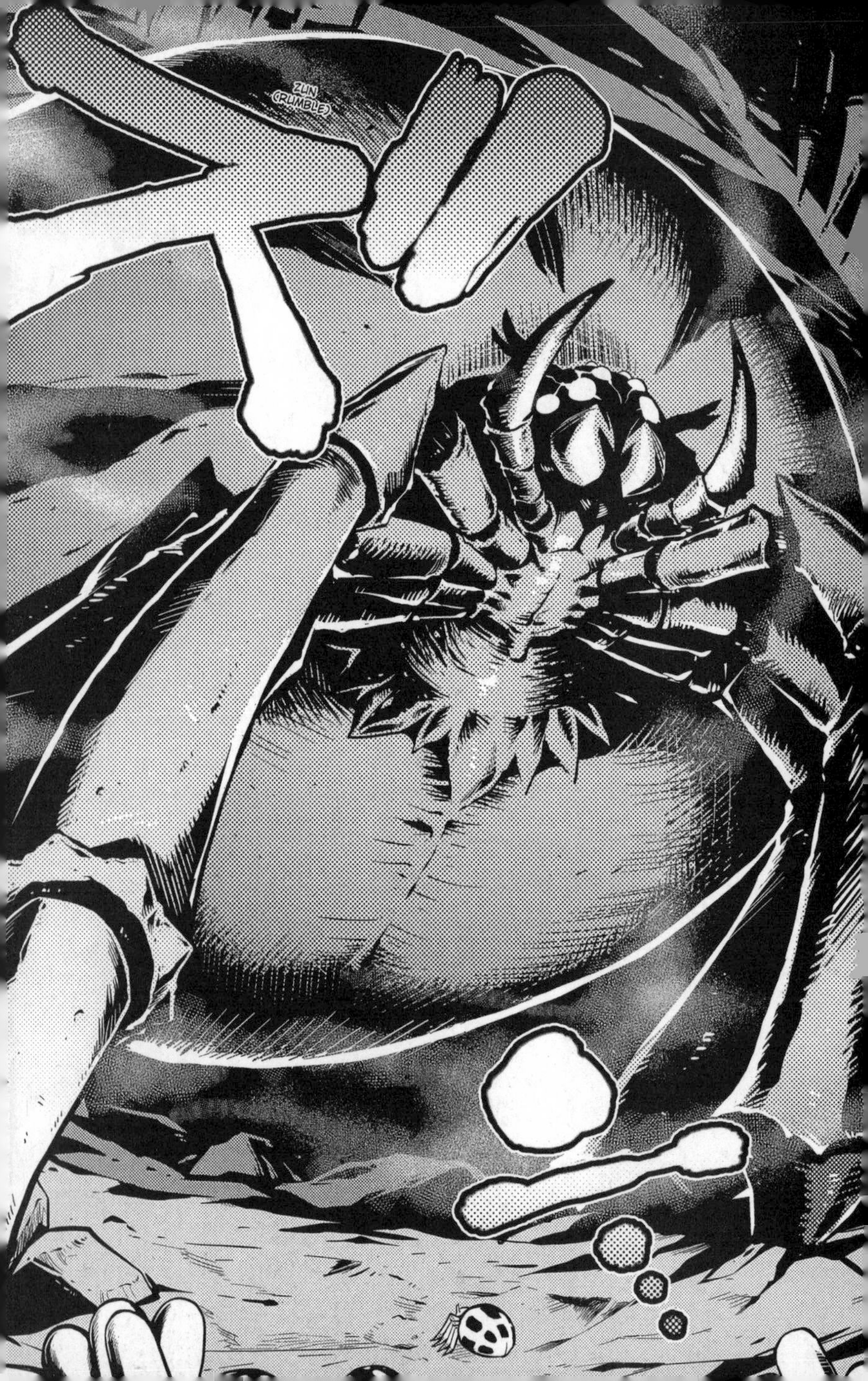
ZUN
(RUMBLE)

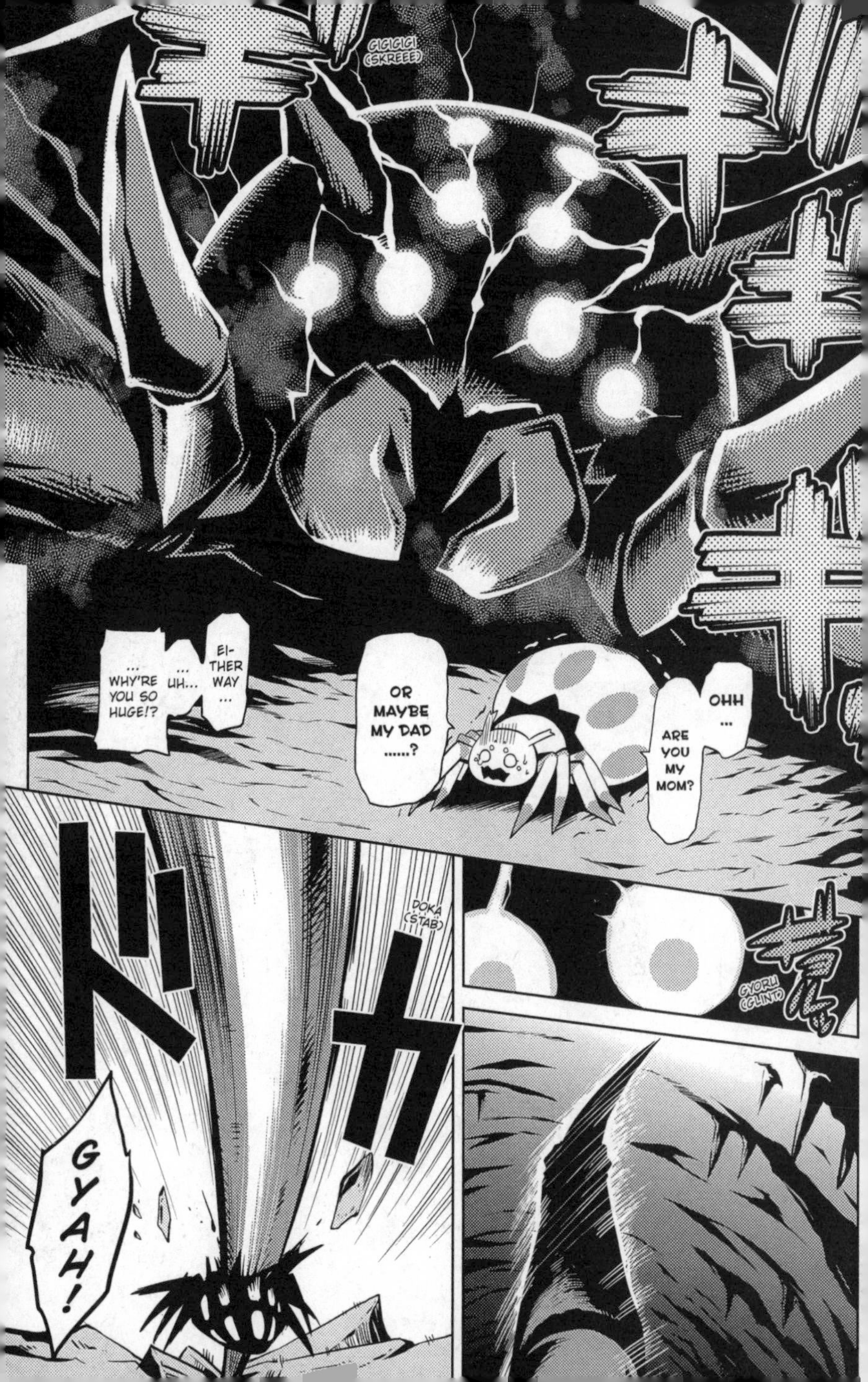
GIGIGIGI (SKREEE)
OHH ...
ARE YOU MY MOM?
OR MAYBE MY DAD ......?
EI-THER WAY ...
... UH...
... WHY'RE YOU SO HUGE!?
GYORU (GLINT)
DOKA (STAB)
GYAH!

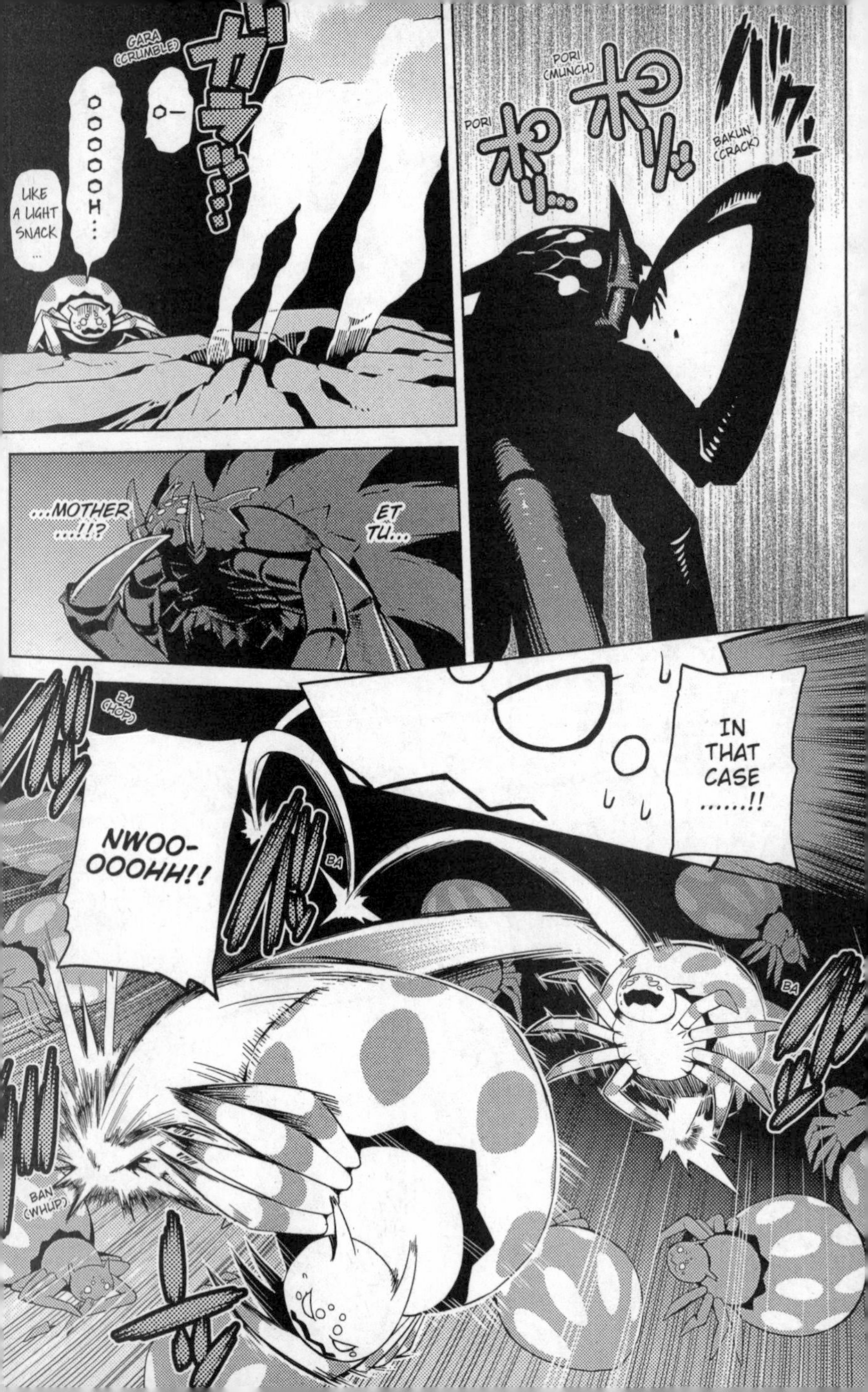
BAKUN (CRACK)
PORI (MUNCH)
PORI
GARA (CRUMBLE)
O-
OOOOOOH...
LIKE A LIGHT SNACK ...
ET TU...
...MOTHER ...!!?
IN THAT CASE ......!!
BA (HOP)
BA
NWOO-OOOHH!!
BA
BAN (WHUP)

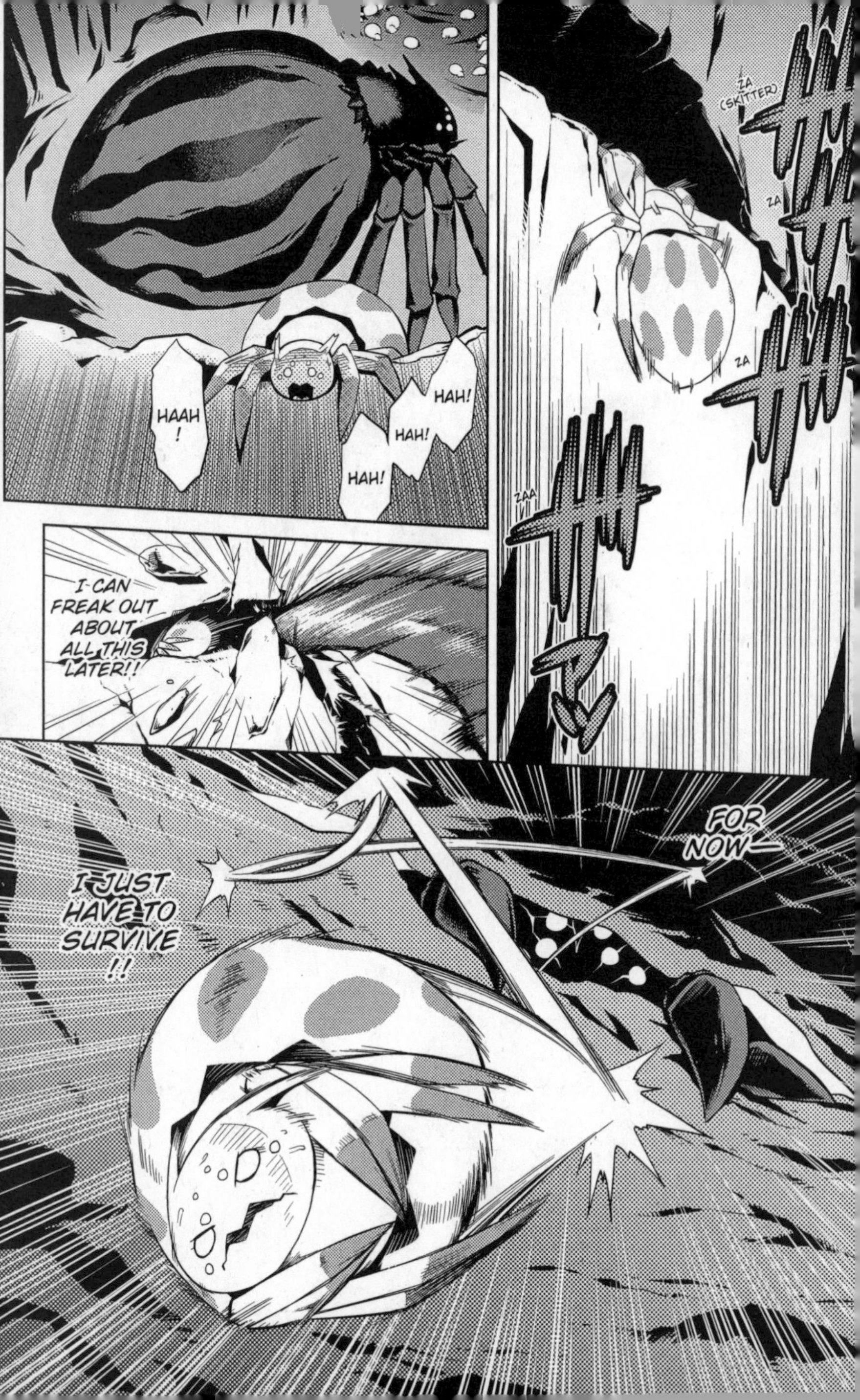
ZA (SKITTER)
ZA
ZA
ZAA
HAH!
HAH!
HAAH!
HAH!
I-CAN FREAK OUT ABOUT ALL THIS LATER!!
FOR NOW—
I JUST HAVE TO SURVIVE!!

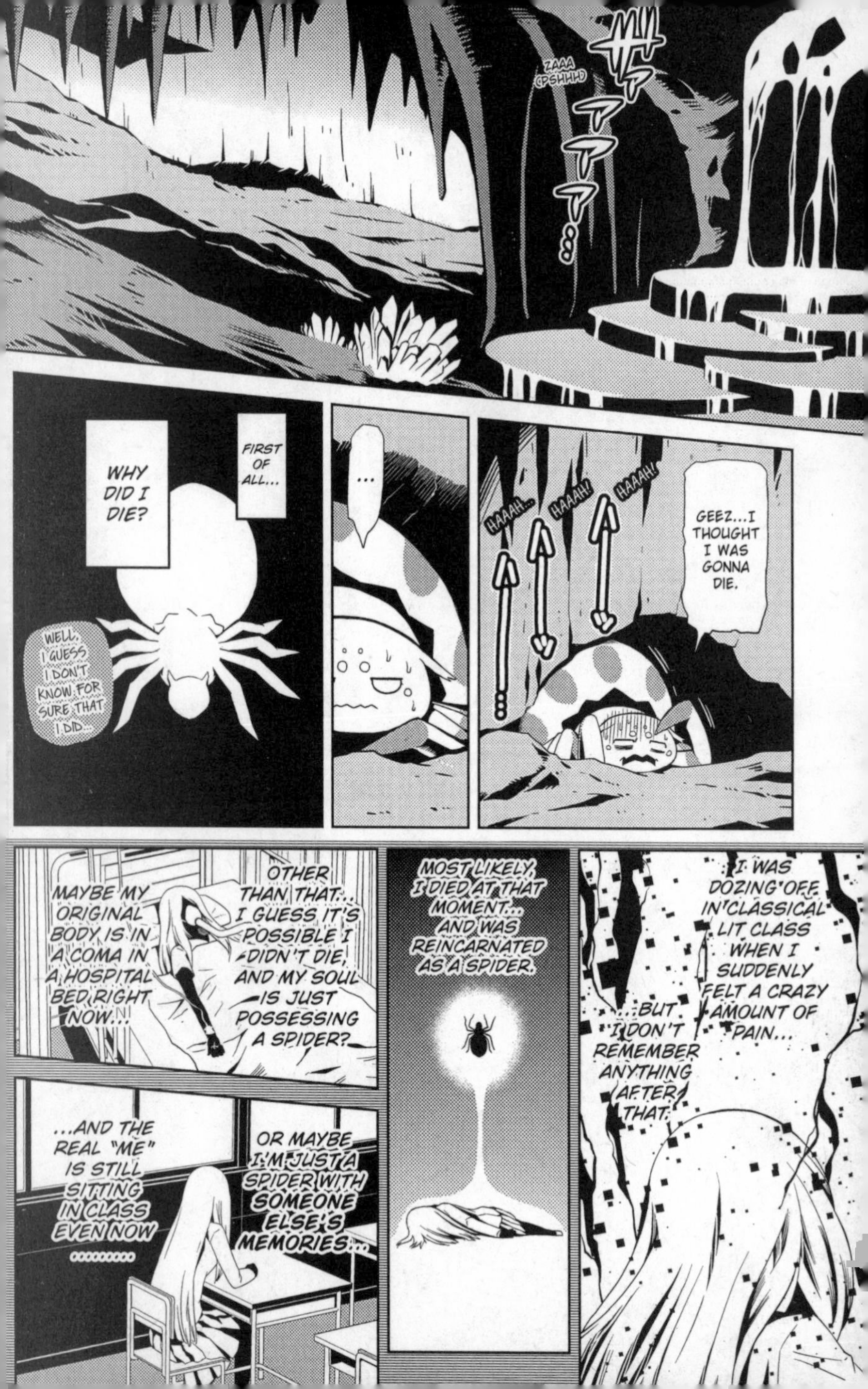
ZAAA (PSHHH)
GEEZ...I THOUGHT I WAS GONNA DIE.
HAAAH!
HAAAH!
HAAAH...
...
FIRST OF ALL...
WHY DID I DIE?
WELL, I GUESS I DON'T KNOW FOR SURE THAT I DID...
I WAS DOZING OFF IN CLASSICAL LIT CLASS WHEN I SUDDENLY FELT A CRAZY AMOUNT OF PAIN...
...BUT I DON'T REMEMBER ANYTHING AFTER THAT.
MOST LIKELY, I DIED AT THAT MOMENT... AND WAS REINCARNATED AS A SPIDER.
OTHER THAN THAT... I GUESS IT'S POSSIBLE I DIDN'T DIE, AND MY SOUL IS JUST POSSESSING A SPIDER?
MAYBE MY ORIGINAL BODY IS IN A COMA IN A HOSPITAL BED RIGHT NOW...!!
OR MAYBE I'M JUST A SPIDER WITH SOMEONE ELSE'S MEMORIES...
...AND THE REAL "ME" IS STILL SITTING IN CLASS EVEN NOW.........

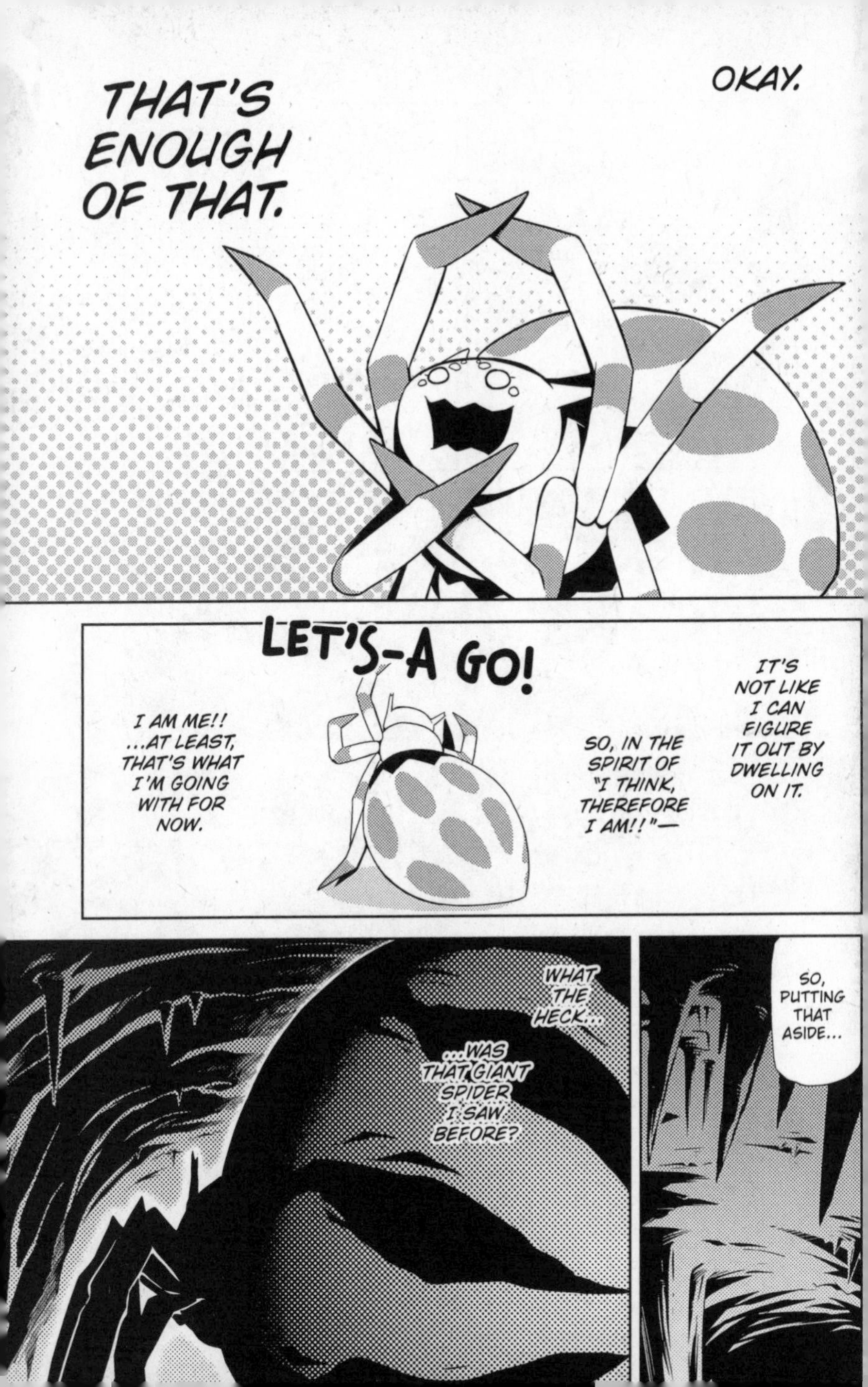
OKAY.
THAT'S ENOUGH OF THAT.
IT'S NOT LIKE I CAN FIGURE IT OUT BY DWELLING ON IT.
SO, IN THE SPIRIT OF "I THINK, THEREFORE I AM!!"—
I AM ME!! ...AT LEAST, THAT'S WHAT I'M GOING WITH FOR NOW.
LET'S-A GO!
SO, PUTTING THAT ASIDE...
WHAT THE HECK...
...WAS THAT GIANT SPIDER I SAW BEFORE?

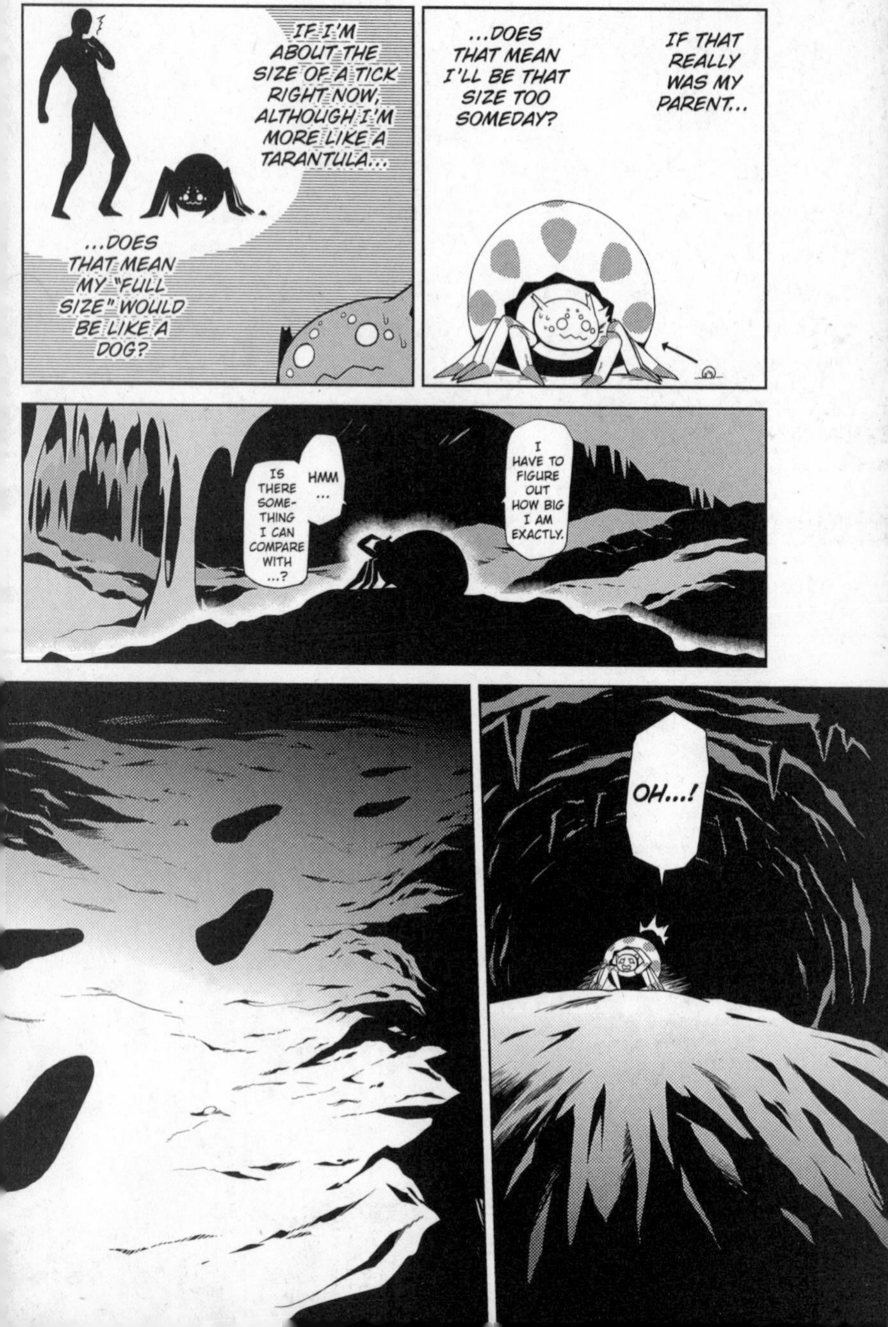
IF THAT REALLY WAS MY PARENT...
...DOES THAT MEAN I'LL BE THAT SIZE TOO SOMEDAY?
IF I'M ABOUT THE SIZE OF A TICK RIGHT NOW, ALTHOUGH I'M MORE LIKE A TARANTULA...
...DOES THAT MEAN MY "FULL SIZE" WOULD BE LIKE A DOG?
I HAVE TO FIGURE OUT HOW BIG I AM EXACTLY.
HMM...
IS THERE SOMETHING I CAN COMPARE WITH...?
OH...!

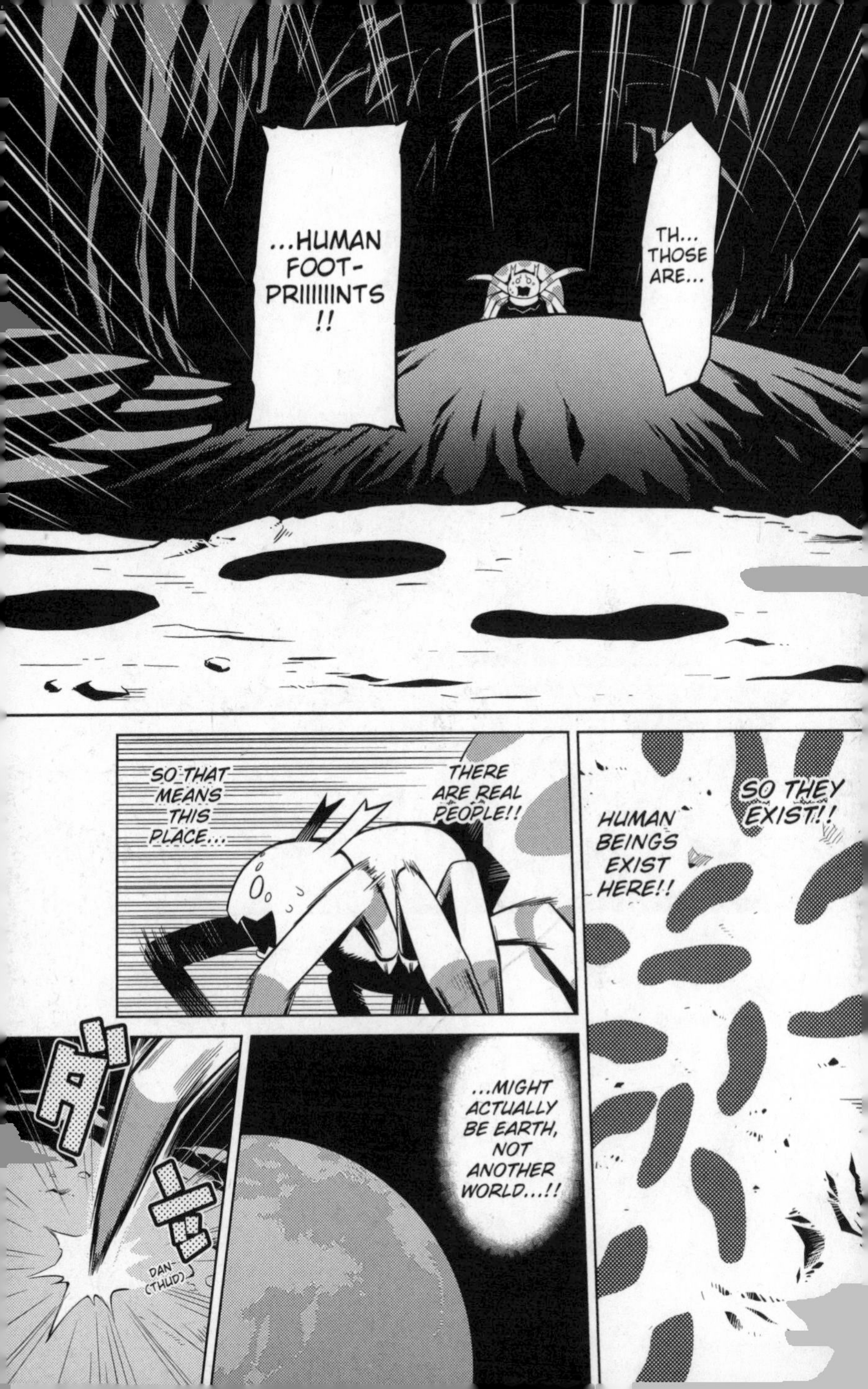
TH... THOSE ARE...
...HUMAN FOOT-PRIIIIIIINTS!!
SO THEY EXIST!!
HUMAN BEINGS EXIST HERE!!
THERE ARE REAL PEOPLE!!
SO THAT MEANS THIS PLACE...
...MIGHT ACTUALLY BE EARTH, NOT ANOTHER WORLD...!!
DAN- (THUD)

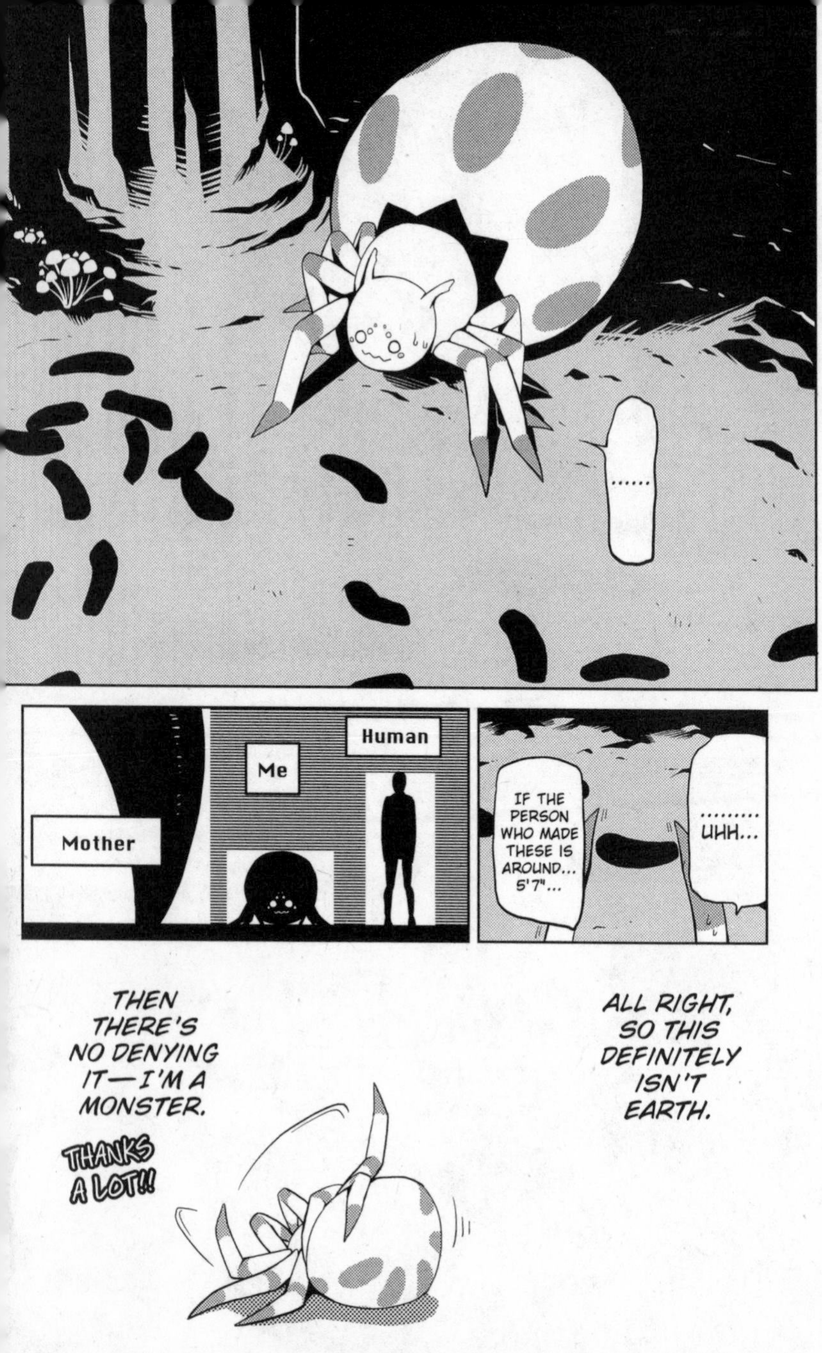
......
....
UHH...
IF THE PERSON WHO MADE THESE IS AROUND... 5'7"...
Human
Me
Mother
ALL RIGHT, SO THIS DEFINITELY ISN'T EARTH.
THEN THERE'S NO DENYING IT—I'M A MONSTER.
THANKS A LOT!!

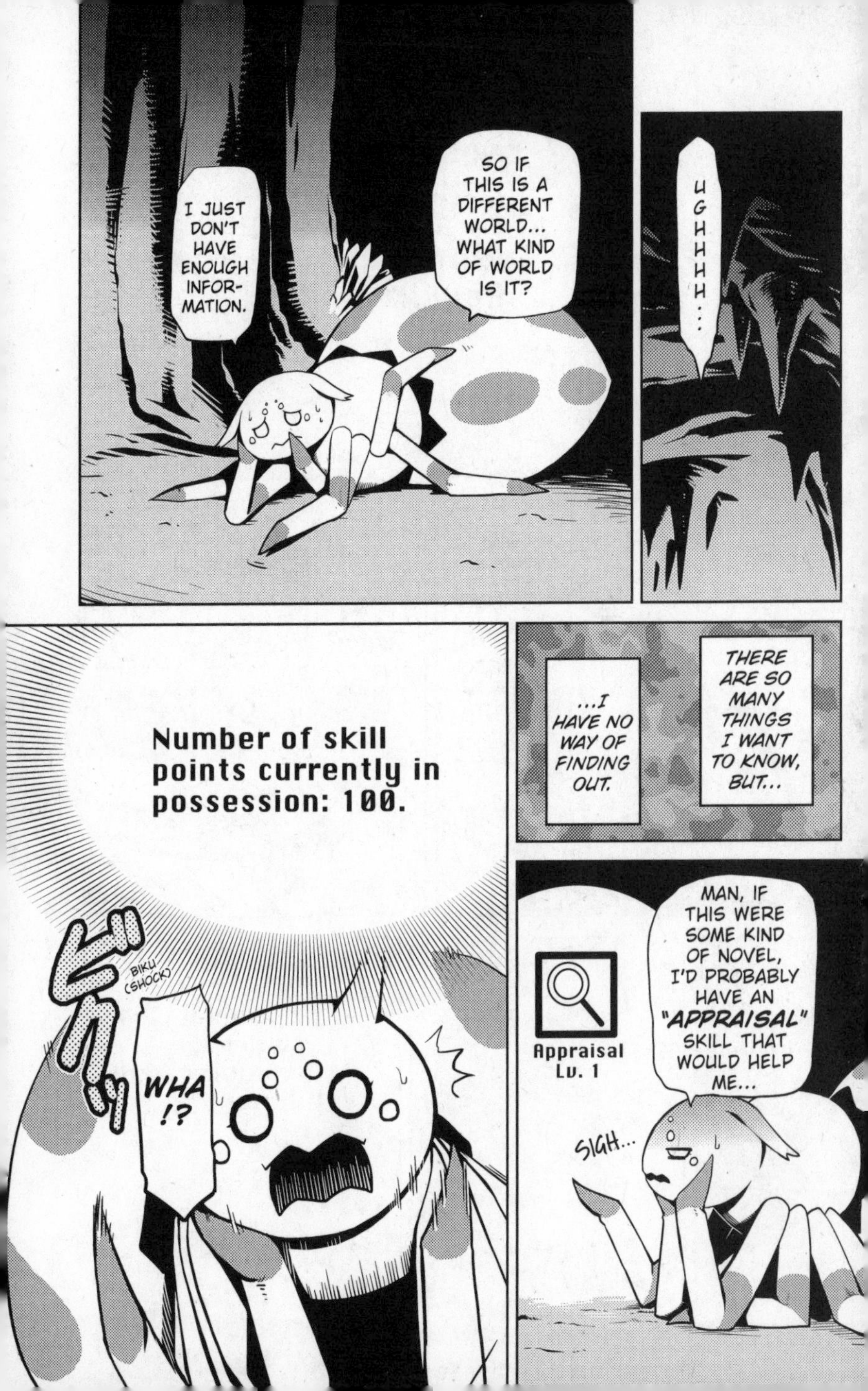
UGHHHH...
SO IF THIS IS A DIFFERENT WORLD... WHAT KIND OF WORLD IS IT?
I JUST DON'T HAVE ENOUGH INFORMATION.
THERE ARE SO MANY THINGS I WANT TO KNOW, BUT...
...I HAVE NO WAY OF FINDING OUT.
MAN, IF THIS WERE SOME KIND OF NOVEL, I'D PROBABLY HAVE AN "APPRAISAL" SKILL THAT WOULD HELP ME...
Appraisal Lv. 1
SIGH...
Number of skill points currently in possession: 100.
BIKU (SHOCK)
WHA!?

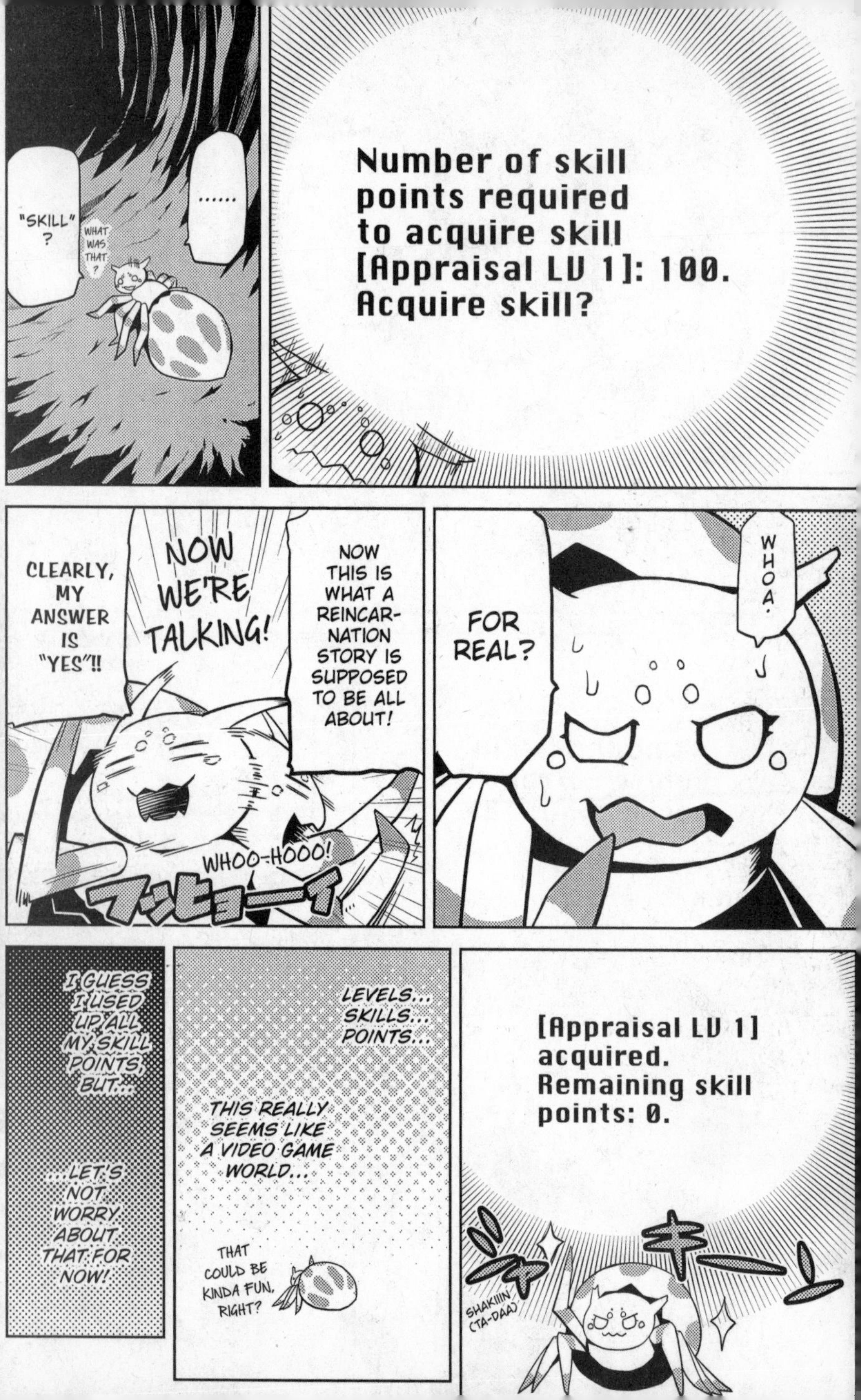
Number of skill points required to acquire skill [Appraisal LV 1]: 100. Acquire skill?
......
"SKILL"?
WHAT WAS THAT?
WHOA.
FOR REAL?
NOW THIS IS WHAT A REINCARNATION STORY IS SUPPOSED TO BE ALL ABOUT!
NOW WE'RE TALKING!
CLEARLY, MY ANSWER IS "YES"!!
WHOO-HOOO!
[Appraisal LV 1] acquired. Remaining skill points: 0.
SHAKIIIN (TA-DAA)
LEVELS... SKILLS... POINTS...
THIS REALLY SEEMS LIKE A VIDEO GAME WORLD...
THAT COULD BE KINDA FUN, RIGHT?
I GUESS I USED UP ALL MY SKILL POINTS, BUT...
...LET'S NOT WORRY ABOUT THAT FOR NOW!

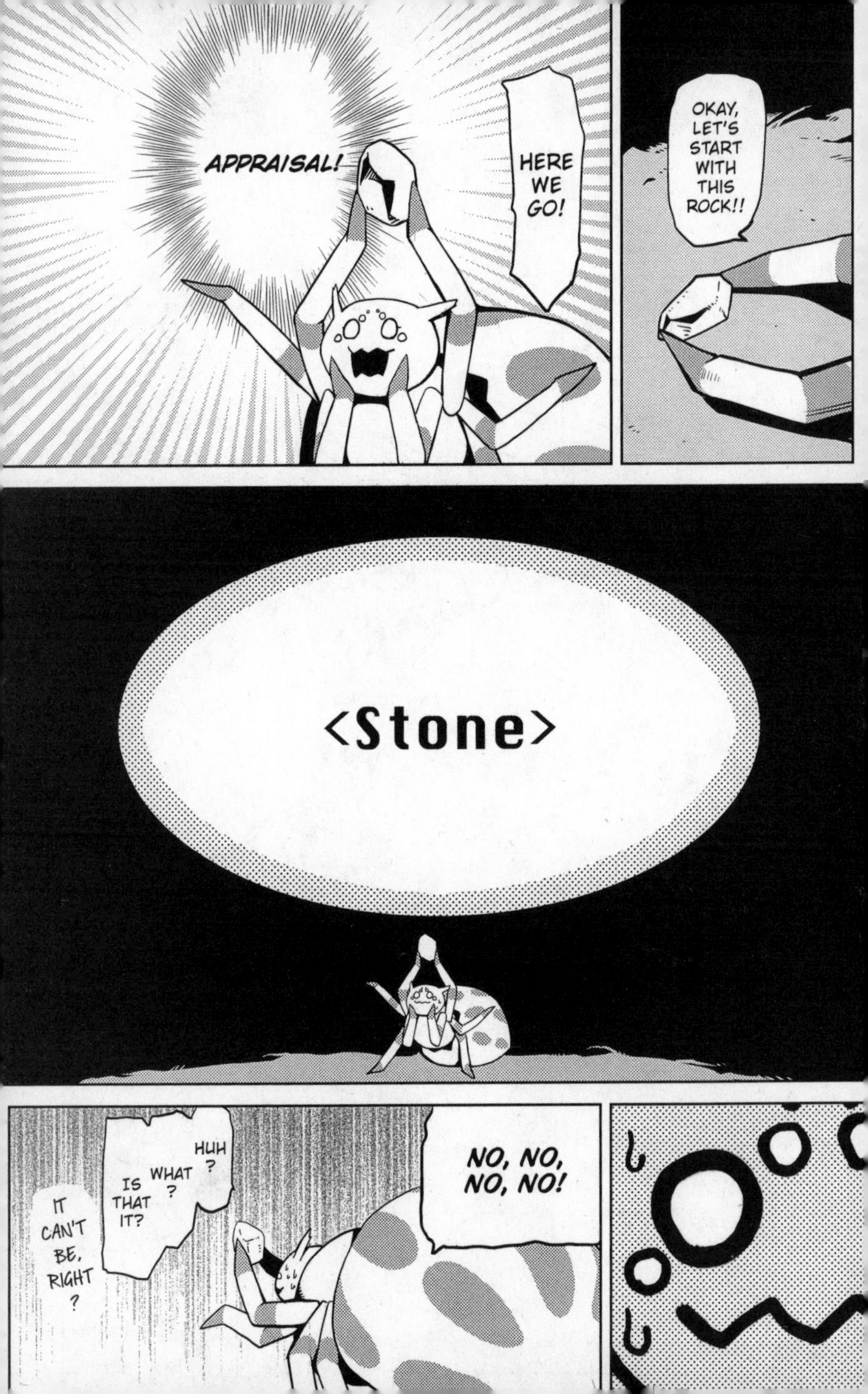
OKAY, LET'S START WITH THIS ROCK!!
HERE WE GO!
APPRAISAL!
<Stone>
NO, NO, NO, NO!
HUH?
WHAT?
IS THAT IT?
IT CAN'T BE, RIGHT?

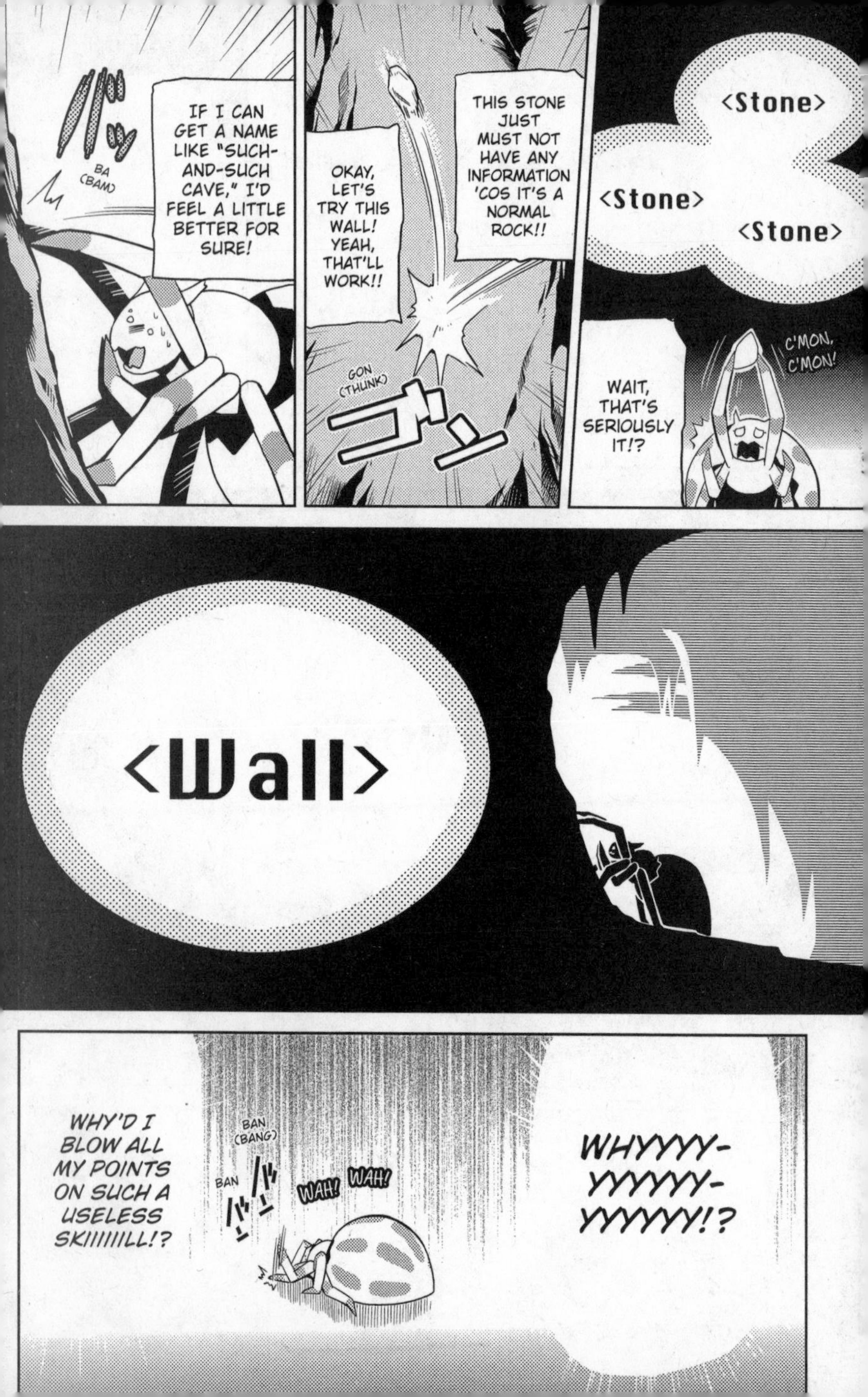

<Stone>
<Stone>
<Stone>
C'MON, C'MON!
WAIT, THAT'S SERIOUSLY IT!?
THIS STONE JUST MUST NOT HAVE ANY INFORMATION 'COS IT'S A NORMAL ROCK!!
OKAY, LET'S TRY THIS WALL! YEAH, THAT'LL WORK!!
GON (THUNK)
IF I CAN GET A NAME LIKE "SUCH-AND-SUCH CAVE," I'D FEEL A LITTLE BETTER FOR SURE!
BA (BAM)
<Wall>
WHYYYYY-YYYYYY-YYYYYY!?
WAH! WAH!
BAN (BANG)
BAN
WHY'D I BLOW ALL MY POINTS ON SUCH A USELESS SKIIIIIILL!?

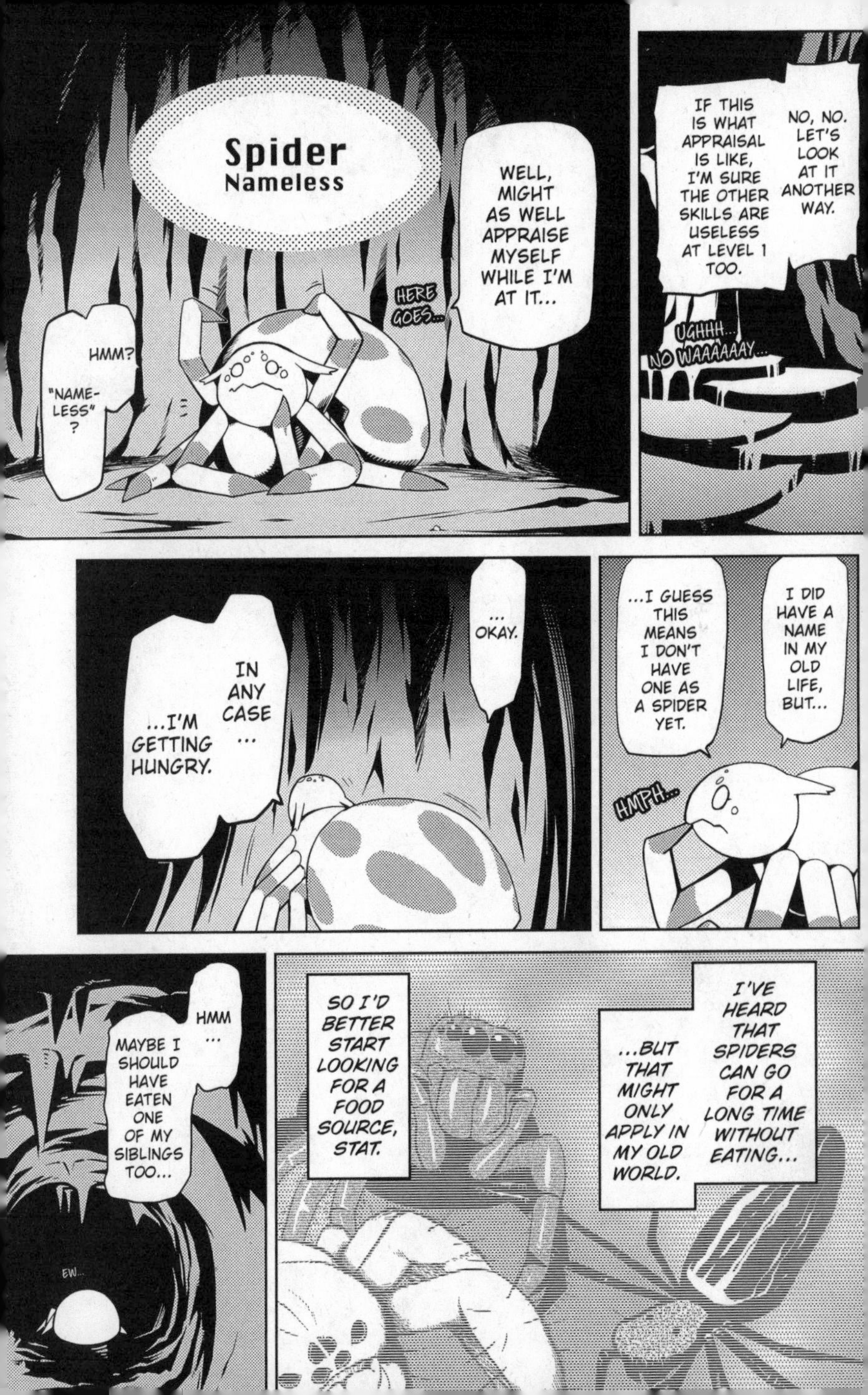
NO, NO. LET'S LOOK AT IT ANOTHER WAY.
IF THIS IS WHAT APPRAISAL IS LIKE, I'M SURE THE OTHER SKILLS ARE USELESS AT LEVEL 1 TOO.
UGHHH... NO WAAAAAAY...
WELL, MIGHT AS WELL APPRAISE MYSELF WHILE I'M AT IT...
HERE GOES...
Spider
Nameless
HMM?
"NAME-LESS"?
I DID HAVE A NAME IN MY OLD LIFE, BUT...
...I GUESS THIS MEANS I DON'T HAVE ONE AS A SPIDER YET.
HMPH...
...OKAY.
IN ANY CASE...
...I'M GETTING HUNGRY.
I'VE HEARD THAT SPIDERS CAN GO FOR A LONG TIME WITHOUT EATING...
...BUT THAT MIGHT ONLY APPLY IN MY OLD WORLD.
SO I'D BETTER START LOOKING FOR A FOOD SOURCE, STAT.
HMM...
MAYBE I SHOULD HAVE EATEN ONE OF MY SIBLINGS TOO...
EW...

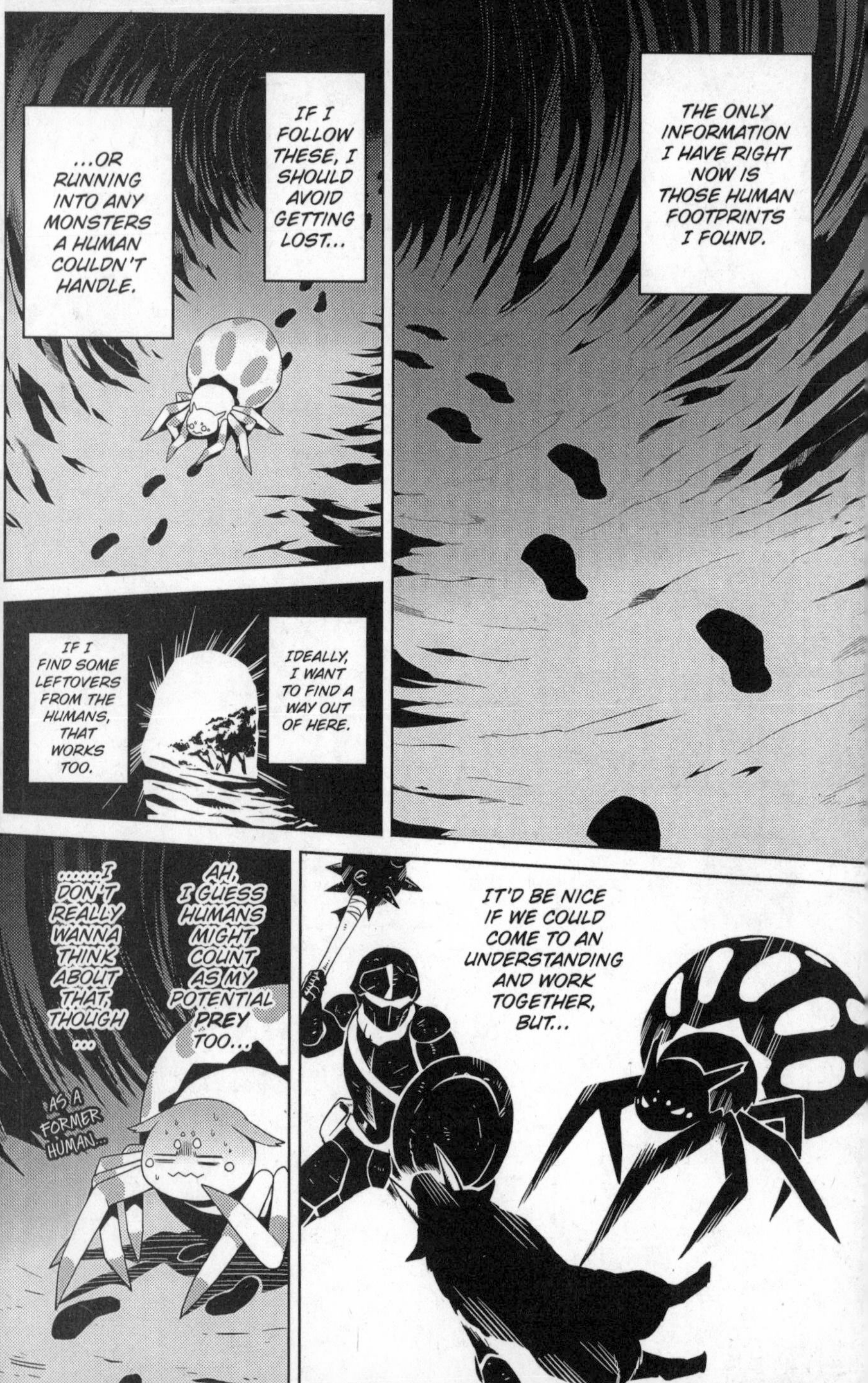
THE ONLY INFORMATION I HAVE RIGHT NOW IS THOSE HUMAN FOOTPRINTS I FOUND.
IF I FOLLOW THESE, I SHOULD AVOID GETTING LOST...
...OR RUNNING INTO ANY MONSTERS A HUMAN COULDN'T HANDLE.
IDEALLY, I WANT TO FIND A WAY OUT OF HERE.
IF I FIND SOME LEFTOVERS FROM THE HUMANS, THAT WORKS TOO.
IT'D BE NICE IF WE COULD COME TO AN UNDERSTANDING AND WORK TOGETHER, BUT...
AH, I GUESS HUMANS MIGHT COUNT AS MY POTENTIAL PREY TOO...
......I DON'T REALLY WANNA THINK ABOUT THAT, THOUGH...
AS A FORMER HUMAN...

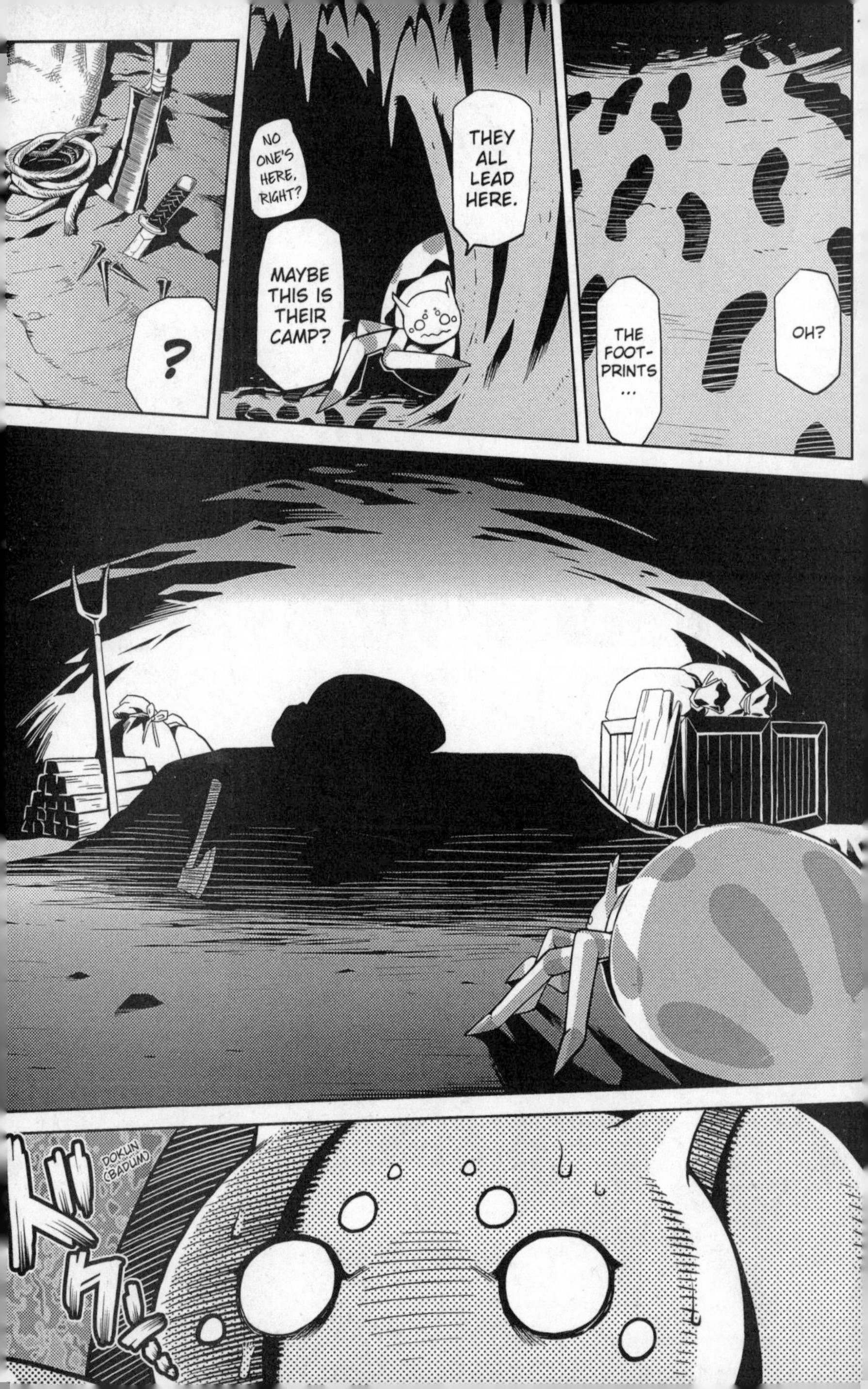
OH?
THE FOOT-PRINTS...
THEY ALL LEAD HERE.
NO ONE'S HERE, RIGHT?
MAYBE THIS IS THEIR CAMP?
?
DOKUN (BADUM)

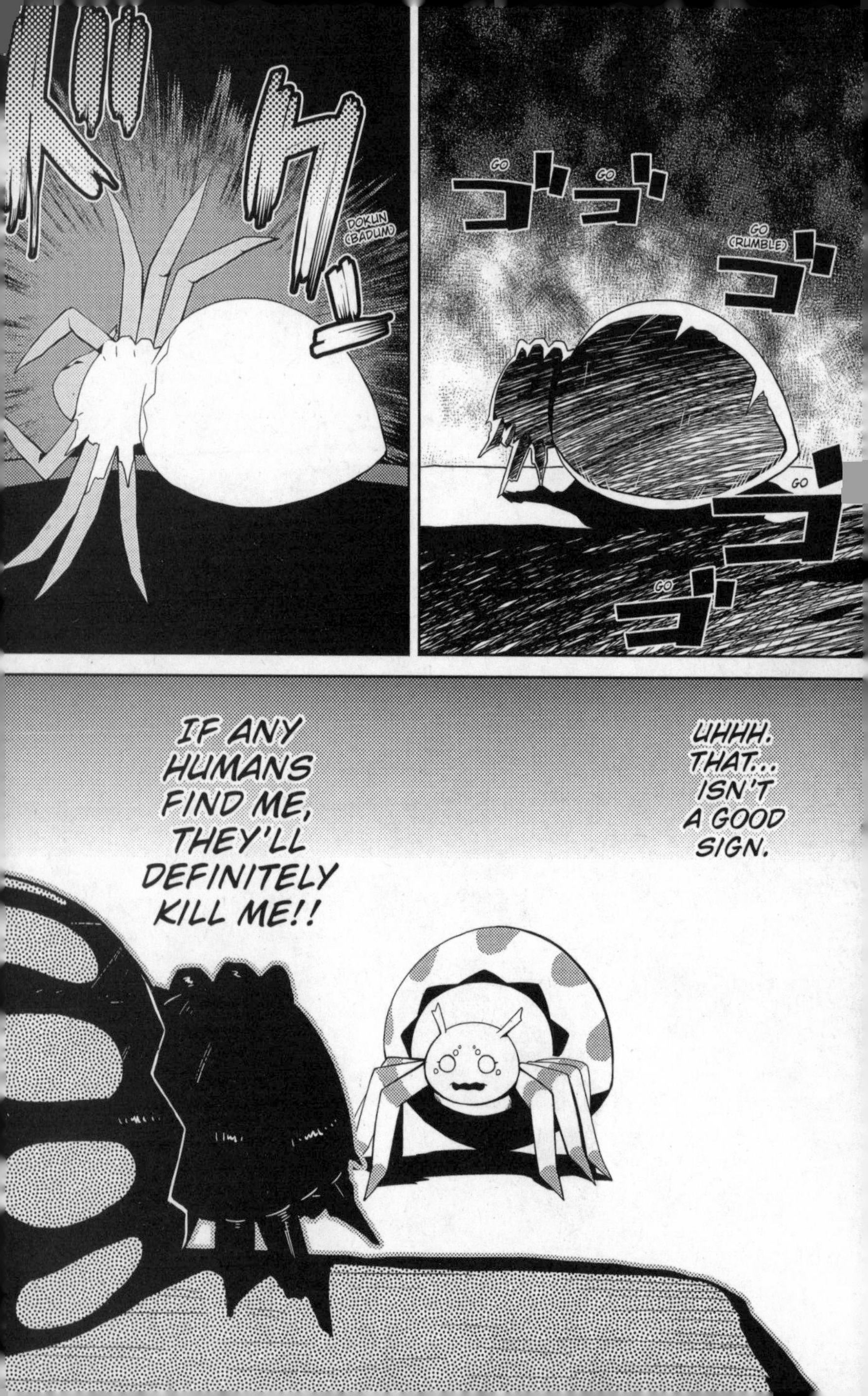
GO
GO
GO (RUMBLE)
GO
GO
DOKUN (BADUM)
UHHH. THAT... ISN'T A GOOD SIGN.
IF ANY HUMANS FIND ME, THEY'LL DEFINITELY KILL ME!!

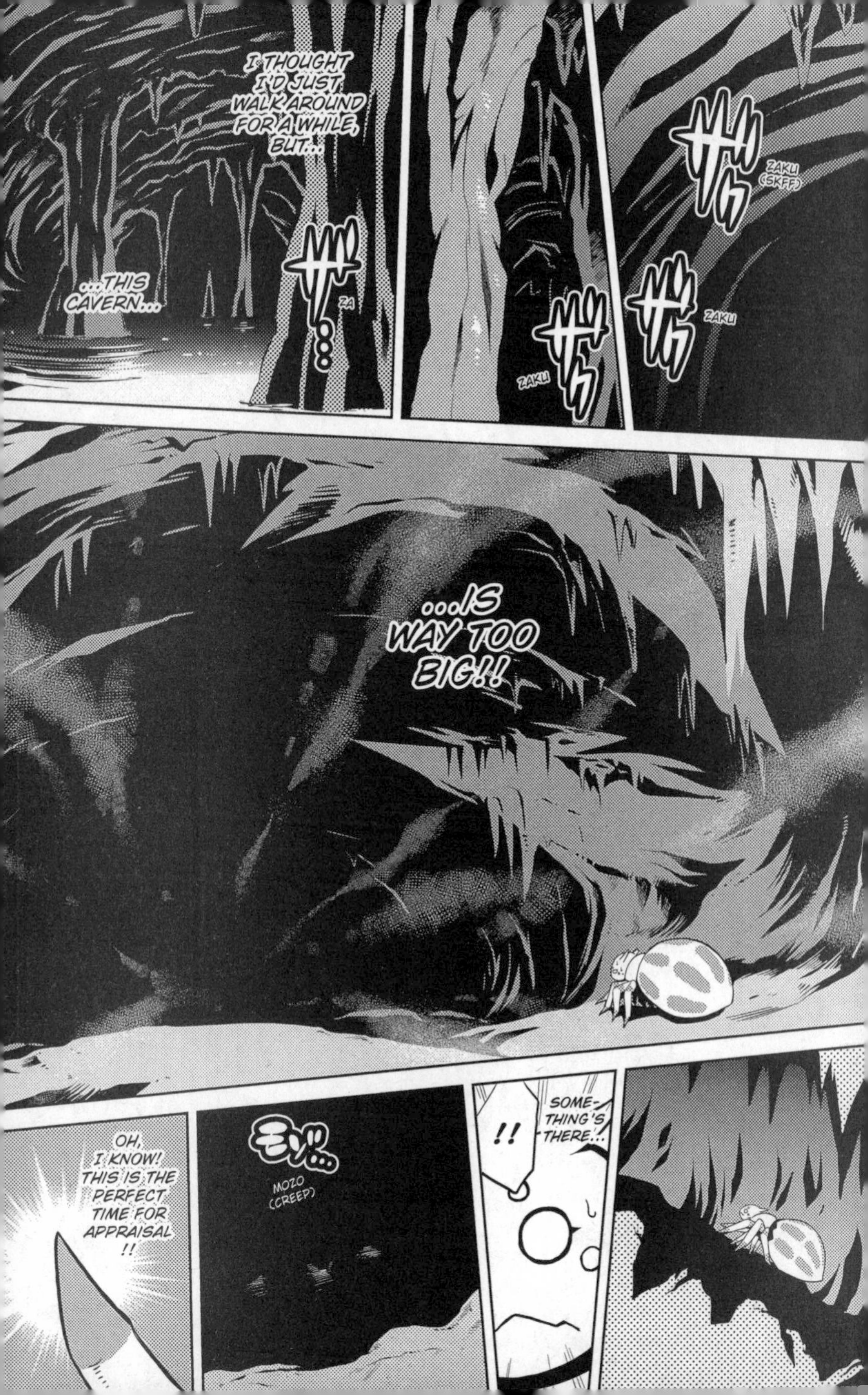
ZAKU (SKFF)
ZAKU
ZAKU
I THOUGHT I'D JUST WALK AROUND FOR A WHILE, BUT...
ZA
...THIS CAVERN...
...IS WAY TOO BIG!!
SOME-THING'S THERE...
!!
MOZO (CREEP)
OH, I KNOW! THIS IS THE PERFECT TIME FOR APPRAISAL!!

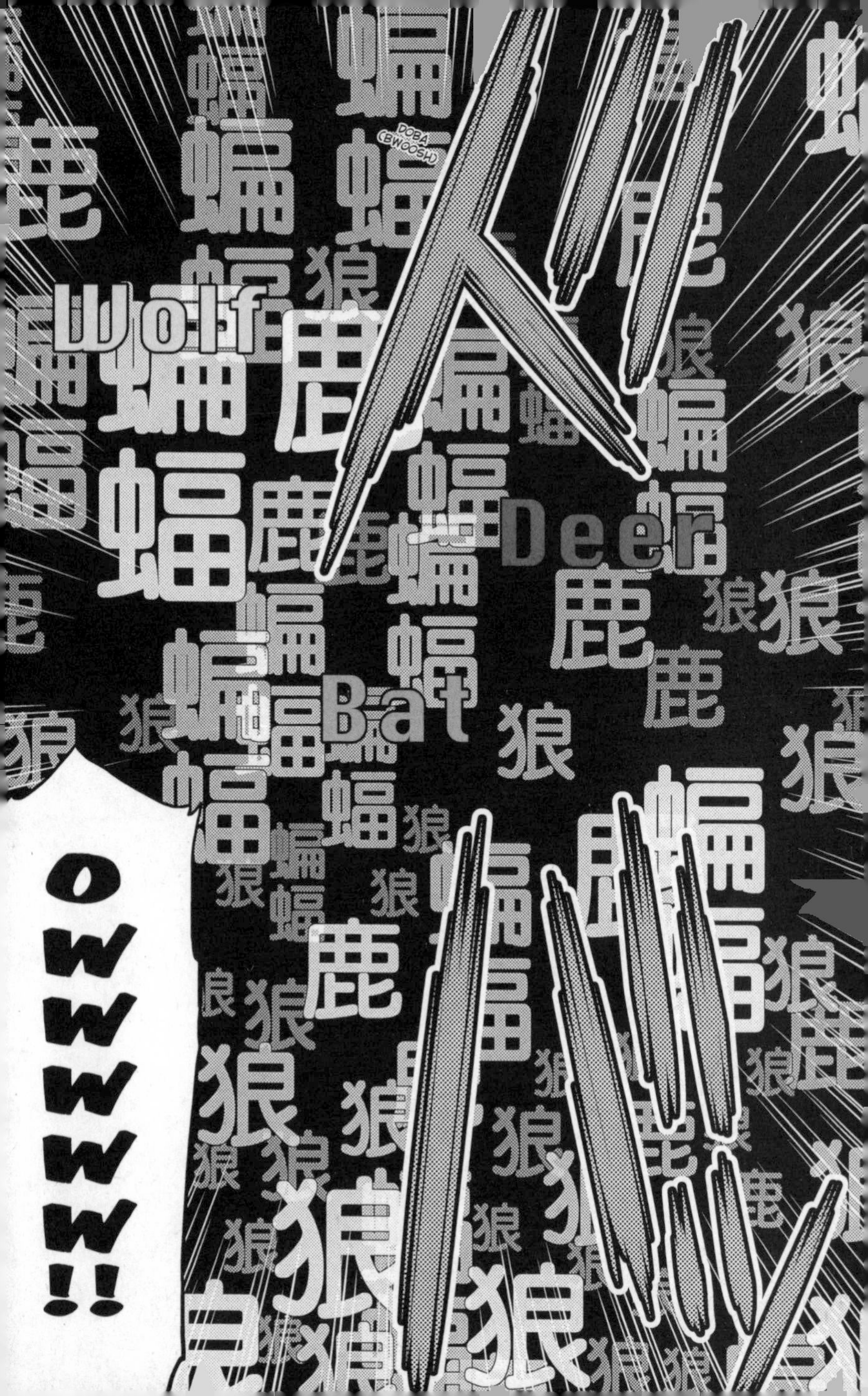
DOBA (BWOOSH)
Wolf
Deer
Bat
OWWWWWWW!!

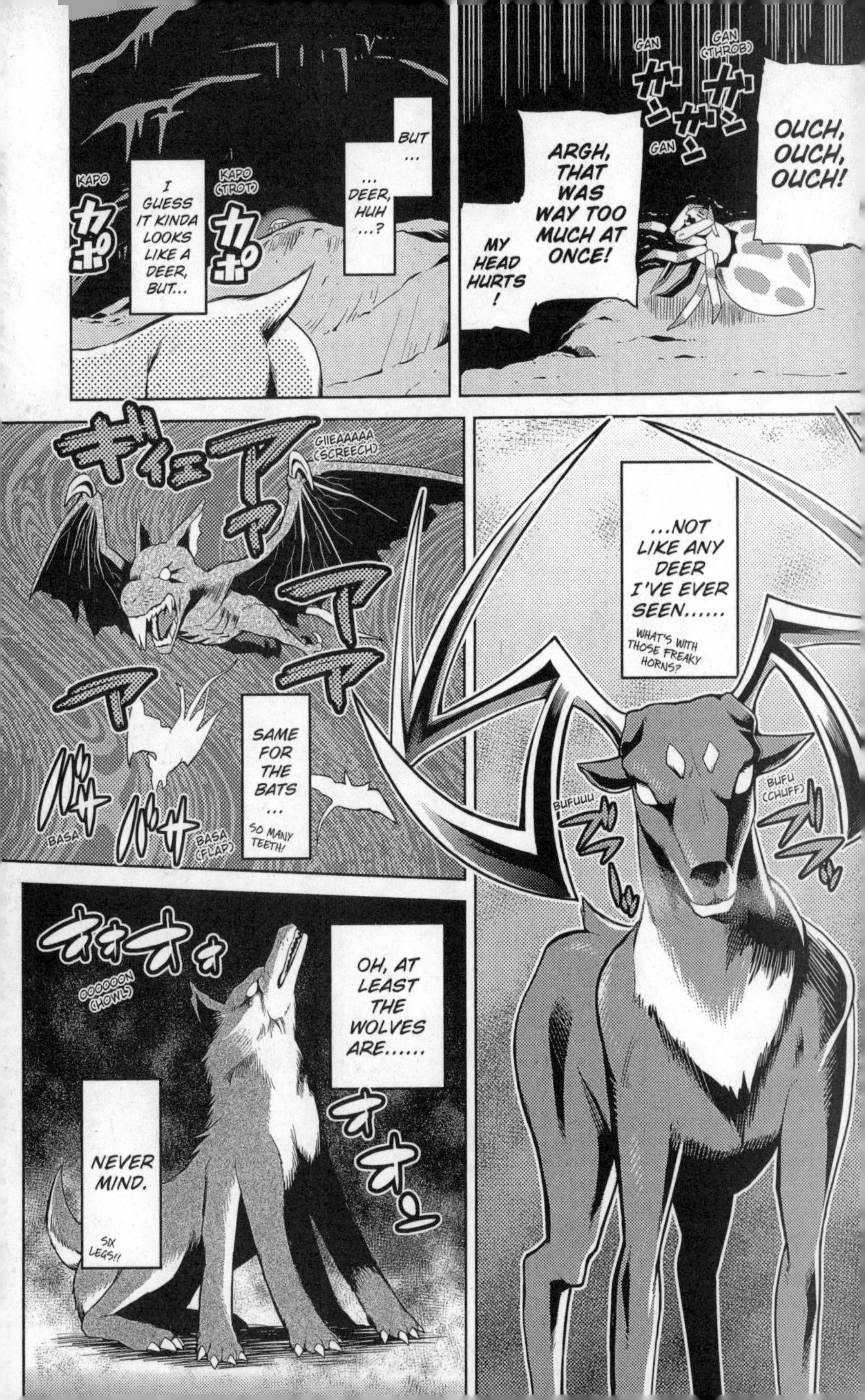
OUCH, OUCH, OUCH!
GAN (THROB)
GAN
GAN
ARGH, THAT WAS WAY TOO MUCH AT ONCE!
MY HEAD HURTS!
BUT...
...DEER, HUH...?
KAPO (TROT)
I GUESS IT KINDA LOOKS LIKE A DEER, BUT...
KAPO
...NOT LIKE ANY DEER I'VE EVER SEEN......
WHAT'S WITH THOSE FREAKY HORNS?
BUFU (CHUFF)
BUFUUU
GIIEAAAAA (SCREECH)
SAME FOR THE BATS...
SO MANY TEETH!
BASA (FLAP)
BASA
OH, AT LEAST THE WOLVES ARE......
OOOOOON (HOWL)
NEVER MIND.
SIX LEGS!!

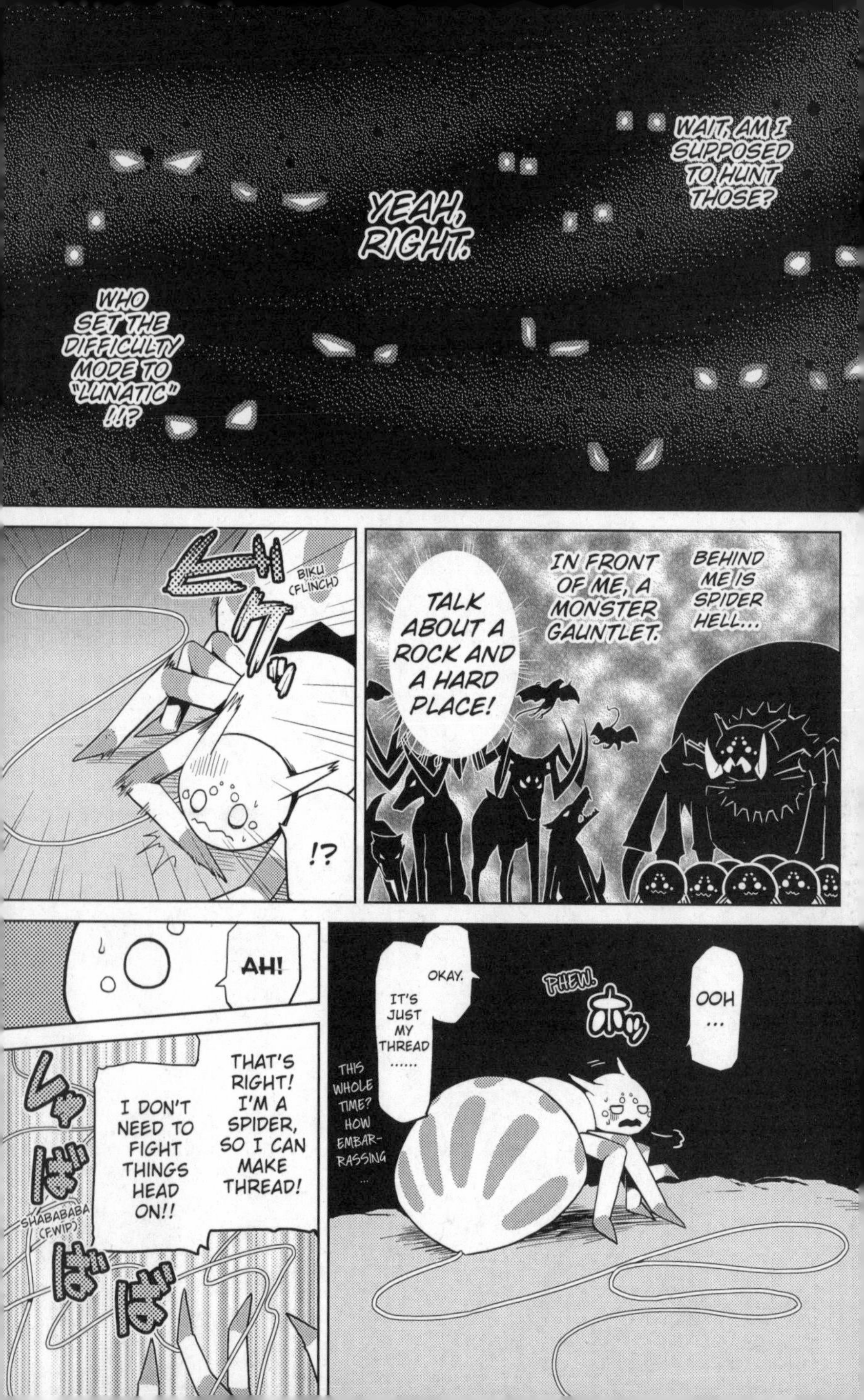
WAIT, AM I SUPPOSED TO HUNT THOSE?
YEAH, RIGHT.
WHO SET THE DIFFICULTY MODE TO "LUNATIC" !!?
BEHIND ME IS SPIDER HELL...
IN FRONT OF ME, A MONSTER GAUNTLET.
TALK ABOUT A ROCK AND A HARD PLACE!
BIKU (FLINCH)
!?
OOH ...
PHEW.
OKAY.
IT'S JUST MY THREAD ......
THIS WHOLE TIME? HOW EMBARRASSING ...
AH!
THAT'S RIGHT! I'M A SPIDER, SO I CAN MAKE THREAD!
I DON'T NEED TO FIGHT THINGS HEAD ON!!
SHABABABA (FWIP)

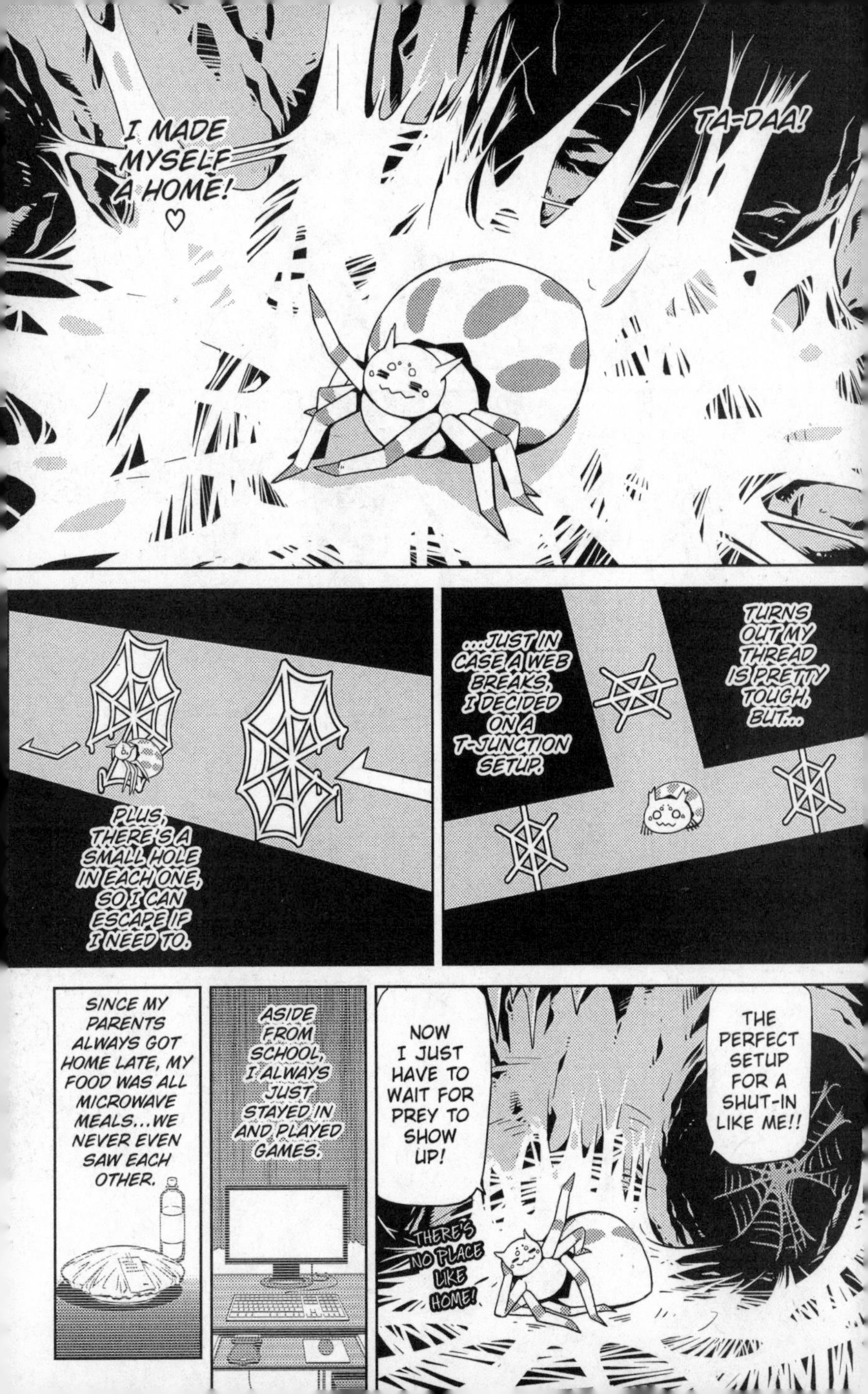
TA-DAA!
I MADE MYSELF A HOME! ♡
TURNS OUT MY THREAD IS PRETTY TOUGH, BUT...
...JUST IN CASE A WEB BREAKS, I DECIDED ON A T-JUNCTION SETUP.
PLUS, THERE'S A SMALL HOLE IN EACH ONE, SO I CAN ESCAPE IF I NEED TO.
THE PERFECT SETUP FOR A SHUT-IN LIKE ME!!
NOW I JUST HAVE TO WAIT FOR PREY TO SHOW UP!
THERE'S NO PLACE LIKE HOME!
ASIDE FROM SCHOOL, I ALWAYS JUST STAYED IN AND PLAYED GAMES.
SINCE MY PARENTS ALWAYS GOT HOME LATE, MY FOOD WAS ALL MICROWAVE MEALS...WE NEVER EVEN SAW EACH OTHER.

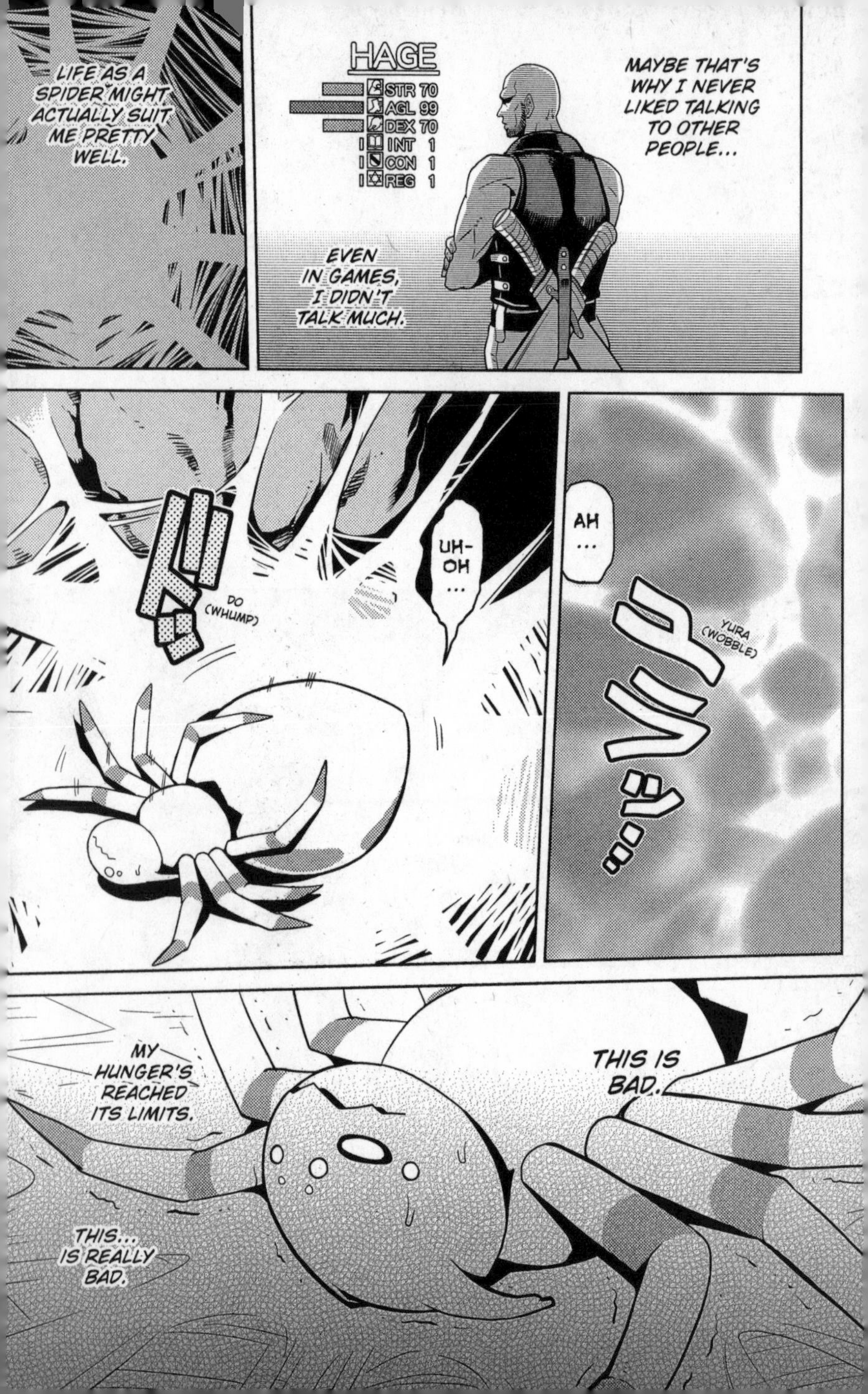
MAYBE THAT'S WHY I NEVER LIKED TALKING TO OTHER PEOPLE...
HAGE
STR 70
AGL 99
DEX 70
INT 1
CON 1
REG 1
EVEN IN GAMES, I DIDN'T TALK MUCH.
LIFE AS A SPIDER MIGHT ACTUALLY SUIT ME PRETTY WELL.
AH...
ユラッ...
YURA (WOBBLE)
UH-OH...
ドッ
DO (WHUMP)
THIS IS BAD.
MY HUNGER'S REACHED ITS LIMITS.
THIS... IS REALLY BAD.

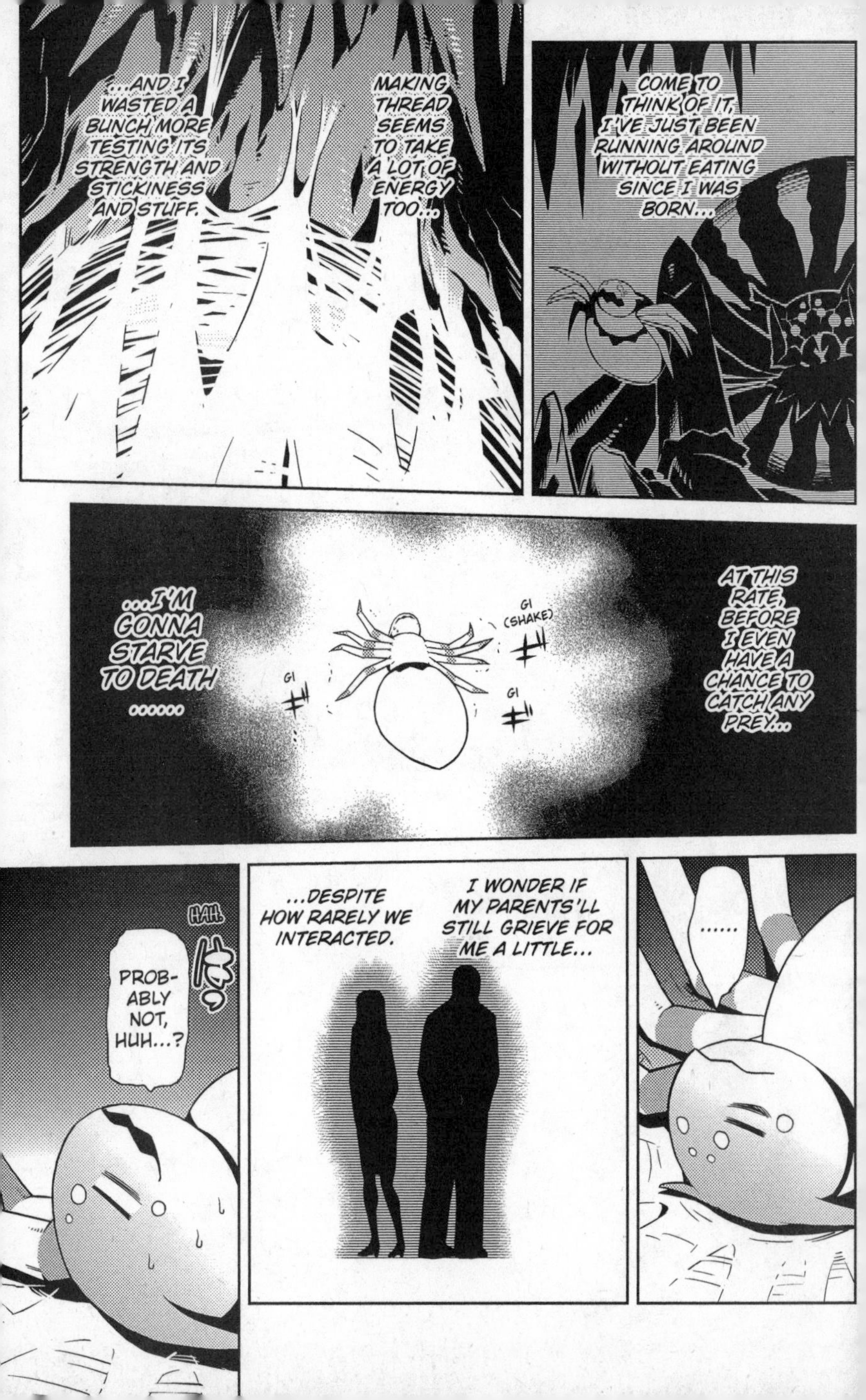
COME TO THINK OF IT, I'VE JUST BEEN RUNNING AROUND WITHOUT EATING SINCE I WAS BORN...
MAKING THREAD SEEMS TO TAKE A LOT OF ENERGY TOO...
...AND I WASTED A BUNCH MORE TESTING ITS STRENGTH AND STICKINESS AND STUFF.
AT THIS RATE, BEFORE I EVEN HAVE A CHANCE TO CATCH ANY PREY...
GI (SHAKE)
GI
GI
...I'M GONNA STARVE TO DEATH ......
......
I WONDER IF MY PARENTS'LL STILL GRIEVE FOR ME A LITTLE...
...DESPITE HOW RARELY WE INTERACTED.
HAH.
PROB-ABLY NOT, HUH...?

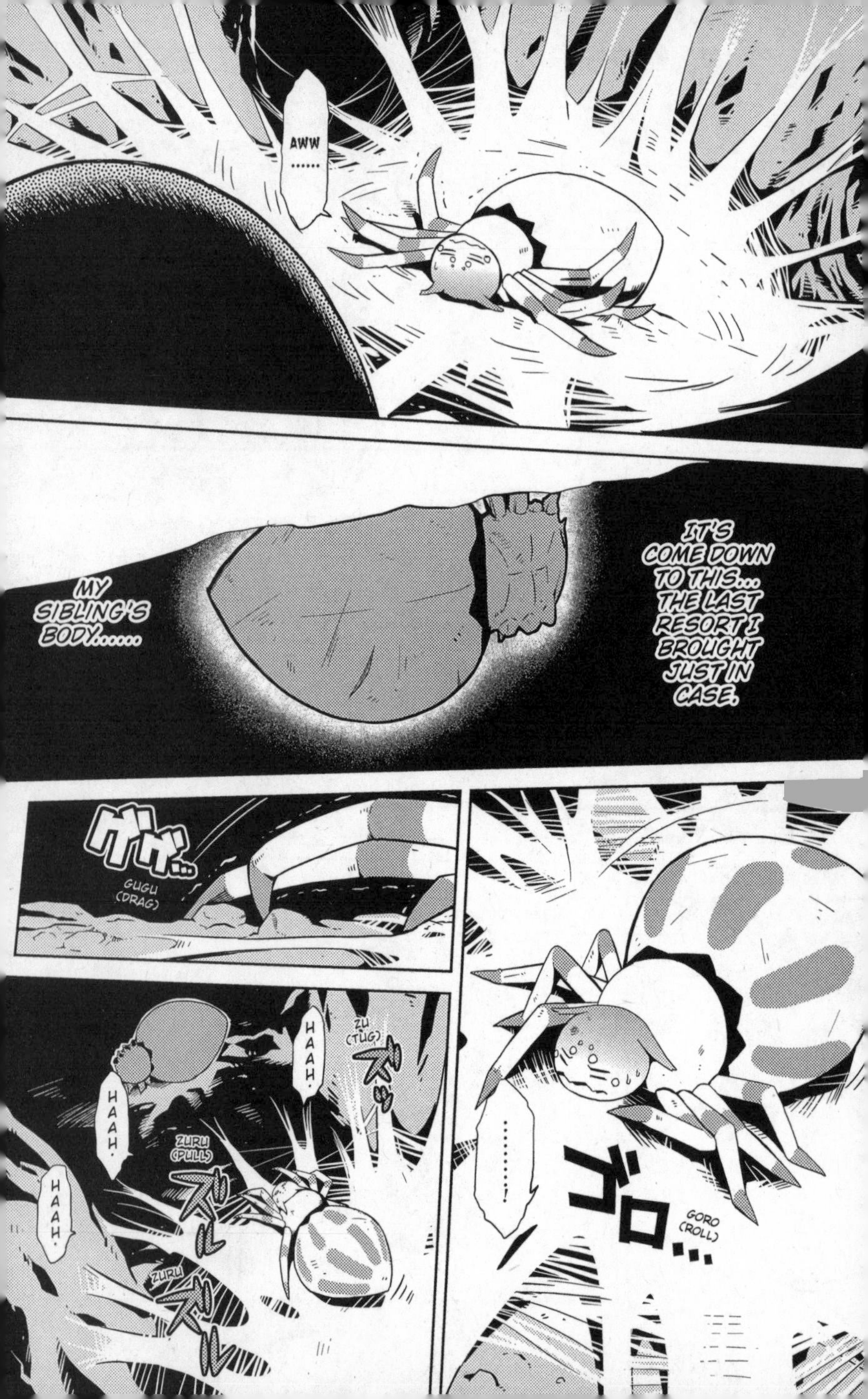
AWW ......
IT'S COME DOWN TO THIS... THE LAST RESORT I BROUGHT JUST IN CASE.
MY SIBLING'S BODY......
......!
ゴロ…
GORO (ROLL)
ググ…
GUGU (DRAG)
HAAH.
ZU (TUG)
HAAH.
ZURU (PULL)
HAAH.
ZURU

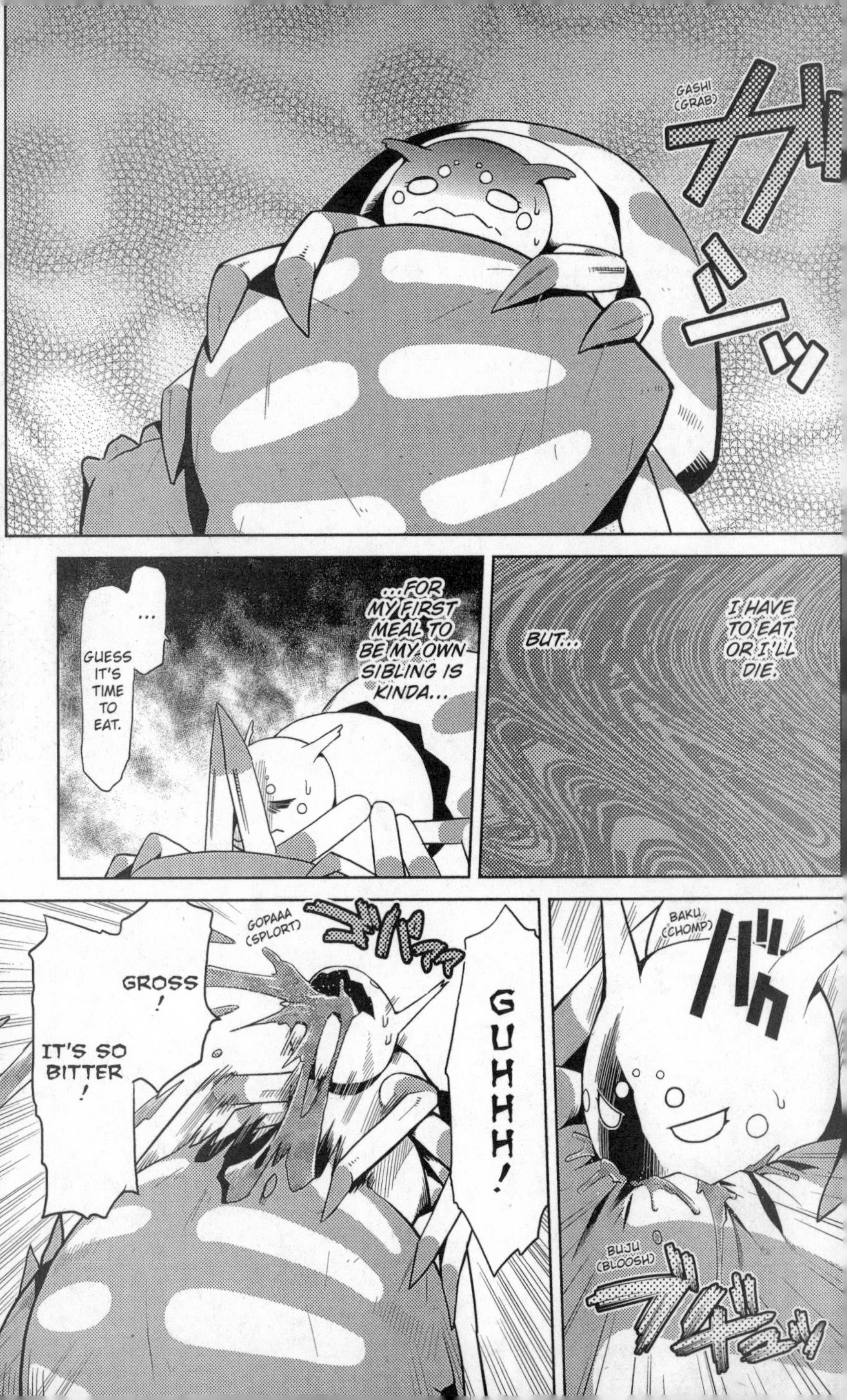
GASHI (GRAB)
I HAVE TO EAT, OR I'LL DIE.
BUT...
...FOR MY FIRST MEAL TO BE MY OWN SIBLING IS KINDA...
...
GUESS IT'S TIME TO EAT.
BAKU (CHOMP)
BUJU (BLOOSH)
GOPAAA (SPLORT)
GUHHH!
GROSS!
IT'S SO BITTER!

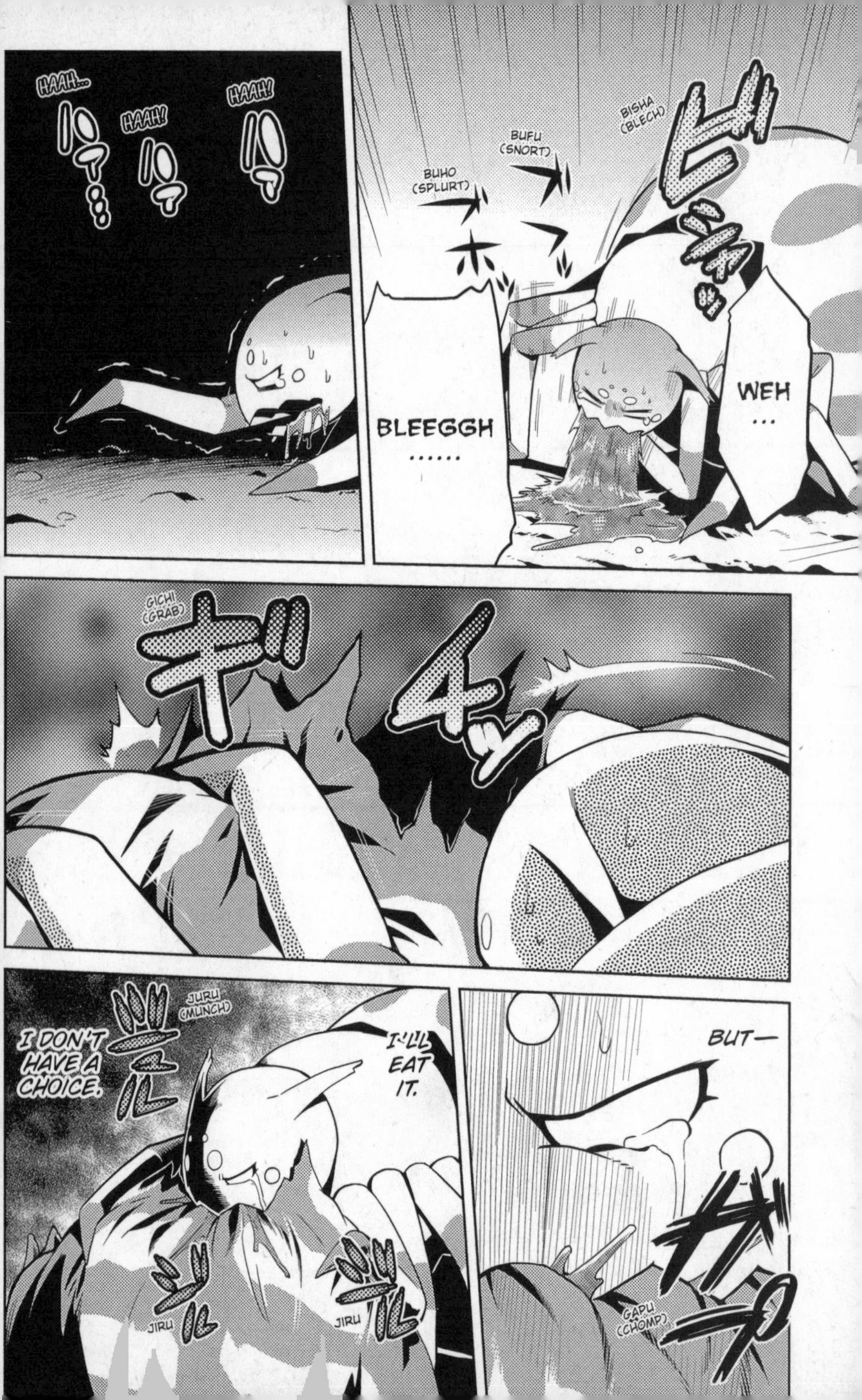

BISHA (BLECH)
WEH...
BUFU (SNORT)
BUHO (SPLURT)
BLEEGGH......
HAAH!
HAAH!
HAAH...
GICHI (GRAB)
BUT—
GAPU (CHOMP)
JURU (MUNCH)
I'LL EAT IT.
I DON'T HAVE A CHOICE.
JIRU
JIRU

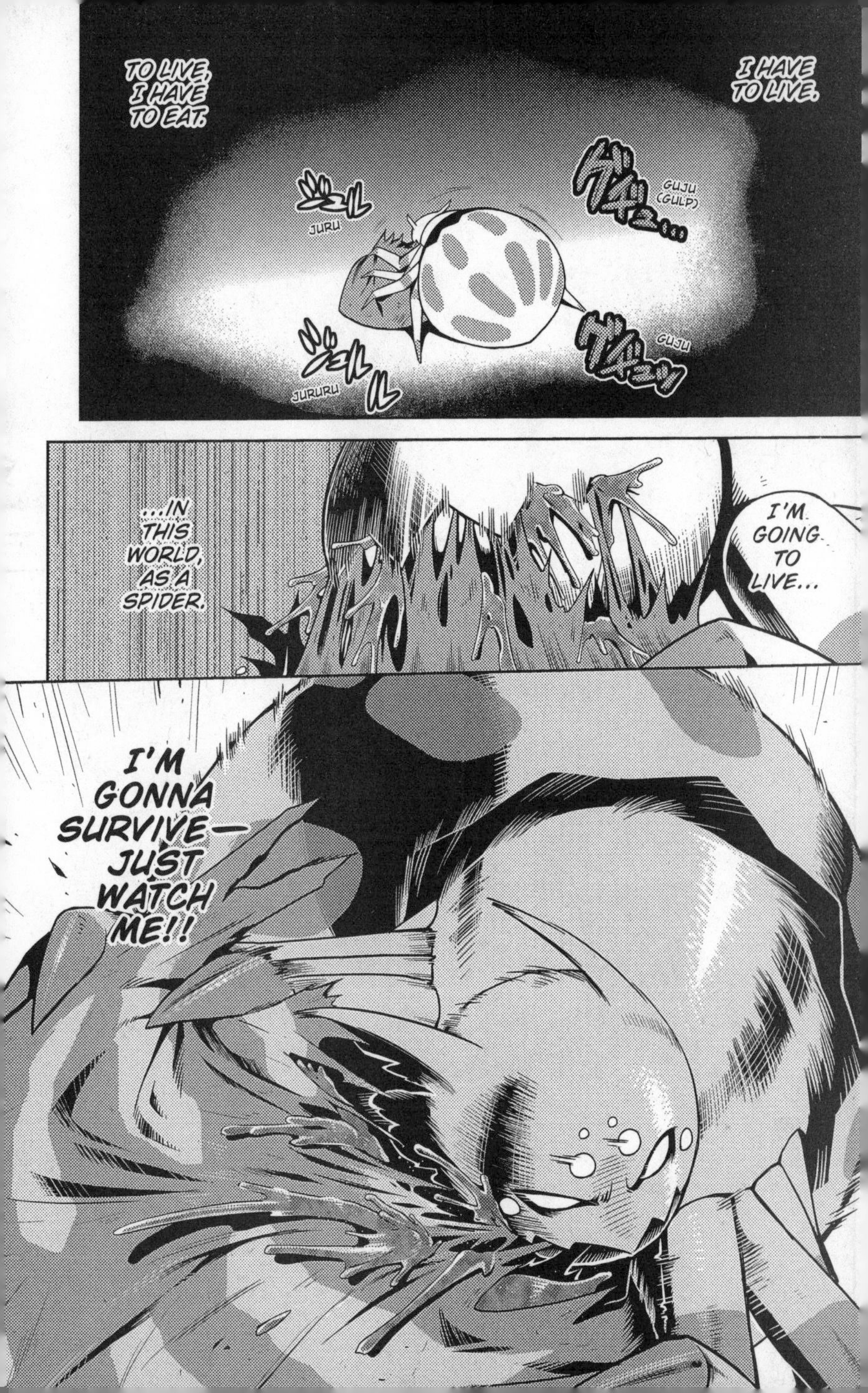
I HAVE TO LIVE.
TO LIVE, I HAVE TO EAT.
GUJU (GULP)
JURU
GUJU
JURURU
I'M GOING TO LIVE...
...IN THIS WORLD, AS A SPIDER.
I'M GONNA SURVIVE—JUST WATCH ME!!

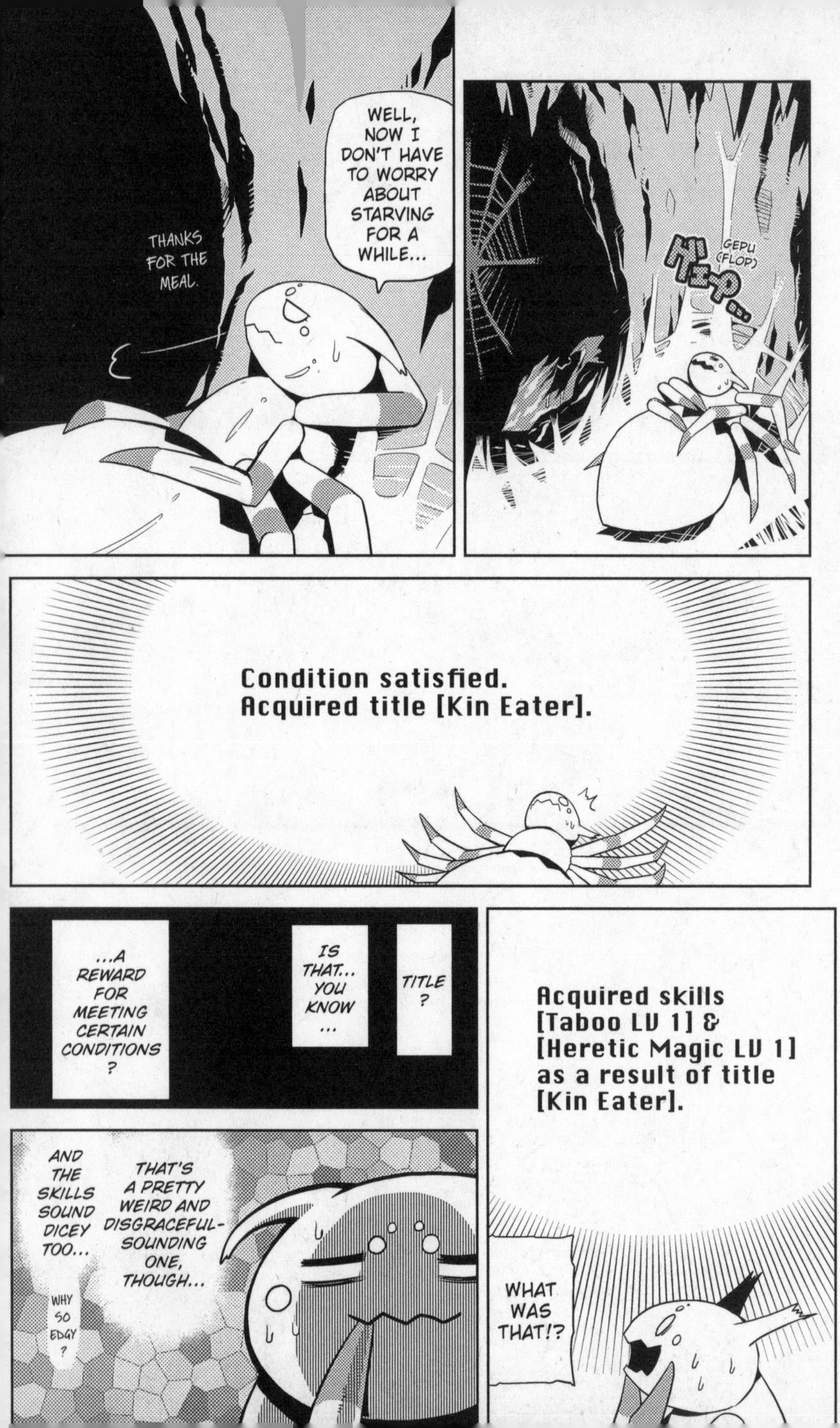
GEPU
(FLOP)
WELL, NOW I DON'T HAVE TO WORRY ABOUT STARVING FOR A WHILE...
THANKS FOR THE MEAL.
Condition satisfied.
Acquired title [Kin Eater].
Acquired skills [Taboo LV 1] & [Heretic Magic LV 1] as a result of title [Kin Eater].
WHAT WAS THAT!?
TITLE?
IS THAT... YOU KNOW...
...A REWARD FOR MEETING CERTAIN CONDITIONS?
THAT'S A PRETTY WEIRD AND DISGRACEFUL-SOUNDING ONE, THOUGH...
AND THE SKILLS SOUND DICEY TOO...
WHY SO EDGY?

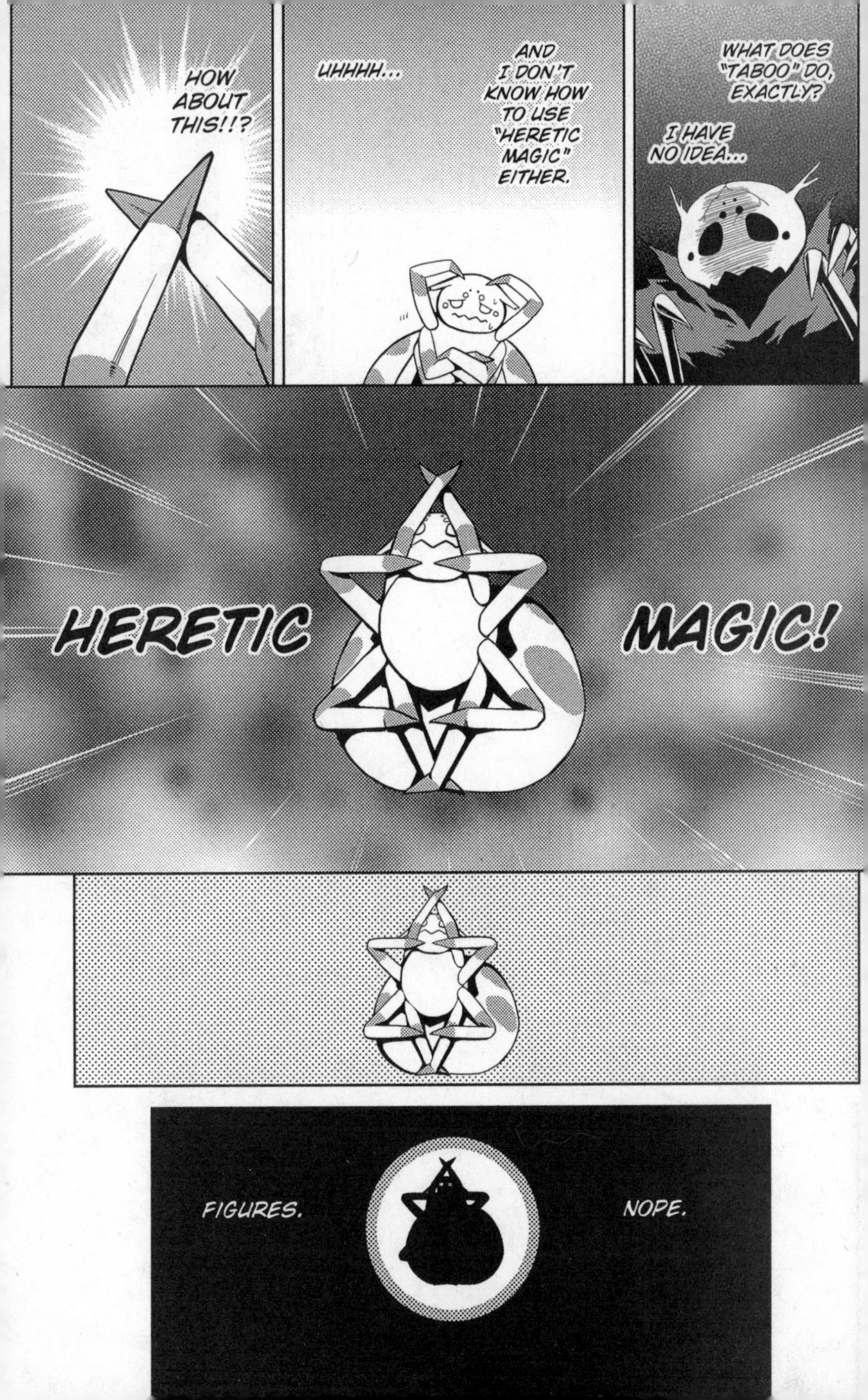
WHAT DOES "TABOO" DO, EXACTLY?
I HAVE NO IDEA...
AND I DON'T KNOW HOW TO USE "HERETIC MAGIC" EITHER.
UHHHH...
HOW ABOUT THIS!!?
HERETIC MAGIC!
NOPE.
FIGURES.

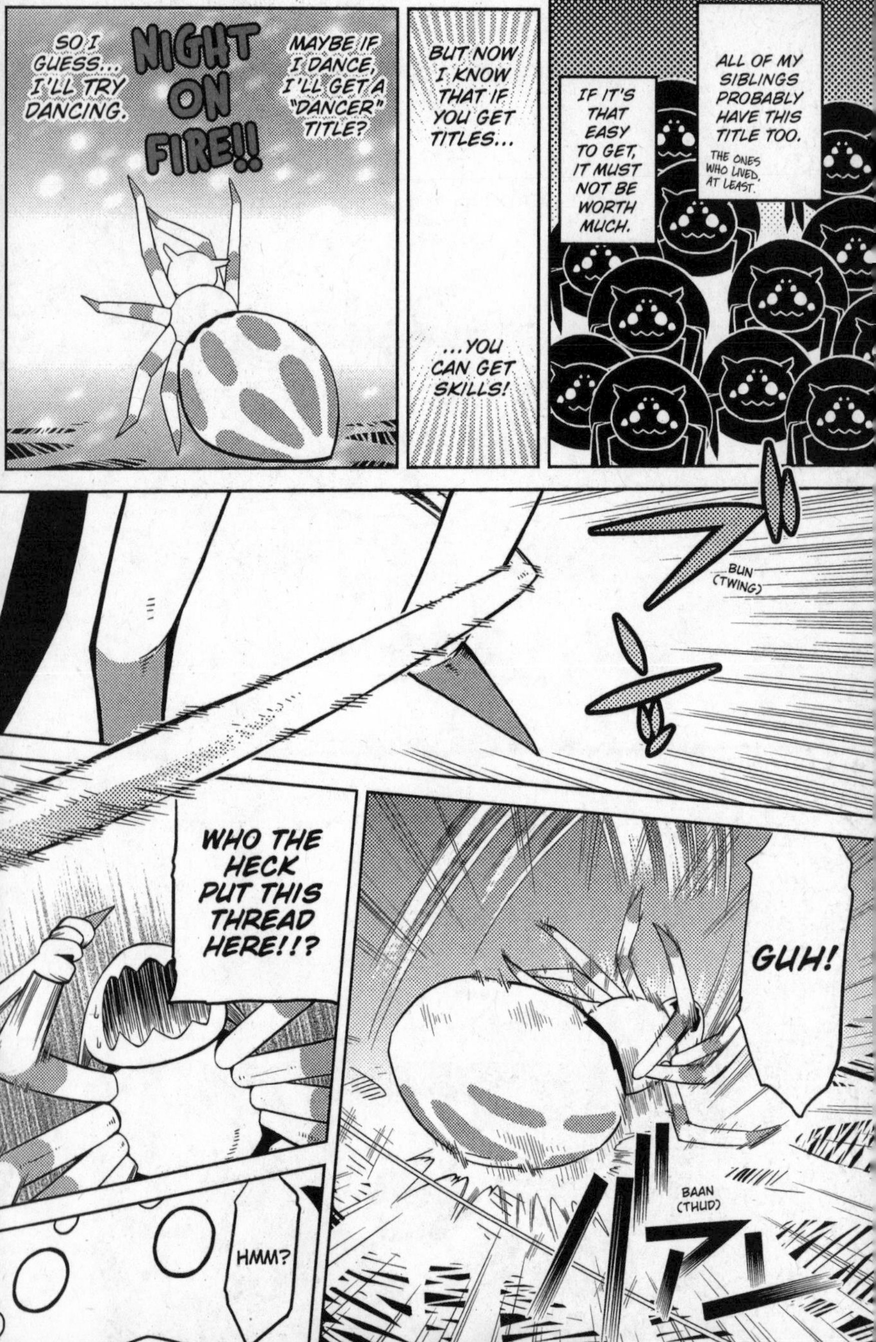
ALL OF MY SIBLINGS PROBABLY HAVE THIS TITLE TOO.
THE ONES WHO LIVED, AT LEAST.
IF IT'S THAT EASY TO GET, IT MUST NOT BE WORTH MUCH.
BUT NOW I KNOW THAT IF YOU GET TITLES...
...YOU CAN GET SKILLS!
MAYBE IF I DANCE, I'LL GET A "DANCER" TITLE?
NIGHT ON FIRE!!
SO I GUESS... I'LL TRY DANCING.
BUN (TWING)
GUH!
BAAN (THUD)
WHO THE HECK PUT THIS THREAD HERE!!?
HMM?

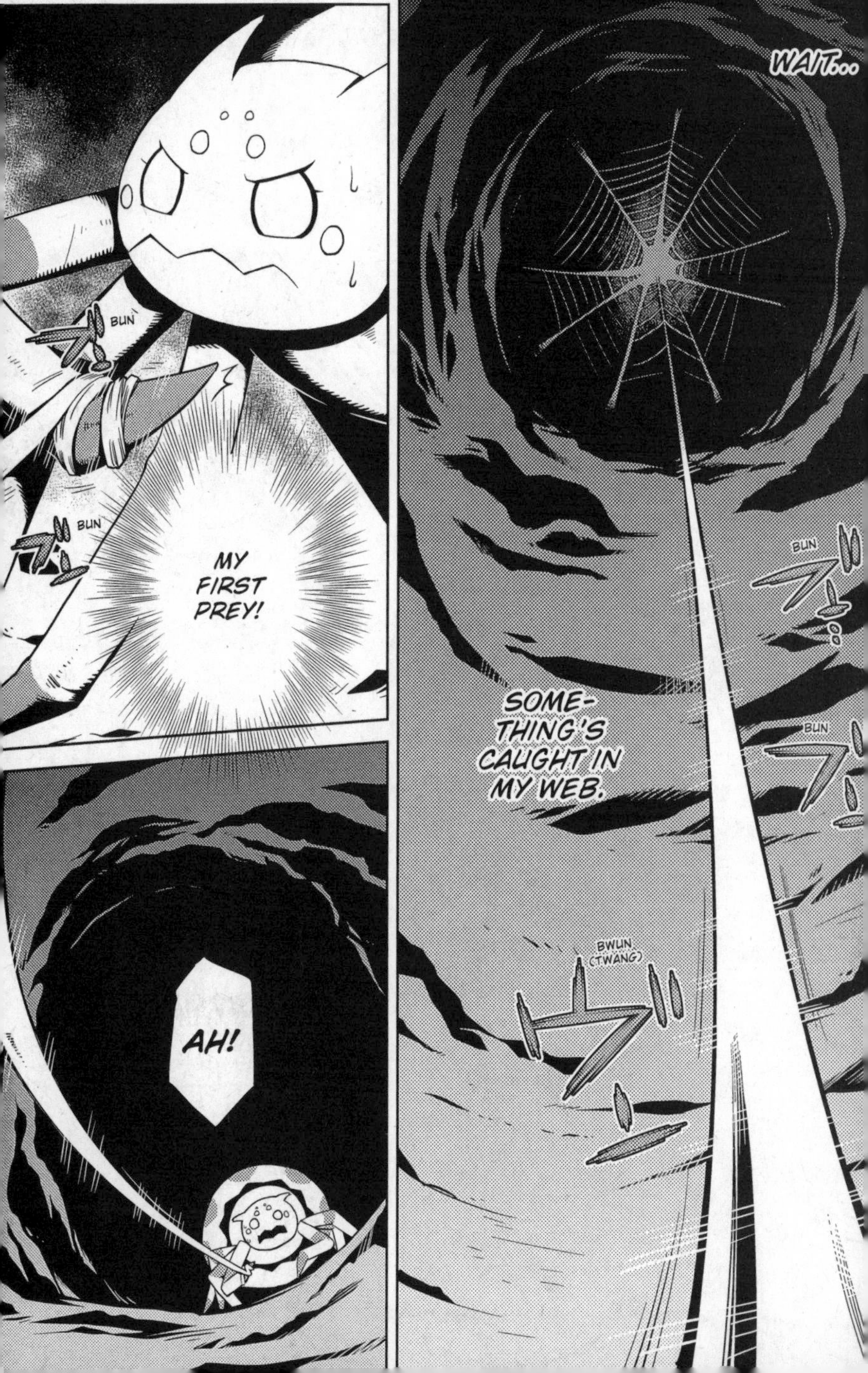
WAIT...
BUN
SOME-THING'S CAUGHT IN MY WEB.
BUN
BWUN (TWANG)
BUN
BUN
MY FIRST PREY!
AH!

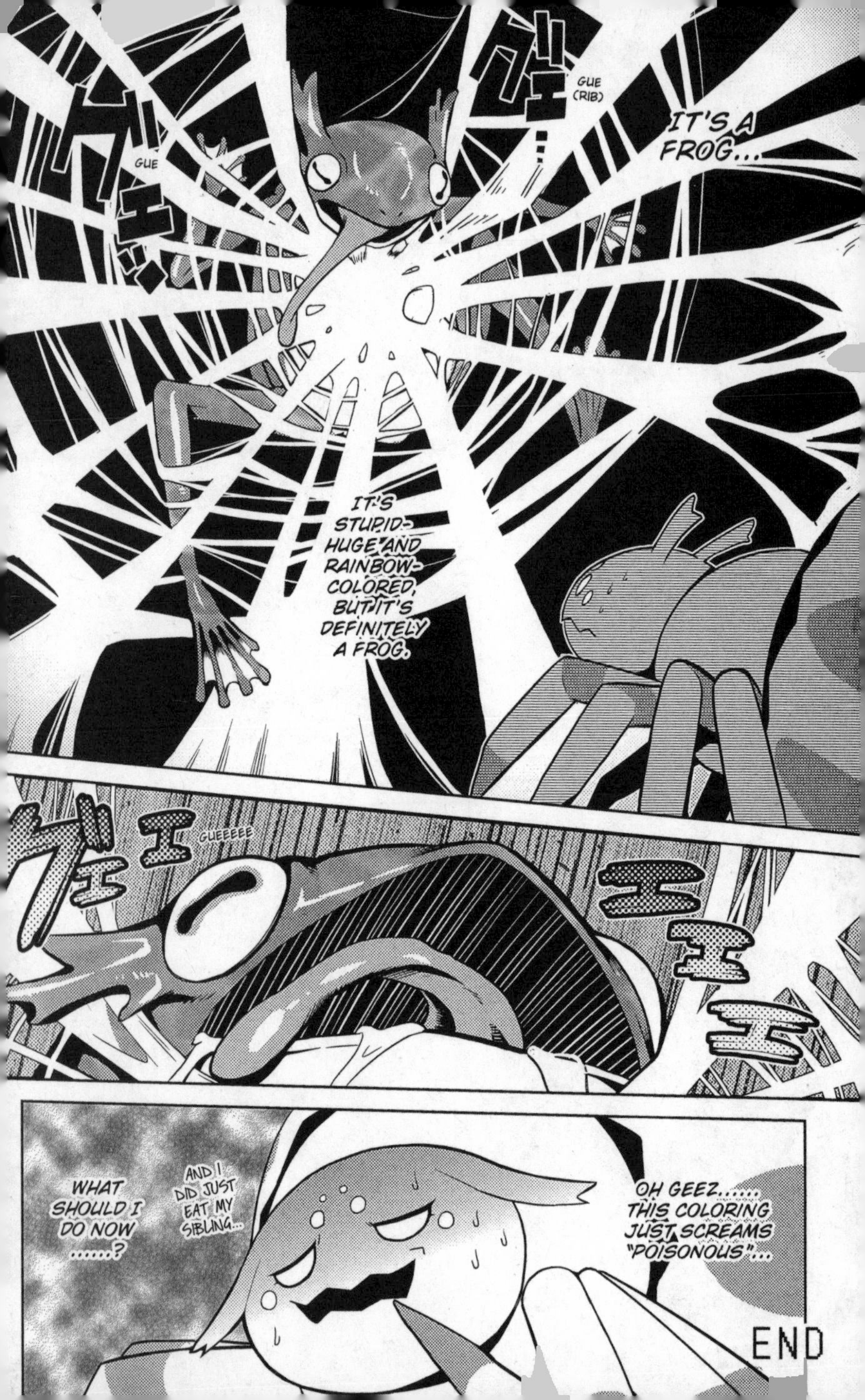
GUE (RIB)
IT'S A FROG...
GUE
IT'S STUPID-HUGE AND RAINBOW-COLORED, BUT IT'S DEFINITELY A FROG.
GUEEEEE
OH GEEZ...... THIS COLORING JUST SCREAMS "POISONOUS"...
AND I DID JUST EAT MY SIBLING...
WHAT SHOULD I DO NOW ......?
END

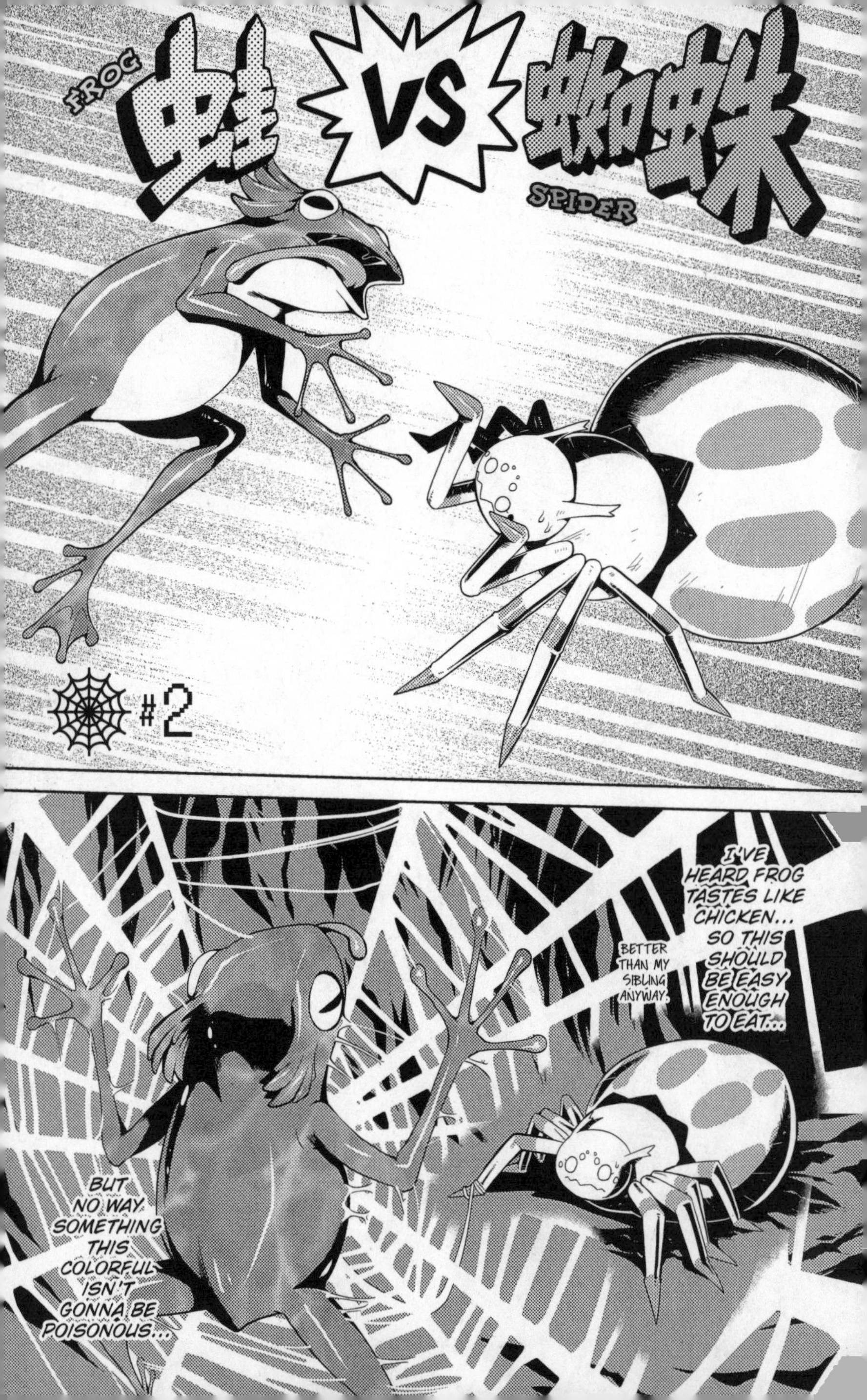
FROG
蛙
VS
蜘蛛
SPIDER
#2
I'VE HEARD FROG TASTES LIKE CHICKEN... SO THIS SHOULD BE EASY ENOUGH TO EAT...
BETTER THAN MY SIBLING ANYWAY.
BUT NO WAY SOMETHING THIS COLORFUL ISN'T GONNA BE POISONOUS...

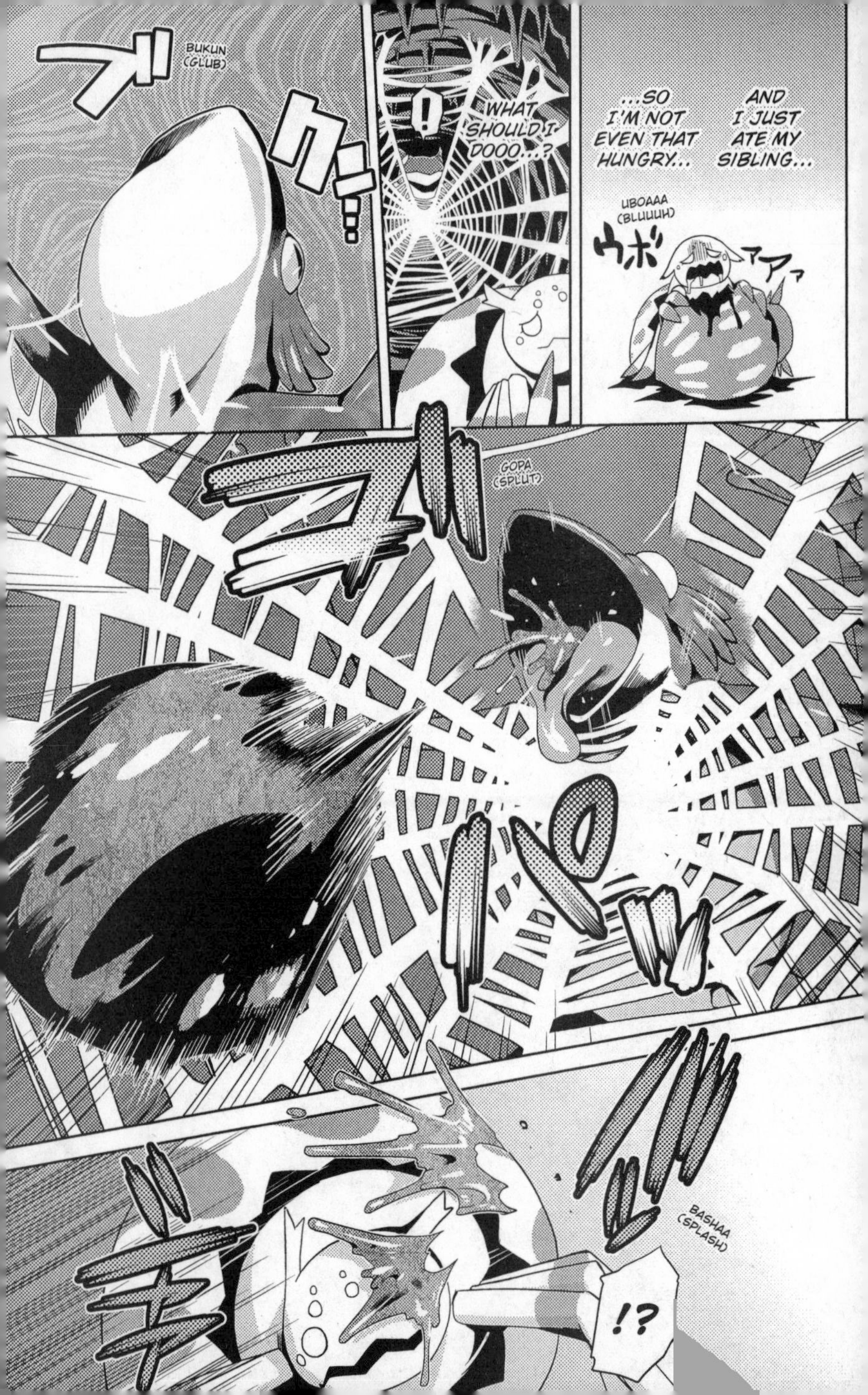

AND I JUST ATE MY SIBLING...
...SO I'M NOT EVEN THAT HUNGRY...
UBOAAA (BLUUUH)
ウボアアァ
!
WHAT SHOULD I DOOO...?
BUKUN (GLUB)
GOPA (SPLUT)
BASHAA (SPLASH)
!?

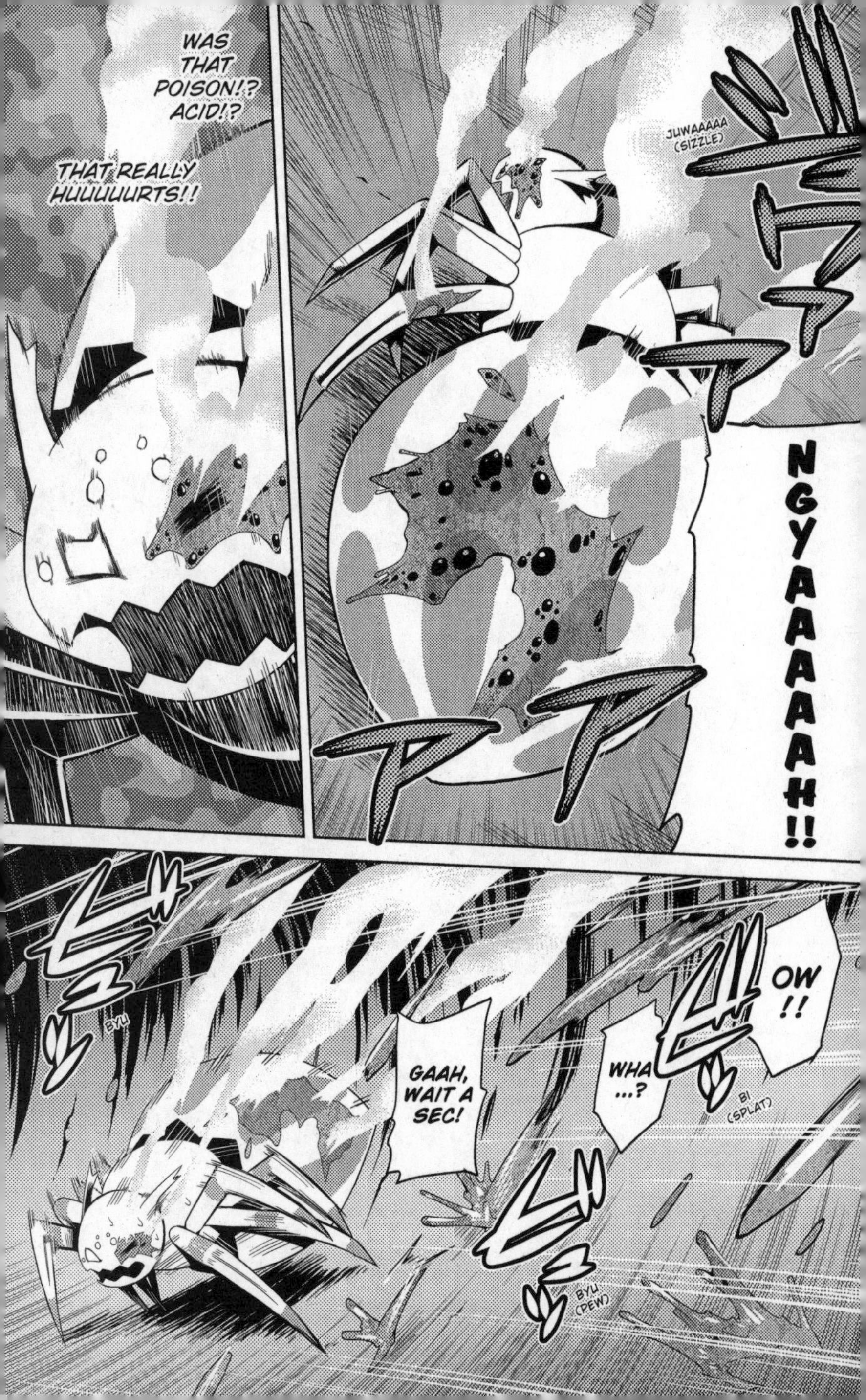
JUWAAAAA (SIZZLE)
NGYAAAAAAH!!
WAS THAT POISON!? ACID!?
THAT REALLY HUUUUURTS!!
OW!!
BI (SPLAT)
WHA...?
GAAH, WAIT A SEC!
BYU (PEW)
BYU

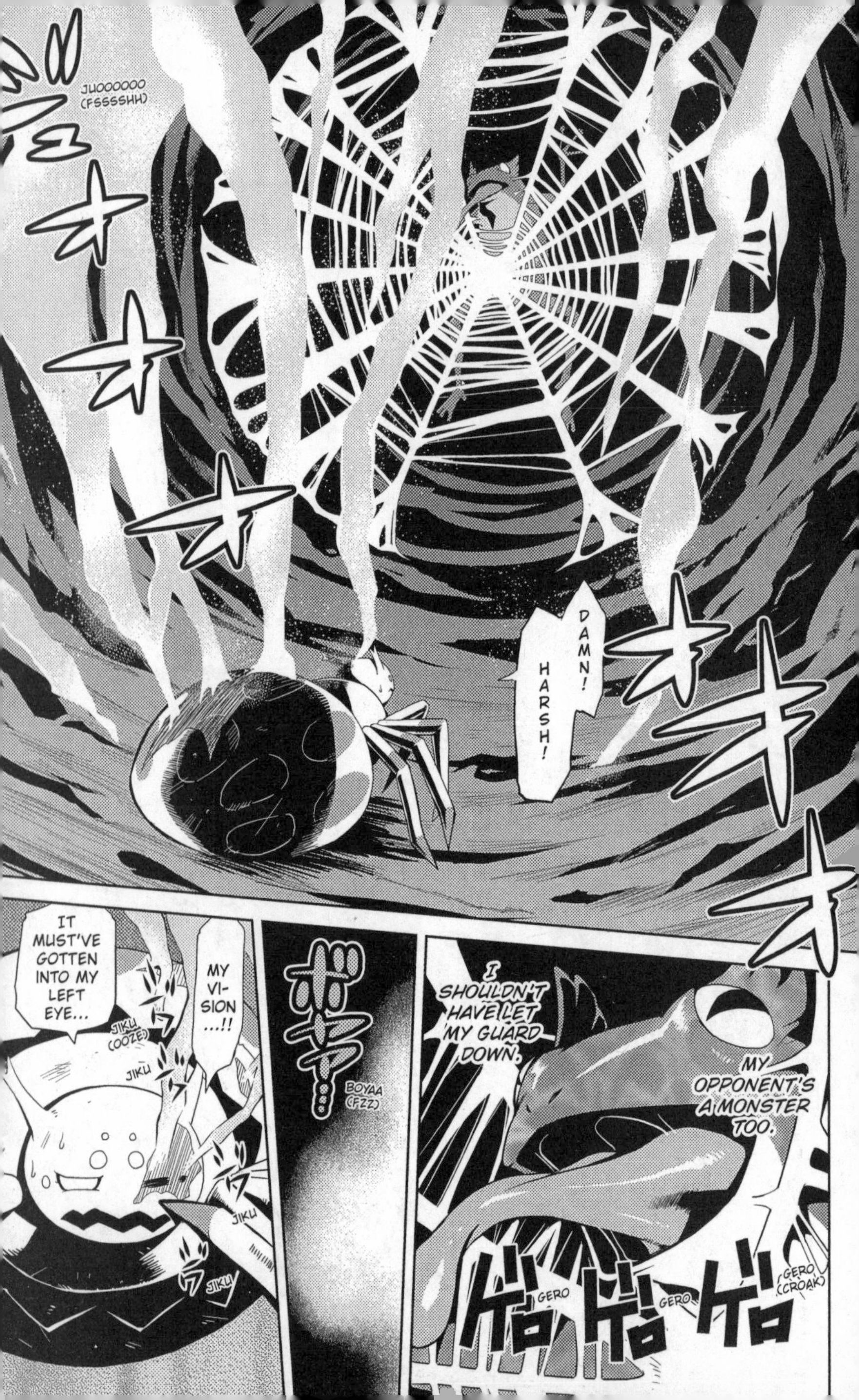
JUOOOOOO (FSSSSHH)
DAMN! HARSH!
I SHOULDN'T HAVE LET MY GUARD DOWN.
MY OPPONENT'S A MONSTER TOO.
GERO
GERO
GERO (CROAK)
BOYAA (FZZ)
MY VI-SION ...!!
IT MUST'VE GOTTEN INTO MY LEFT EYE...
JIKU (OOZE)
JIKU
JIKU
JIKU

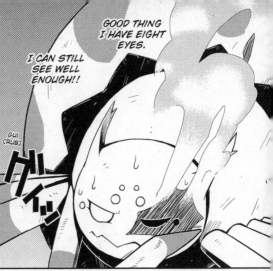

GOOD THING I HAVE EIGHT EYES.
I CAN STILL SEE WELL ENOUGH!!
GUI (RUB)
SO THIS IS WHAT IT FEELS LIKE TO HAVE ACID DUMPED ON YOU...
I'M NOT GONNA MELT, AM I!?
Proficiency has reached the required level. Acquired skill [Acid Resistance LV 1].
WHOA !!
BIKU (FLINCH)
SHUN (SHOOM)
AH... THE PAIN'S LETTING UP A LITTLE.
SO YOU CAN GET SKILLS WITHOUT SPENDING POINTS TOO?
Acid Damage
Acid Resistance
Skill Points
Appraisal
Title
Taboo, Heretic Magic
IN THAT CASE...

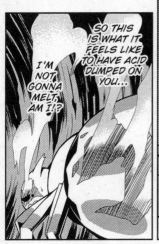

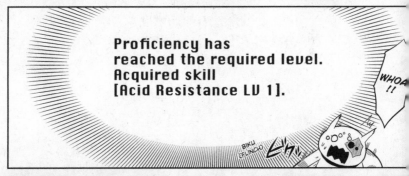

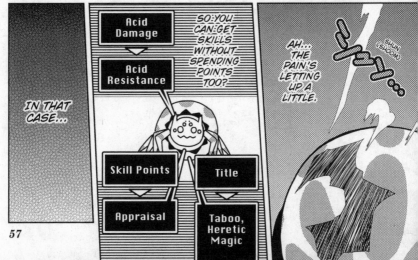

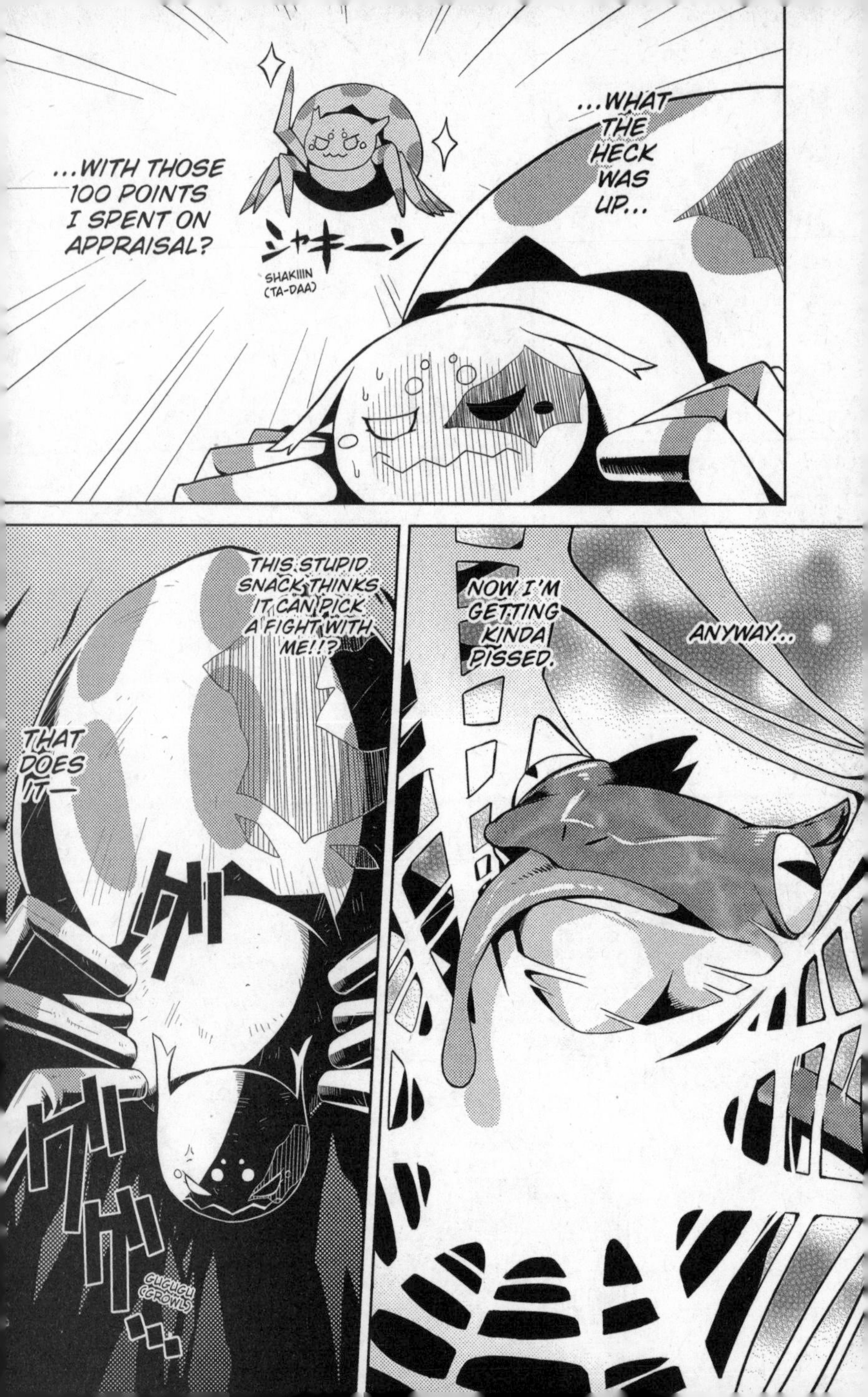
...WHAT THE HECK WAS UP...
...WITH THOSE 100 POINTS I SPENT ON APPRAISAL?
シャキーン
SHAKIIIN (TA-DAA)
ANYWAY...
NOW I'M GETTING KINDA PISSED.
THIS STUPID SNACK THINKS IT CAN PICK A FIGHT WITH ME!!?
THAT DOES IT—
GUGUGU (GROWL)

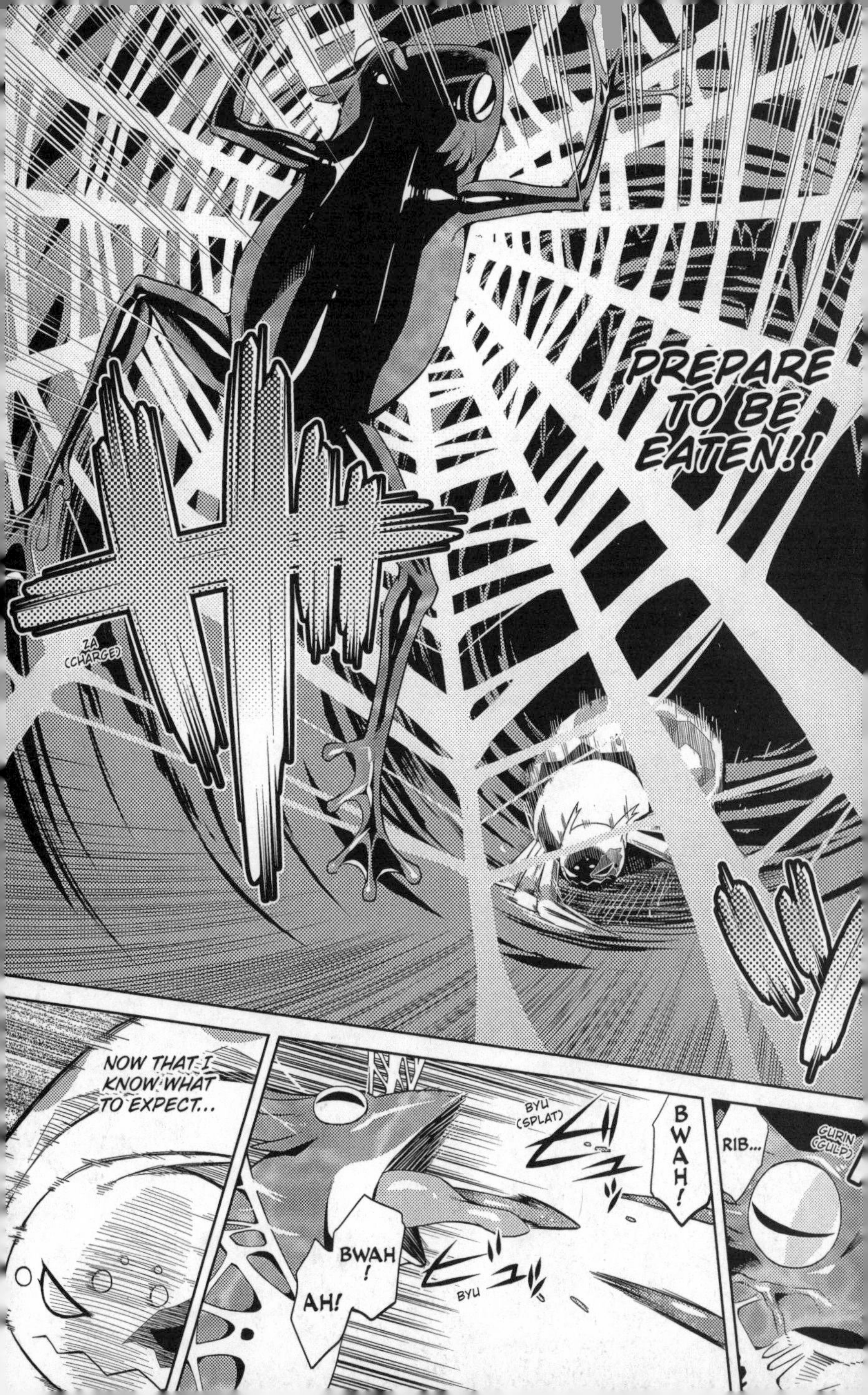
PREPARE TO BE EATEN!!
ZA (CHARGE)
GURIN (GULP)
RIB...
BWAH!
BYU (SPLAT)
BWAH!
BYU
AH!
NOW THAT I KNOW WHAT TO EXPECT...

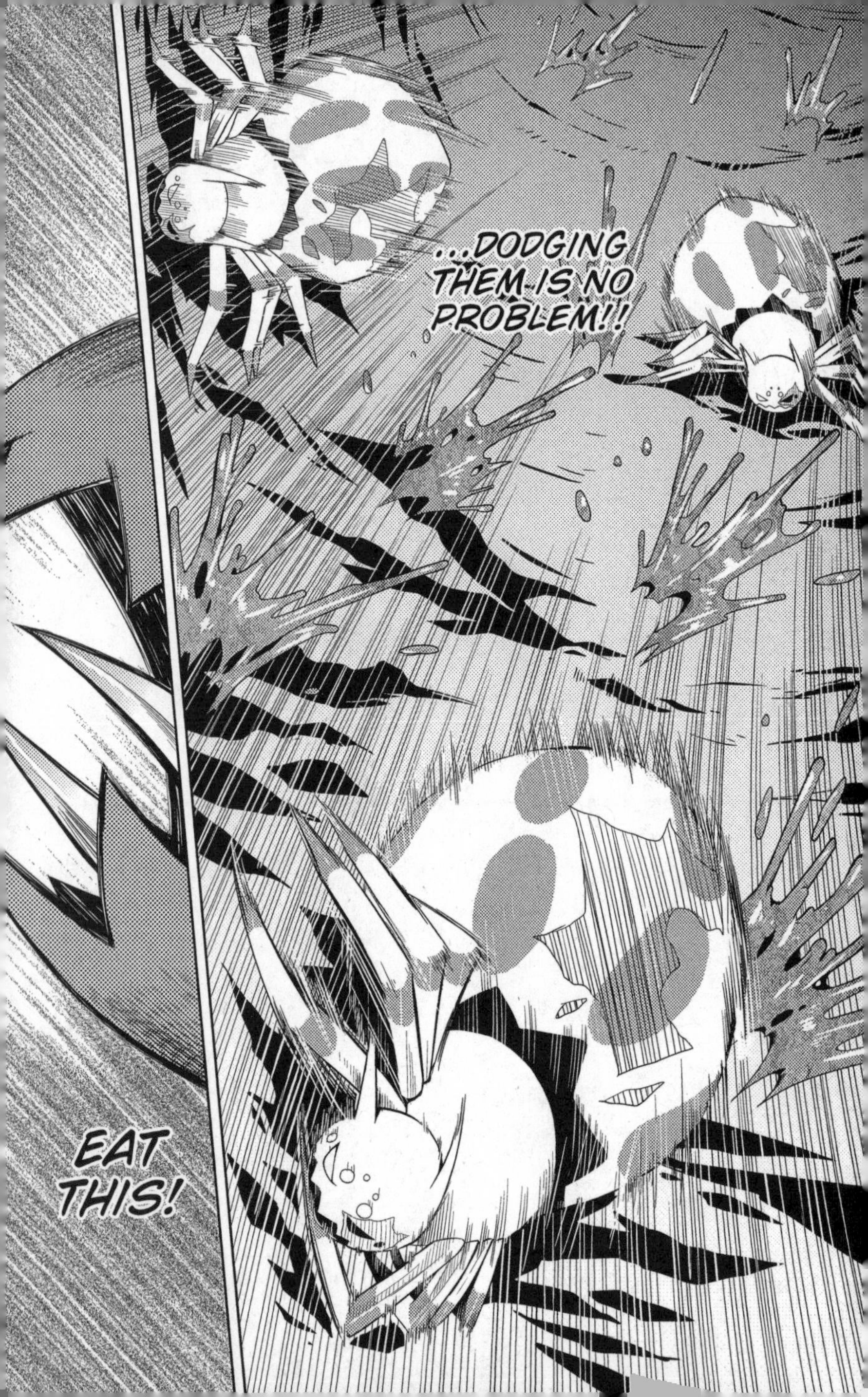
...DODGING THEM IS NO PROBLEM!!
EAT THIS!

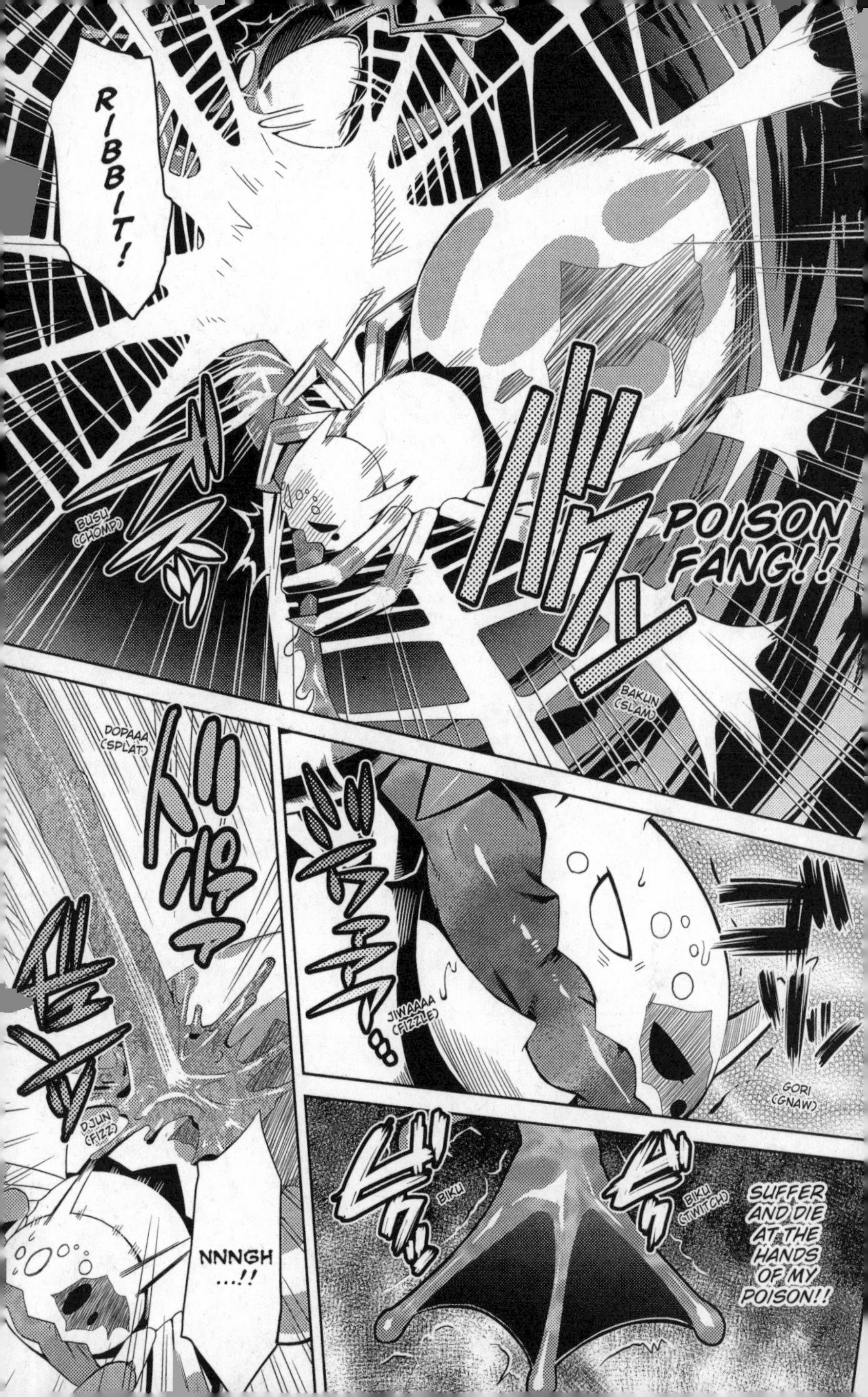

RIBBIT!
POISON FANG!!
BUSU (CHOMP)
BAKUN (SLAM)
GORI (GNAW)
JIWAAAA (FIZZLE)
SUFFER AND DIE AT THE HANDS OF MY POISON!!
BIKU (TWITCH)
BIKU
DOPAAA (SPLAT)
DJUN (FIZZ)
NNNGH ...!!

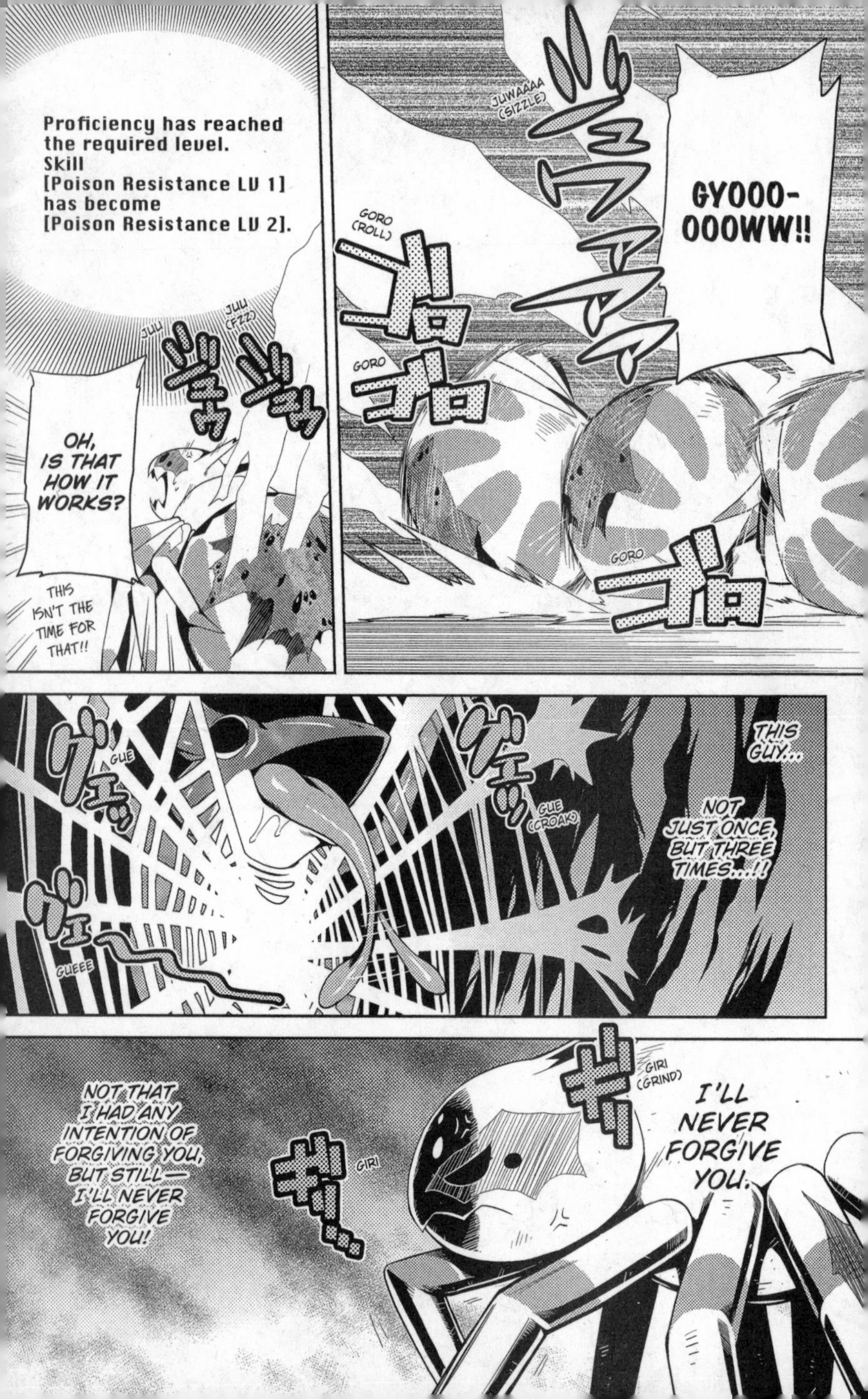
GYOOO-OOOWW!!
JUWAAAA (SIZZLE)
GORO (ROLL)
GORO
GORO
Proficiency has reached the required level.
Skill
[Poison Resistance LV 1]
has become
[Poison Resistance LV 2].
JUU (FZZ)
JUU
OH, IS THAT HOW IT WORKS?
THIS ISN'T THE TIME FOR THAT!!
THIS GUY...
NOT JUST ONCE, BUT THREE TIMES...!!
GUE (CROAK)
GUE
GUEEE
I'LL NEVER FORGIVE YOU.
GIRI (GRIND)
GIRI
NOT THAT I HAD ANY INTENTION OF FORGIVING YOU, BUT STILL— I'LL NEVER FORGIVE YOU!

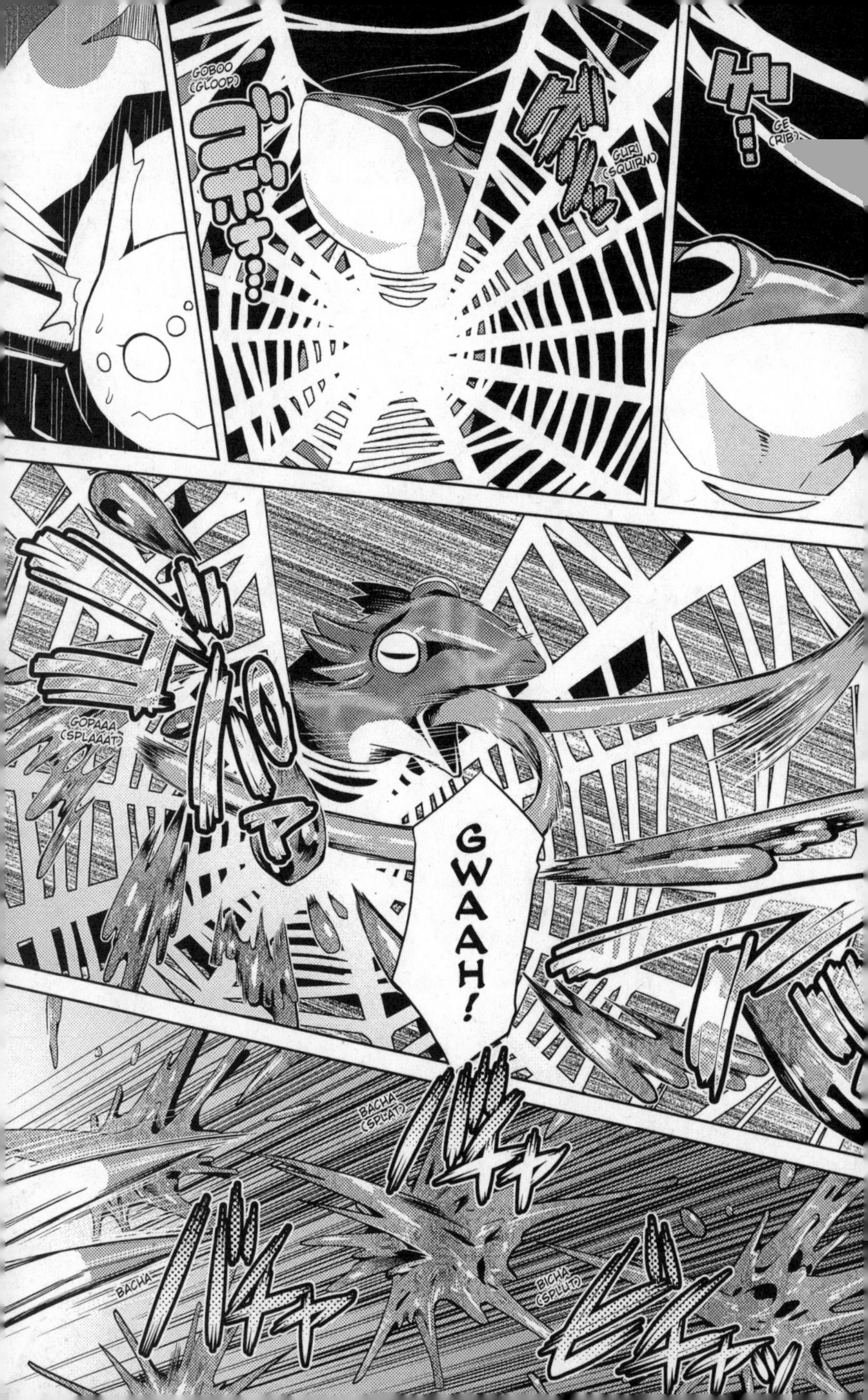
GE (RIB)
GURI (SQUIRM)
GOBOO (GLOOP)
GWAAH!
GOPAAA (SPLAAAT)
BACHA (SPLAT)
BICHA (SPLUT)
BACHA

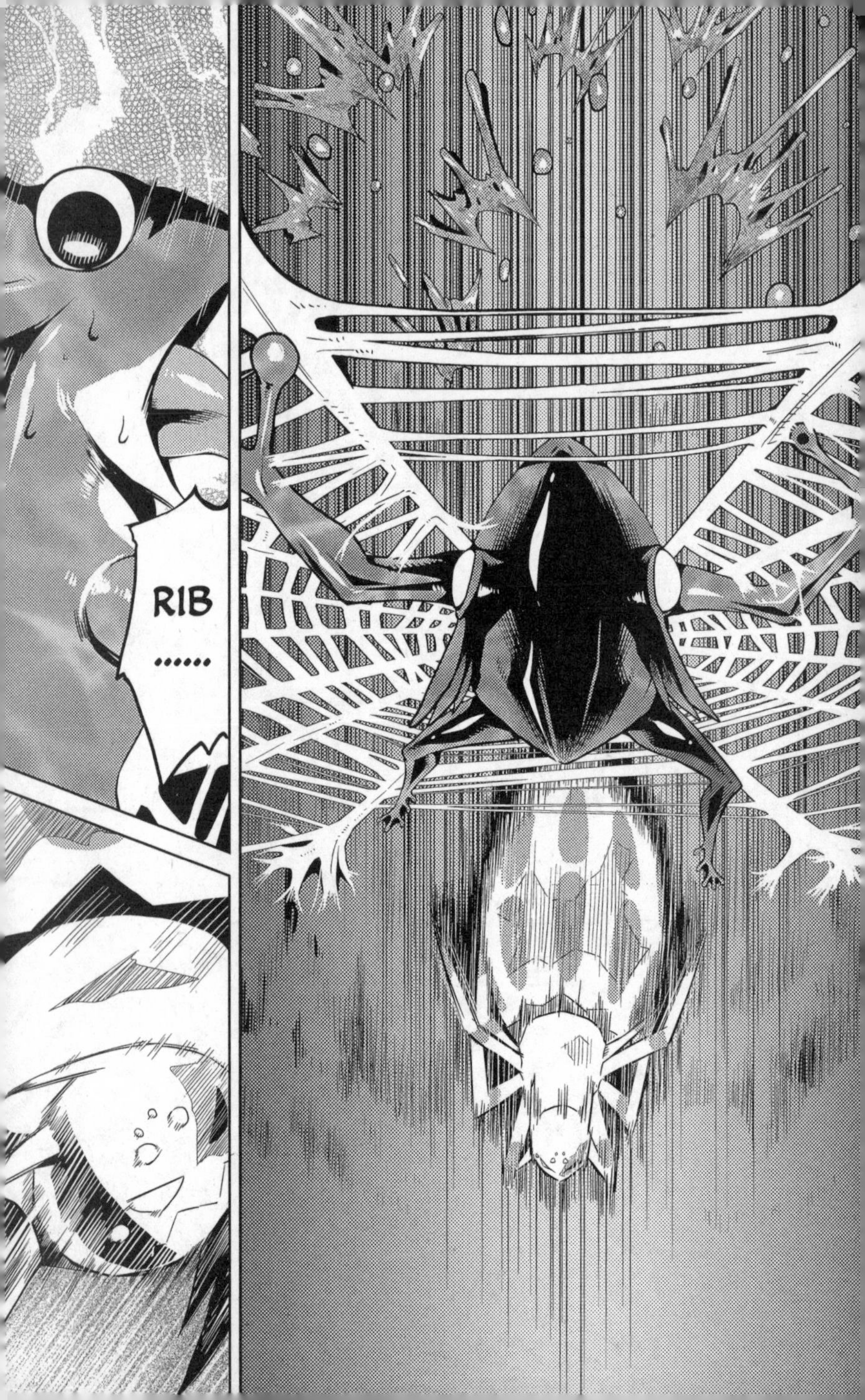
RIB ......

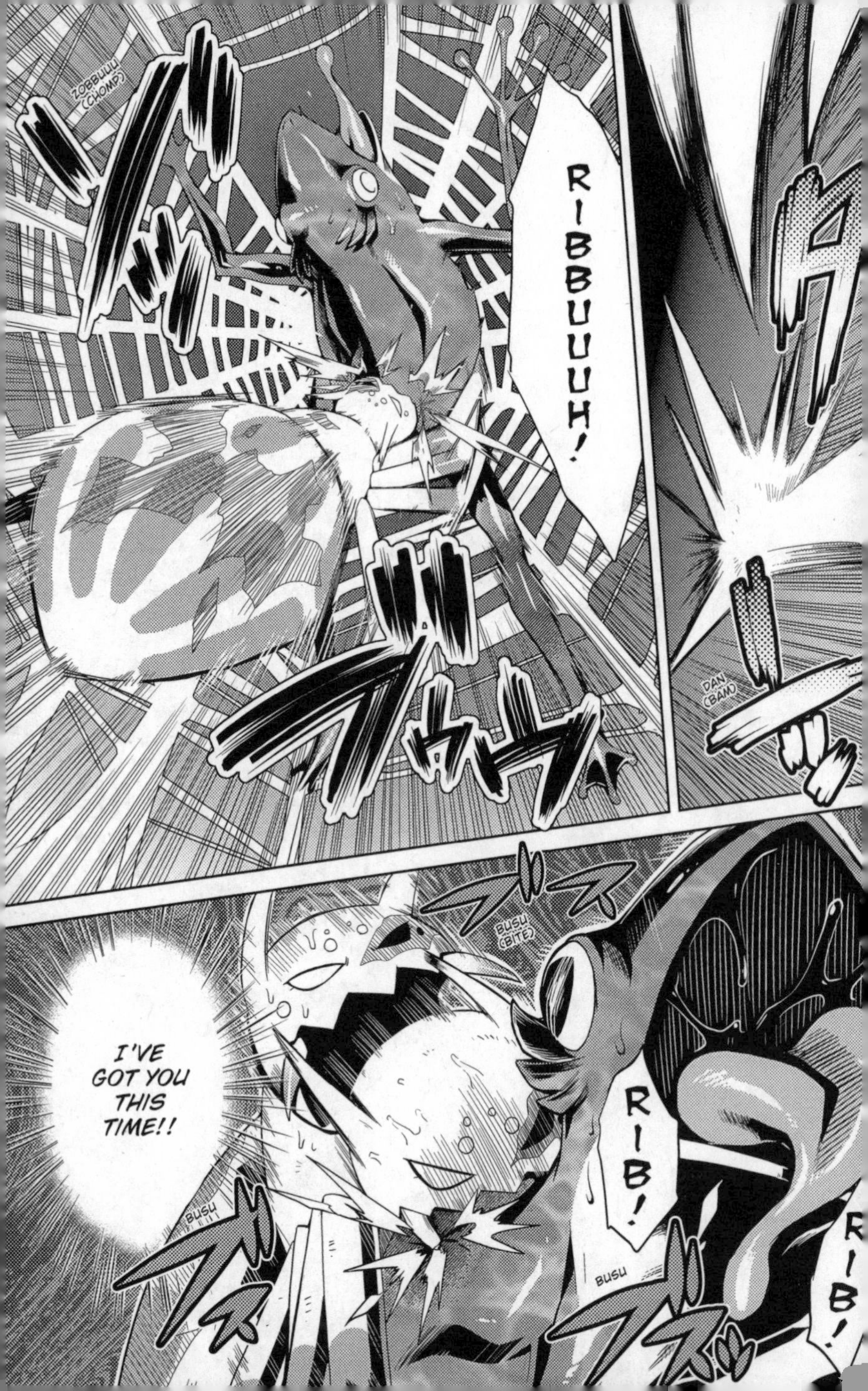
DAN (BAM)
ZOBBUUU (CHOMP)
RIBBUUUH!
BUSU (BITE)
RIB!
RIB!
BUSU
I'VE GOT YOU THIS TIME!!
BUSU

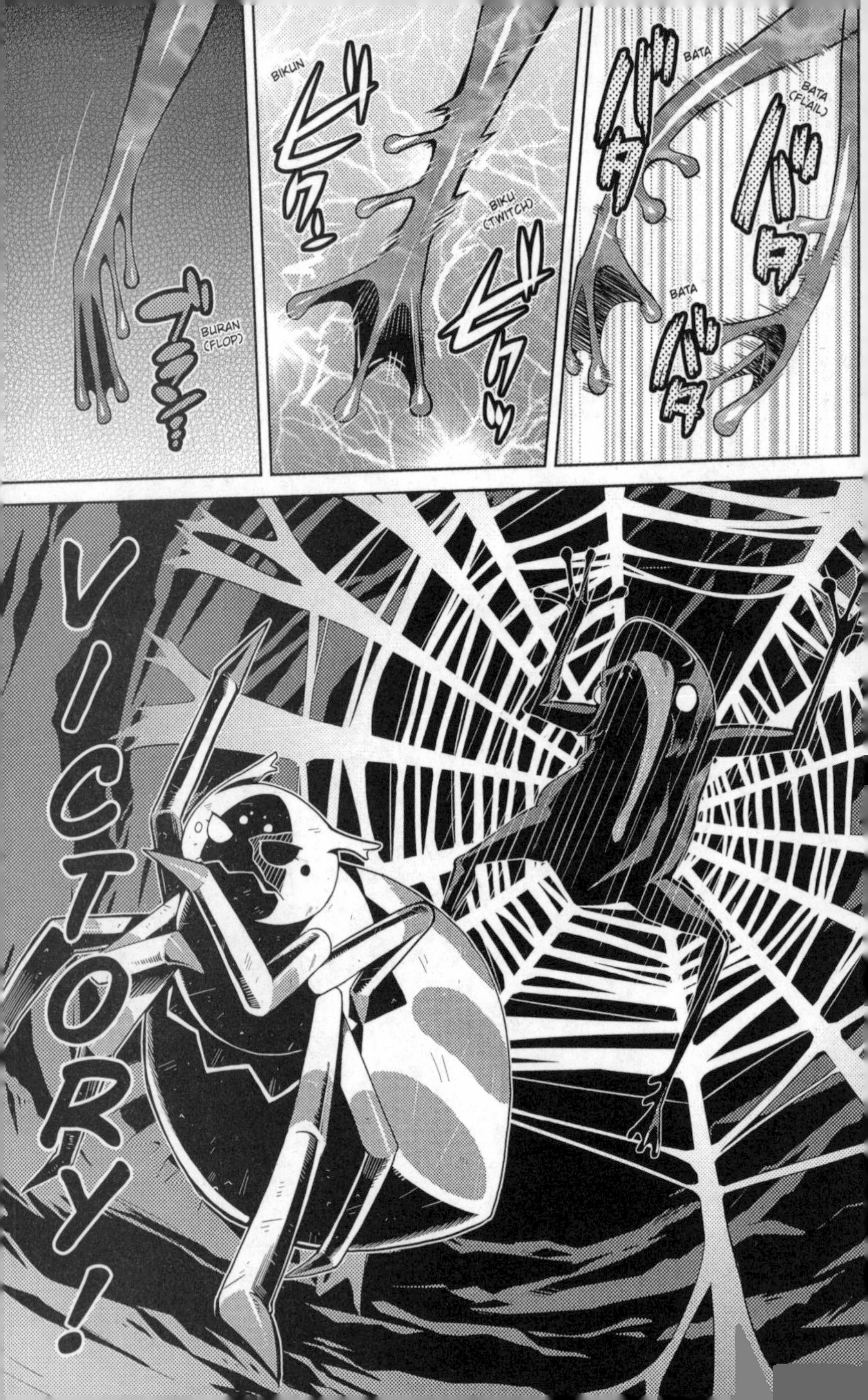

BATA
BATA (FLAIL)
BATA
BIKUN
BIKU (TWITCH)
BURAN (FLOP)
VICTORY!

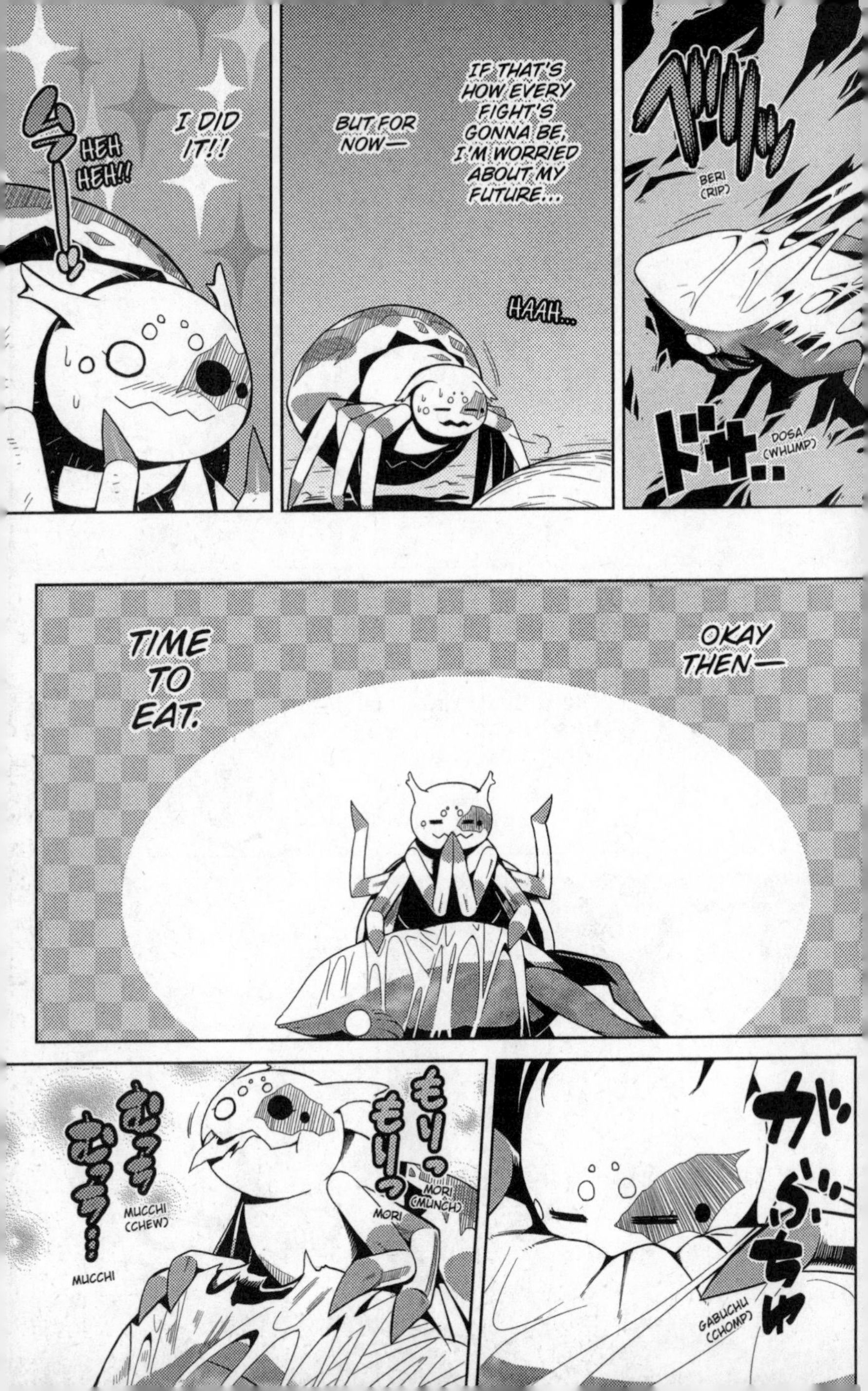

BERI (RIP)
ドサ..
DOSA (WHUMP)
IF THAT'S HOW EVERY FIGHT'S GONNA BE, I'M WORRIED ABOUT MY FUTURE...
BUT FOR NOW—
HAAH...
I DID IT!!
HEH HEH!!
OKAY THEN—
TIME TO EAT.
GABUCHU (CHOMP)
もりっ もりっ
MORI (MUNCH)
MORI
MUCCHI (CHEW)
MUCCHI

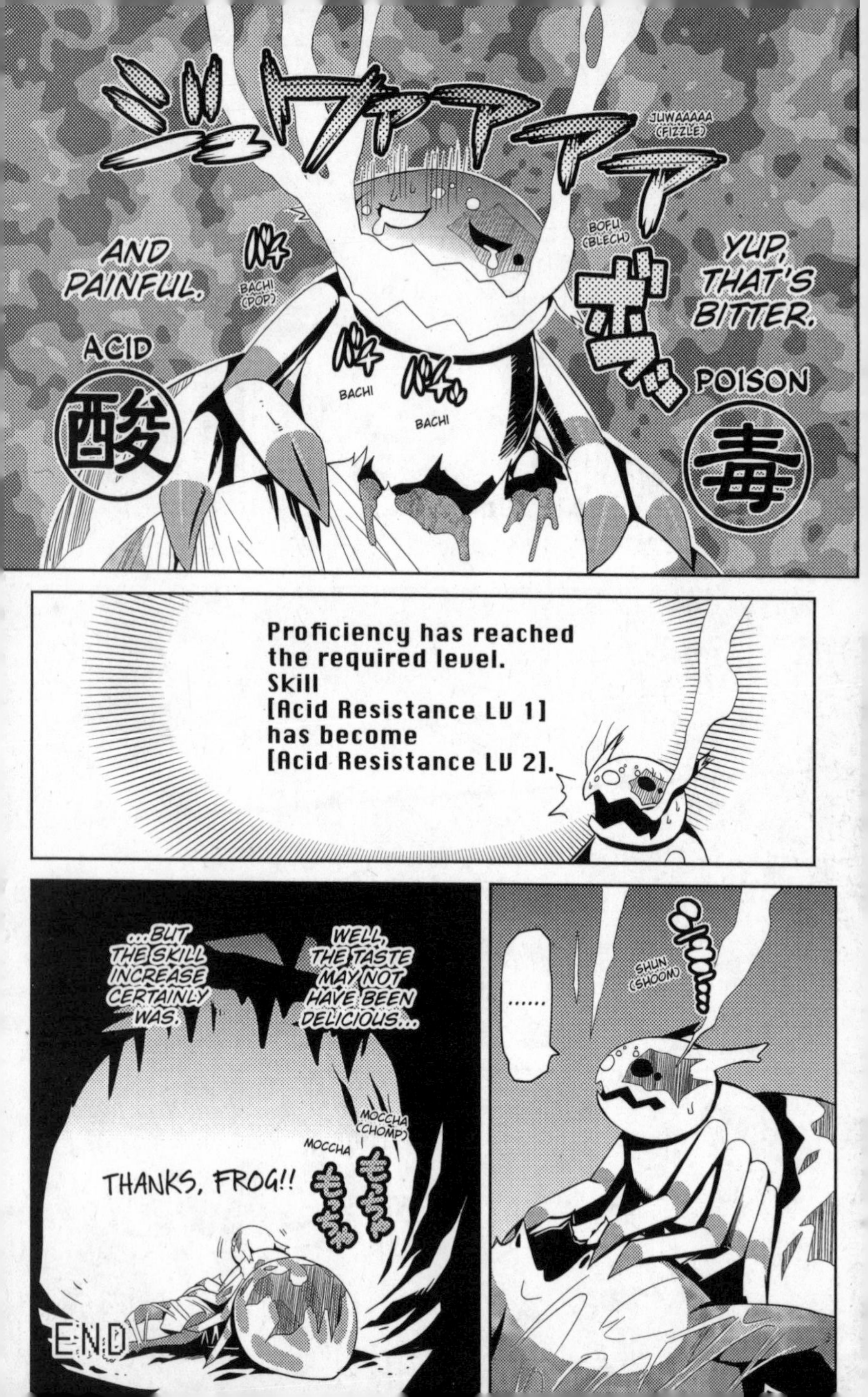
JUWAAAAA (FIZZLE)
YUP, THAT'S BITTER.
BOFU (BLECH)
POISON
毒
AND PAINFUL.
BACHI (POP)
BACHI
BACHI
ACID
酸
Proficiency has reached the required level. Skill [Acid Resistance LV 1] has become [Acid Resistance LV 2].
SHUN (SHOOM)
......
WELL, THE TASTE MAY NOT HAVE BEEN DELICIOUS...
...BUT THE SKILL INCREASE CERTAINLY WAS.
MOCCHA (CHOMP)
MOCCHA
THANKS, FROG!!
END

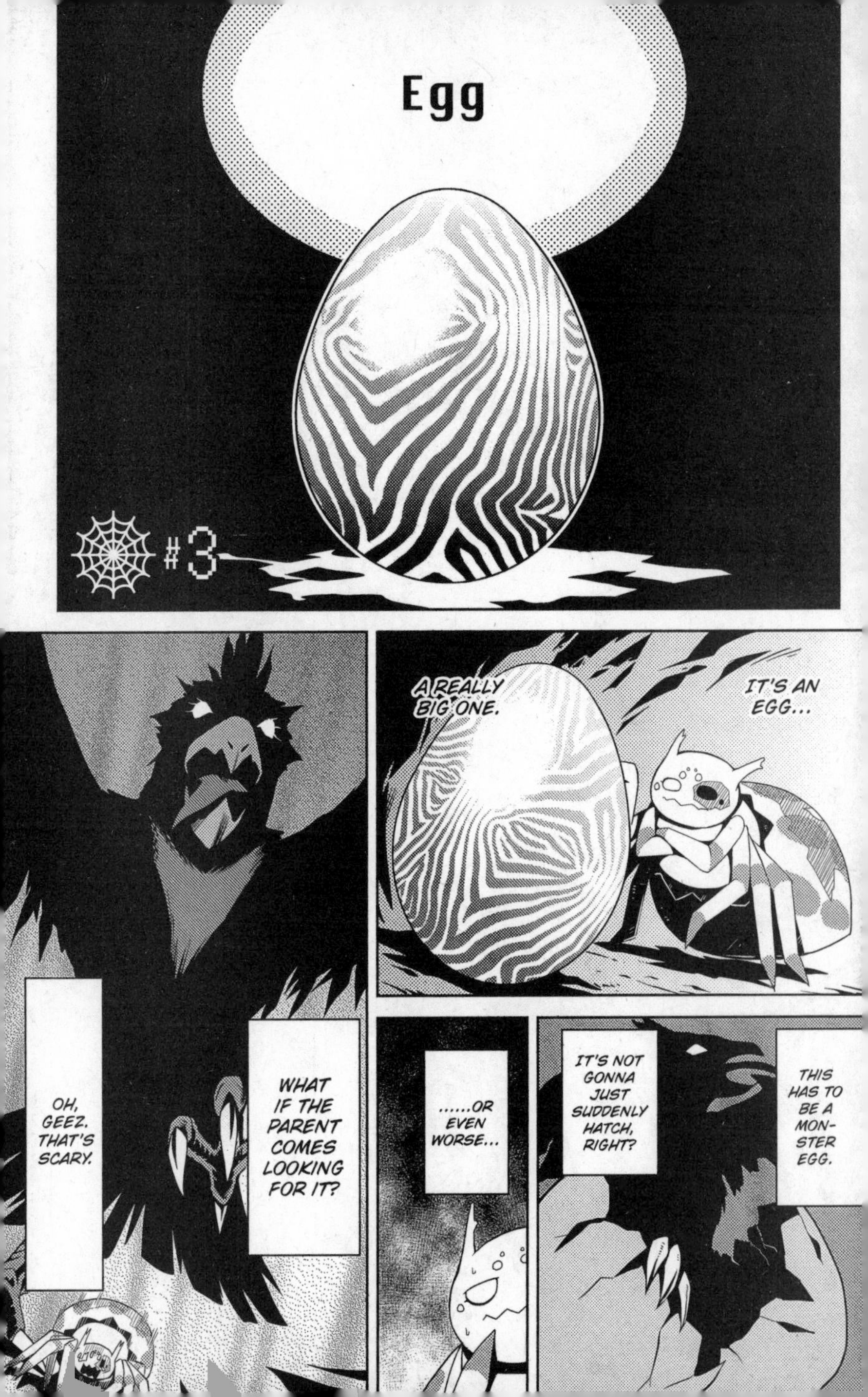
Egg
#3
IT'S AN EGG...
A REALLY BIG ONE.
THIS HAS TO BE A MON-STER EGG.
IT'S NOT GONNA JUST SUDDENLY HATCH, RIGHT?
......OR EVEN WORSE...
WHAT IF THE PARENT COMES LOOKING FOR IT?
OH, GEEZ. THAT'S SCARY.

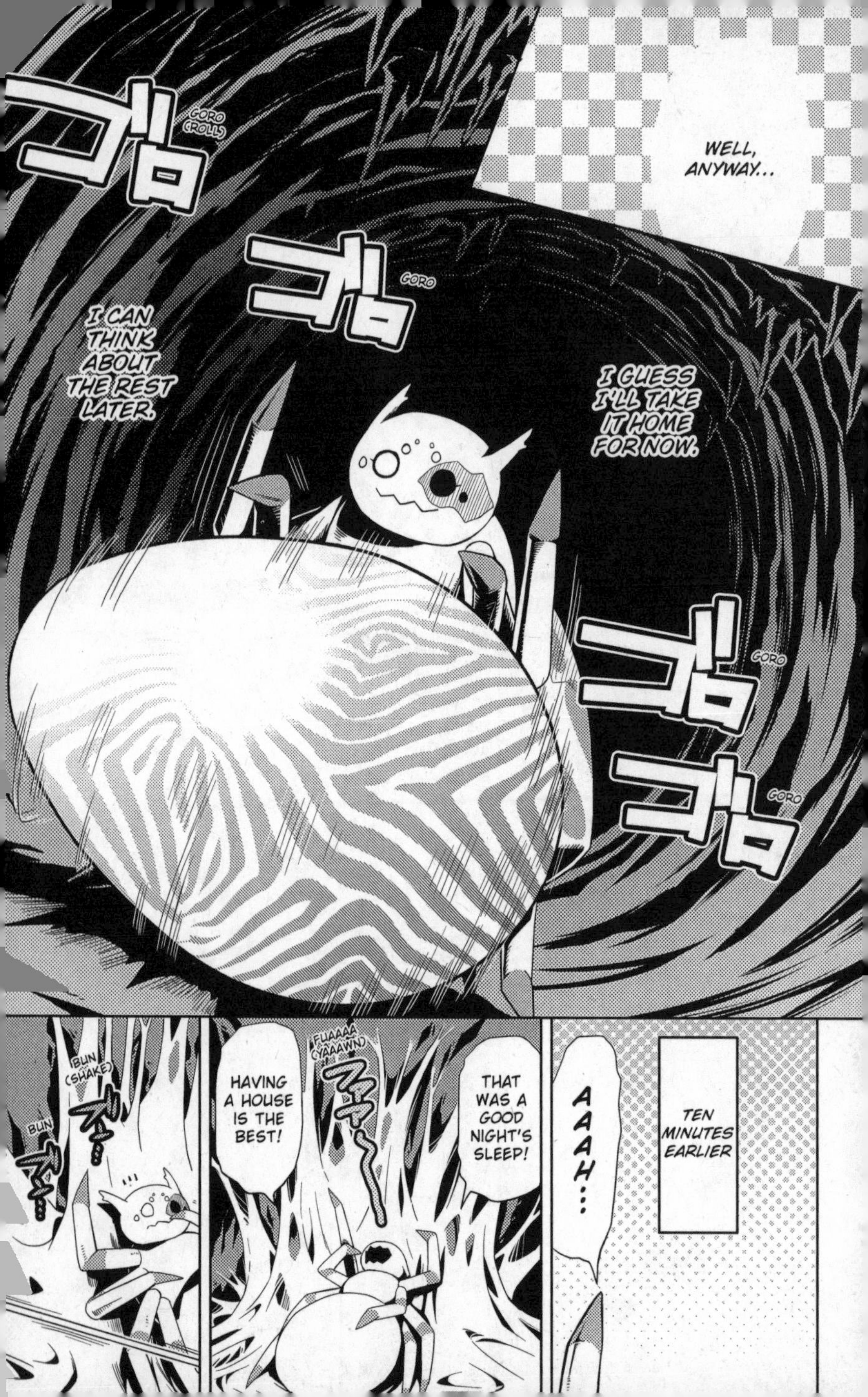

WELL, ANYWAY...
I GUESS I'LL TAKE IT HOME FOR NOW.
I CAN THINK ABOUT THE REST LATER.
GORO (ROLL)
GORO
GORO
GORO
TEN MINUTES EARLIER
AAAH...
THAT WAS A GOOD NIGHT'S SLEEP!
FUAAAA (YAAAWN)
HAVING A HOUSE IS THE BEST!
BUN (SHAKE)
BUN

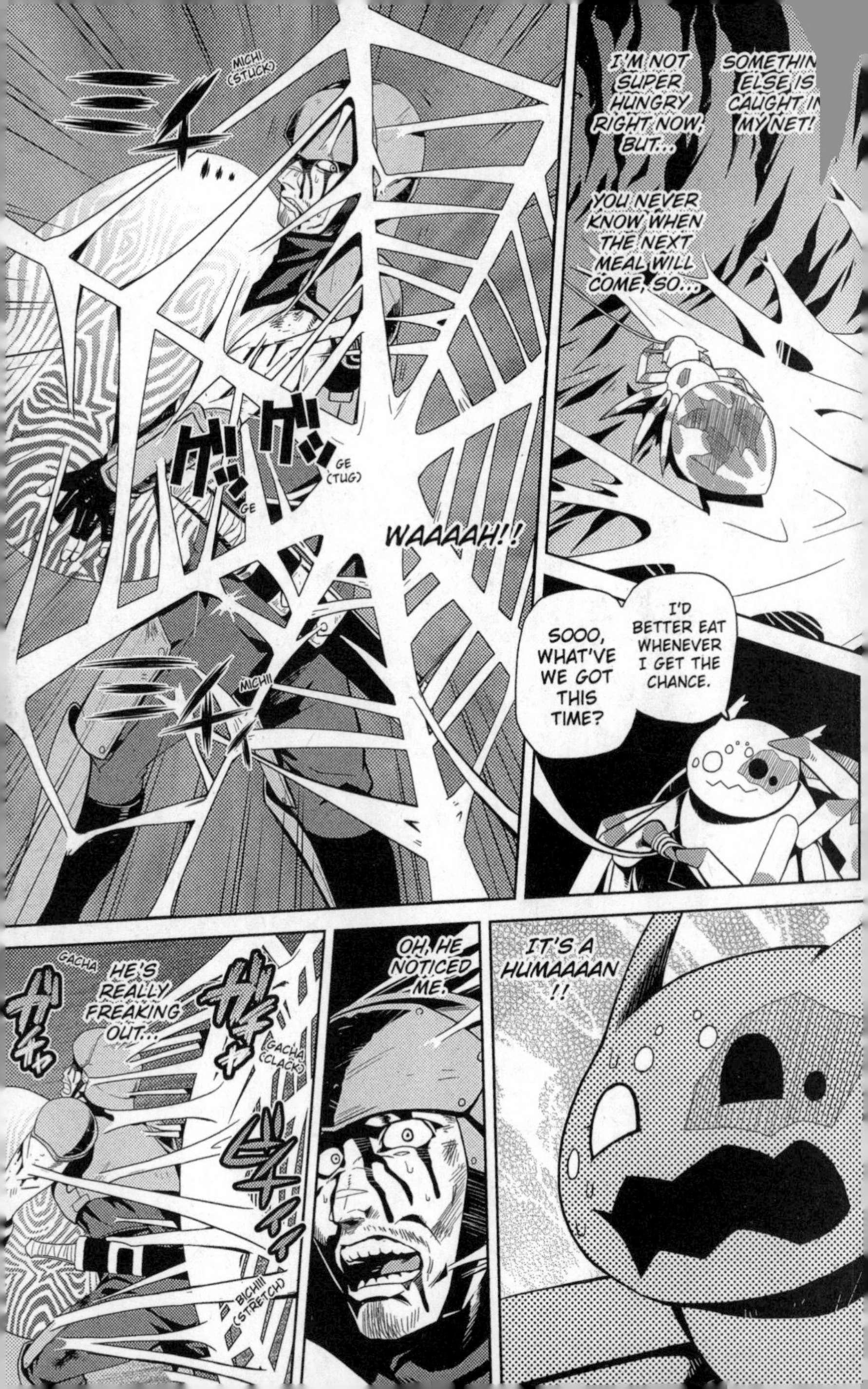
SOMETHIN ELSE IS CAUGHT IN MY NET!
I'M NOT SUPER HUNGRY RIGHT NOW, BUT...
YOU NEVER KNOW WHEN THE NEXT MEAL WILL COME, SO...
I'D BETTER EAT WHENEVER I GET THE CHANCE.
SOOO, WHAT'VE WE GOT THIS TIME?
MICHI (STUCK)
GE (TUG)
GE
WAAAAH!!
MICHII
IT'S A HUMAAAAN!!
OH, HE NOTICED ME.
BICHIII (STRETCH)
GACHA (CLACK)
HE'S REALLY FREAKING OUT...
GACHA

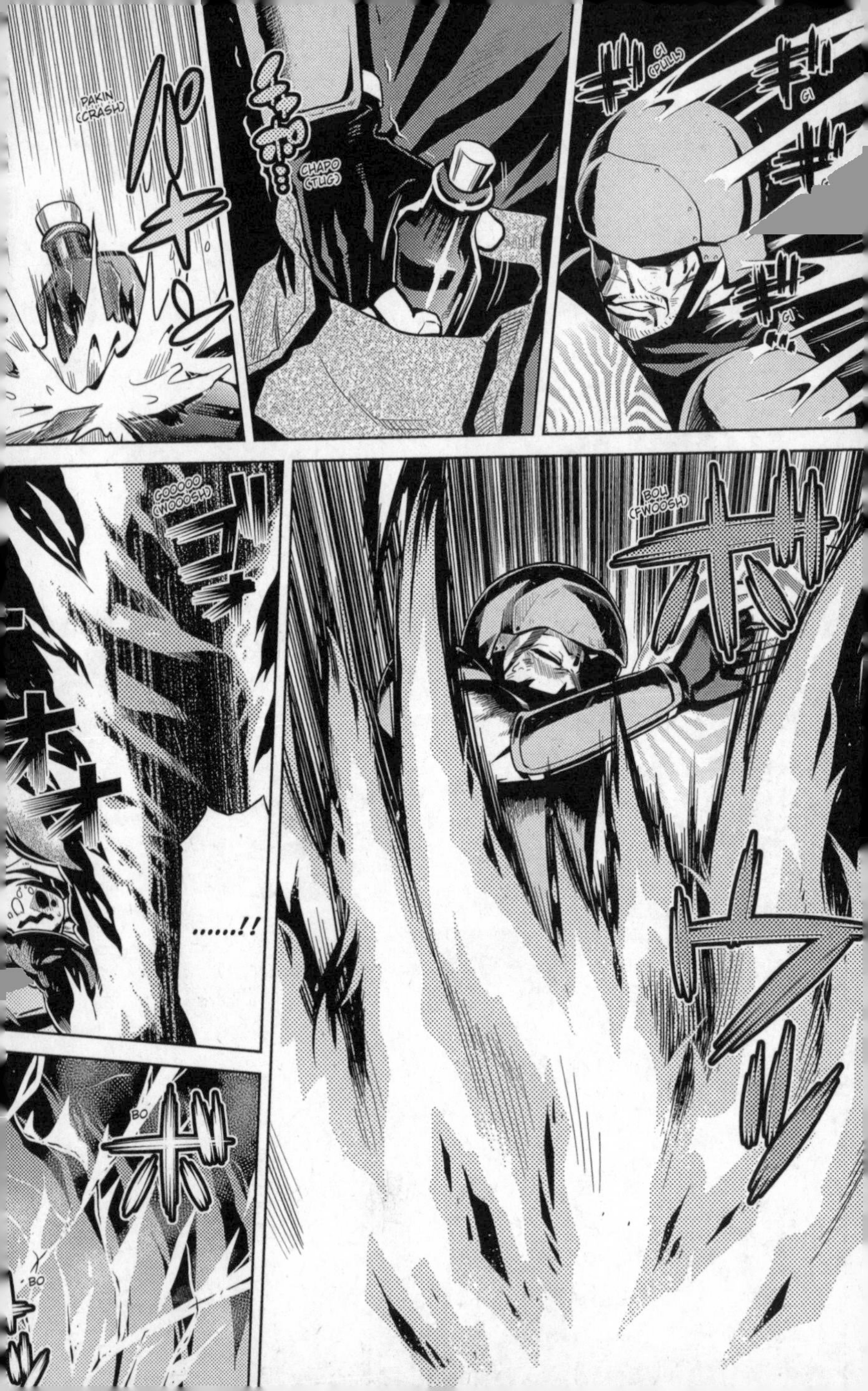
GI
(PULL)
GI
GI
CHAPO
(TUG)
PAKIN
(CRASH)
BOU
(FWOOSH)
GOOOOO
(WOOOSH)
......!!
BO
BO

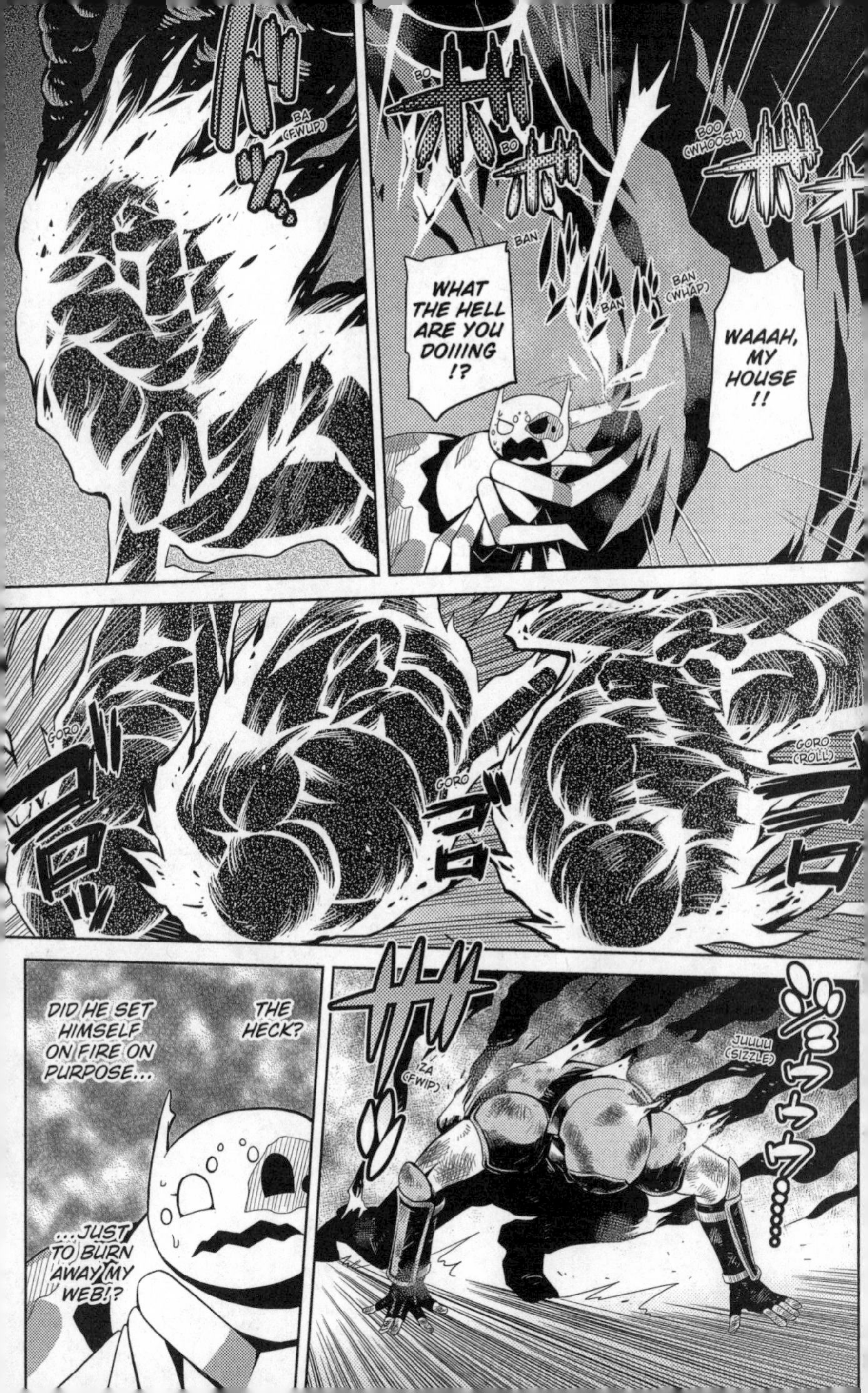
BOO (WHOOSH)
BO
BO
WAAAH, MY HOUSE!!
BAN (WHAP)
BAN
BAN
WHAT THE HELL ARE YOU DOIIING!?
BA (FWUP)
GORO (ROLL)
GORO
GORO
JUUUU (SIZZLE)
ZA (FWIP)
THE HECK?
DID HE SET HIMSELF ON FIRE ON PURPOSE...
...JUST TO BURN AWAY MY WEB!?

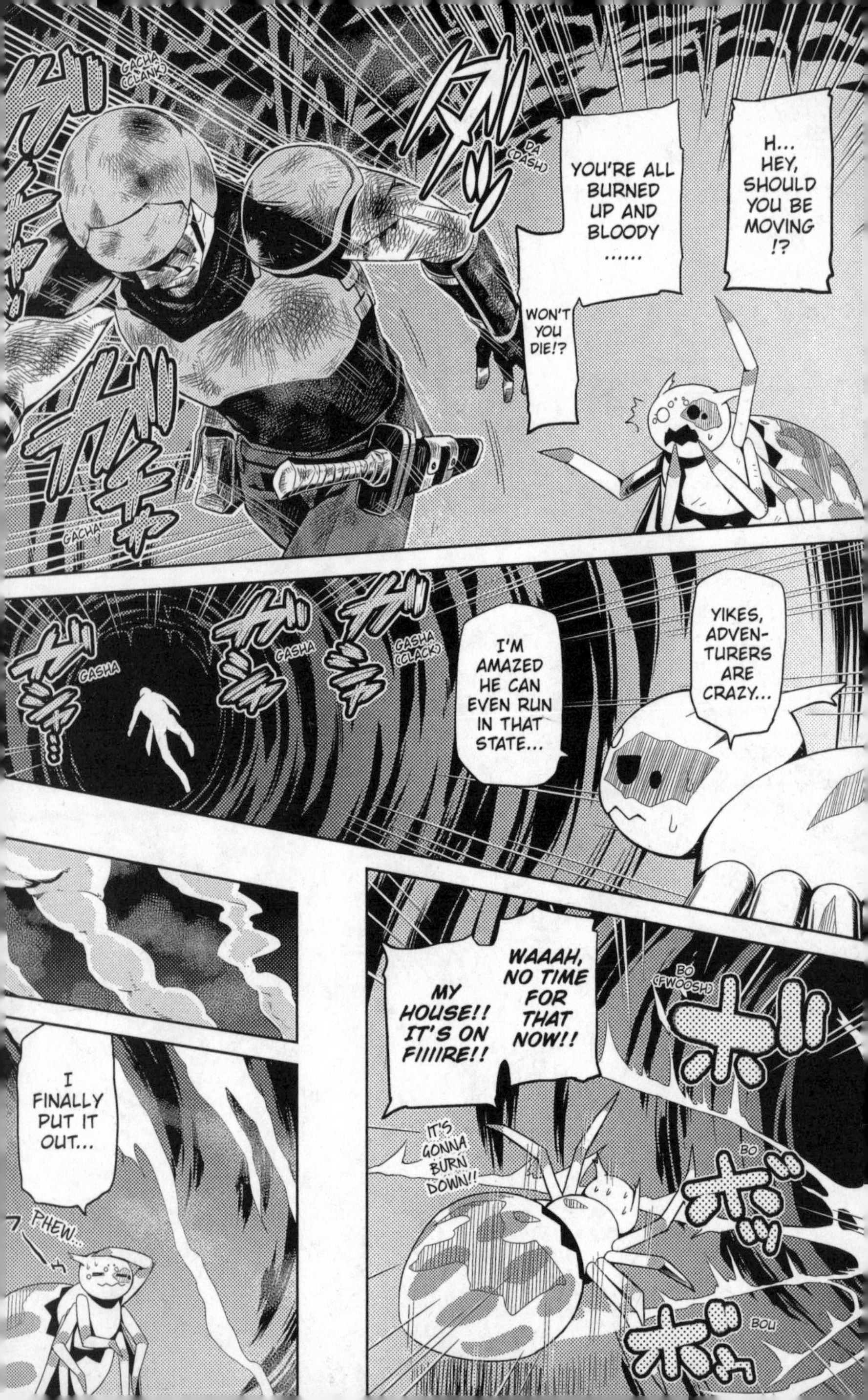
H... HEY, SHOULD YOU BE MOVING!?
YOU'RE ALL BURNED UP AND BLOODY ......
WON'T YOU DIE!?
DA (DASH)
GACHA (CLANK)
GACHA
YIKES, ADVENTURERS ARE CRAZY...
I'M AMAZED HE CAN EVEN RUN IN THAT STATE...
GASHA (CLACK)
GASHA
GASHA
WAAAH, NO TIME FOR THAT NOW!!
MY HOUSE!! IT'S ON FIIIIRE!!
BO (FWOOSH)
IT'S GONNA BURN DOWN!!
BO
BOU
I FINALLY PUT IT OUT...
PHEW...

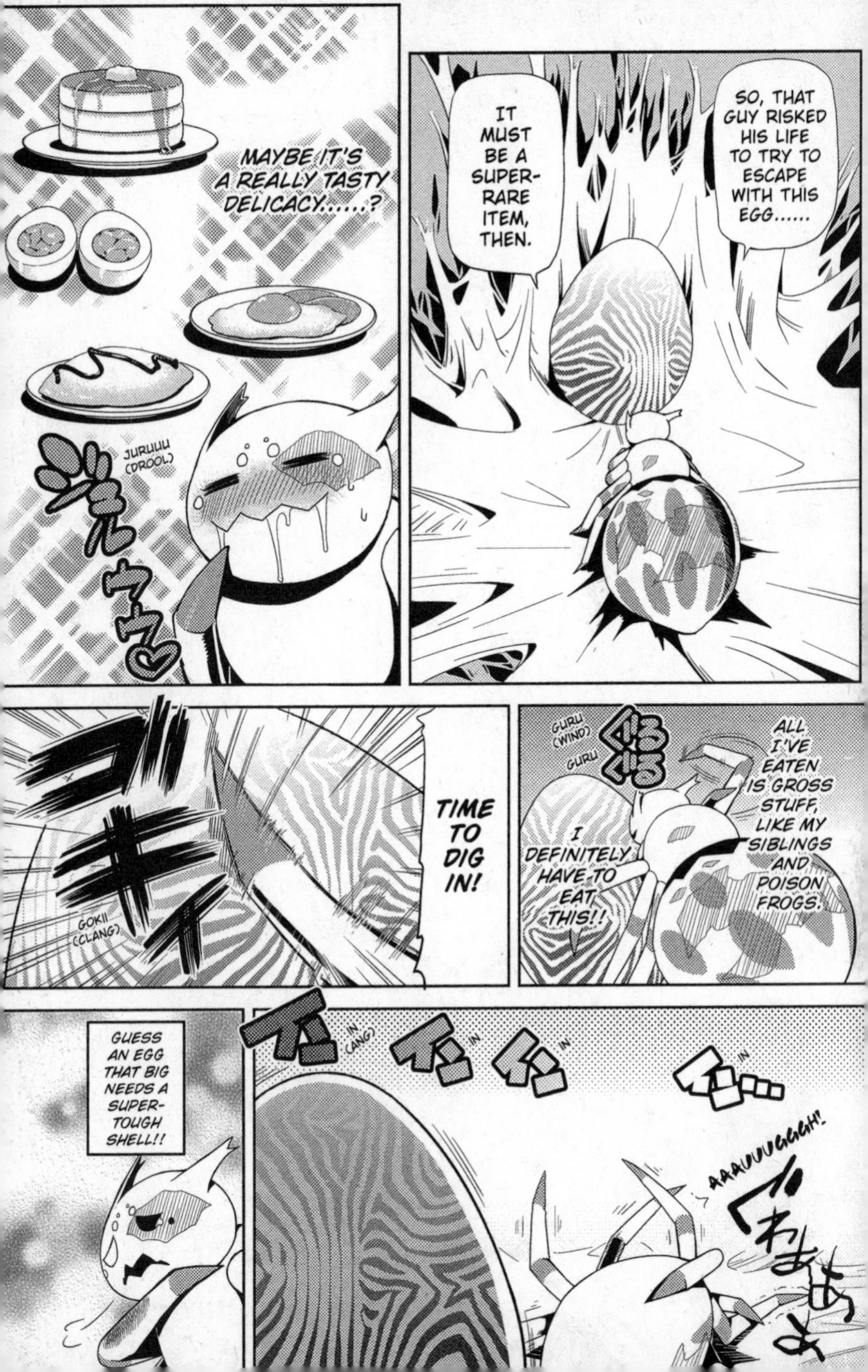
SO, THAT GUY RISKED HIS LIFE TO TRY TO ESCAPE WITH THIS EGG......
IT MUST BE A SUPER-RARE ITEM, THEN.
MAYBE IT'S A REALLY TASTY DELICACY......?
JURUUU (DROOL)
ALL I'VE EATEN IS GROSS STUFF, LIKE MY SIBLINGS AND POISON FROGS.
GURU (WIND)
GURU
I DEFINITELY HAVE TO EAT THIS!!
TIME TO DIG IN!
GOKII (CLANG)
IN (ANG)
IN
IN
IN
AAAUUUGGGH!
GUESS AN EGG THAT BIG NEEDS A SUPER-TOUGH SHELL!!

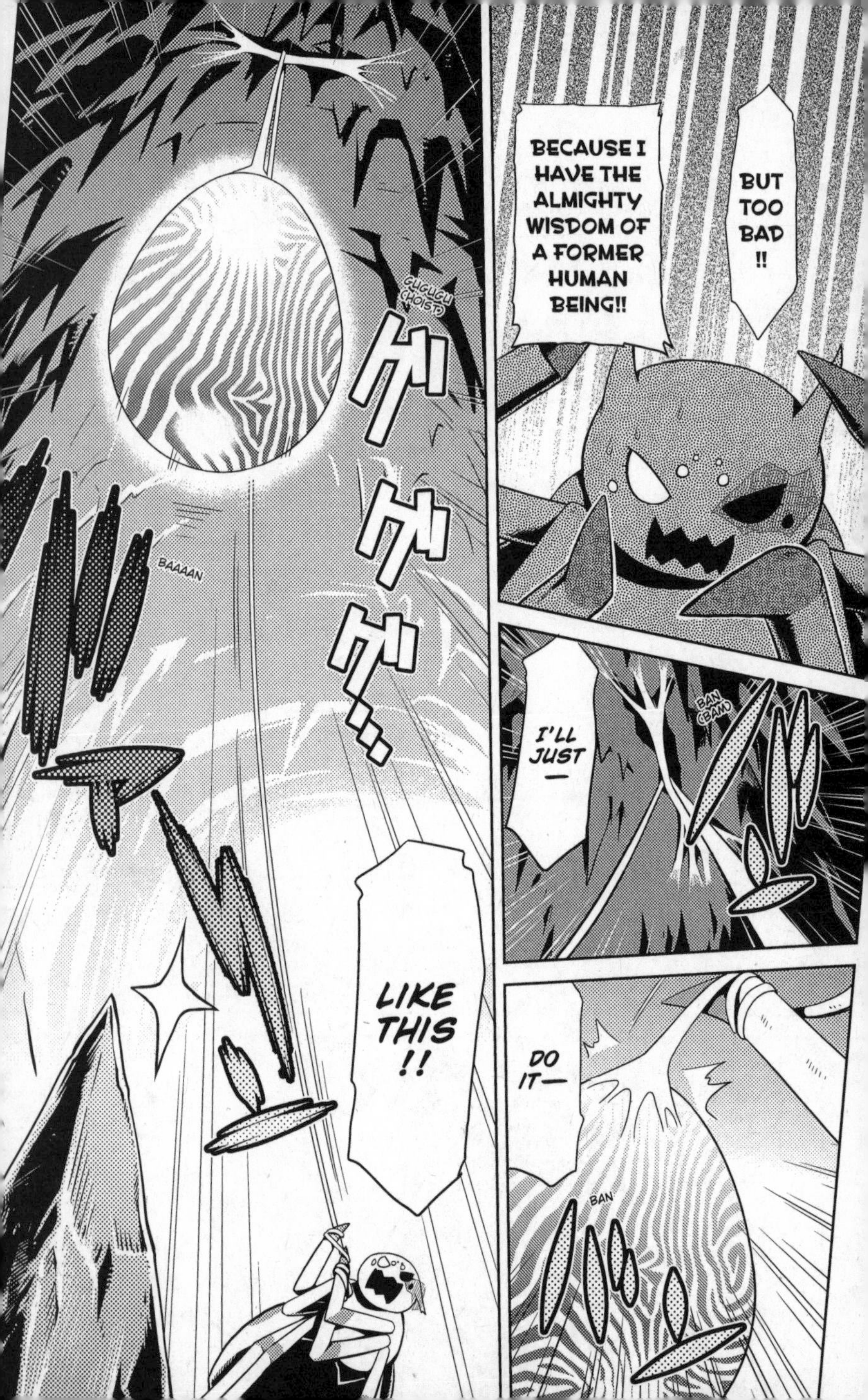
BUT TOO BAD !!
BECAUSE I HAVE THE ALMIGHTY WISDOM OF A FORMER HUMAN BEING!!
BAN (BAM)
I'LL JUST—
DO IT—
BAN
GUGUGU (HOIST)
BAAAAN
LIKE THIS !!

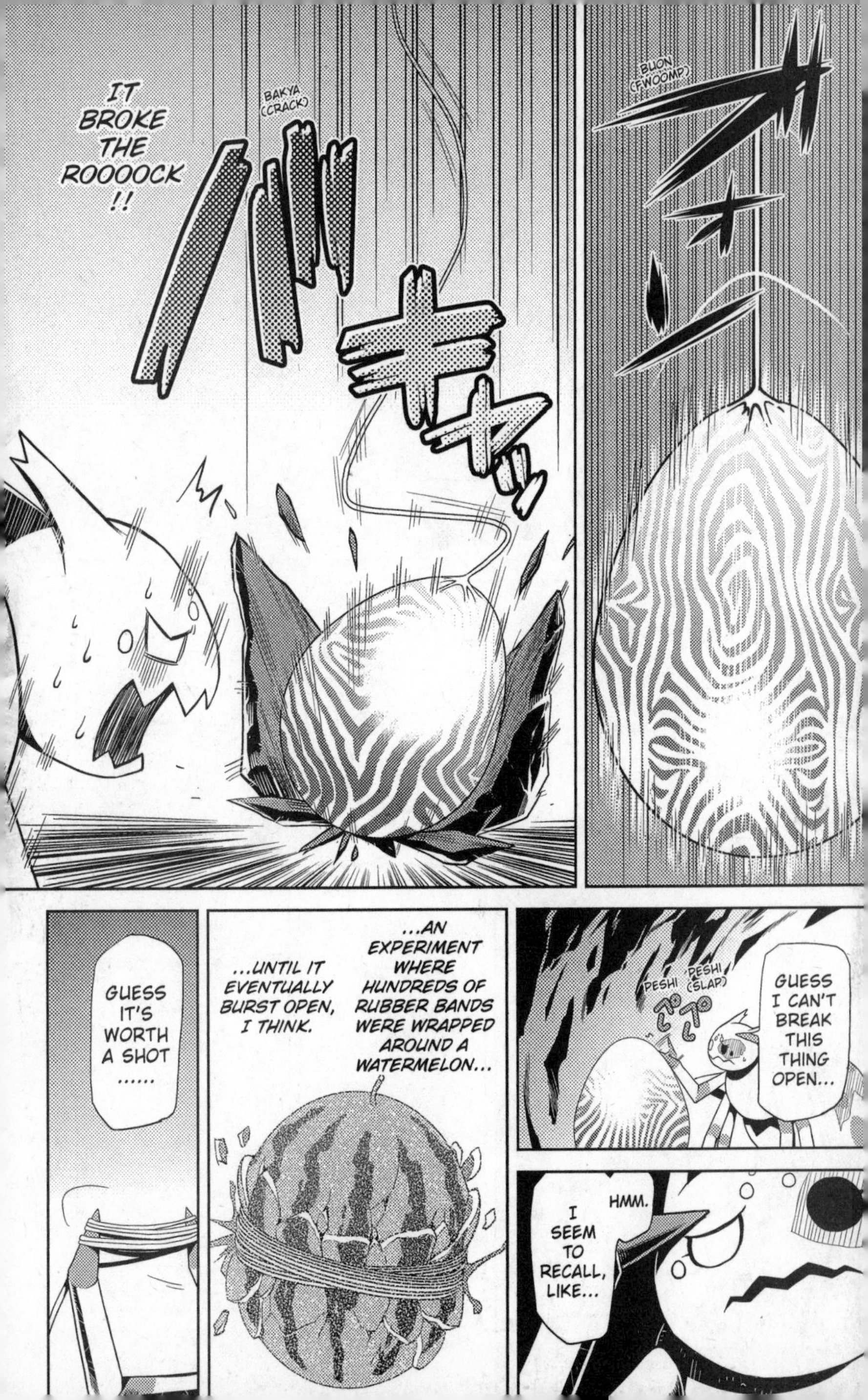
BUON (FWOOMP)
BAKYA (CRACK)
IT BROKE THE ROOOOCK!!
PESHI PESHI (SLAP)
GUESS I CAN'T BREAK THIS THING OPEN...
HMM.
I SEEM TO RECALL, LIKE...
...AN EXPERIMENT WHERE HUNDREDS OF RUBBER BANDS WERE WRAPPED AROUND A WATERMELON...
...UNTIL IT EVENTUALLY BURST OPEN, I THINK.
GUESS IT'S WORTH A SHOT ......

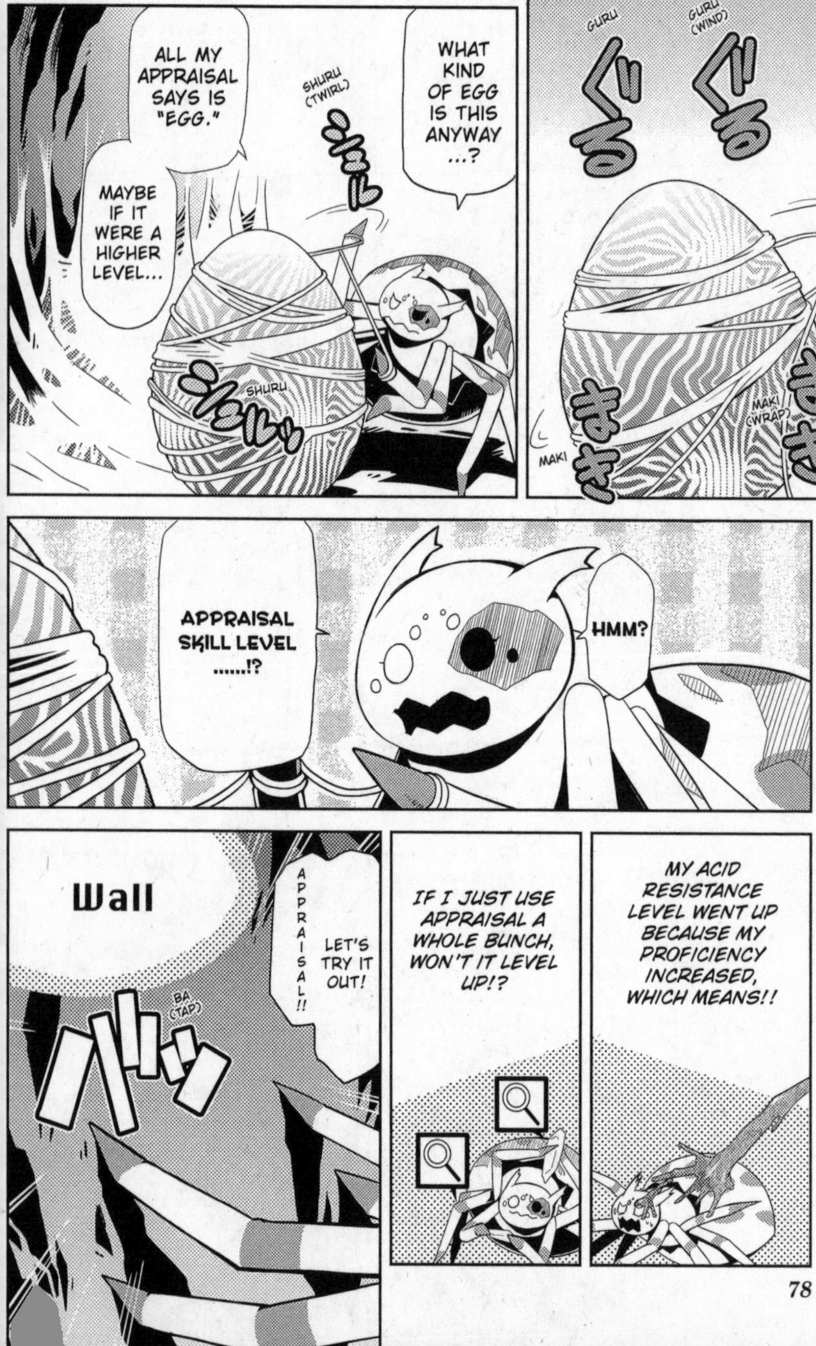
GURU (WIND)
GURU
ぐる
ぐる
MAKI (WRAP)
MAKI
まき
まき
WHAT KIND OF EGG IS THIS ANYWAY ...?
SHURU (TWIRL)
ALL MY APPRAISAL SAYS IS "EGG."
MAYBE IF IT WERE A HIGHER LEVEL...
SHURU
HMM?
APPRAISAL SKILL LEVEL ......!?
MY ACID RESISTANCE LEVEL WENT UP BECAUSE MY PROFICIENCY INCREASED, WHICH MEANS!!
IF I JUST USE APPRAISAL A WHOLE BUNCH, WON'T IT LEVEL UP!?
LET'S TRY IT OUT!
APPRAISAL!!
Wall
BA (TAP)

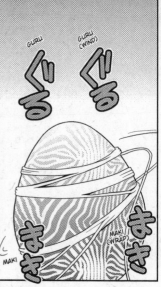

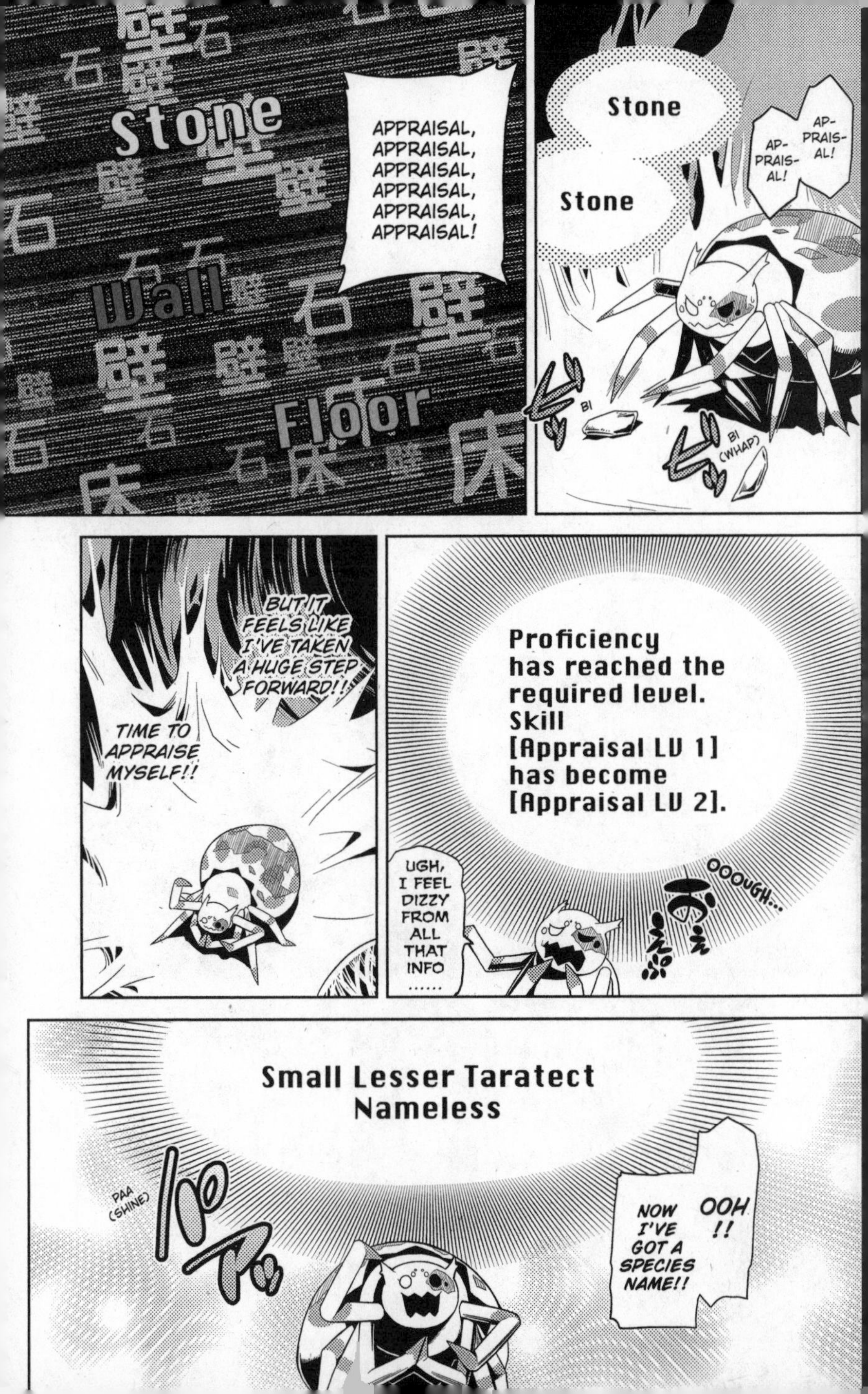
AP-PRAIS-AL!
AP-PRAIS-AL!
Stone
Stone
BI
BI (WHAP)
APPRAISAL, APPRAISAL, APPRAISAL, APPRAISAL, APPRAISAL, APPRAISAL!
Stone
Wall
Floor
Proficiency has reached the required level. Skill [Appraisal LV 1] has become [Appraisal LV 2].
OOOUGH...
UGH, I FEEL DIZZY FROM ALL THAT INFO ......
BUT IT FEELS LIKE I'VE TAKEN A HUGE STEP FORWARD!!
TIME TO APPRAISE MYSELF!!
Small Lesser Taratect
Nameless
OOH!!
NOW I'VE GOT A SPECIES NAME!!
PAA (SHINE)

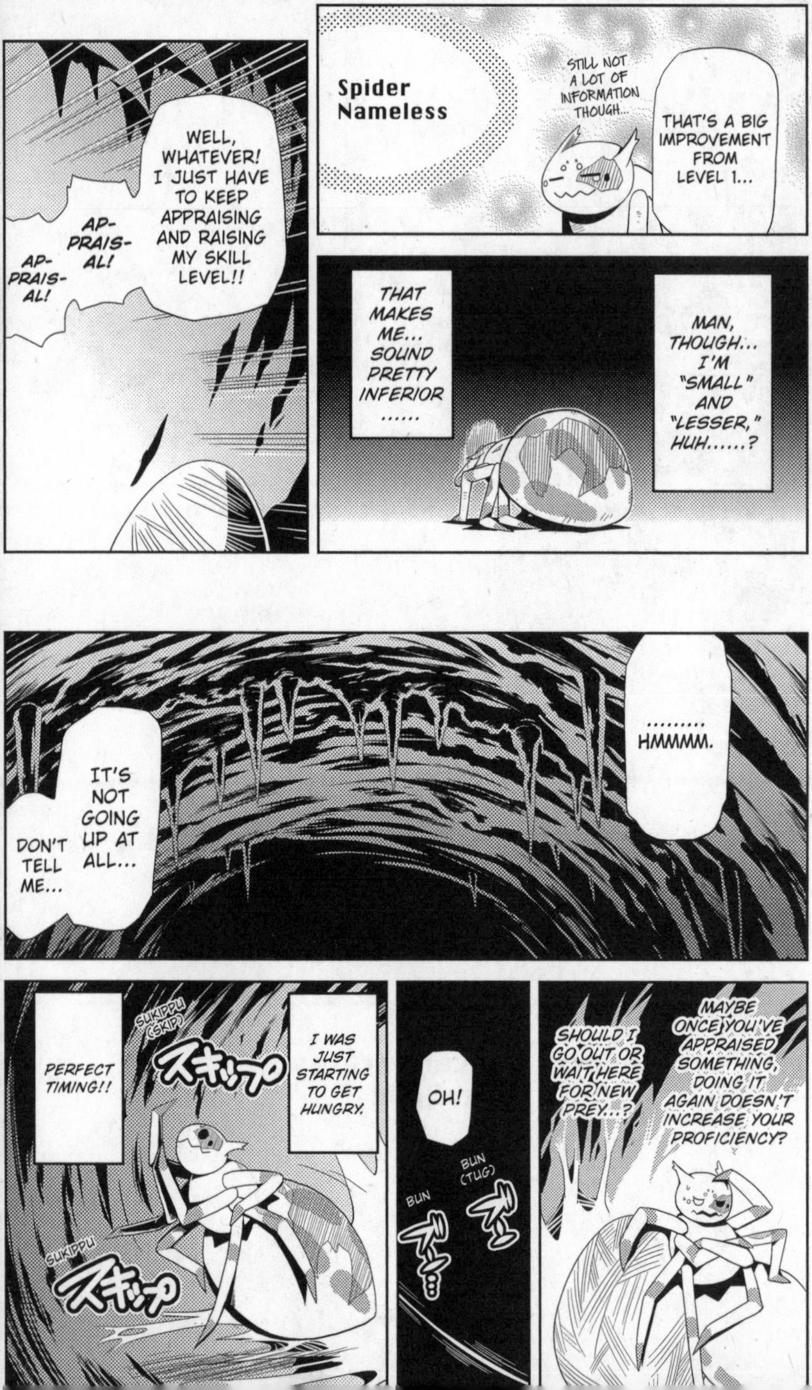
THAT'S A BIG IMPROVEMENT FROM LEVEL 1...
STILL NOT A LOT OF INFORMATION THOUGH...
Spider Nameless
MAN, THOUGH... I'M "SMALL" AND "LESSER," HUH......?
THAT MAKES ME... SOUND PRETTY INFERIOR ......
WELL, WHATEVER! I JUST HAVE TO KEEP APPRAISING AND RAISING MY SKILL LEVEL!!
AP-PRAIS-AL!
AP-PRAIS-AL!
.... HMMMM.
IT'S NOT GOING UP AT ALL...
DON'T TELL ME...
MAYBE ONCE YOU'VE APPRAISED SOMETHING, DOING IT AGAIN DOESN'T INCREASE YOUR PROFICIENCY?
SHOULD I GO OUT OR WAIT HERE FOR NEW PREY...?
OH!
BUN (TUG)
BUN
I WAS JUST STARTING TO GET HUNGRY.
SUKIPPU (SKIP)
スキップ
PERFECT TIMING!!
SUKIPPU
スキップ

Elroe Frog

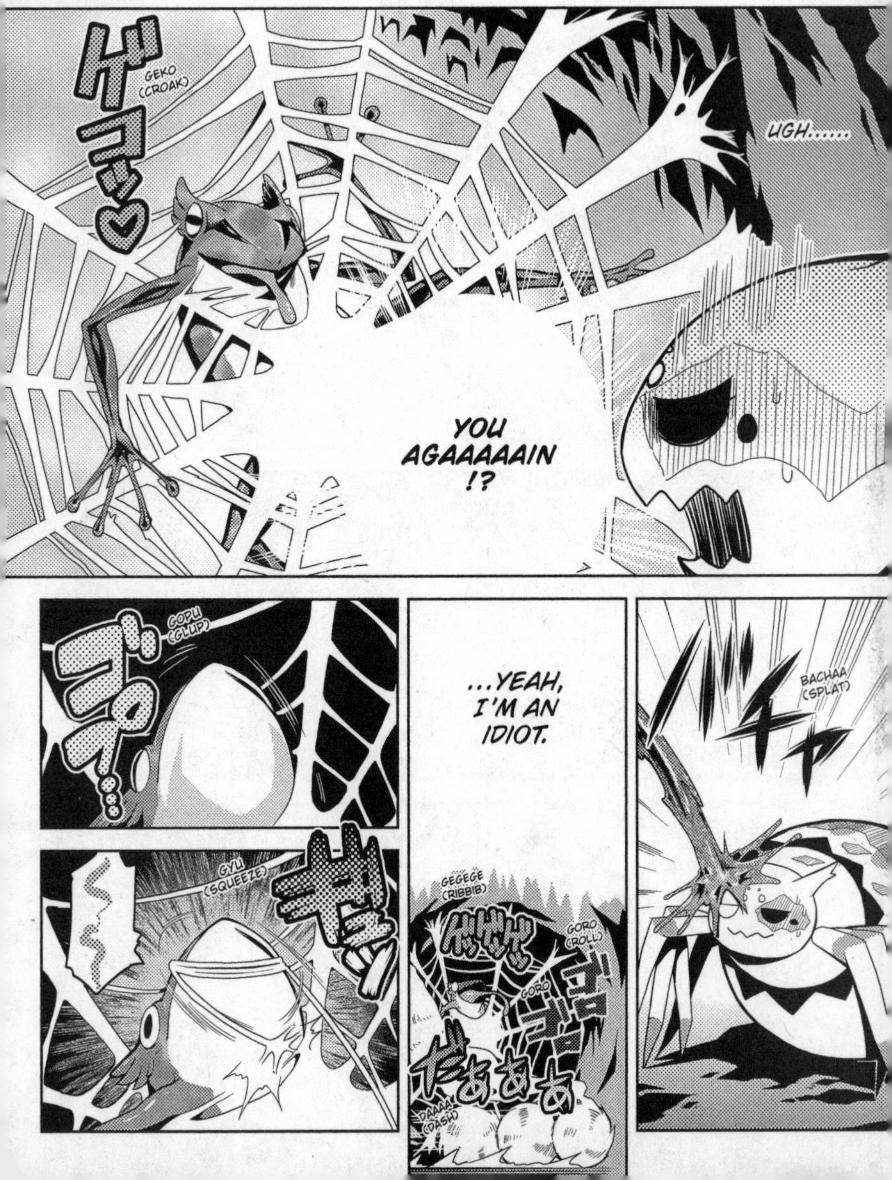
UGH......
GEKO (CROAK)
YOU AGAAAAAIN!?
BACHAA (SPLAT)
...YEAH, I'M AN IDIOT.
GEGEGE (RIBBIT)
GORO (ROLL)
GORO
DAAAA (DASH)
GOPU (GLUP)
GYU (SQUEEZE)

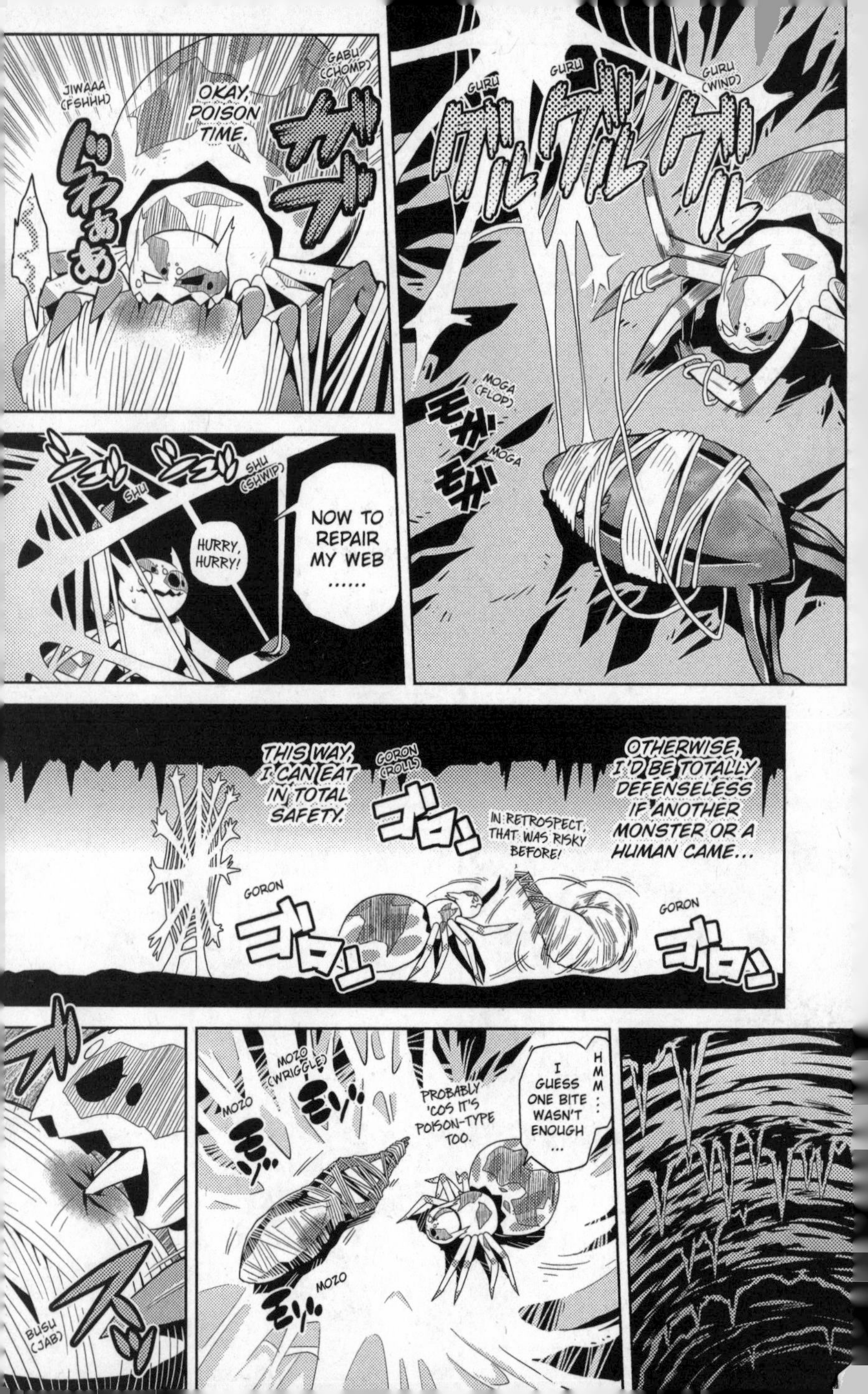
GURU (WIND)
GURU
GURU
MOGA (FLOP)
MOGA
GABU (CHOMP)
OKAY, POISON TIME.
JIWAAA (FSHHH)
NOW TO REPAIR MY WEB ......
SHU (SHWIP)
HURRY, HURRY!
SHU
OTHERWISE, I'D BE TOTALLY DEFENSELESS IF ANOTHER MONSTER OR A HUMAN CAME...
IN RETROSPECT, THAT WAS RISKY BEFORE!
GORON (ROLL)
THIS WAY, I CAN EAT IN TOTAL SAFETY.
GORON
GORON
HMM...
I GUESS ONE BITE WASN'T ENOUGH...
PROBABLY 'COS IT'S POISON-TYPE TOO.
MOZO (WRIGGLE)
MOZO
MOZO
BUSU (JAB)

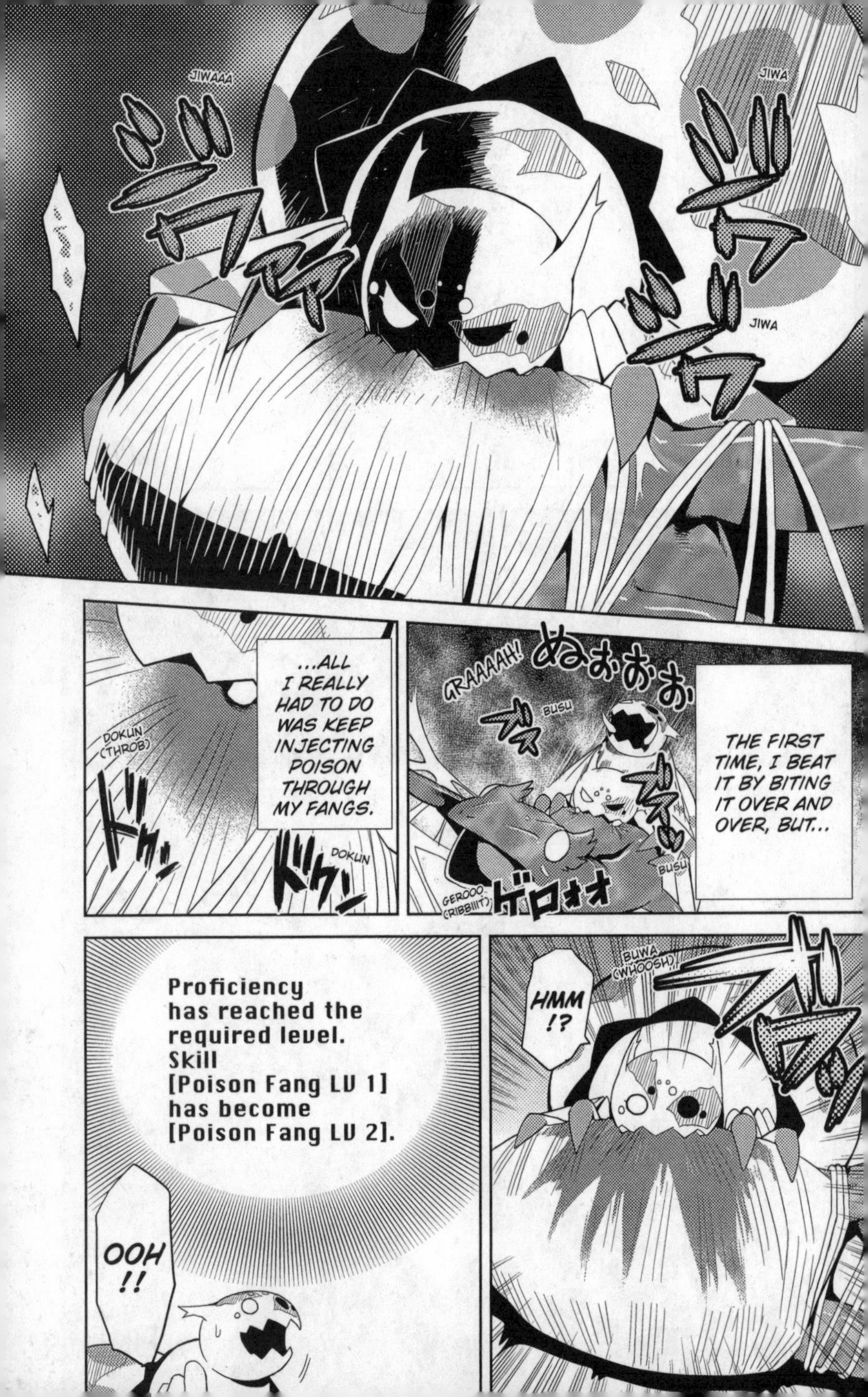
JIWA
JIWA
JIWAAA
...
THE FIRST TIME, I BEAT IT BY BITING IT OVER AND OVER, BUT...
GRAAAAH!
ぬおおお
BUSU
BUSU
GEROOO (RIBBIIIT)
ゲロォオ
...ALL I REALLY HAD TO DO WAS KEEP INJECTING POISON THROUGH MY FANGS.
DOKUN (THROB)
DOKUN
BUWA (WHOOSH)
HMM !?
Proficiency has reached the required level. Skill [Poison Fang LV 1] has become [Poison Fang LV 2].
OOH !!

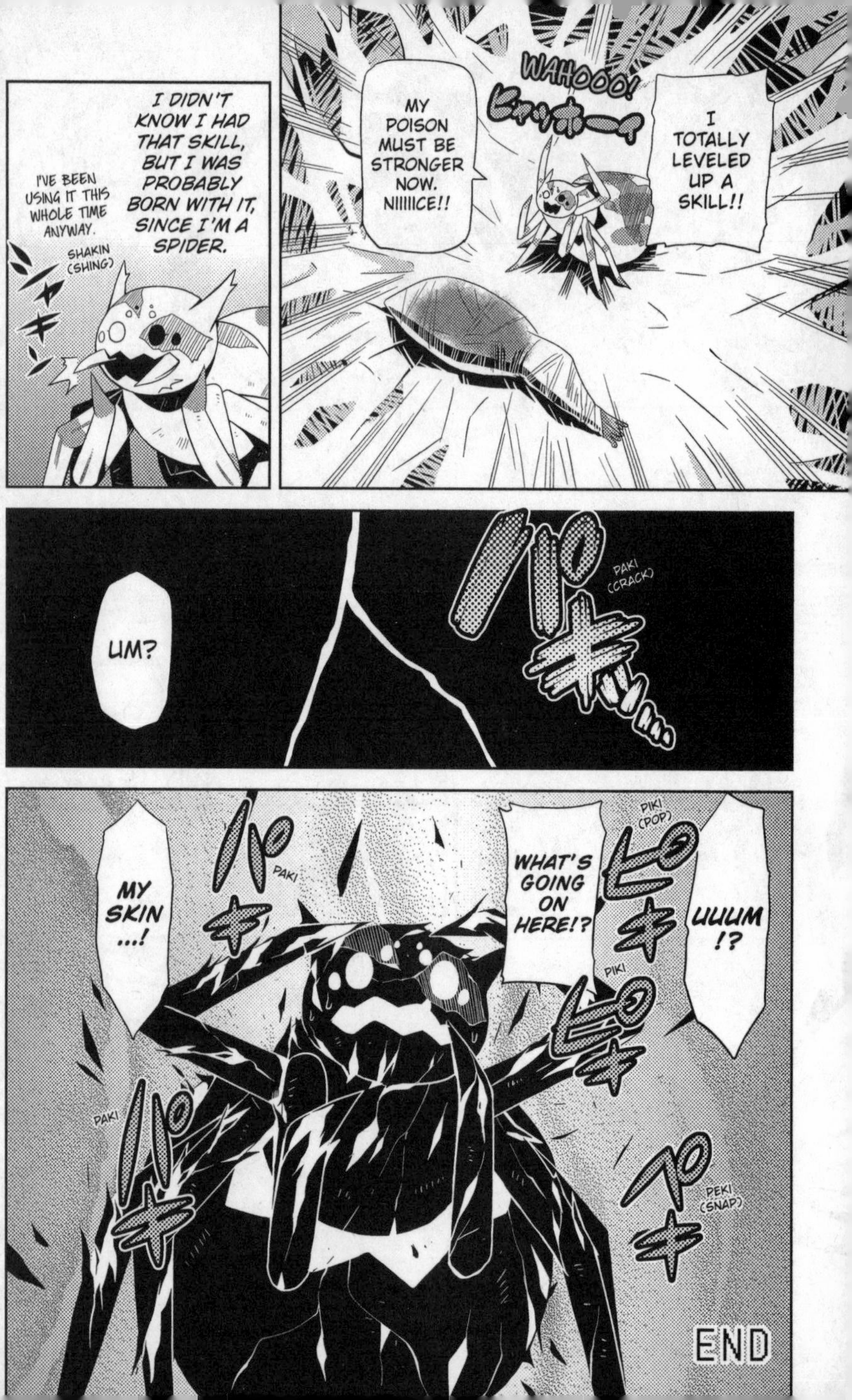
WAHOOO!
I TOTALLY LEVELED UP A SKILL!!
MY POISON MUST BE STRONGER NOW. NIIIIICE!!
I DIDN'T KNOW I HAD THAT SKILL, BUT I WAS PROBABLY BORN WITH IT, SINCE I'M A SPIDER.
I'VE BEEN USING IT THIS WHOLE TIME ANYWAY.
SHAKIN (SHING)
PAKI (CRACK)
UM?
UUUM!?
PIKI (POP)
PIKI
WHAT'S GOING ON HERE!?
PAKI
MY SKIN...!
PEKI (SNAP)
PAKI
END

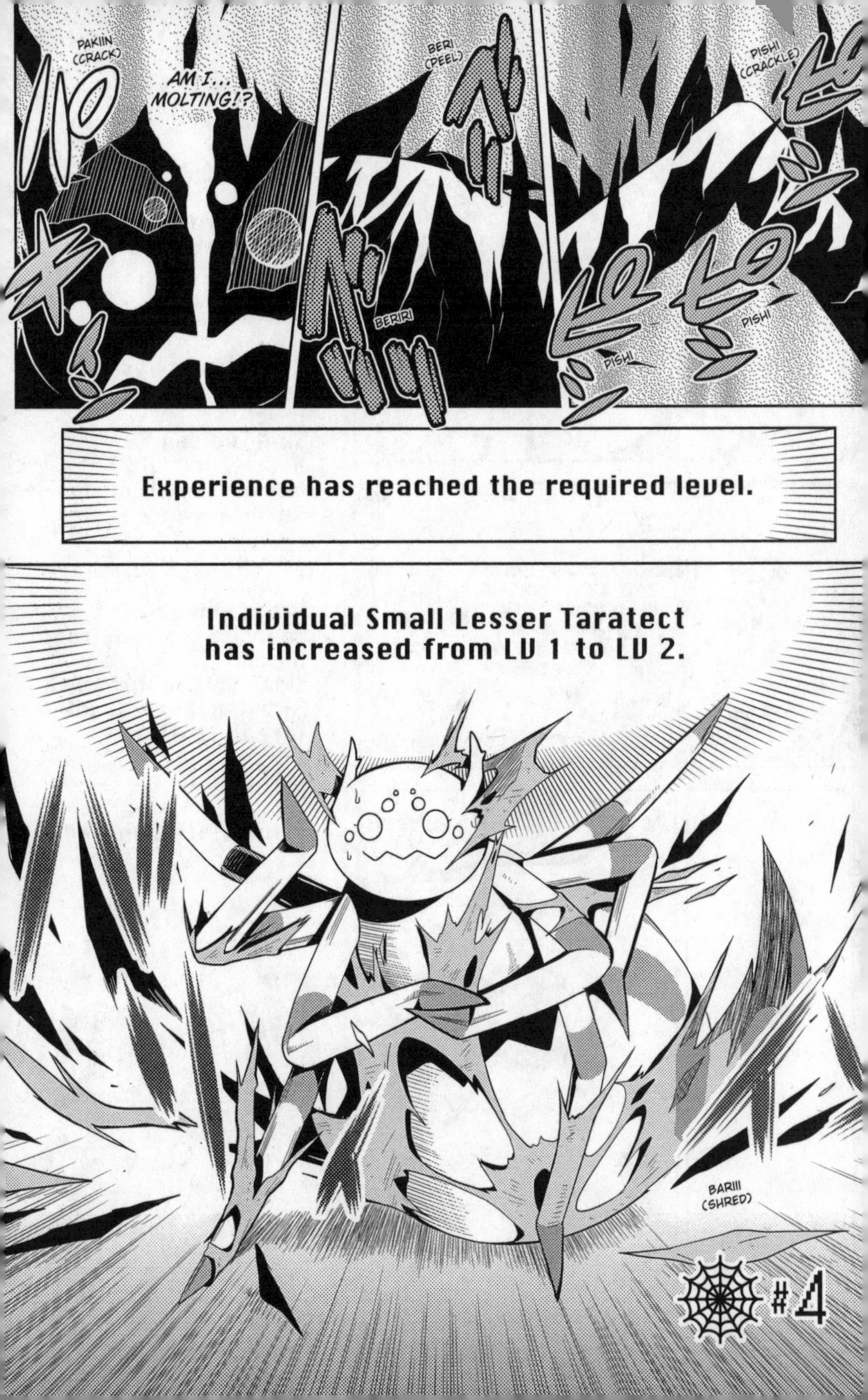

PISHI (CRACKLE)
PISHI
PISHI
BERI (PEEL)
BERIRI
PAKIIN (CRACK)
AM I... MOLTING!?
Experience has reached the required level.
Individual Small Lesser Taratect has increased from LV 1 to LV 2.
BARIII (SHRED)
#4

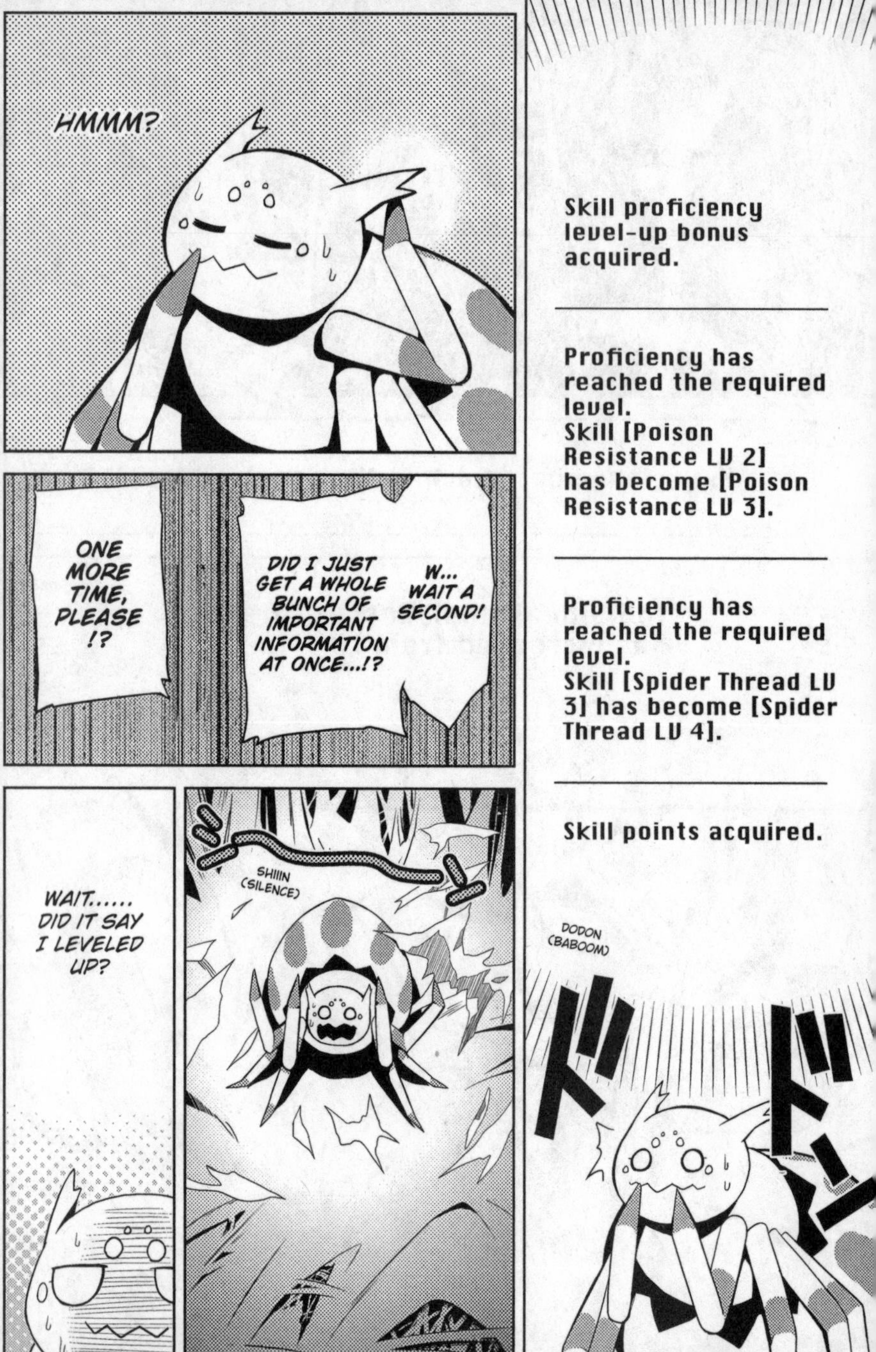
Skill proficiency level-up bonus acquired.
Proficiency has reached the required level. Skill [Poison Resistance LV 2] has become [Poison Resistance LV 3].
Proficiency has reached the required level. Skill [Spider Thread LV 3] has become [Spider Thread LV 4].
Skill points acquired.
DODON (BABOOM)
ドドン
HMMM?
W... WAIT A SECOND!
DID I JUST GET A WHOLE BUNCH OF IMPORTANT INFORMATION AT ONCE...!?
ONE MORE TIME, PLEASE!?
SHIIIN (SILENCE)
WAIT...... DID IT SAY I LEVELED UP?

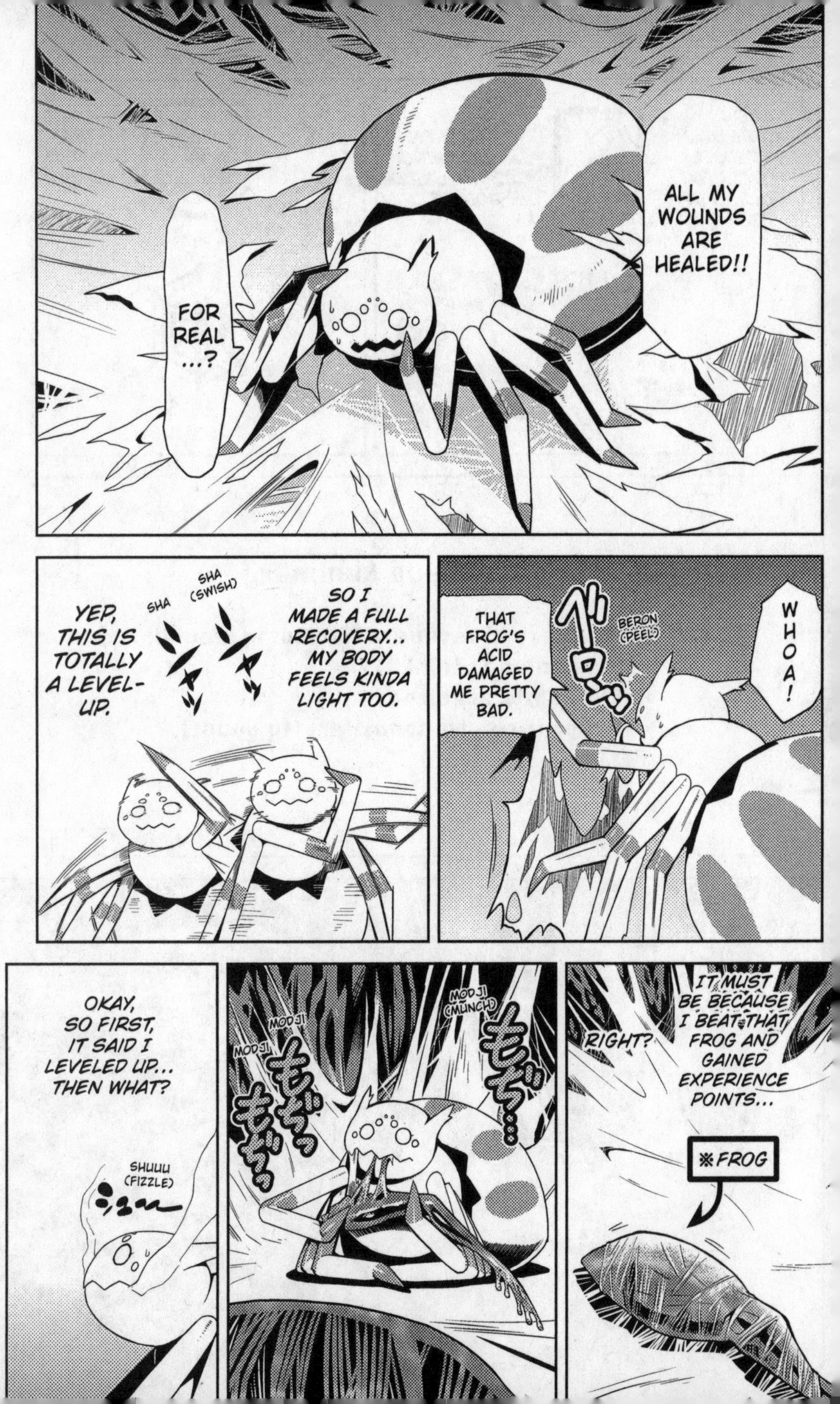
ALL MY WOUNDS ARE HEALED!!
FOR REAL ...?
WHOA!
BERON (PEEL)
THAT FROG'S ACID DAMAGED ME PRETTY BAD.
SO I MADE A FULL RECOVERY... MY BODY FEELS KINDA LIGHT TOO.
SHA (SWISH)
SHA
YEP, THIS IS TOTALLY A LEVEL-UP.
IT MUST BE BECAUSE I BEAT THAT FROG AND GAINED EXPERIENCE POINTS...
RIGHT?
※FROG
MODJI (MUNCH)
MODJI
MODJI
OKAY, SO FIRST, IT SAID I LEVELED UP... THEN WHAT?
SHUUU (FIZZLE)

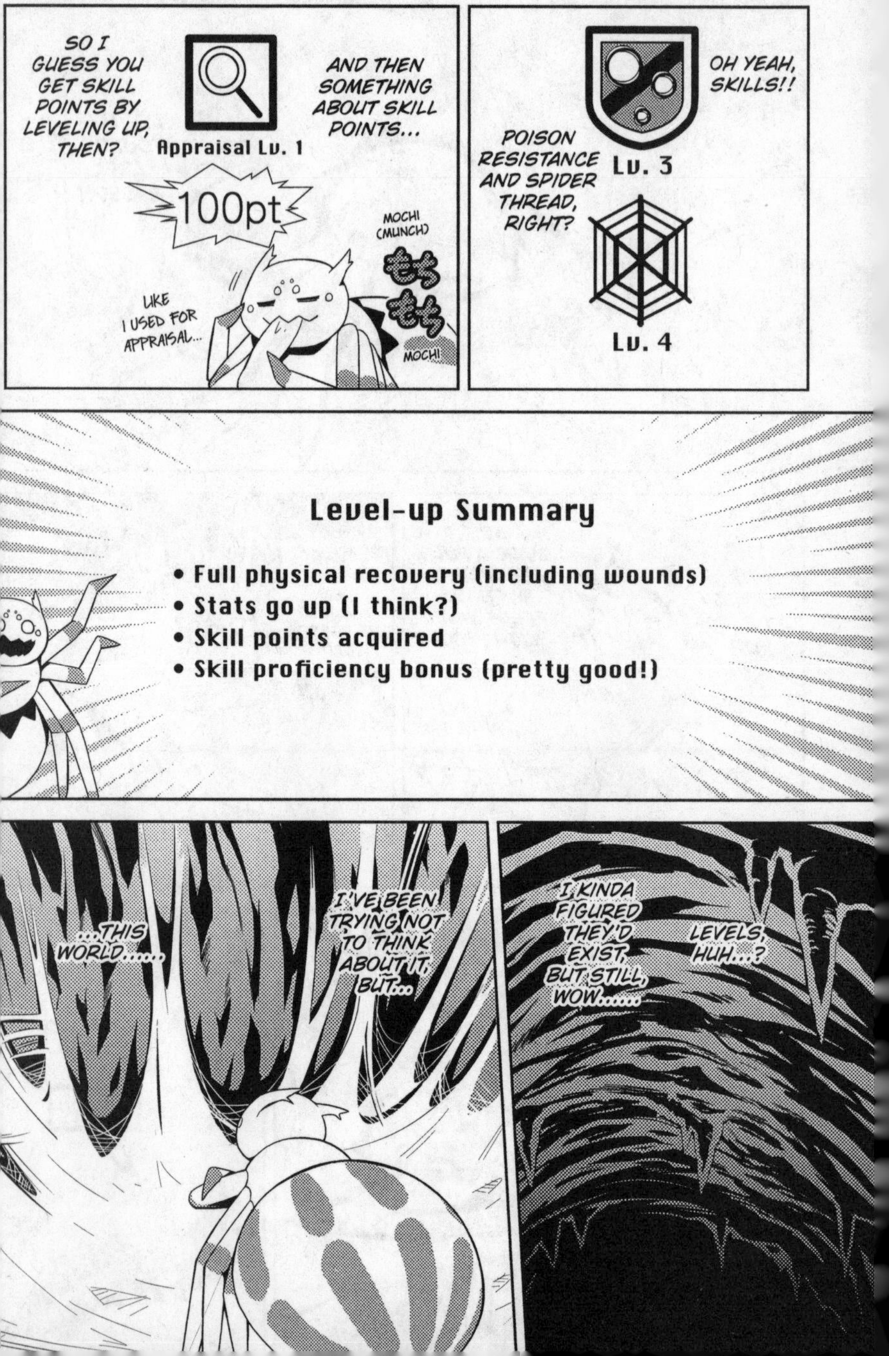
OH YEAH, SKILLS!!
POISON RESISTANCE AND SPIDER THREAD, RIGHT?
Lv. 3
Lv. 4
AND THEN SOMETHING ABOUT SKILL POINTS...
Appraisal Lv. 1
SO I GUESS YOU GET SKILL POINTS BY LEVELING UP, THEN?
100pt
MOCHI (MUNCH)
もち もち
MOCHI
LIKE I USED FOR APPRAISAL...
Level-up Summary
• Full physical recovery (including wounds)
• Stats go up (I think?)
• Skill points acquired
• Skill proficiency bonus (pretty good!)
LEVELS, HUH...?
I KINDA FIGURED THEY'D EXIST, BUT STILL, WOW......
I'VE BEEN TRYING NOT TO THINK ABOUT IT, BUT...
...THIS WORLD......

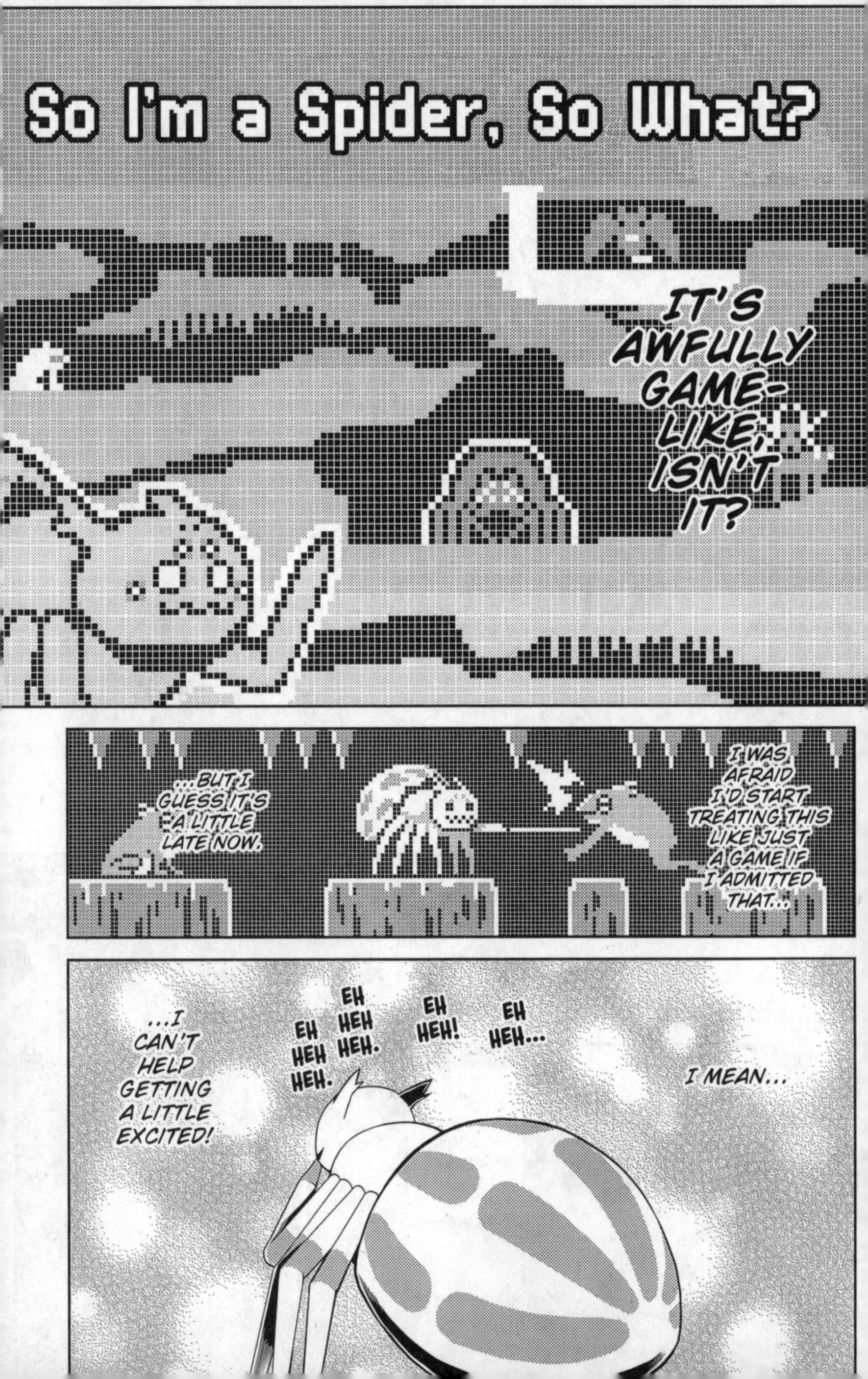
So I'm a Spider, So What?
IT'S AWFULLY GAME-LIKE, ISN'T IT?
I WAS AFRAID I'D START TREATING THIS LIKE JUST A GAME IF I ADMITTED THAT...
...BUT I GUESS IT'S A LITTLE LATE NOW.
I MEAN...
EH HEH...
EH HEH!
EH HEH HEH.
EH HEH HEH.
...I CAN'T HELP GETTING A LITTLE EXCITED!

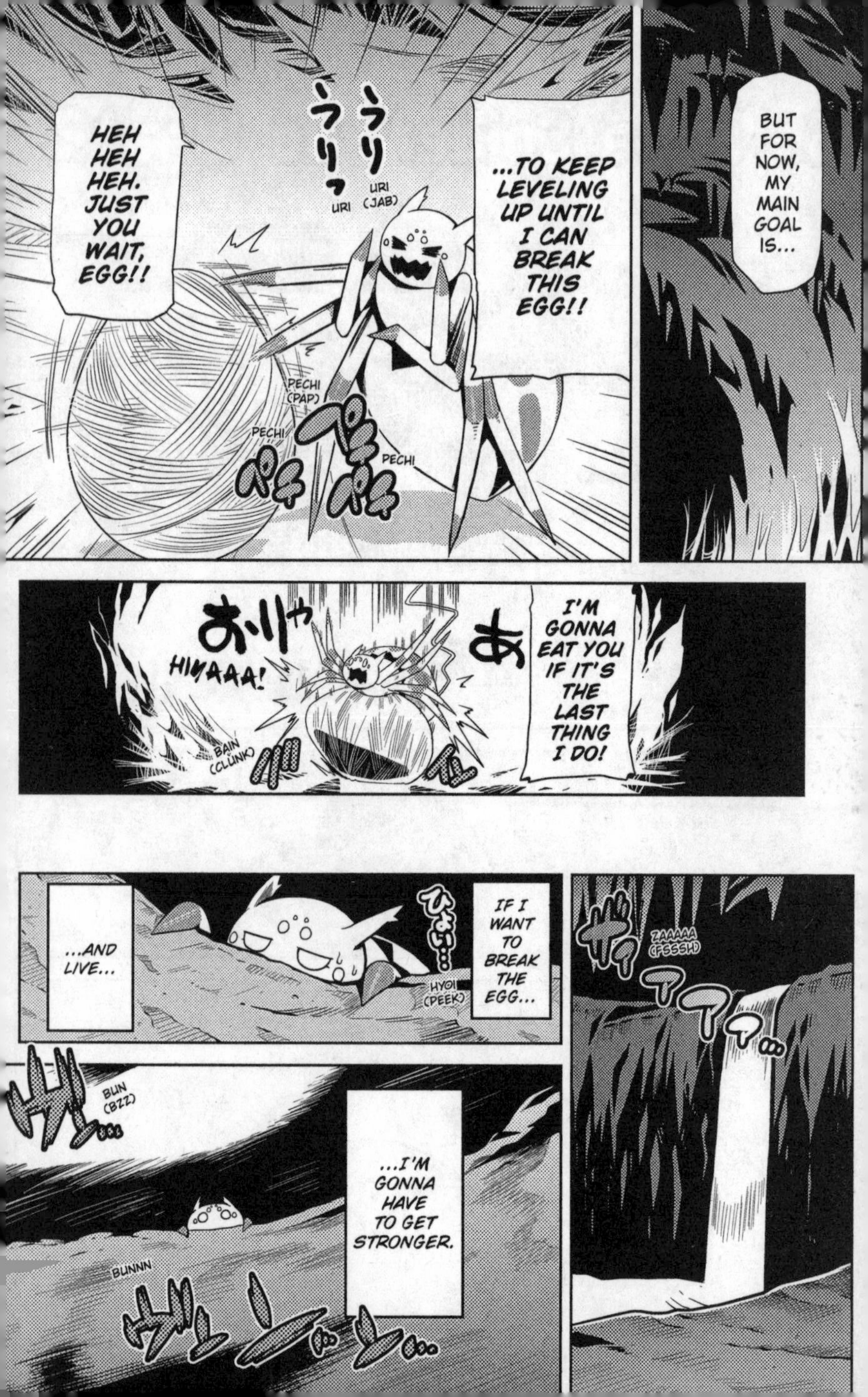
BUT FOR NOW, MY MAIN GOAL IS...
...TO KEEP LEVELING UP UNTIL I CAN BREAK THIS EGG!!
URI (JAB)
URI
HEH HEH HEH. JUST YOU WAIT, EGG!!
PECHI (PAP)
PECHI
PECHI
I'M GONNA EAT YOU IF IT'S THE LAST THING I DO!
HIYAAA!
BAIN (CLUNK)
ZAAAAA (PSSSH)
IF I WANT TO BREAK THE EGG...
HYOI (PEEK)
...AND LIVE...
...I'M GONNA HAVE TO GET STRONGER.
BUN (BZZ)
BUNNN

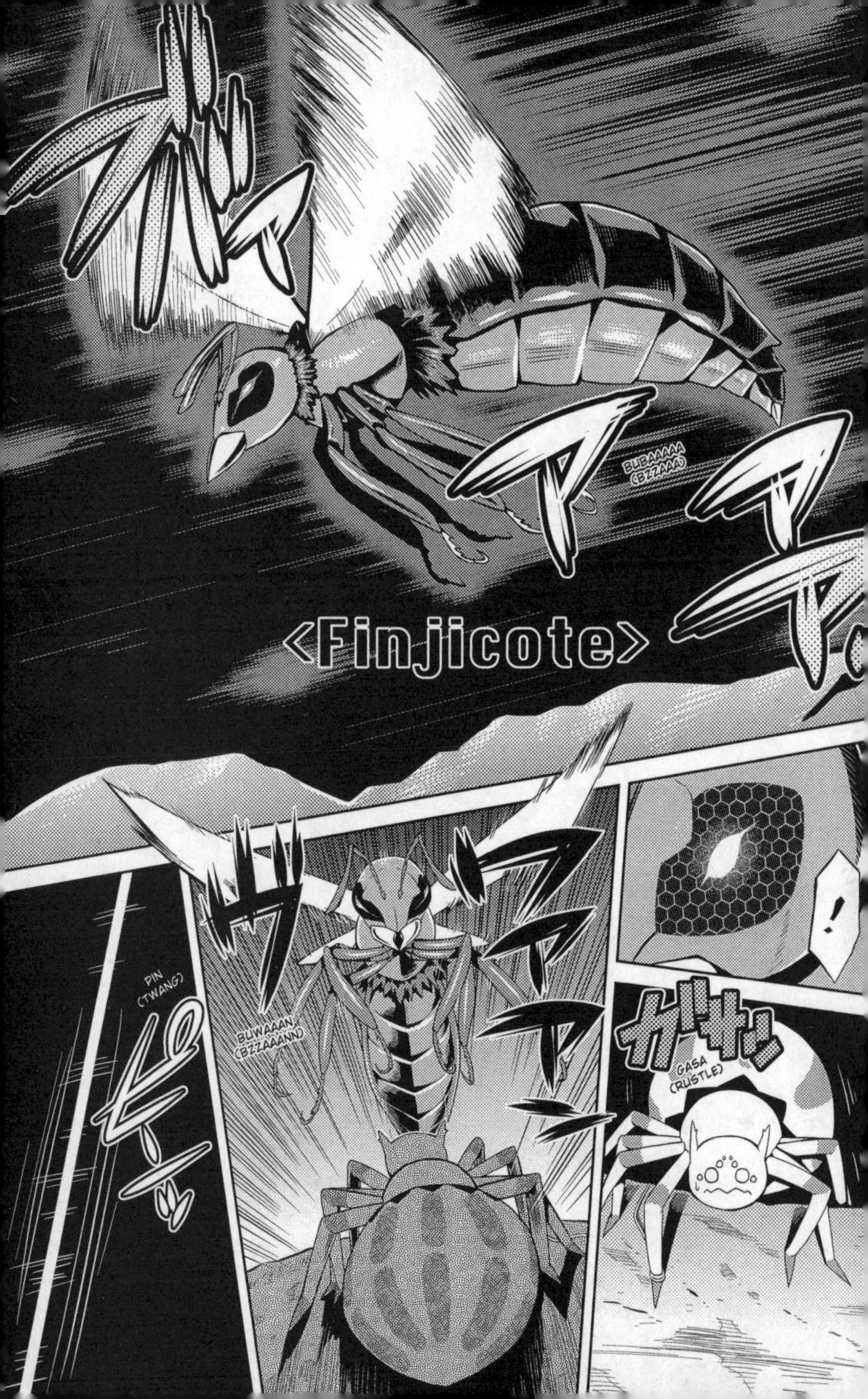
BUBAAAAA (BZZAAA)
<Finjicote>
!
GASA (RUSTLE)
BUWAAAN (BZZAAANN)
PIN (TWANG)

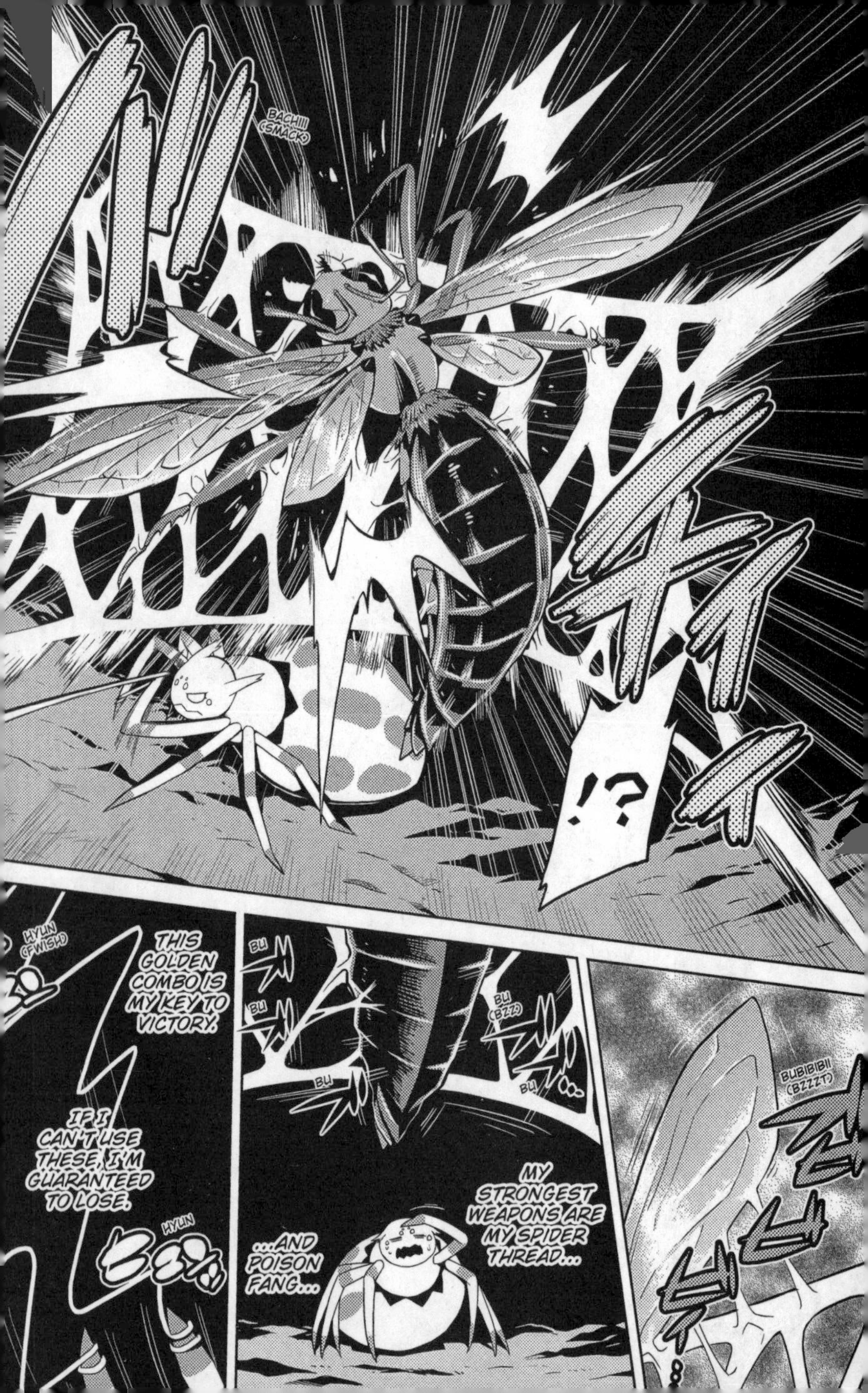
BACHI!! (SMACK)
!?
BUBIBIBII (BZZZT)
BU (BZZ)
BU
BU
BU
BU
MY STRONGEST WEAPONS ARE MY SPIDER THREAD...
...AND POISON FANG...
THIS GOLDEN COMBO IS MY KEY TO VICTORY.
HYUN (FWISH)
IF I CAN'T USE THESE, I'M GUARANTEED TO LOSE.
HYUN

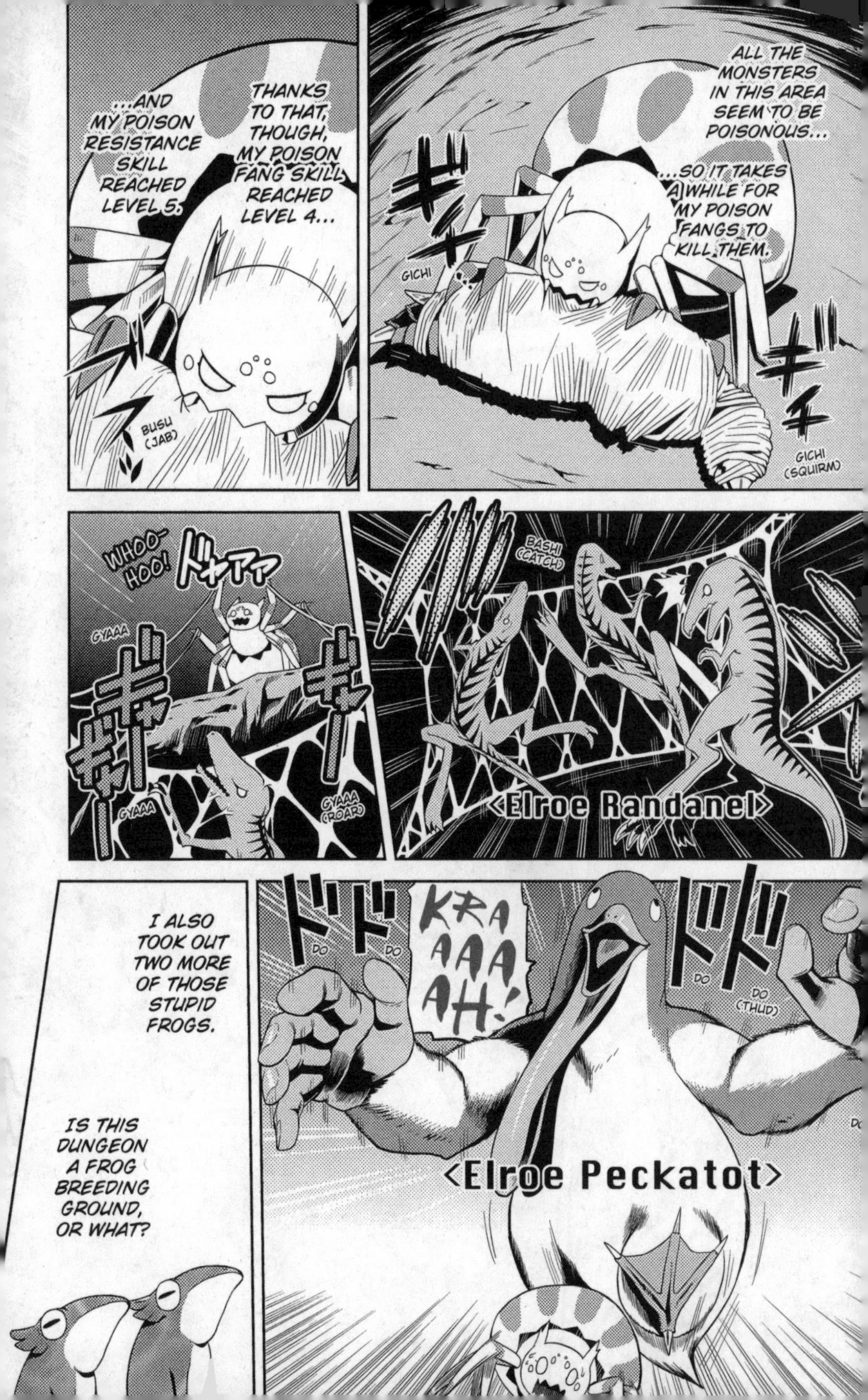
ALL THE MONSTERS IN THIS AREA SEEM TO BE POISONOUS...
...SO IT TAKES A WHILE FOR MY POISON FANGS TO KILL THEM.
GICHI
GICHI (SQUIRM)
THANKS TO THAT, THOUGH, MY POISON FANG SKILL REACHED LEVEL 4...
...AND MY POISON RESISTANCE SKILL REACHED LEVEL 5.
BUSU (JAB)
BASHI (CATCH)
<Elroe Randanel>
WHOO-HOO!
GYAAA
GYAAA
GYAAA (ROAR)
KRAAAAAAH!
DO
DO
DO
DO (THUD)
<Elroe Peckatot>
I ALSO TOOK OUT TWO MORE OF THOSE STUPID FROGS.
IS THIS DUNGEON A FROG BREEDING GROUND, OR WHAT?

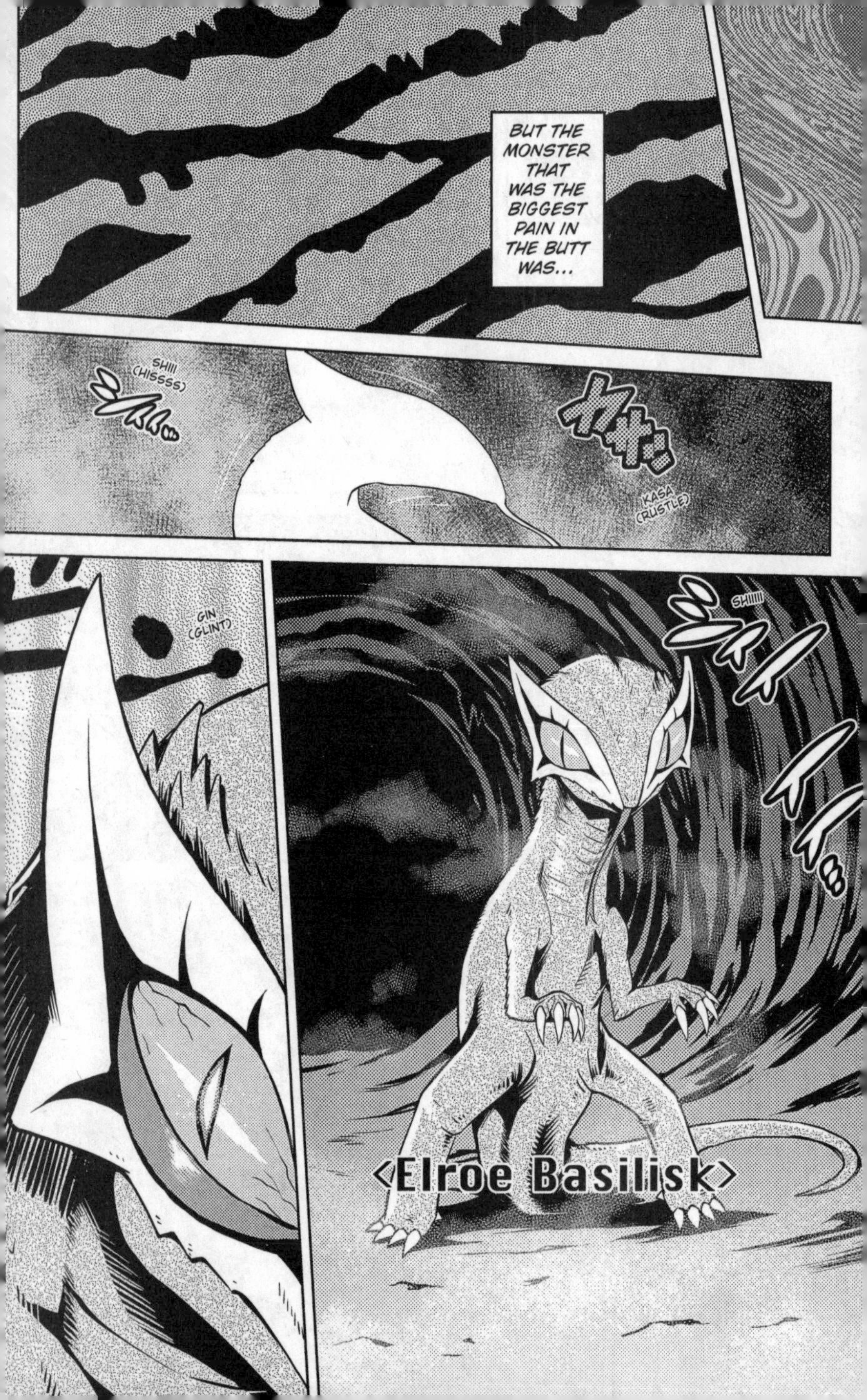
BUT THE MONSTER THAT WAS THE BIGGEST PAIN IN THE BUTT WAS...
KASA (RUSTLE)
SHIII (HISSSS)
SHIIII
GIN (GLINT)
‹Elroe Basilisk›

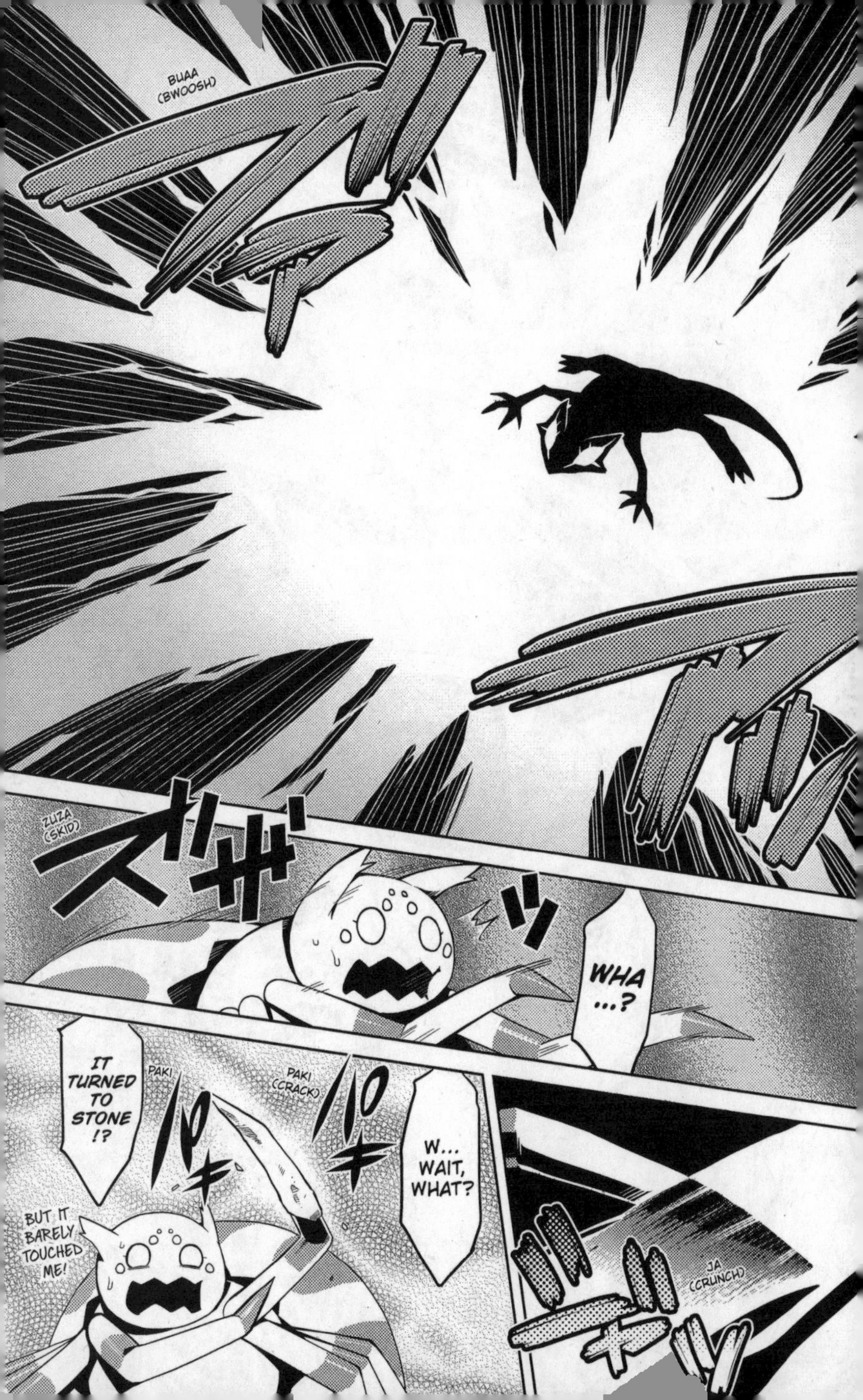
BUAA (BWOOSH)
ZUZA (SKID)
WHA ...?
W... WAIT, WHAT?
PAKI
PAKI (CRACK)
IT TURNED TO STONE !?
BUT IT BARELY TOUCHED ME!
JA (CRUNCH)

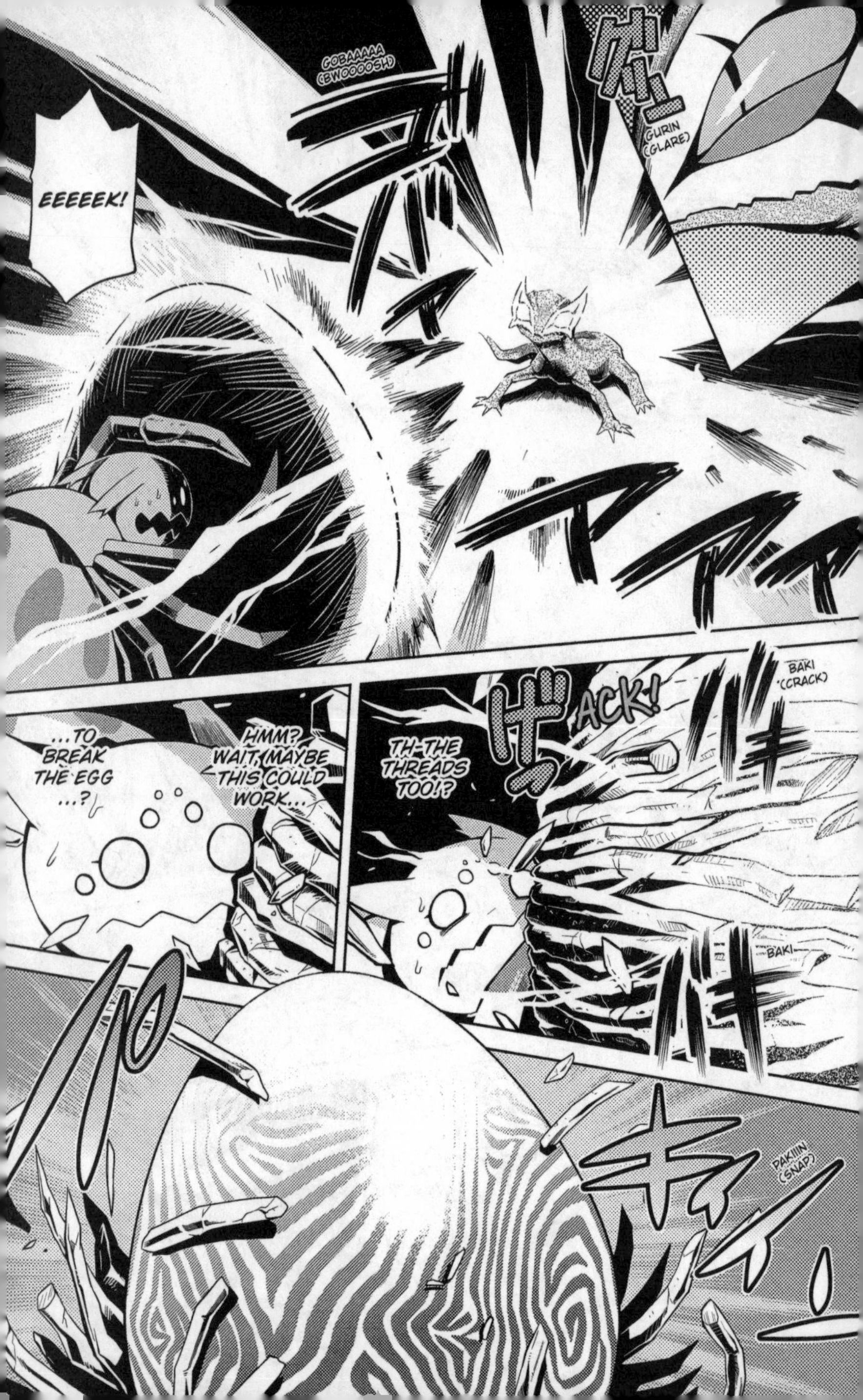
GURIN (GLARE)
GOBAAAAA (BWOOOOSH)
EEEEEK!
BAKI (CRACK)
ACK!
TH-THE THREADS TOO!?
BAKI
HMM? WAIT, MAYBE THIS COULD WORK...
...TO BREAK THE EGG ...?
PAKIIIN (SNAP)

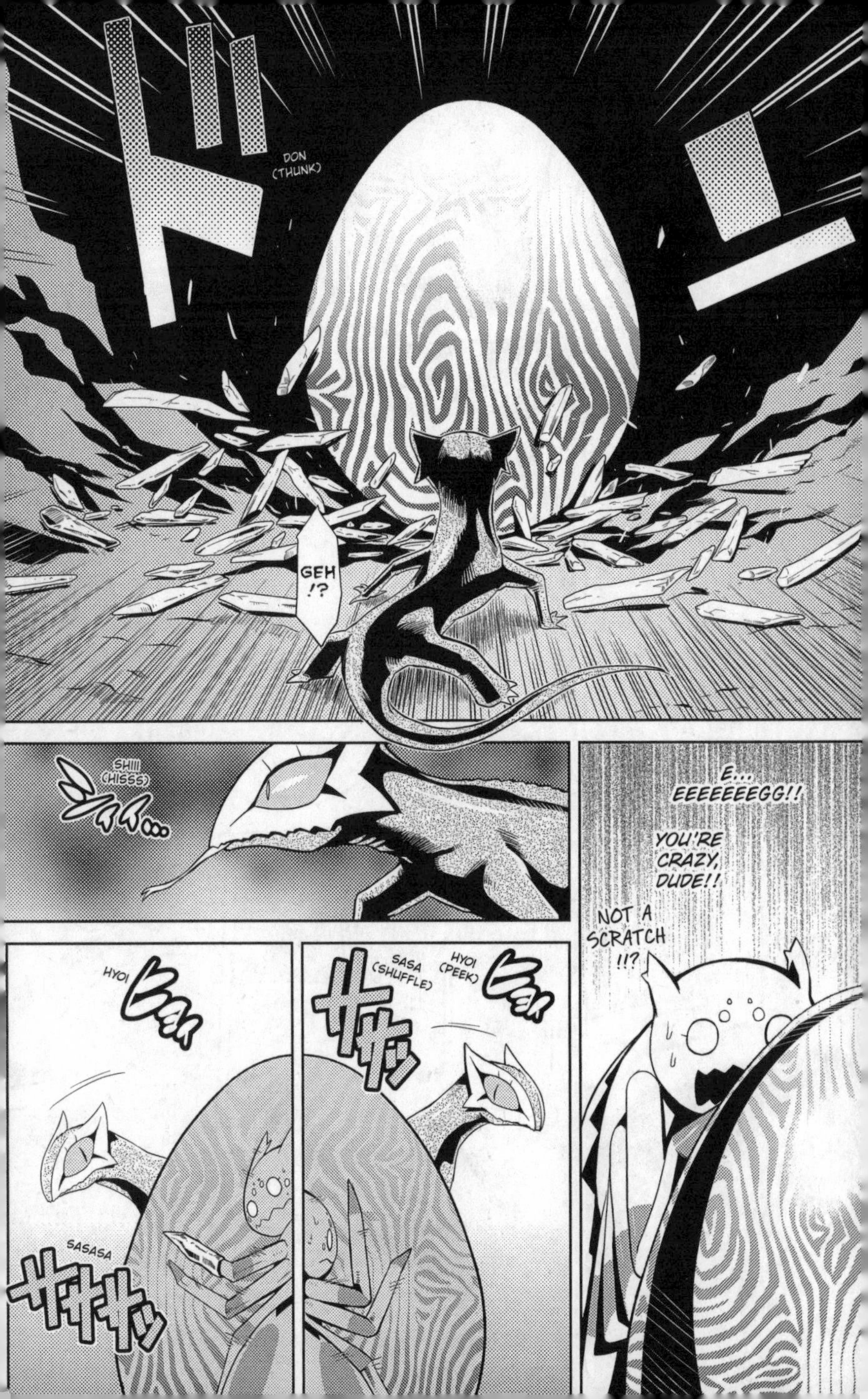
DON
(THUNK)
GEH
!?
E...
EEEEEEEGG!!
YOU'RE
CRAZY,
DUDE!!
NOT A
SCRATCH
!!?
SHIII
(HISSS)
HYOI
(PEEK)
SASA
(SHUFFLE)
HYOI
SASASA

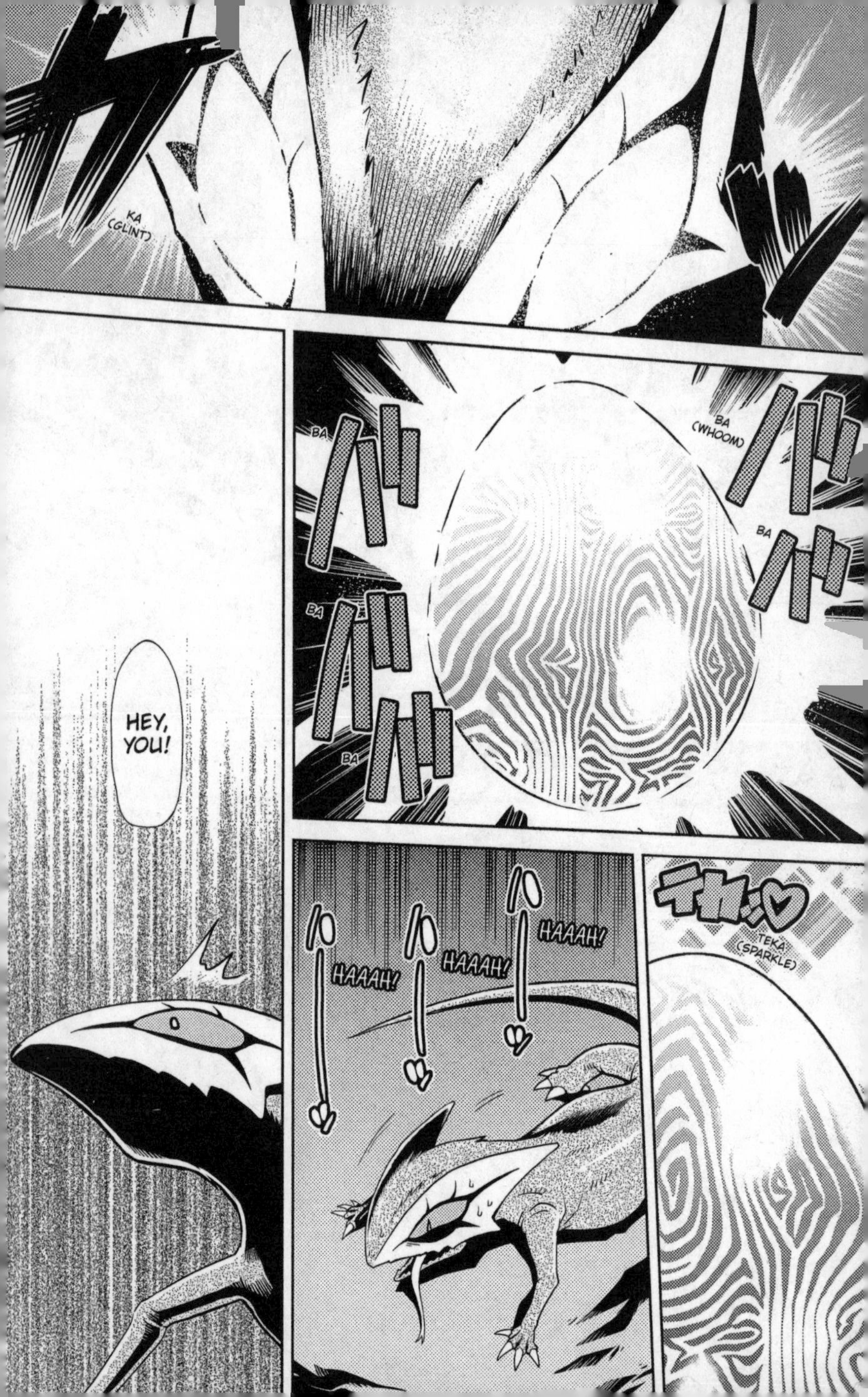
KA (GLINT)
BA (WHOOM)
BA
BA
BA
BA
TEKA (SPARKLE)
HAAAH!
HAAAH!
HAAAH!
HEY, YOU!

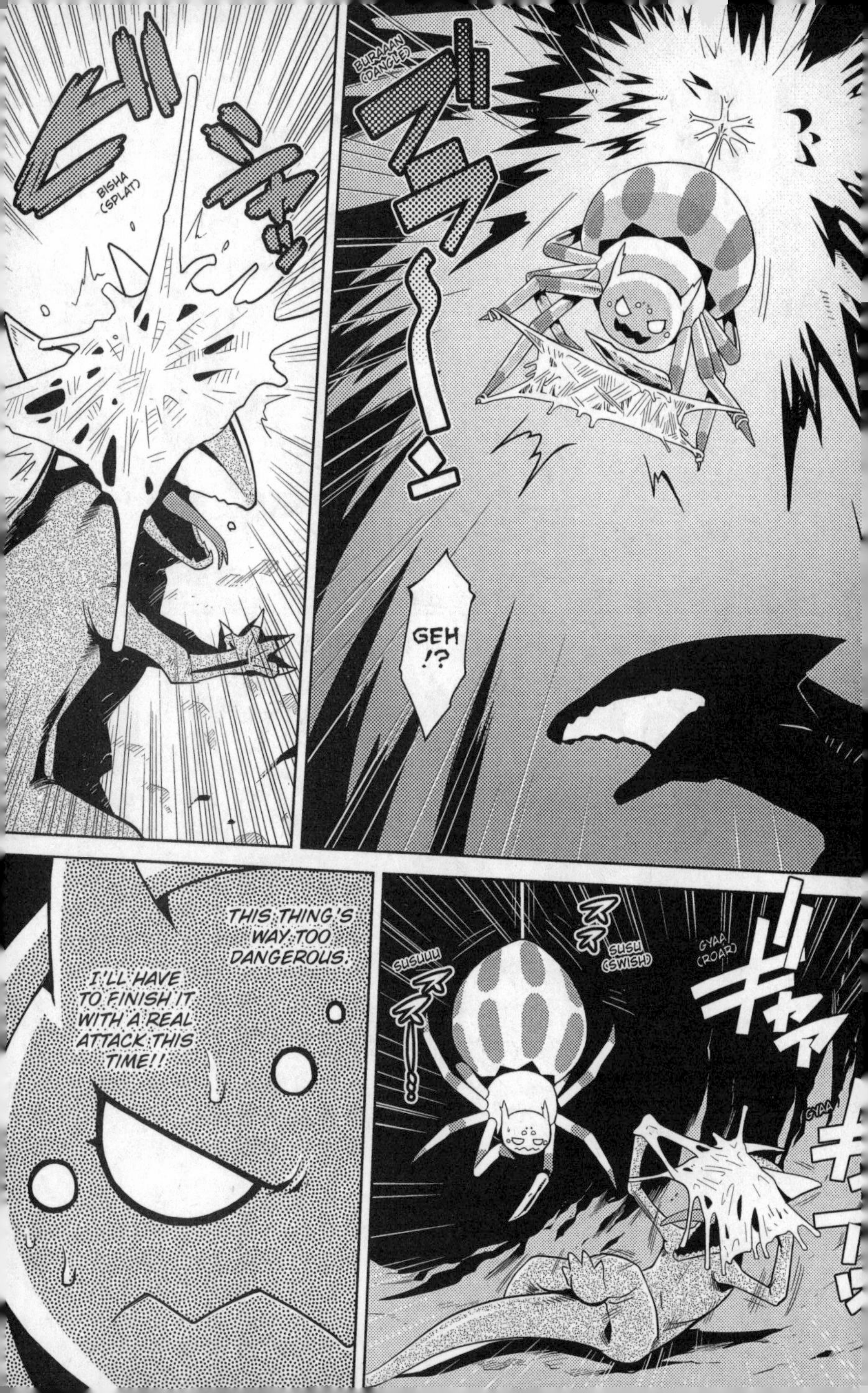
BURAAAN (DANGLE)
GEH !?
BISHA (SPLAT)
GYAA (ROAR)
GYAA
SUSU (SWISH)
SUSULU
THIS THING'S WAY TOO DANGEROUS.
I'LL HAVE TO FINISH IT WITH A REAL ATTACK THIS TIME!!

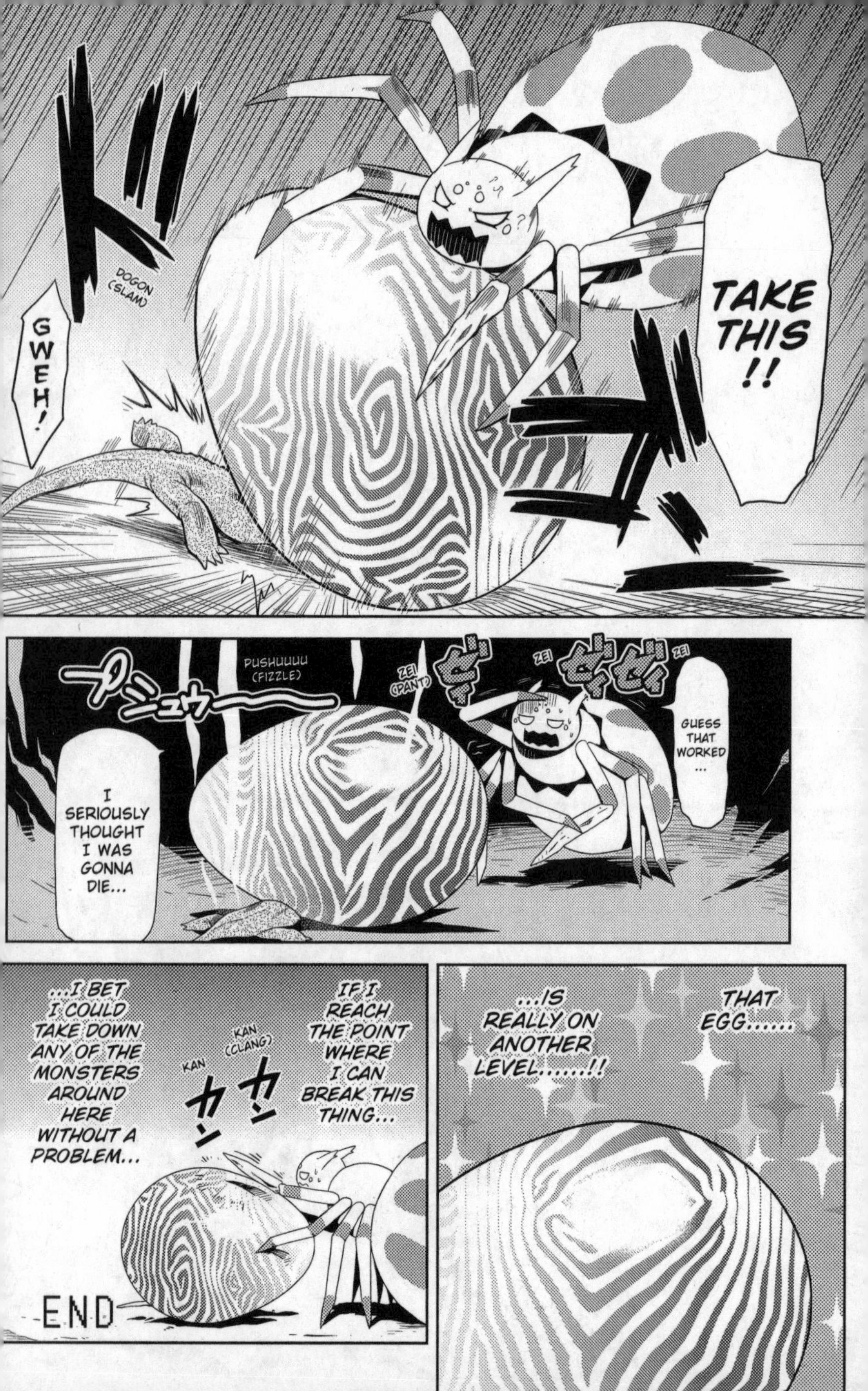
TAKE THIS!!
DOGON (SLAM)
GWEH!
ZEI
ZEI
ZEI (PANT)
GUESS THAT WORKED ...
PUSHUUUU (FIZZLE)
I SERIOUSLY THOUGHT I WAS GONNA DIE...
THAT EGG......
...IS REALLY ON ANOTHER LEVEL......!!
IF I REACH THE POINT WHERE I CAN BREAK THIS THING...
KAN (CLANG)
KAN
...I BET I COULD TAKE DOWN ANY OF THE MONSTERS AROUND HERE WITHOUT A PROBLEM...
END

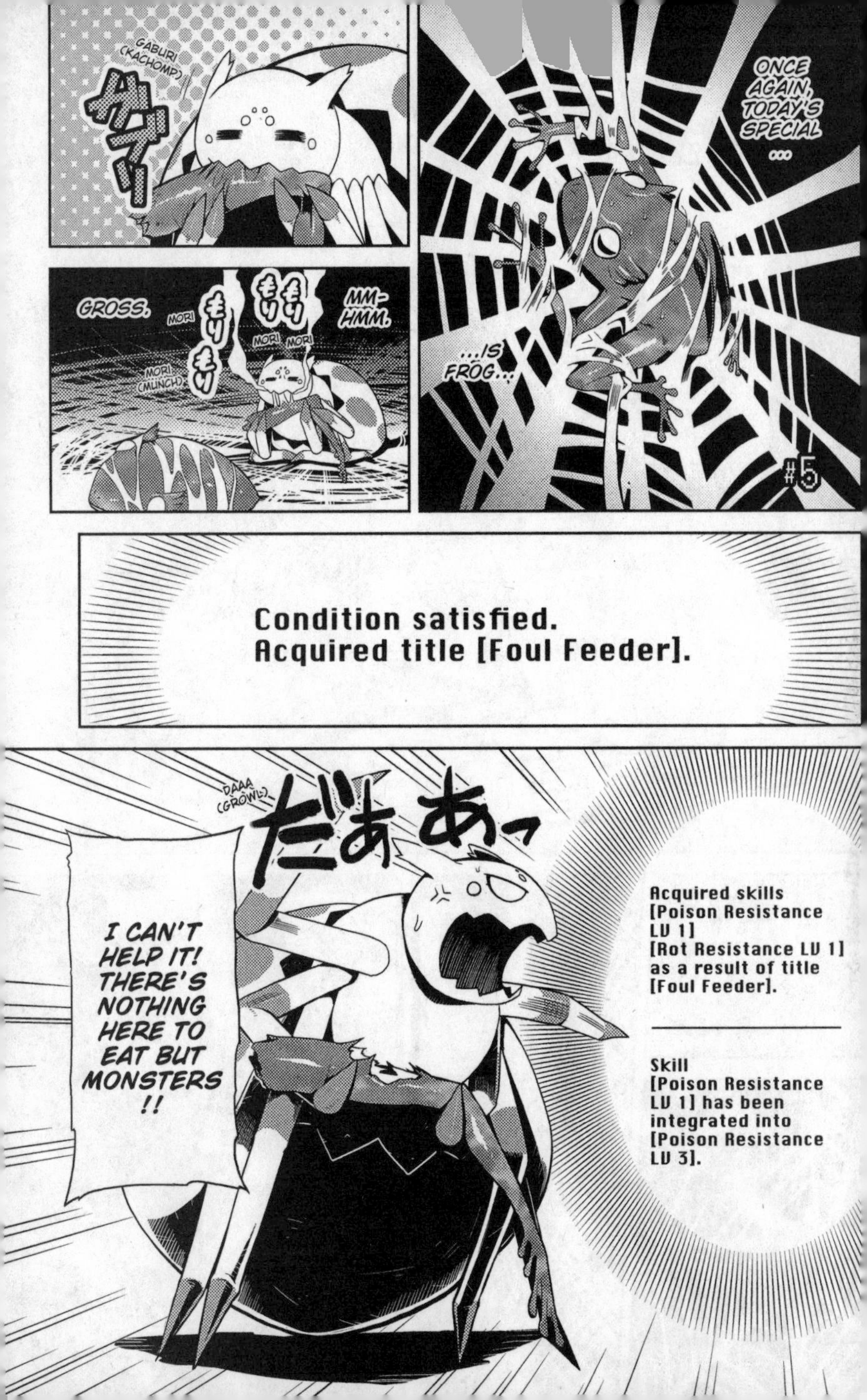
ONCE AGAIN, TODAY'S SPECIAL ...
...IS FROG...
#5
ガブリ
GABURI (KACHOMP)
MM-HMM.
もりもり
MORI MORI
もりもり
MORI MORI (MUNCH)
GROSS.
Condition satisfied.
Acquired title [Foul Feeder].
だあぁっ
DAAA (GROWL)
Acquired skills [Poison Resistance LV 1] [Rot Resistance LV 1] as a result of title [Foul Feeder].
Skill [Poison Resistance LV 1] has been integrated into [Poison Resistance LV 3].
I CAN'T HELP IT! THERE'S NOTHING HERE TO EAT BUT MONSTERS!!

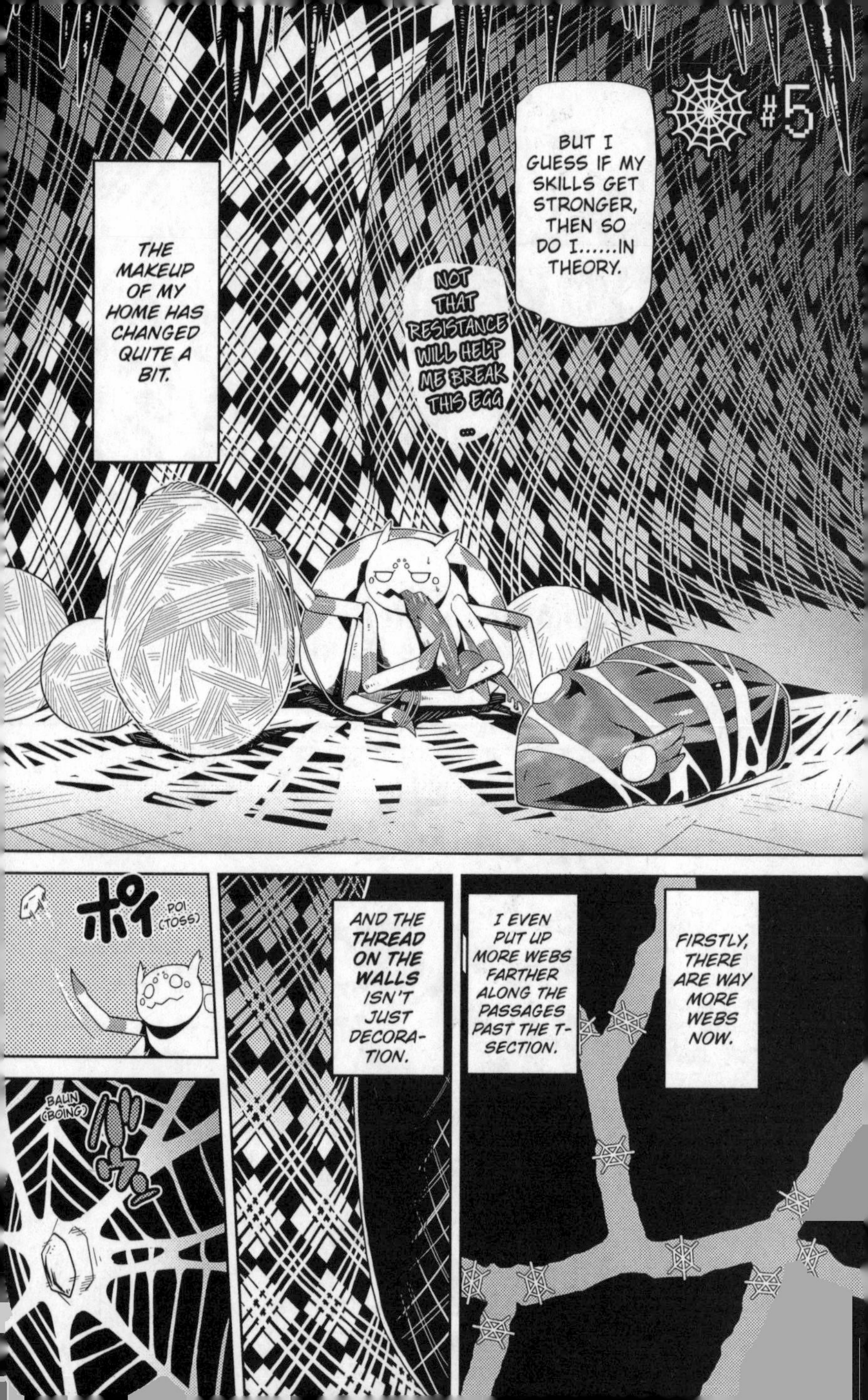
#5
BUT I GUESS IF MY SKILLS GET STRONGER, THEN SO DO I......IN THEORY.
NOT THAT RESISTANCE WILL HELP ME BREAK THIS EGG...
THE MAKEUP OF MY HOME HAS CHANGED QUITE A BIT.
FIRSTLY, THERE ARE WAY MORE WEBS NOW.
I EVEN PUT UP MORE WEBS FARTHER ALONG THE PASSAGES PAST THE T-SECTION.
AND THE THREAD ON THE WALLS ISN'T JUST DECORATION.
ポイ
POI (TOSS)
BAUN (BOING)

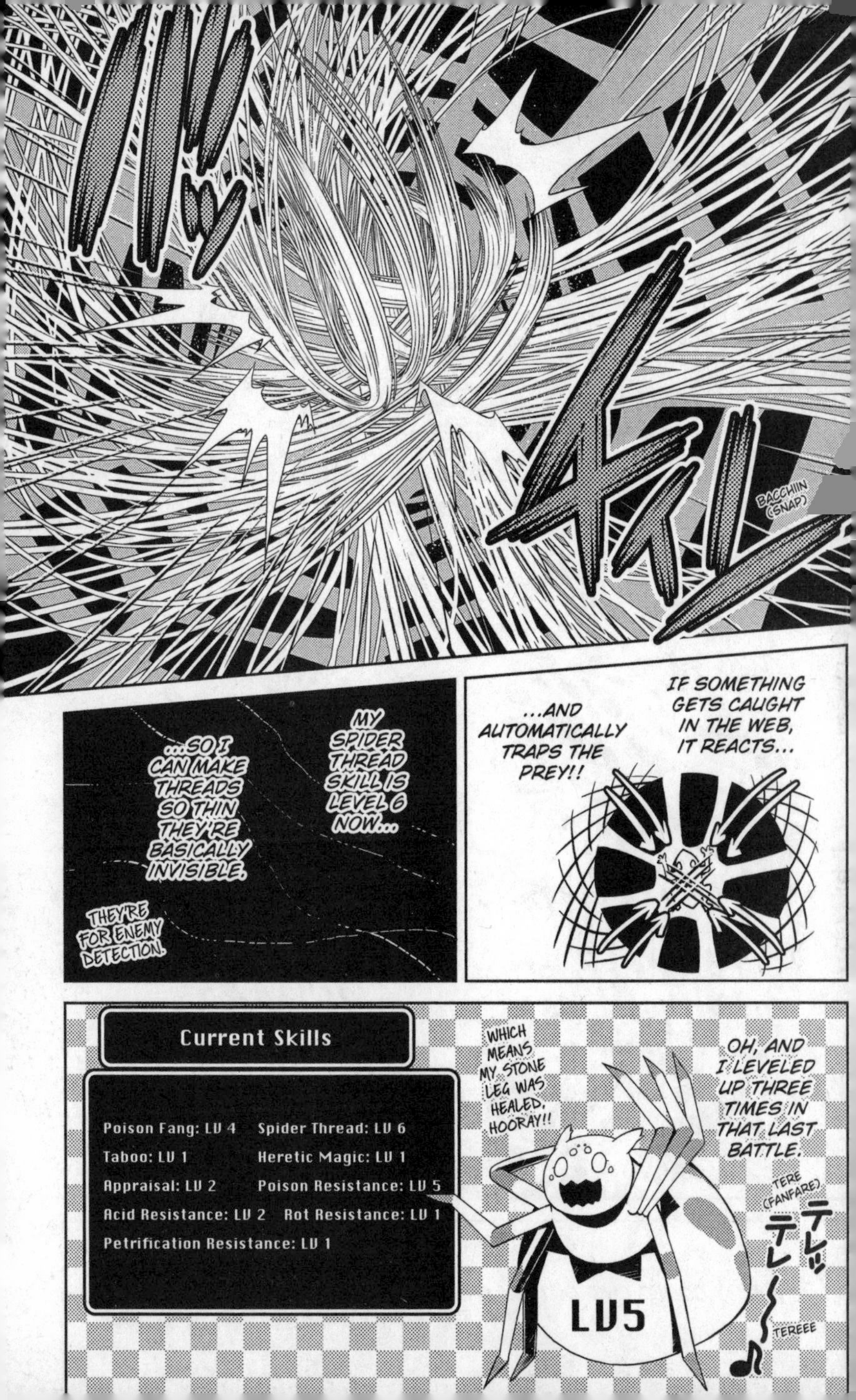
BACCHIIN (SNAP)
IF SOMETHING GETS CAUGHT IN THE WEB, IT REACTS...
...AND AUTOMATICALLY TRAPS THE PREY!!
MY SPIDER THREAD SKILL IS LEVEL 6 NOW...
...SO I CAN MAKE THREADS SO THIN THEY'RE BASICALLY INVISIBLE.
THEY'RE FOR ENEMY DETECTION.
OH, AND I LEVELED UP THREE TIMES IN THAT LAST BATTLE.
TERE (FANFARE)
テレッ
テレー
TEREEE
WHICH MEANS MY STONE LEG WAS HEALED. HOORAY!!
Current Skills
Poison Fang: LV 4
Spider Thread: LV 6
Taboo: LV 1
Heretic Magic: LV 1
Appraisal: LV 2
Poison Resistance: LV 5
Acid Resistance: LV 2
Rot Resistance: LV 1
Petrification Resistance: LV 1
LV5

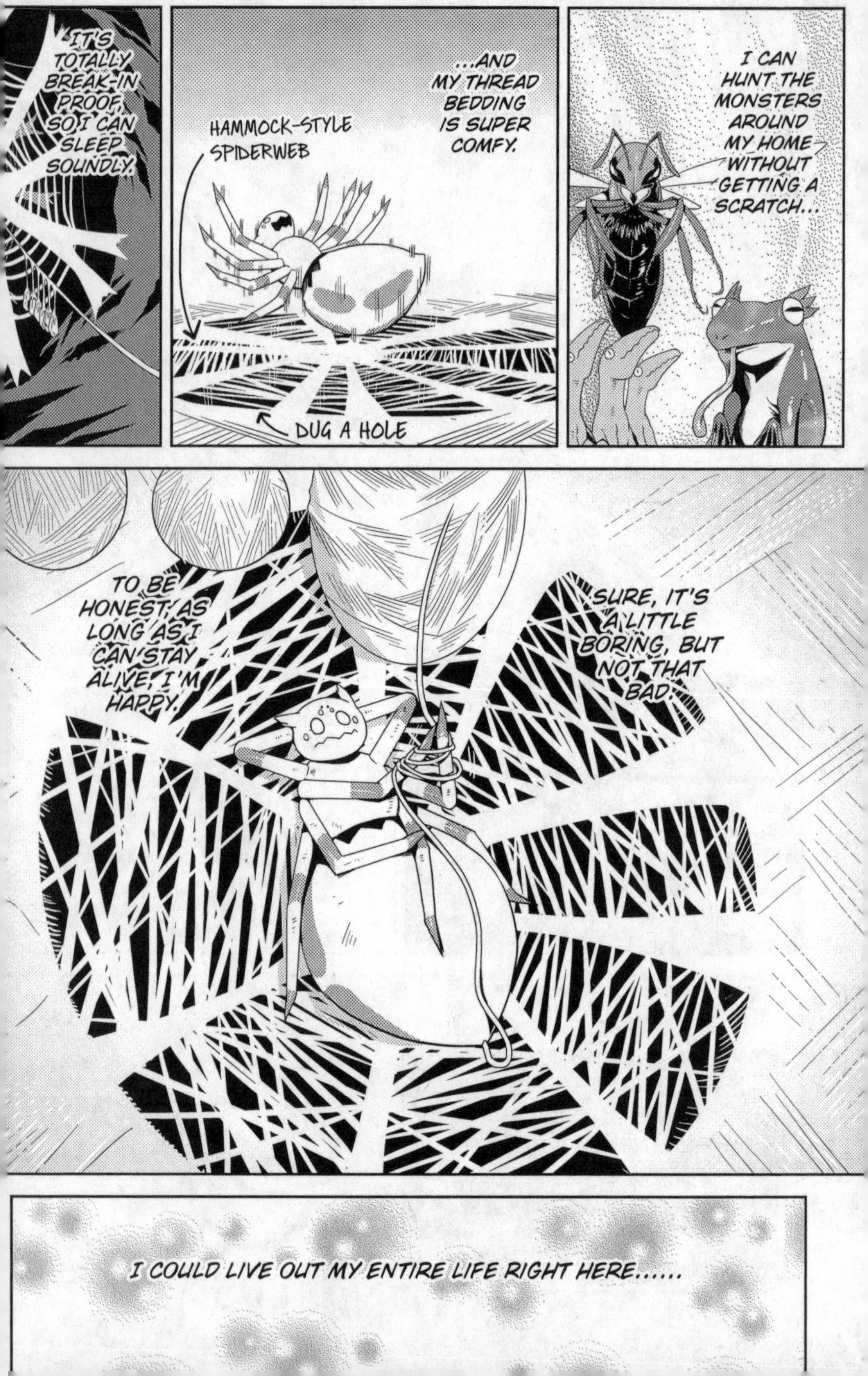
I CAN HUNT THE MONSTERS AROUND MY HOME WITHOUT GETTING A SCRATCH...
...AND MY THREAD BEDDING IS SUPER COMFY.
HAMMOCK-STYLE SPIDERWEB
DUG A HOLE
IT'S TOTALLY BREAK-IN PROOF, SO I CAN SLEEP SOUNDLY.
SURE, IT'S A LITTLE BORING, BUT NOT THAT BAD.
TO BE HONEST, AS LONG AS I CAN STAY ALIVE, I'M HAPPY.
I COULD LIVE OUT MY ENTIRE LIFE RIGHT HERE......

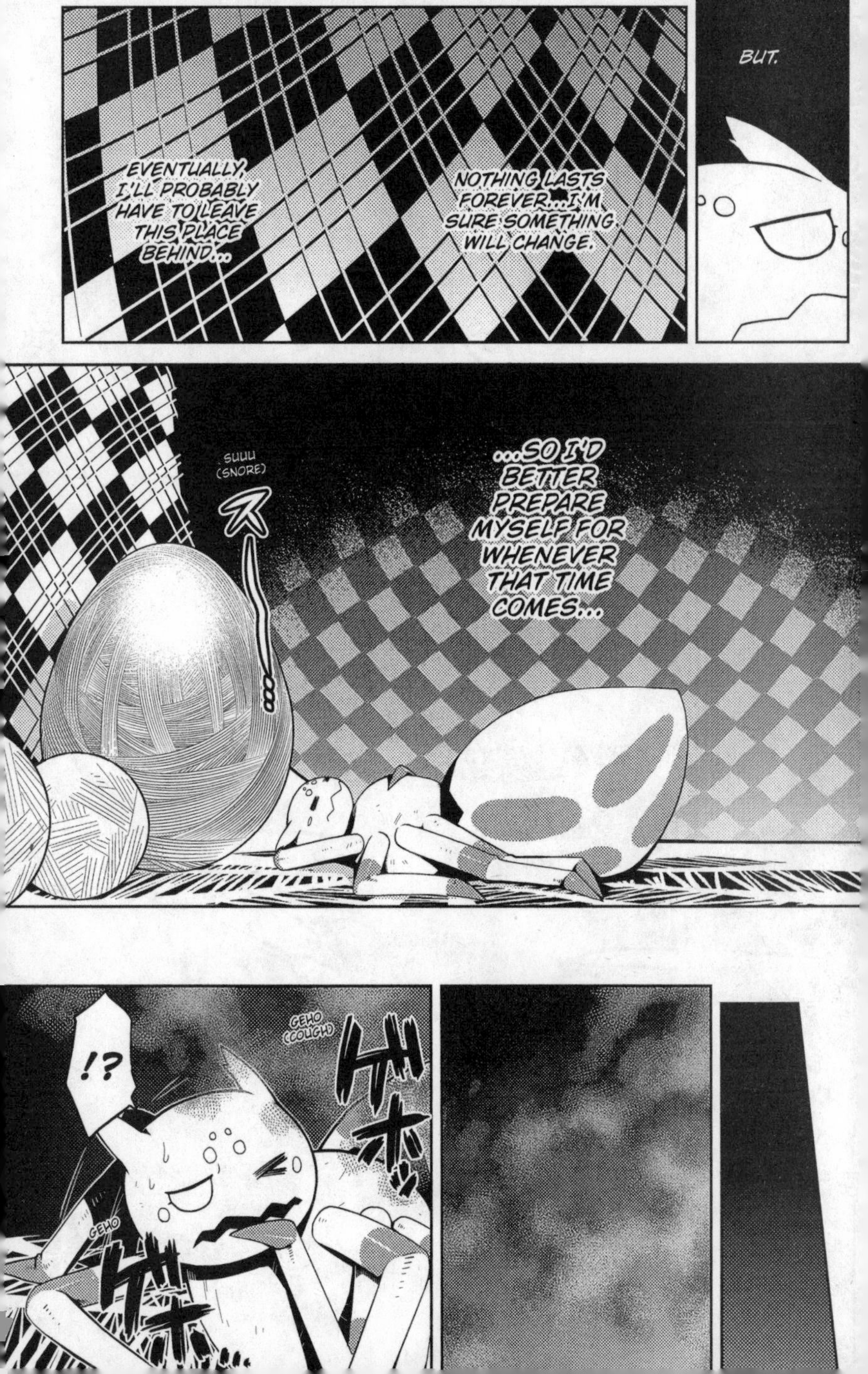
BUT.
NOTHING LASTS FOREVER... I'M SURE SOMETHING WILL CHANGE.
EVENTUALLY, I'LL PROBABLY HAVE TO LEAVE THIS PLACE BEHIND...
...SO I'D BETTER PREPARE MYSELF FOR WHENEVER THAT TIME COMES...
SUUU (SNORE)
GEHO (COUGH)
!?
GEHO

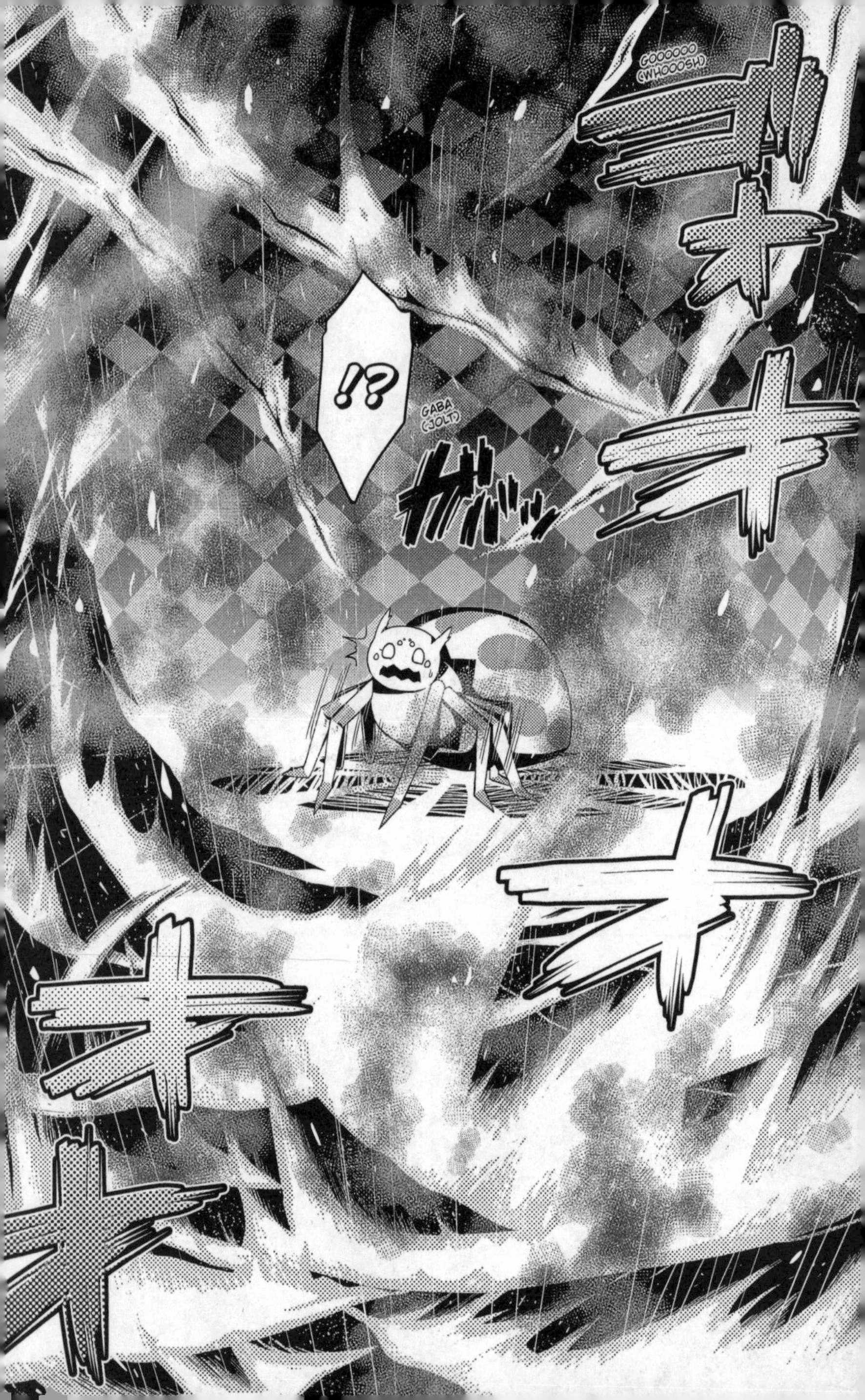
GOOOOOO (WHOOOSH)
!?
GABA (JOLT)

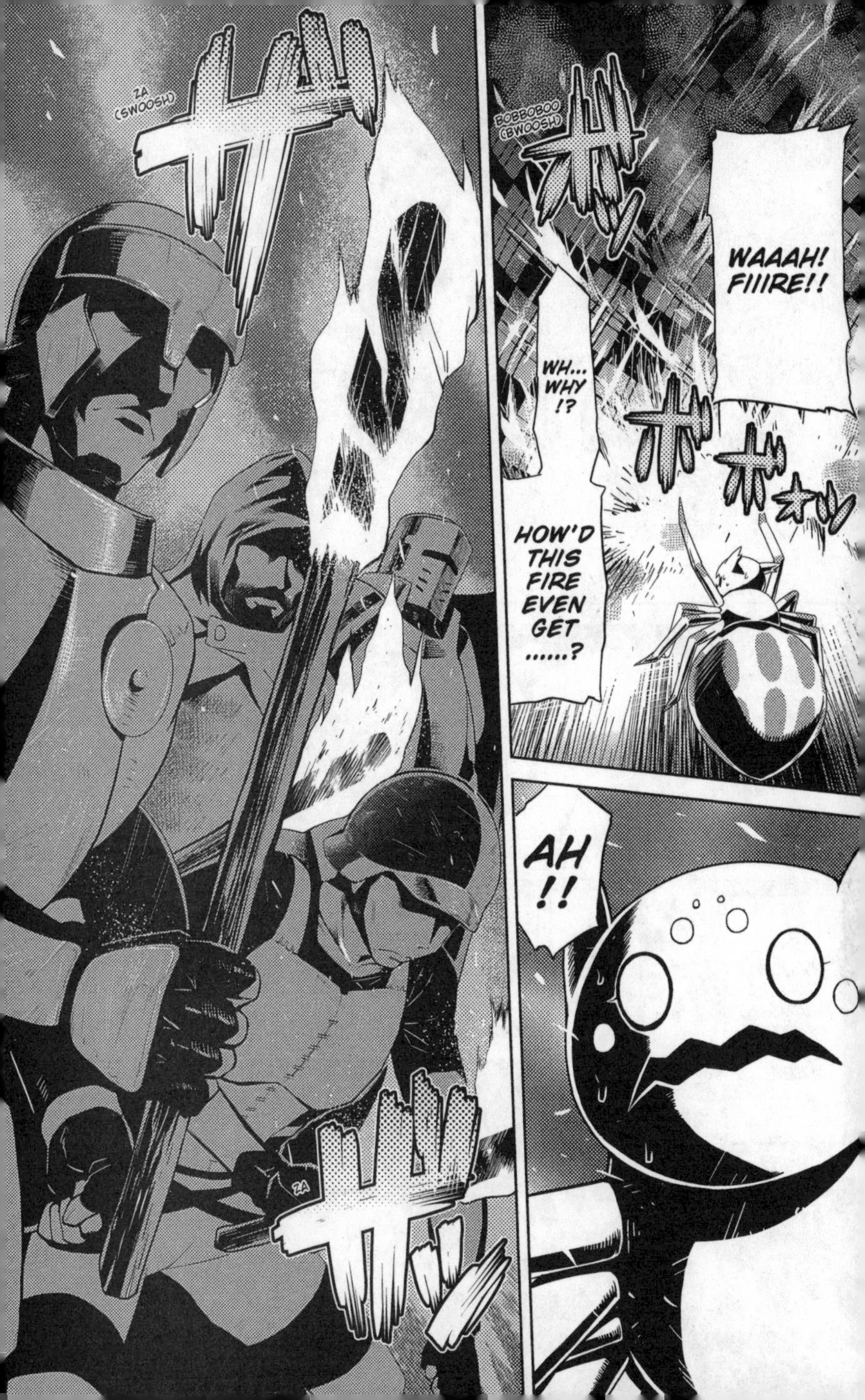
BOBBOBOO (BWOOSH)
WAAAH! FIIIRE!!
WH... WHY !?
HOW'D THIS FIRE EVEN GET ......?
AH !!
ZA (SWOOSH)
ZA

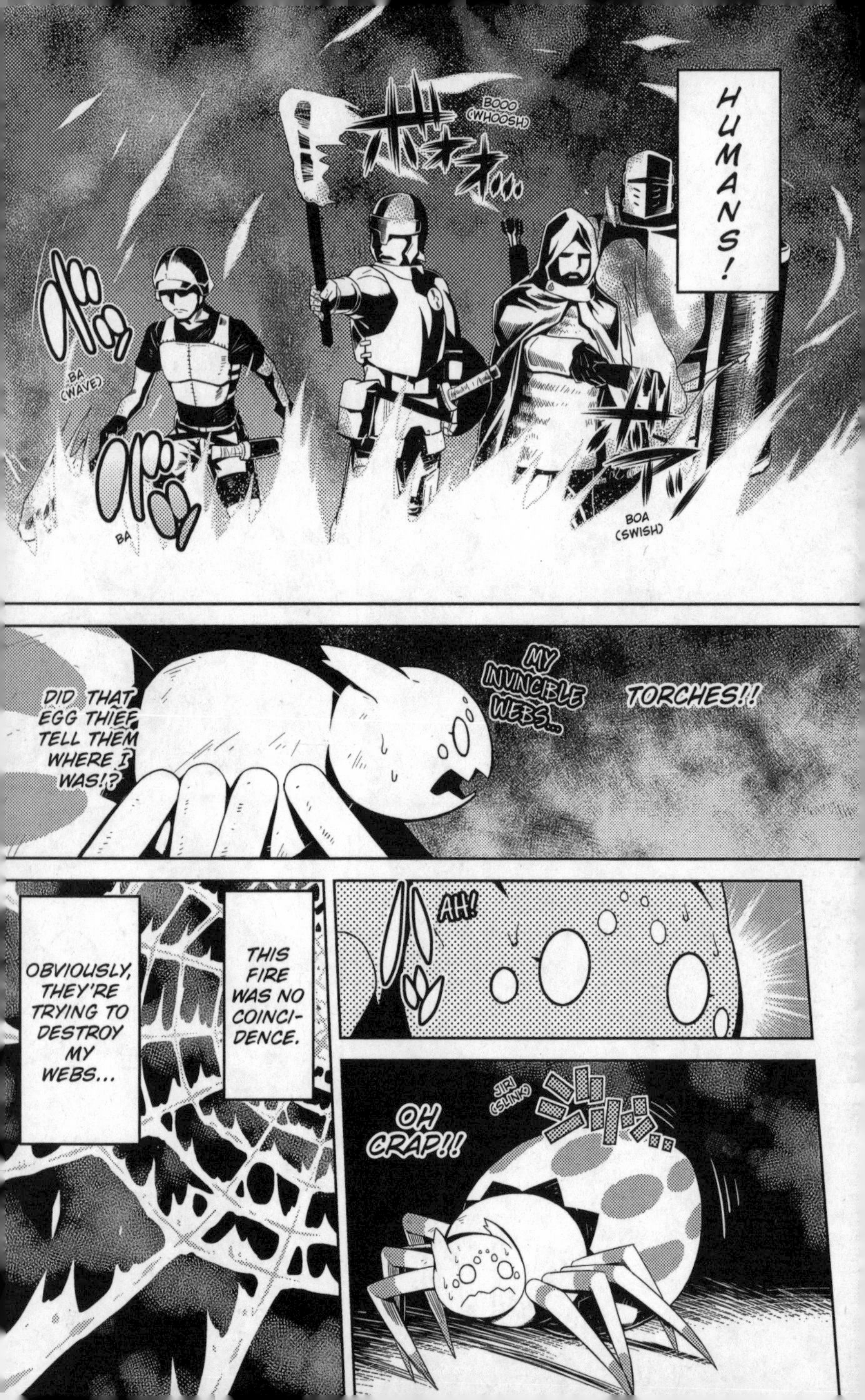
HUMANS!
BOOO (WHOOSH)
BOA (SWISH)
BA (WAVE)
BA
TORCHES!!
MY INVINCIBLE WEBS...
DID THAT EGG THIEF TELL THEM WHERE I WAS!?
AH!
JIRI (SLINK)
OH CRAP!!
THIS FIRE WAS NO COINCIDENCE.
OBVIOUSLY, THEY'RE TRYING TO DESTROY MY WEBS...

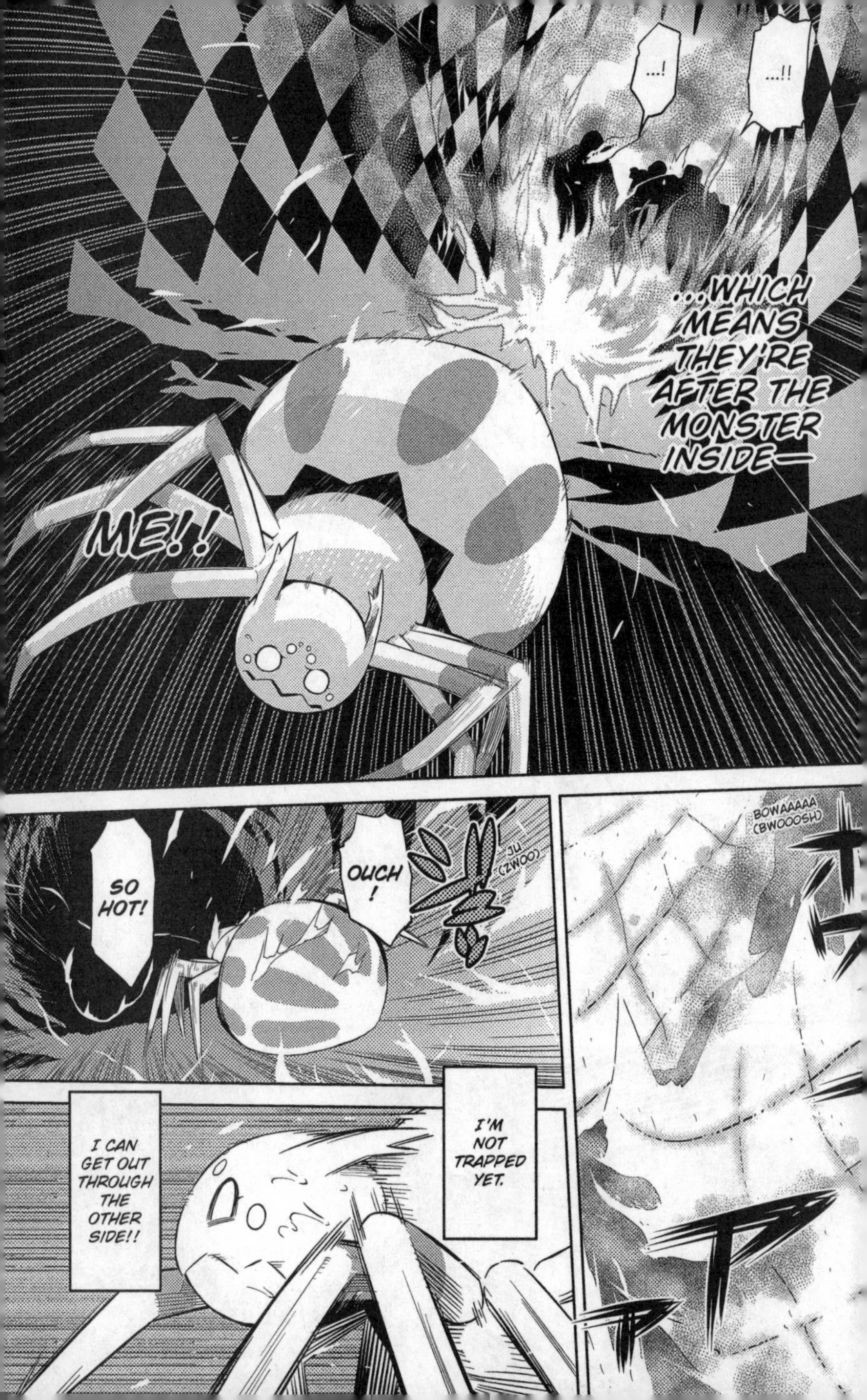

...!!
...!
...WHICH MEANS THEY'RE AFTER THE MONSTER INSIDE—
ME!!
BOWAAAAA (BWOOOSH)
JU (ZOWZ)
OUCH!
SO HOT!
I'M NOT TRAPPED YET.
I CAN GET OUT THROUGH THE OTHER SIDE!!

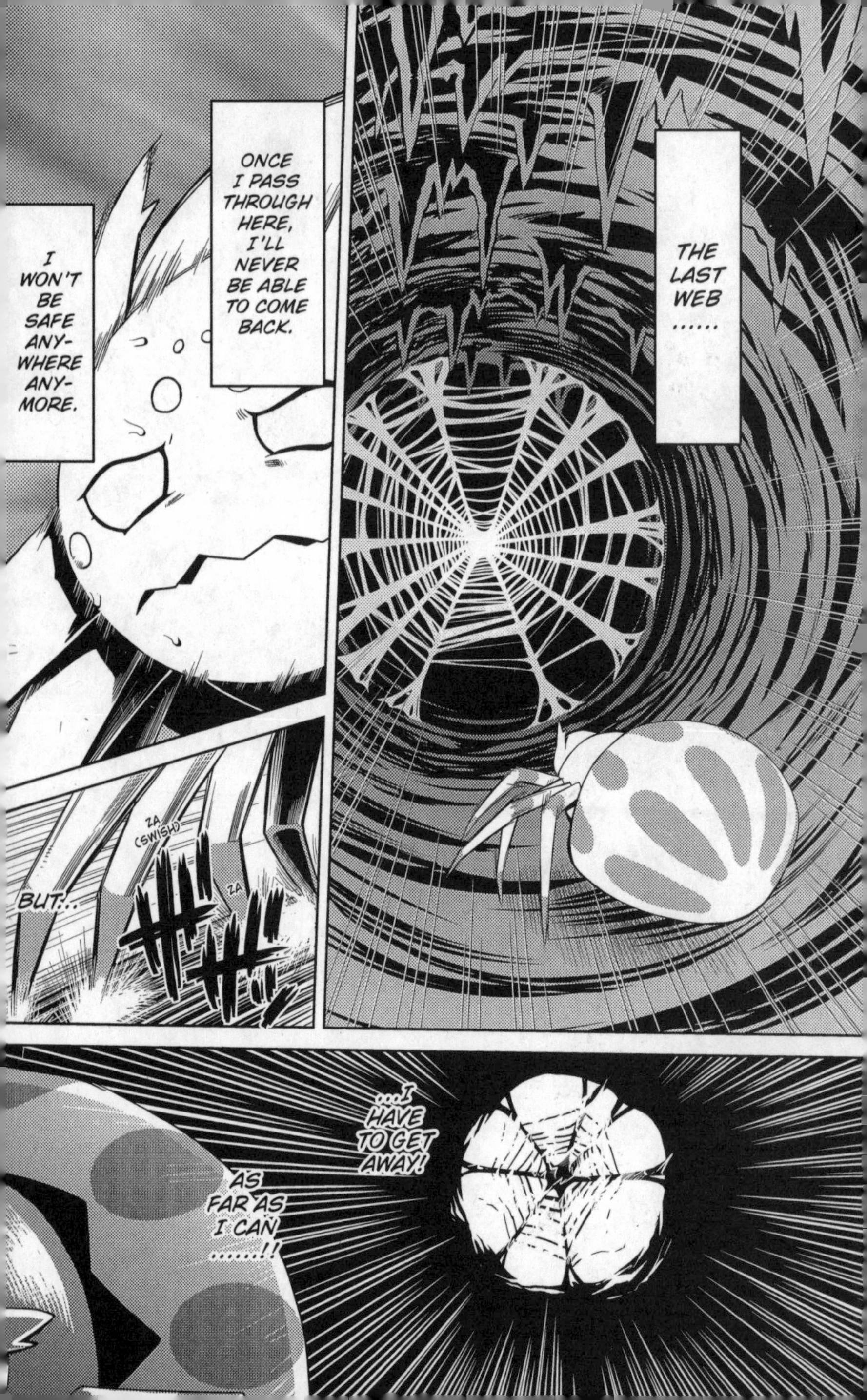
THE LAST WEB ......
ONCE I PASS THROUGH HERE, I'LL NEVER BE ABLE TO COME BACK.
I WON'T BE SAFE ANY-WHERE ANY-MORE.
ZA (SWISH)
ZA
BUT...
...I HAVE TO GET AWAY!
AS FAR AS I CAN ......!!

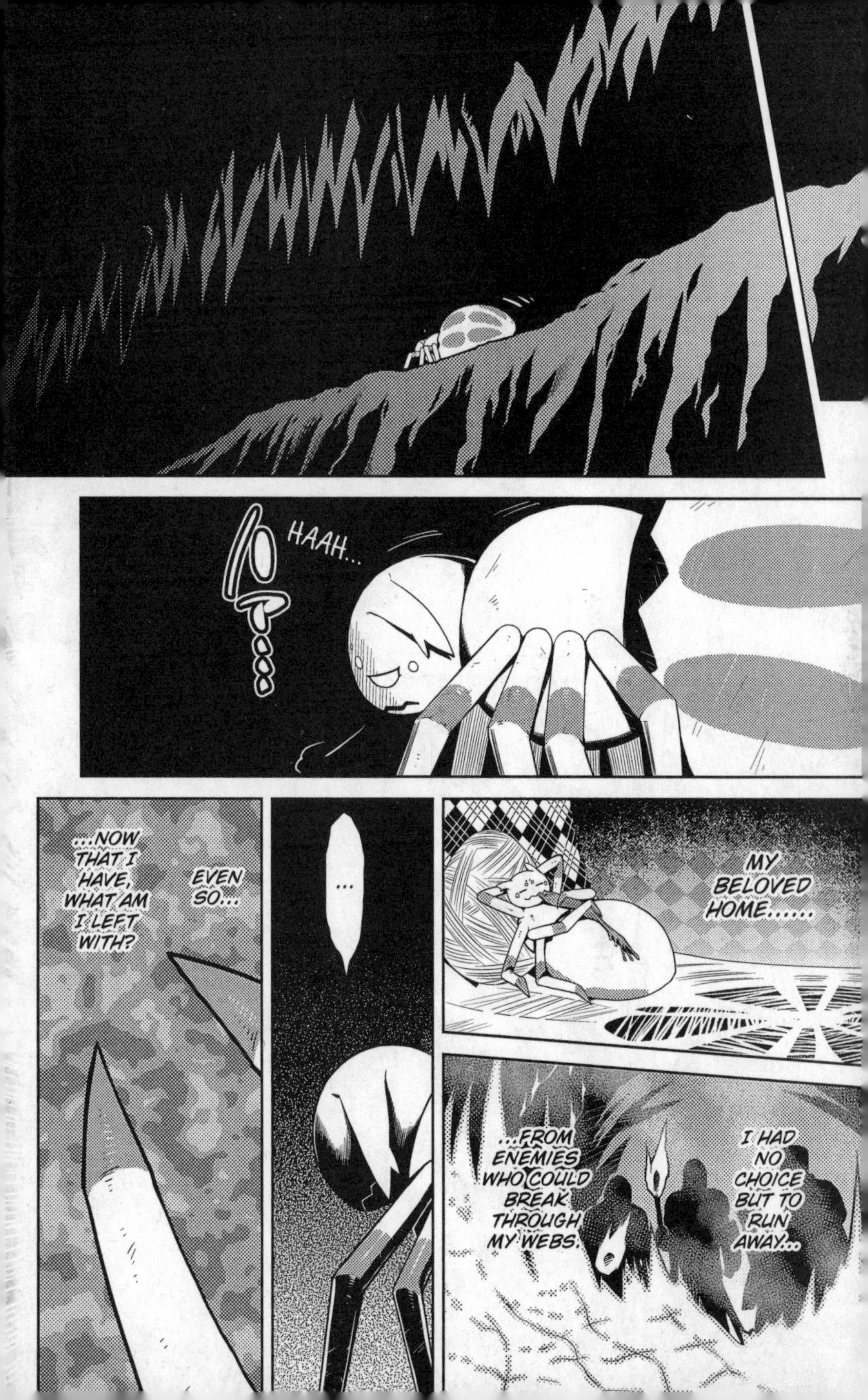

HAAH...
MY BELOVED HOME......
I HAD NO CHOICE BUT TO RUN AWAY...
...FROM ENEMIES WHO COULD BREAK THROUGH MY WEBS.
...
EVEN SO...
...NOW THAT I HAVE, WHAT AM I LEFT WITH?

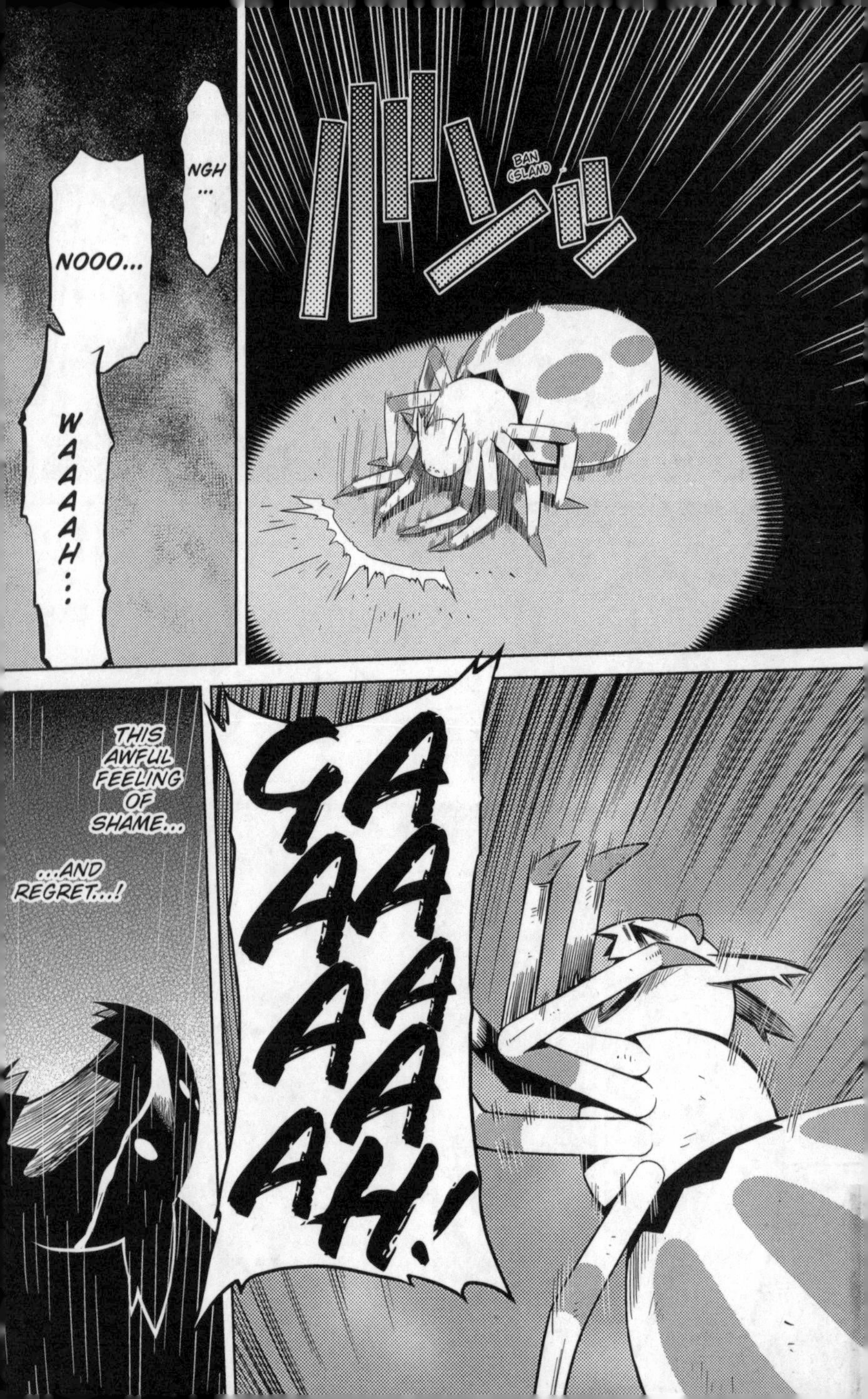
BAN (SLAM)
NGH ...
NOOO...
WAAAAAH...
GAAAAAAAAH!
THIS AWFUL FEELING OF SHAME...
...AND REGRET...!

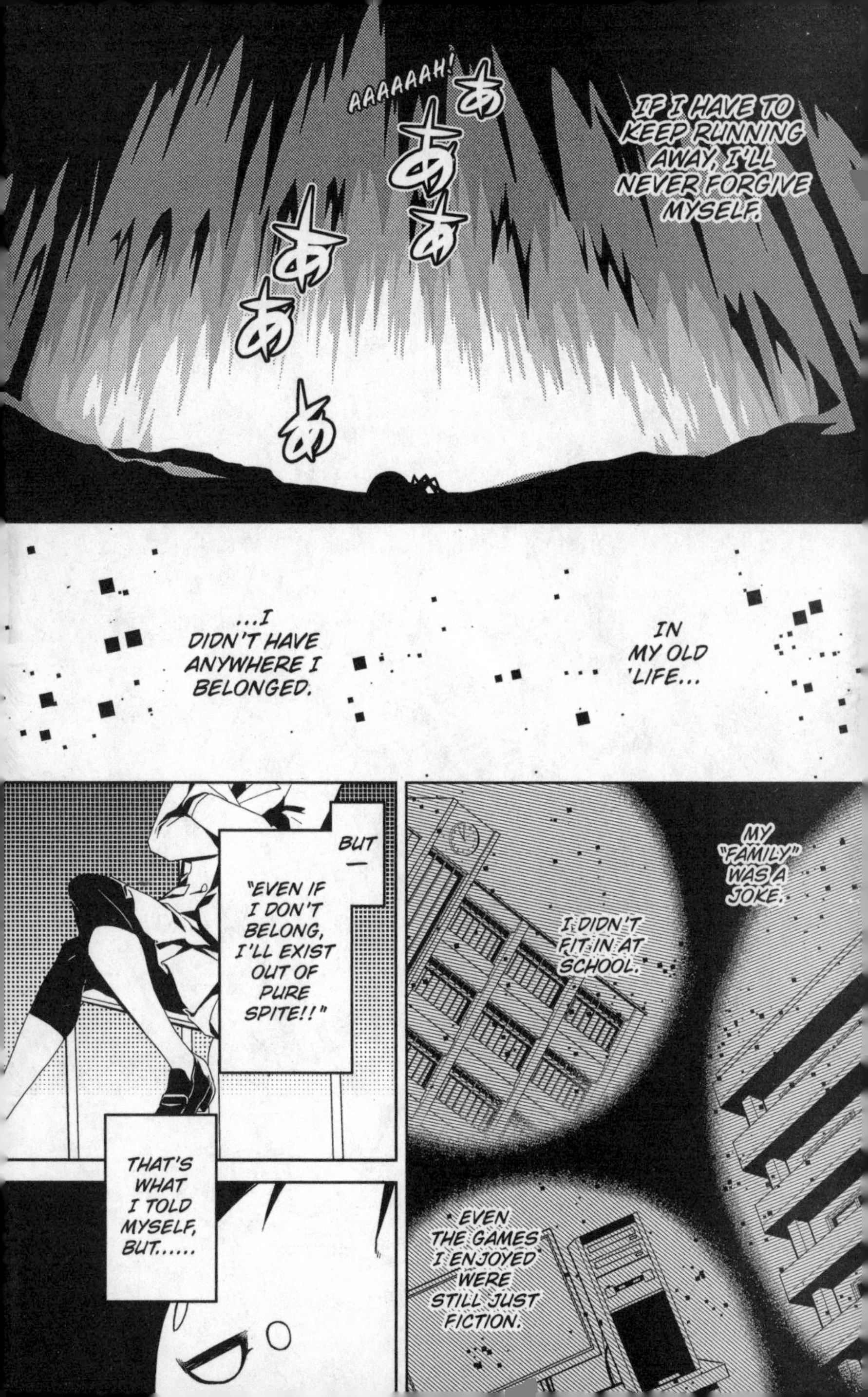

IF I HAVE TO KEEP RUNNING AWAY, I'LL NEVER FORGIVE MYSELF.
AAAAAAH!
ああああああ
IN MY OLD 'LIFE...
...I DIDN'T HAVE ANYWHERE I BELONGED.
MY "FAMILY" WAS A JOKE.
I DIDN'T FIT IN AT SCHOOL.
EVEN THE GAMES I ENJOYED WERE STILL JUST FICTION.
BUT —
"EVEN IF I DON'T BELONG, I'LL EXIST OUT OF PURE SPITE!!"
THAT'S WHAT I TOLD MYSELF, BUT......

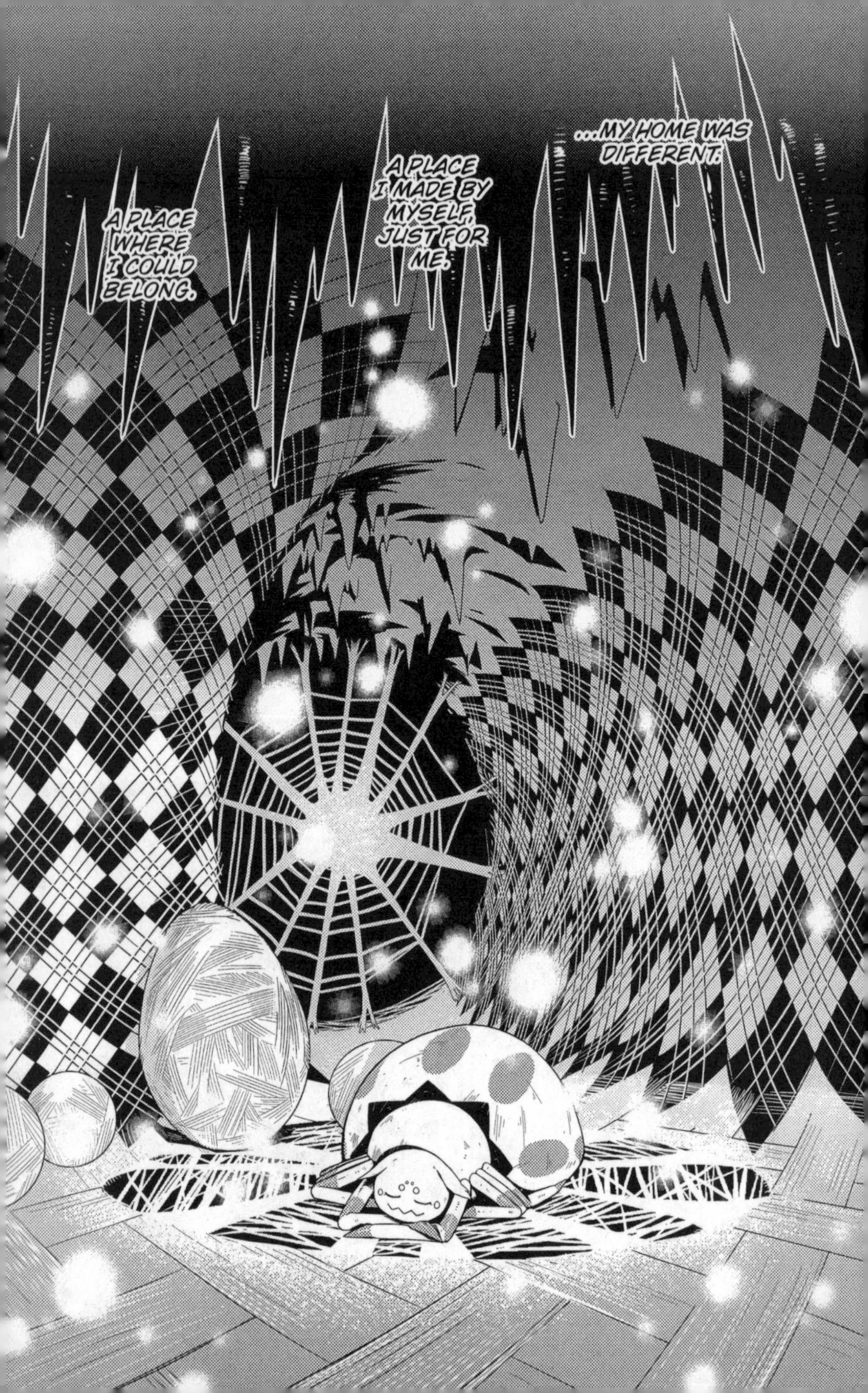
...MY HOME WAS DIFFERENT.
A PLACE I MADE BY MYSELF, JUST FOR ME.
A PLACE WHERE I COULD BELONG.

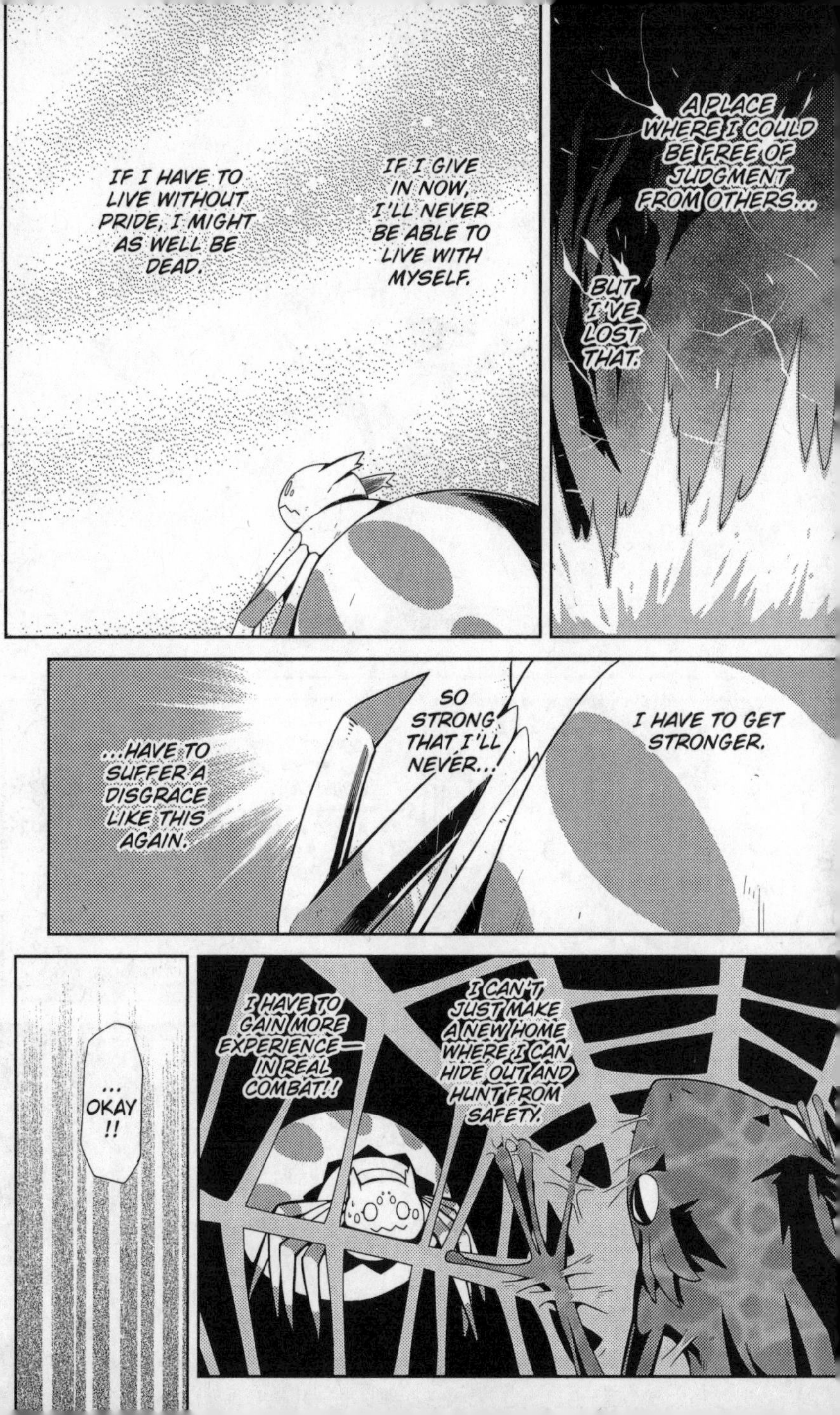
A PLACE WHERE I COULD BE FREE OF JUDGMENT FROM OTHERS...
BUT I'VE LOST THAT.
IF I GIVE IN NOW, I'LL NEVER BE ABLE TO LIVE WITH MYSELF.
IF I HAVE TO LIVE WITHOUT PRIDE, I MIGHT AS WELL BE DEAD.
I HAVE TO GET STRONGER.
SO STRONG THAT I'LL NEVER...
...HAVE TO SUFFER A DISGRACE LIKE THIS AGAIN.
I CAN'T JUST MAKE A NEW HOME WHERE I CAN HIDE OUT AND HUNT FROM SAFETY.
I HAVE TO GAIN MORE EXPERIENCE—IN REAL COMBAT!!
...OKAY!!

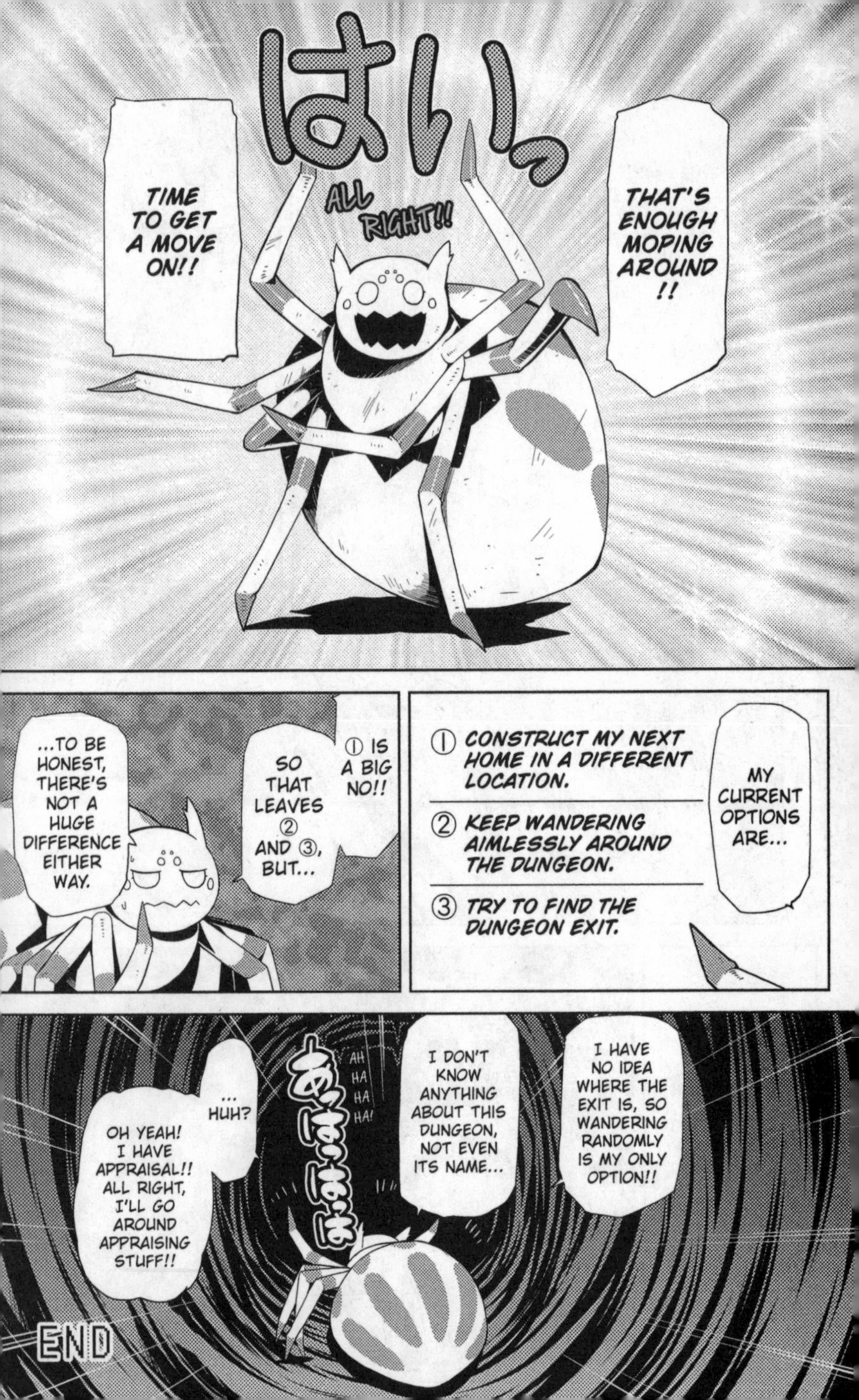
THAT'S ENOUGH MOPING AROUND!!
はいっ
ALL RIGHT!!
TIME TO GET A MOVE ON!!
MY CURRENT OPTIONS ARE...
① CONSTRUCT MY NEXT HOME IN A DIFFERENT LOCATION.
② KEEP WANDERING AIMLESSLY AROUND THE DUNGEON.
③ TRY TO FIND THE DUNGEON EXIT.
① IS A BIG NO!!
SO THAT LEAVES ② AND ③, BUT...
...TO BE HONEST, THERE'S NOT A HUGE DIFFERENCE EITHER WAY.
I HAVE NO IDEA WHERE THE EXIT IS, SO WANDERING RANDOMLY IS MY ONLY OPTION!!
I DON'T KNOW ANYTHING ABOUT THIS DUNGEON, NOT EVEN ITS NAME...
AH HA HA HA!
...HUH?
OH YEAH! I HAVE APPRAISAL!! ALL RIGHT, I'LL GO AROUND APPRAISING STUFF!!
END

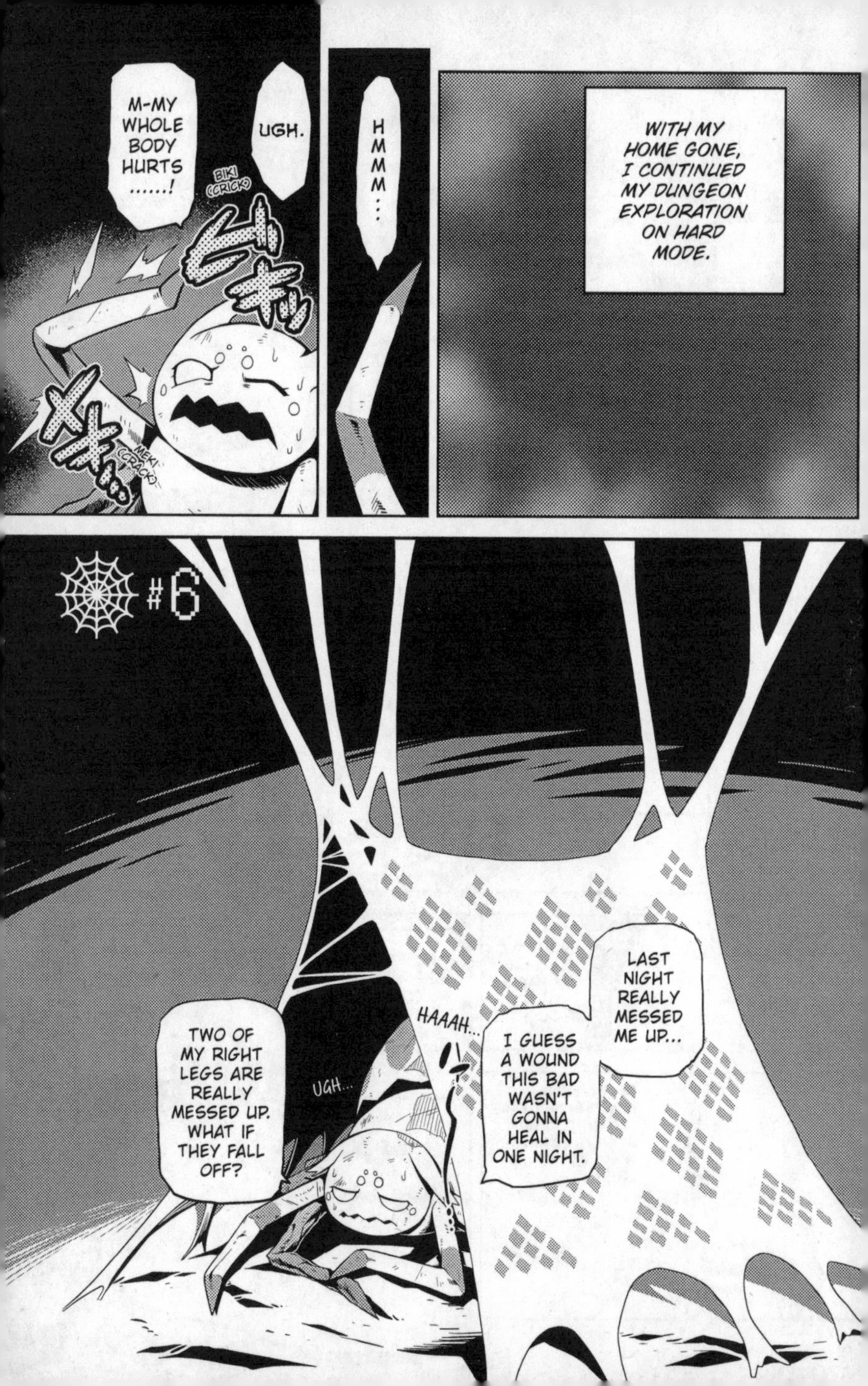
WITH MY HOME GONE, I CONTINUED MY DUNGEON EXPLORATION ON HARD MODE.
HMMM...
UGH.
M-MY WHOLE BODY HURTS ......!
BIKI (CRICK)
MEKI (CRACK)
#6
LAST NIGHT REALLY MESSED ME UP...
I GUESS A WOUND THIS BAD WASN'T GONNA HEAL IN ONE NIGHT.
HAAAH...
TWO OF MY RIGHT LEGS ARE REALLY MESSED UP. WHAT IF THEY FALL OFF?
UGH...

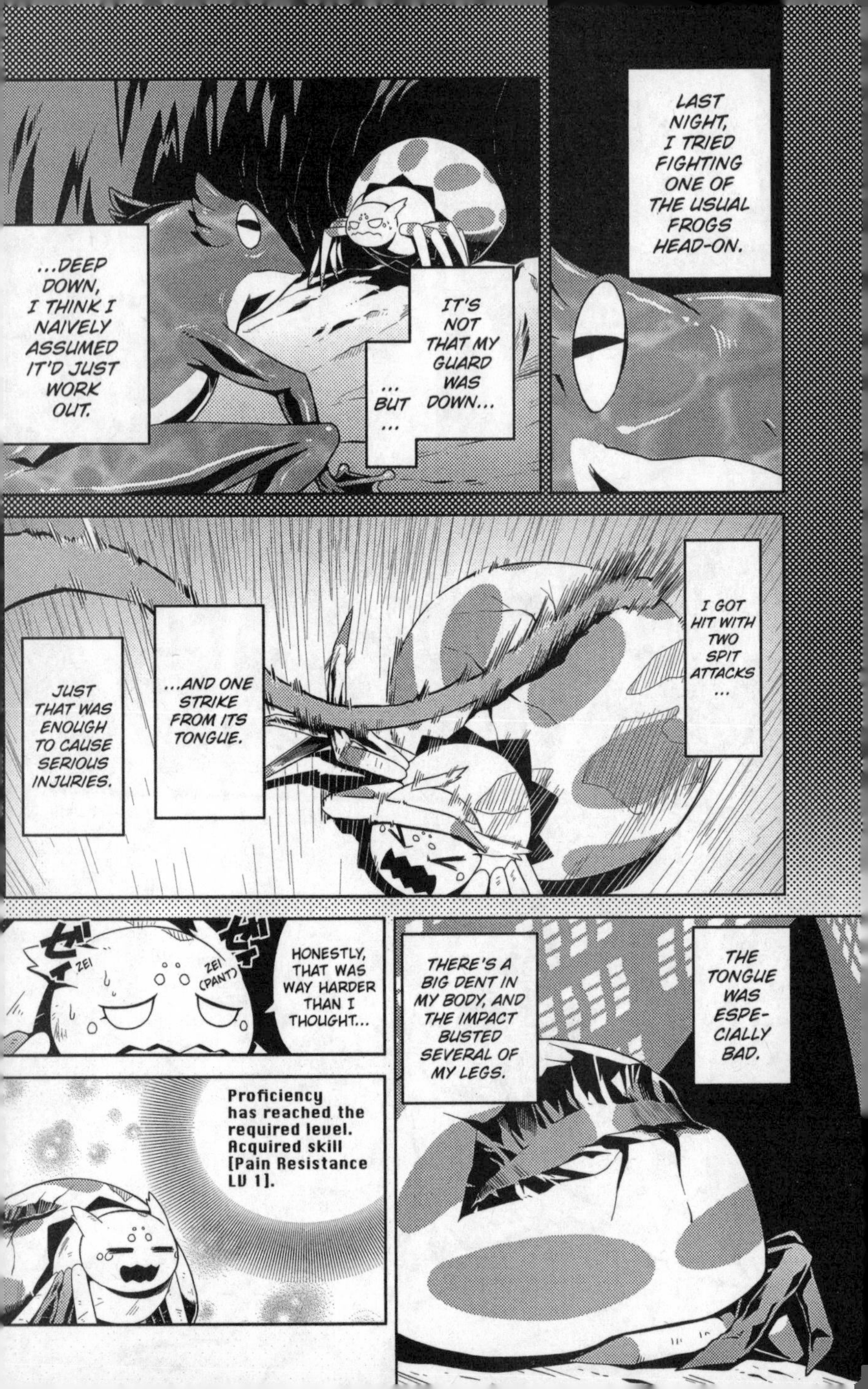
LAST NIGHT, I TRIED FIGHTING ONE OF THE USUAL FROGS HEAD-ON.
IT'S NOT THAT MY GUARD WAS DOWN...
...BUT ...
...DEEP DOWN, I THINK I NAIVELY ASSUMED IT'D JUST WORK OUT.
I GOT HIT WITH TWO SPIT ATTACKS ...
...AND ONE STRIKE FROM ITS TONGUE.
JUST THAT WAS ENOUGH TO CAUSE SERIOUS INJURIES.
THE TONGUE WAS ESPE-CIALLY BAD.
THERE'S A BIG DENT IN MY BODY, AND THE IMPACT BUSTED SEVERAL OF MY LEGS.
HONESTLY, THAT WAS WAY HARDER THAN I THOUGHT...
ZEI (PANT)
ZEI
Proficiency has reached the required level. Acquired skill [Pain Resistance LV 1].

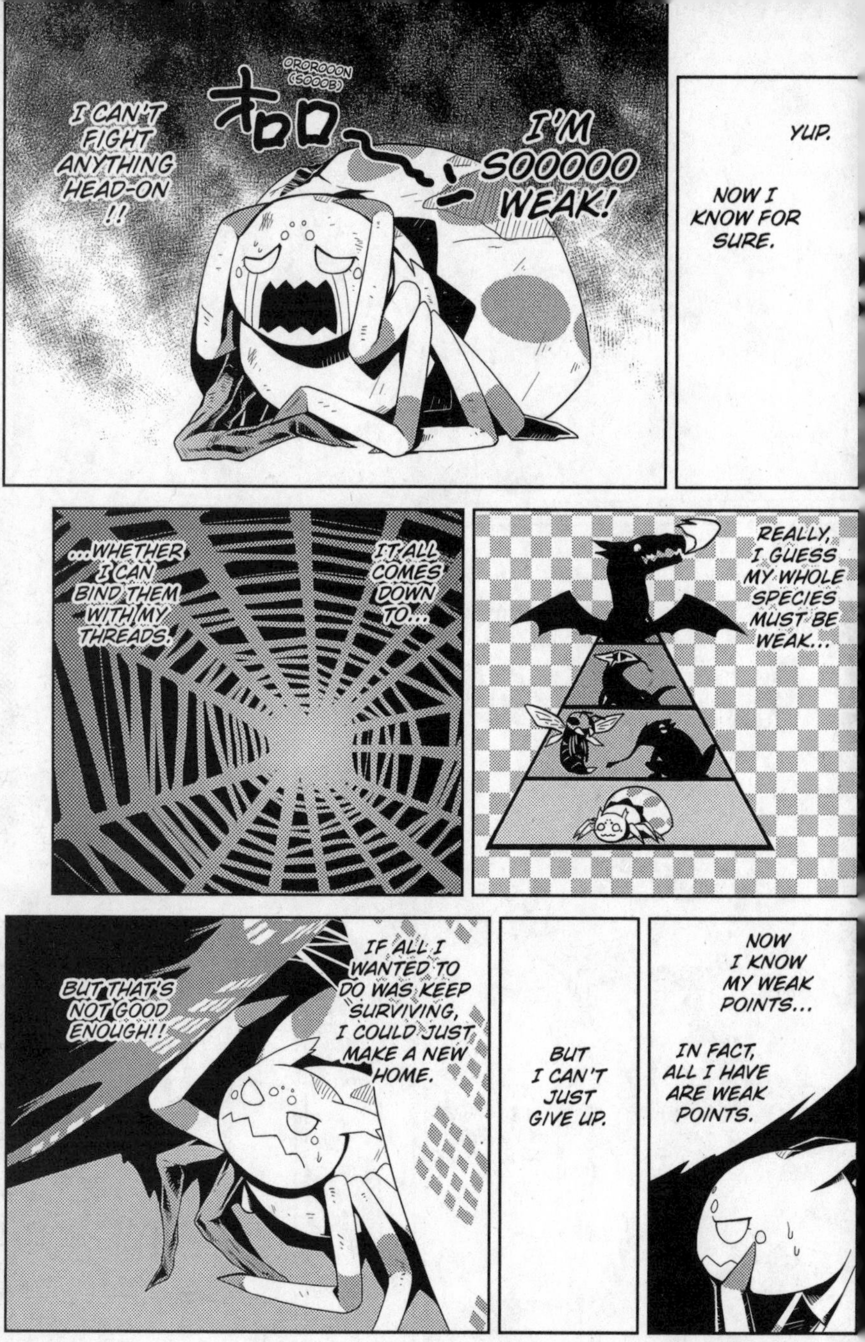
YUP.
NOW I KNOW FOR SURE.
I'M SOOOOO WEAK!
オロロ～～～
ORORooon (SOOOB)
I CAN'T FIGHT ANYTHING HEAD-ON!!
REALLY, I GUESS MY WHOLE SPECIES MUST BE WEAK...
IT ALL COMES DOWN TO...
...WHETHER I CAN BIND THEM WITH MY THREADS.
NOW I KNOW MY WEAK POINTS...
IN FACT, ALL I HAVE ARE WEAK POINTS.
BUT I CAN'T JUST GIVE UP.
IF ALL I WANTED TO DO WAS KEEP SURVIVING, I COULD JUST MAKE A NEW HOME.
BUT THAT'S NOT GOOD ENOUGH!!

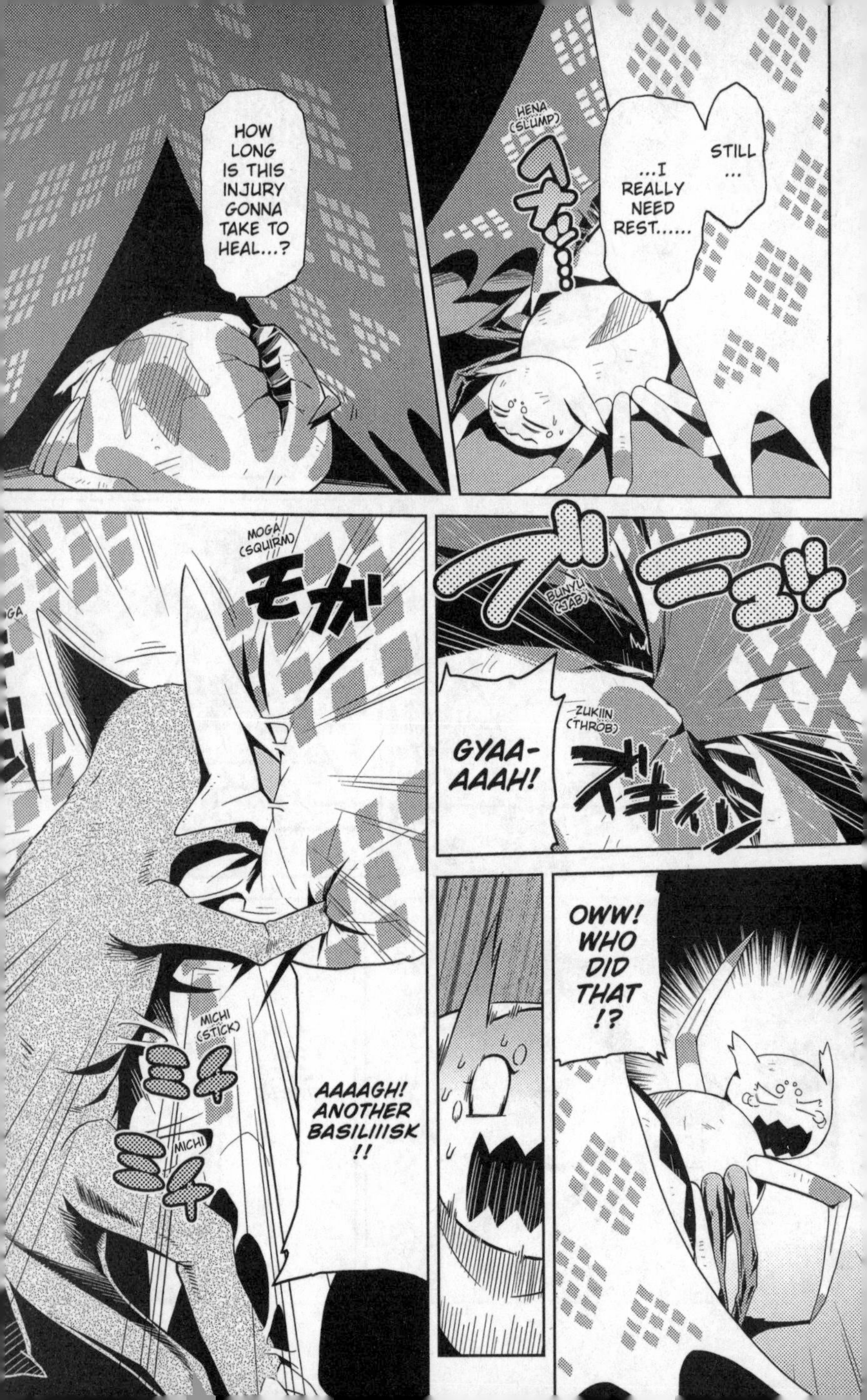
HENA (SLUMP)
STILL ...
...I REALLY NEED REST......
HOW LONG IS THIS INJURY GONNA TAKE TO HEAL...?
BUNYU (JAB)
GYAA-AAAH!
ZUKIIN (THROB)
OWW! WHO DID THAT !?
MOGA (SQUIRM)
MICHI (STICK)
MICHI
AAAAGH! ANOTHER BASILIIISK !!

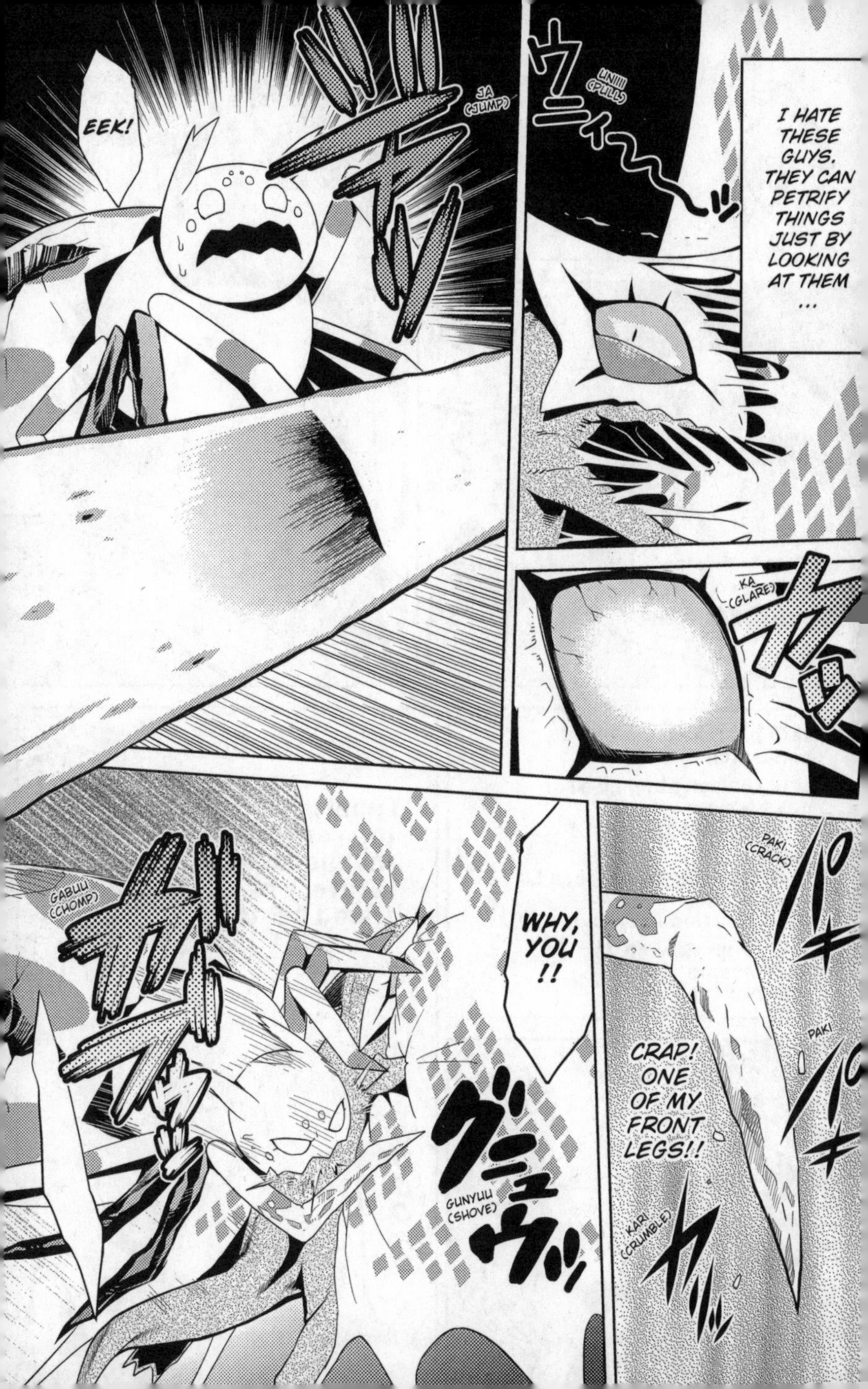
UNIIII (PULL)
I HATE THESE GUYS. THEY CAN PETRIFY THINGS JUST BY LOOKING AT THEM ...
KA (GLARE)
EEK!
JA (JUMP)
PAKI (CRACK)
CRAP! ONE OF MY FRONT LEGS!!
PAKI
KARI (CRUMBLE)
WHY, YOU!!
GUNYUU (SHOVE)
GABUU (CHOMP)

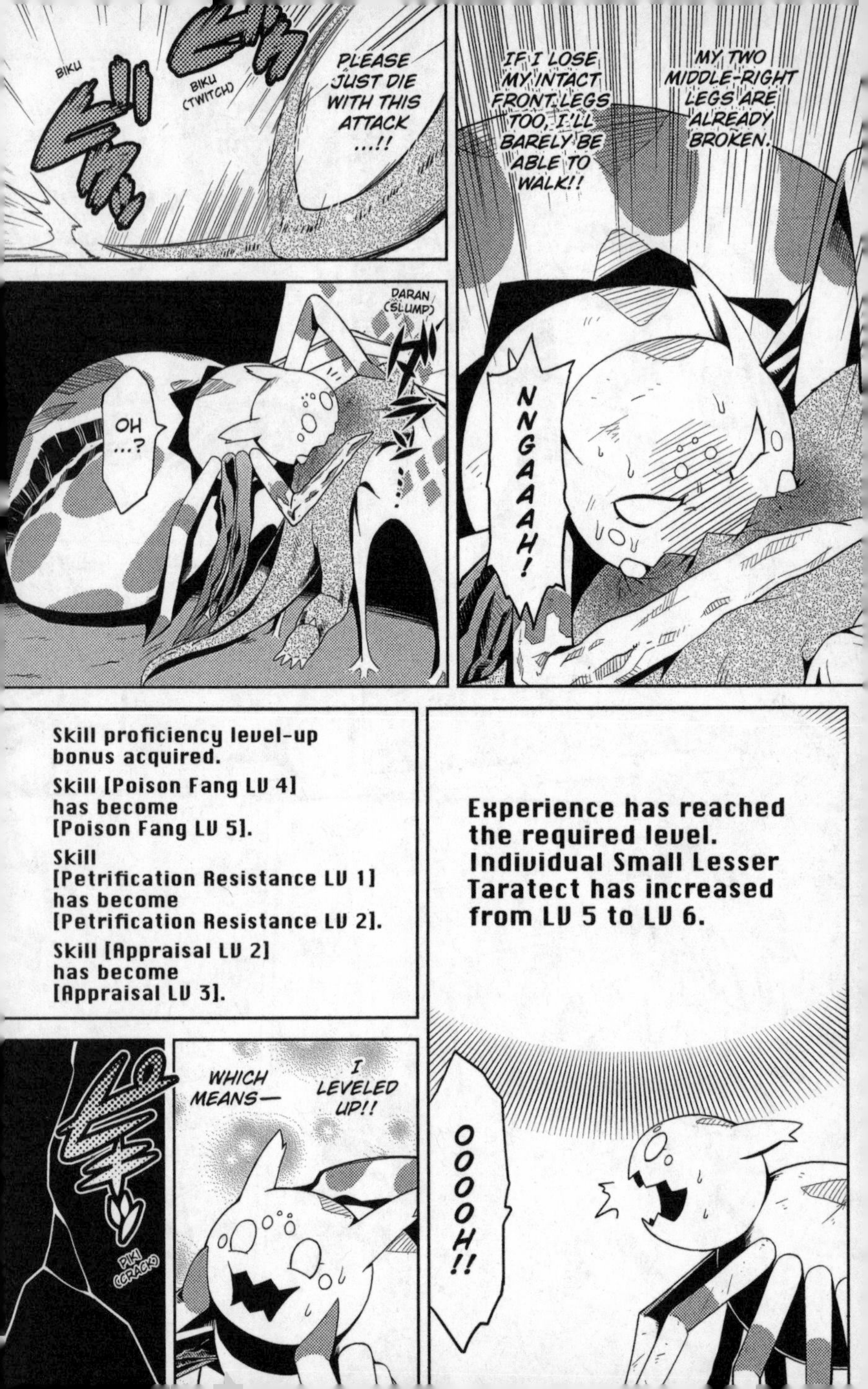
MY TWO MIDDLE-RIGHT LEGS ARE ALREADY BROKEN.
IF I LOSE MY INTACT FRONT LEGS TOO, I'LL BARELY BE ABLE TO WALK!!
NNGAAAAH!
PLEASE JUST DIE WITH THIS ATTACK ...!!
BIKU (TWITCH)
BIKU
DARAN (SLUMP)
OH ...?
Experience has reached the required level. Individual Small Lesser Taratect has increased from LV 5 to LV 6.
Skill proficiency level-up bonus acquired.
Skill [Poison Fang LV 4] has become [Poison Fang LV 5].
Skill [Petrification Resistance LV 1] has become [Petrification Resistance LV 2].
Skill [Appraisal LV 2] has become [Appraisal LV 3].
OOOOOH!!
I LEVELED UP!!
WHICH MEANS—
PIKI (CRACK)

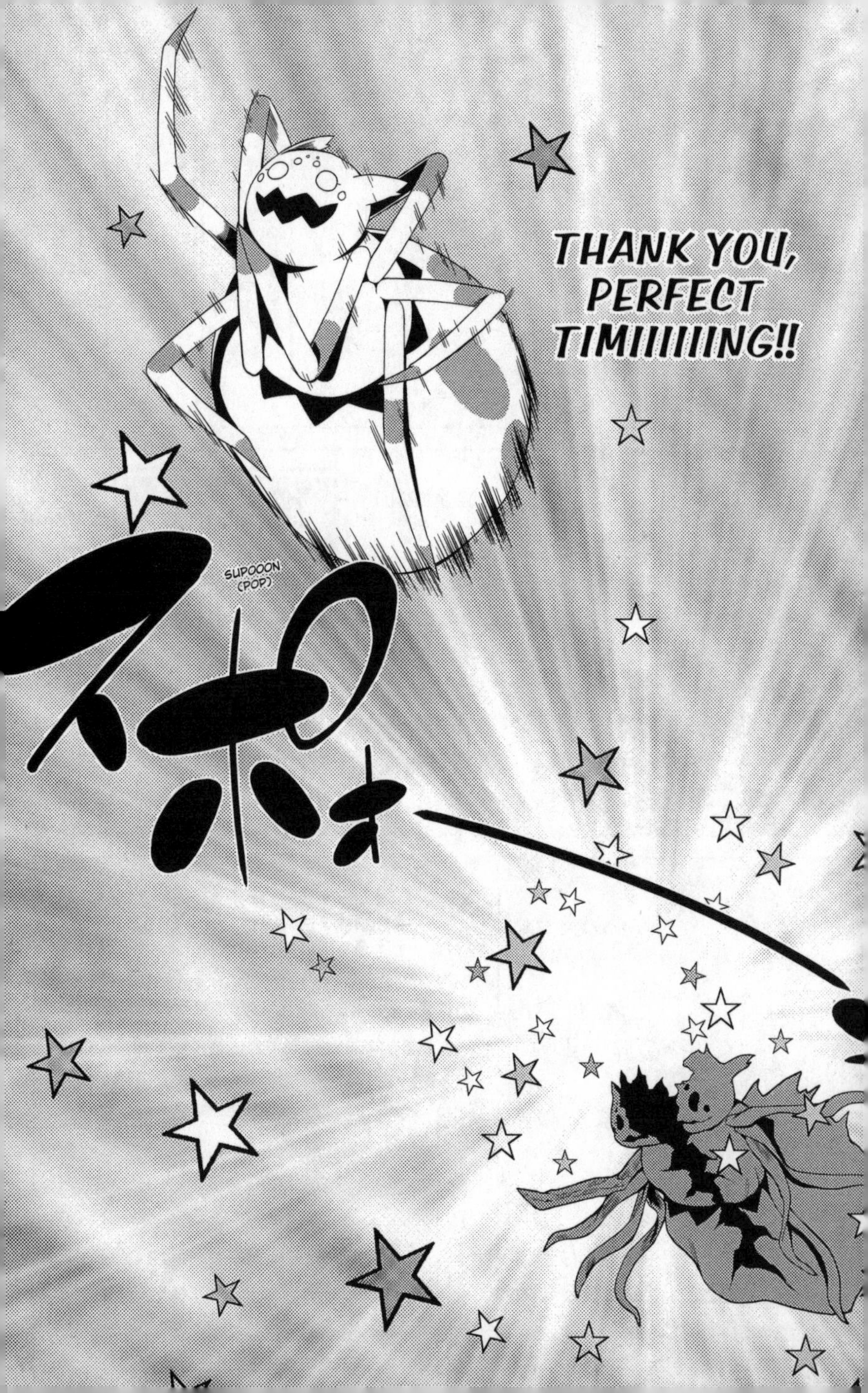
THANK YOU, PERFECT TIMIIIIIING!!
スポォ
SUPOOON (POP)

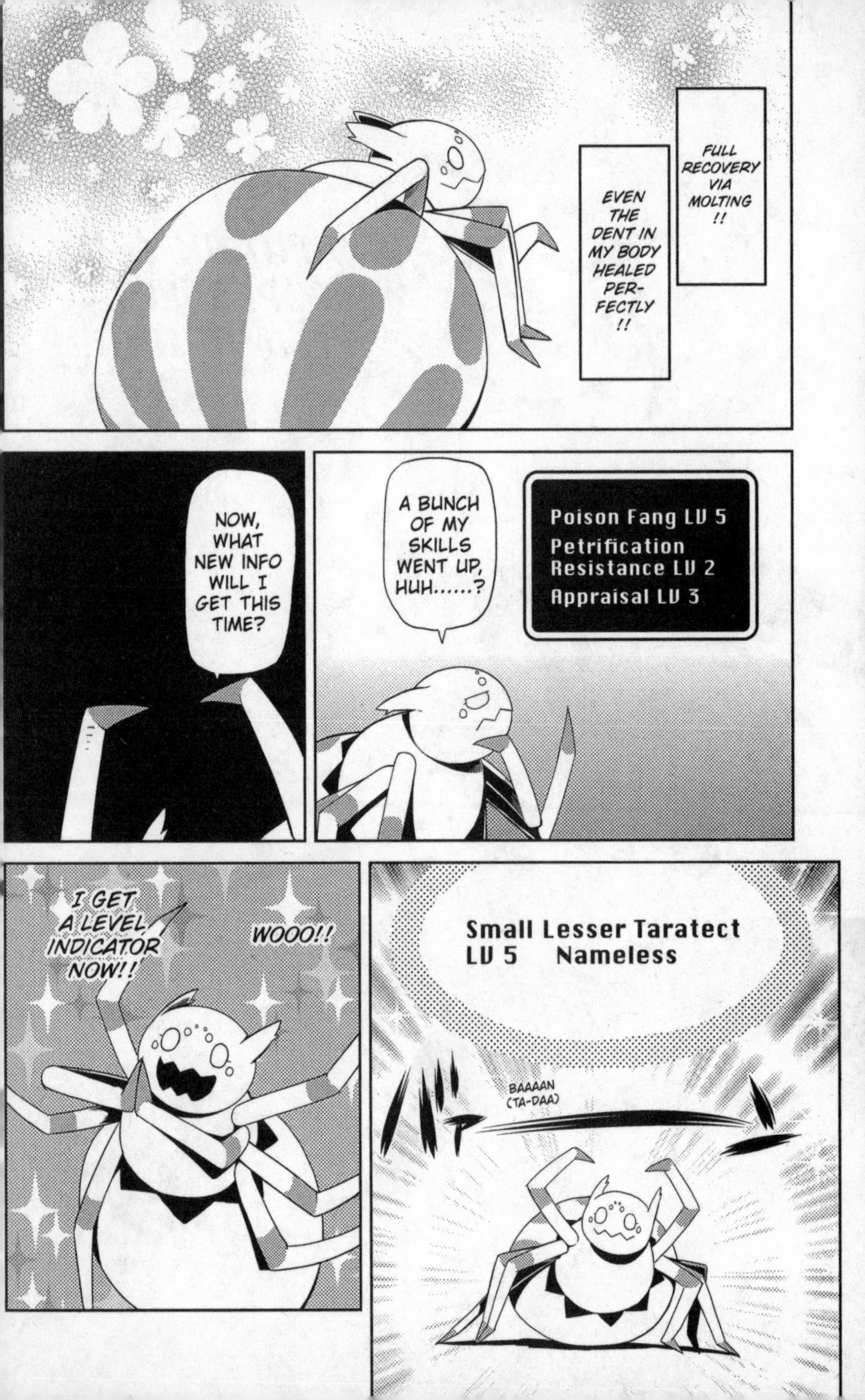
FULL RECOVERY VIA MOLTING!!
EVEN THE DENT IN MY BODY HEALED PER-FECTLY!!
Poison Fang LV 5
Petrification Resistance LV 2
Appraisal LV 3
A BUNCH OF MY SKILLS WENT UP, HUH......?
NOW, WHAT NEW INFO WILL I GET THIS TIME?
Small Lesser Taratect LV 5 Nameless
BAAAAN (TA-DAA)
WOOO!!
I GET A LEVEL INDICATOR NOW!!

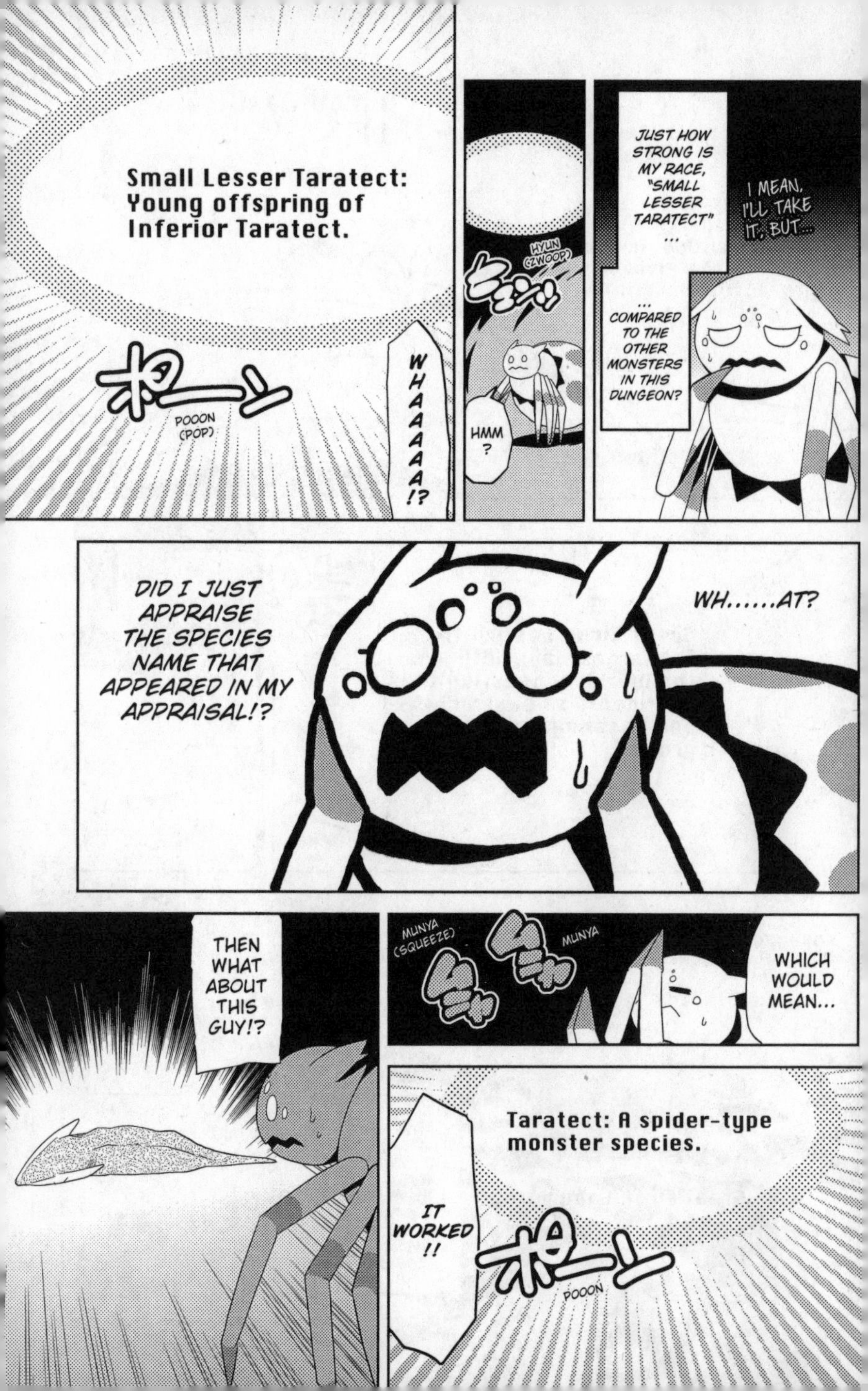
I MEAN, I'LL TAKE IT, BUT...
JUST HOW STRONG IS MY RACE, "SMALL LESSER TARATECT" ... ... COMPARED TO THE OTHER MONSTERS IN THIS DUNGEON?
HYUN (ZWOOP)
HMM?
Small Lesser Taratect: Young offspring of Inferior Taratect.
WHAAAAAAA!?
POOON (POP)
WH......AT?
DID I JUST APPRAISE THE SPECIES NAME THAT APPEARED IN MY APPRAISAL!?
WHICH WOULD MEAN...
MUNYA
MUNYA (SQUEEZE)
Taratect: A spider-type monster species.
IT WORKED!!
POOON
THEN WHAT ABOUT THIS GUY!?

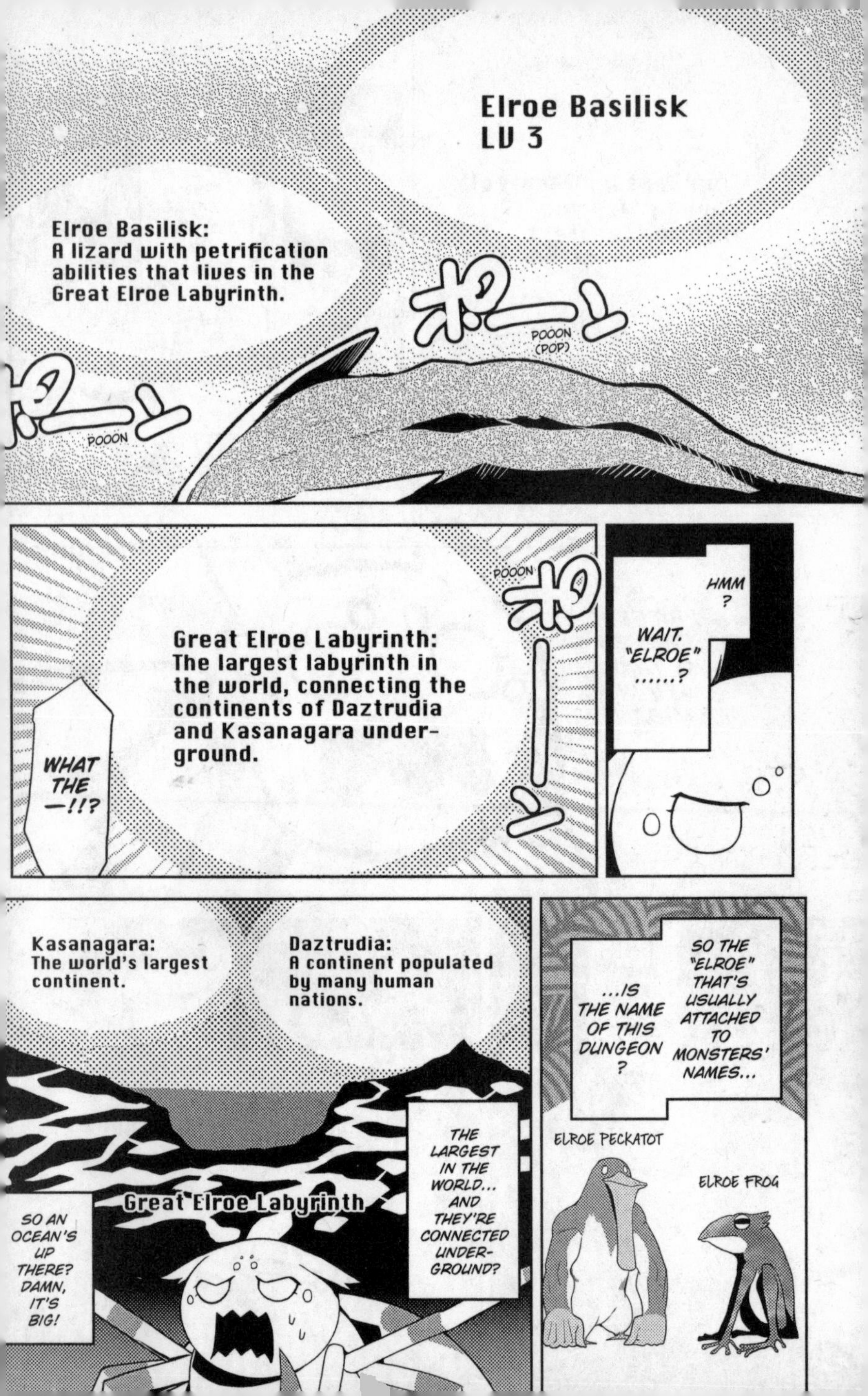
Elroe Basilisk LV 3
POOON (POP)
Elroe Basilisk: A lizard with petrification abilities that lives in the Great Elroe Labyrinth.
POOON
HMM?
WAIT. "ELROE"......?
POOON
Great Elroe Labyrinth: The largest labyrinth in the world, connecting the continents of Daztrudia and Kasanagara under-ground.
WHAT THE—!!?
SO THE "ELROE" THAT'S USUALLY ATTACHED TO MONSTERS' NAMES...
...IS THE NAME OF THIS DUNGEON?
ELROE PECKATOT
ELROE FROG
Daztrudia: A continent populated by many human nations.
Kasanagara: The world's largest continent.
THE LARGEST IN THE WORLD... AND THEY'RE CONNECTED UNDER-GROUND?
Great Elroe Labyrinth
SO AN OCEAN'S UP THERE? DAMN, IT'S BIG!

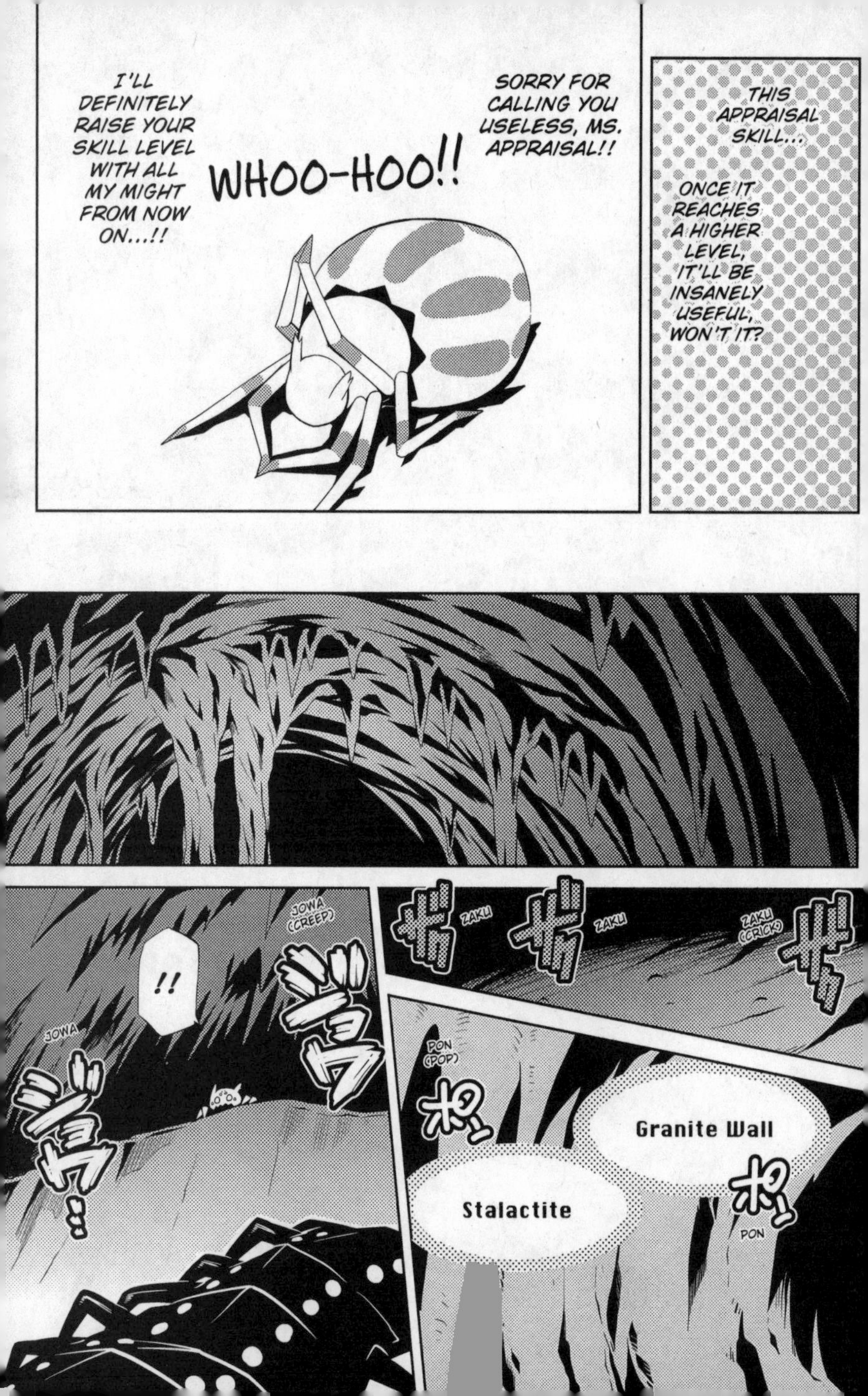

THIS APPRAISAL SKILL...
ONCE IT REACHES A HIGHER LEVEL, IT'LL BE INSANELY USEFUL, WON'T IT?
SORRY FOR CALLING YOU USELESS, MS. APPRAISAL!!
WHOO-HOO!!
I'LL DEFINITELY RAISE YOUR SKILL LEVEL WITH ALL MY MIGHT FROM NOW ON...!!
ZAKU (CRICK)
ZAKU
ZAKU
Granite Wall
PON
PON (POP)
Stalactite
JOWA (CREEP)
!!
JOWA

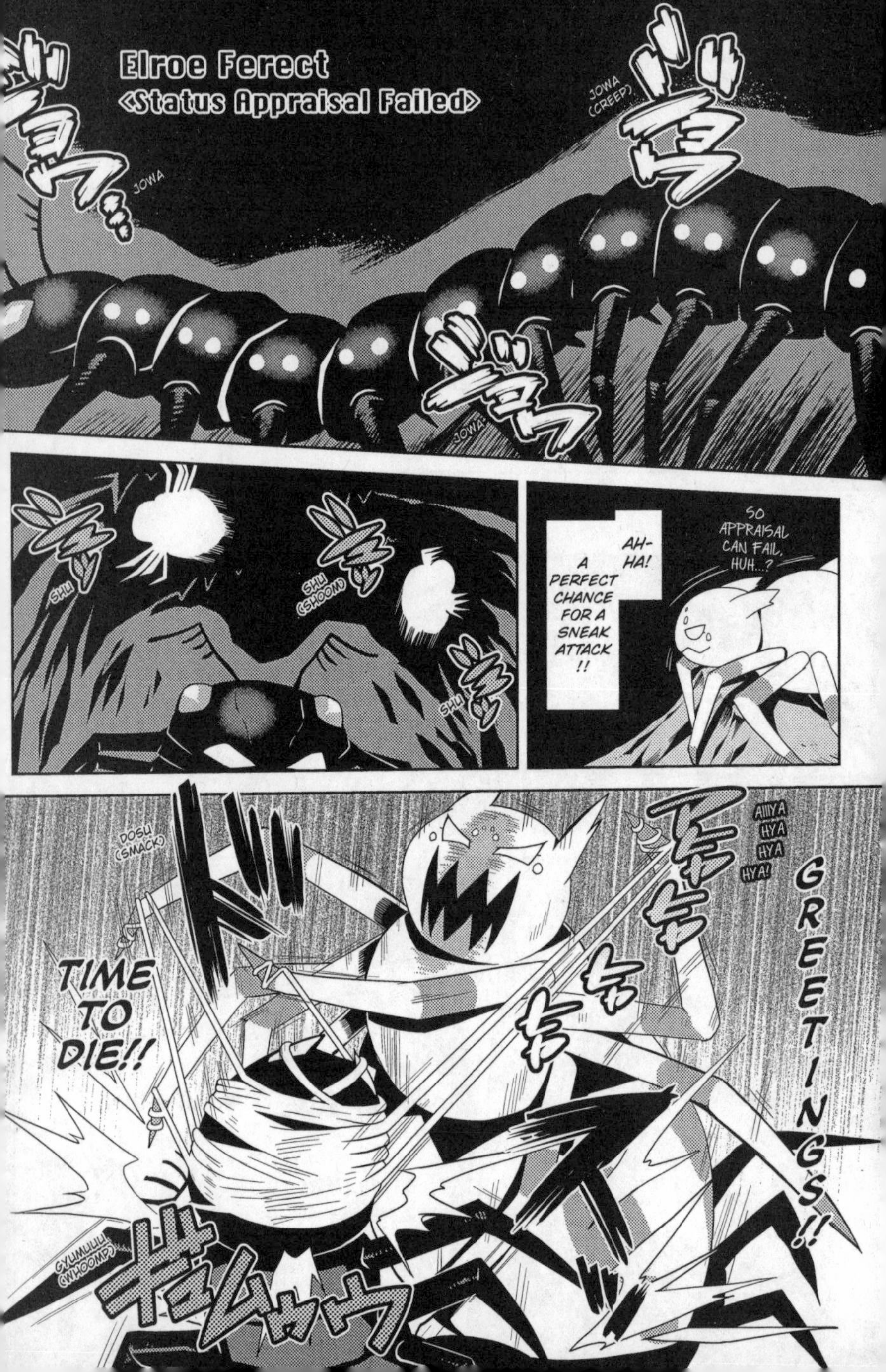
JOWA (CREEP)
Elroe Ferect
«Status Appraisal Failed»
JOWA
JOWA
SO APPRAISAL CAN FAIL, HUH...?
AH-HA!
A PERFECT CHANCE FOR A SNEAK ATTACK!!
SHU (SHOOM)
SHU
SHU
AIIIYA HYA HYA HYA!
GREETINGS!!
DOSU (SMACK)
TIME TO DIE!!
GYUMULU (WHOOMP)

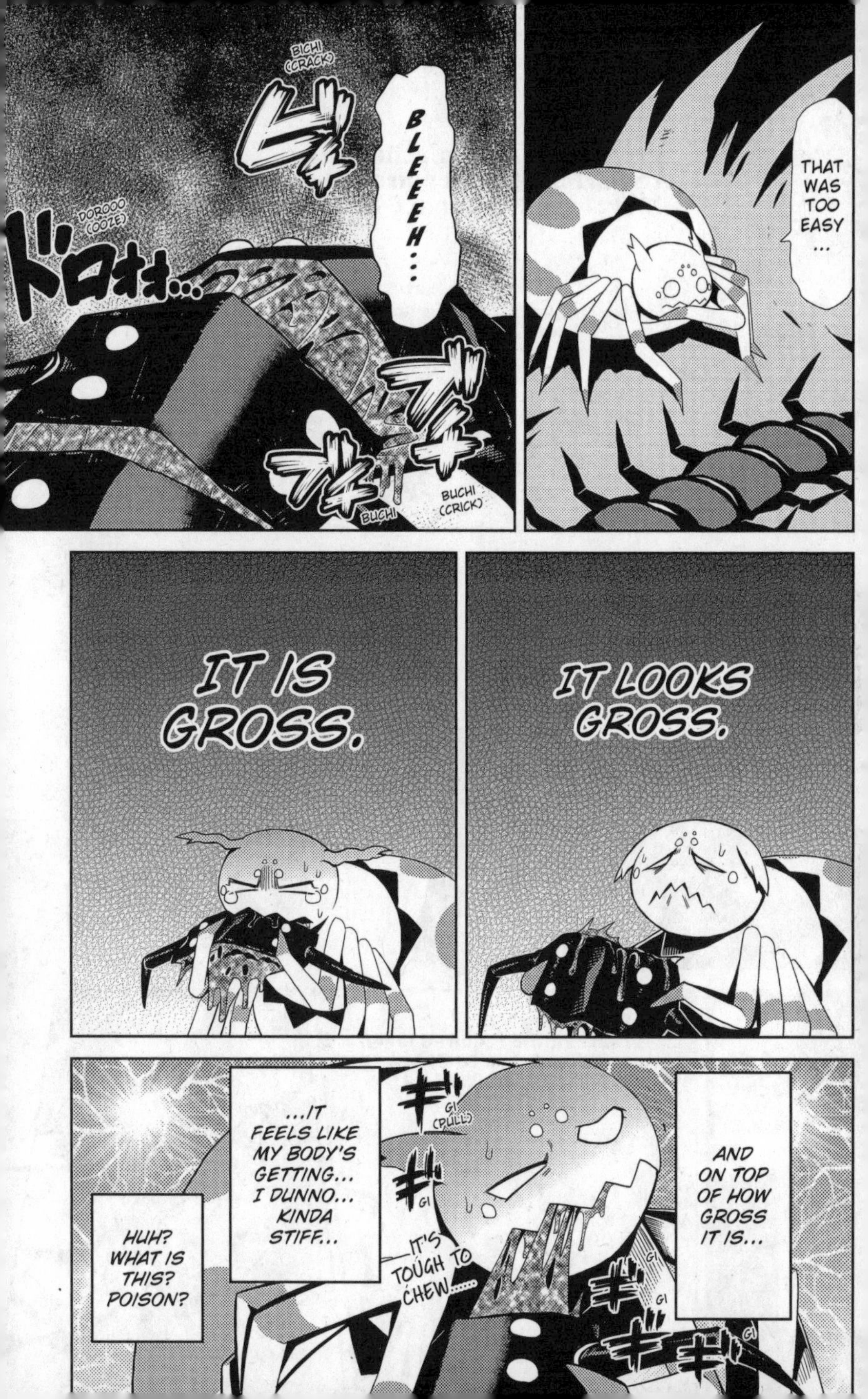
THAT WAS TOO EASY ...
BLEEEEH...
BICHI (CRACK)
DOROOO (OOZE)
BUCHI (CRICK)
BUCHI
IT LOOKS GROSS.
IT IS GROSS.
AND ON TOP OF HOW GROSS IT IS...
GI
GI
GI
GI (PULL)
GI
IT'S TOUGH TO CHEW......
...IT FEELS LIKE MY BODY'S GETTING... I DUNNO... KINDA STIFF...
HUH? WHAT IS THIS? POISON?

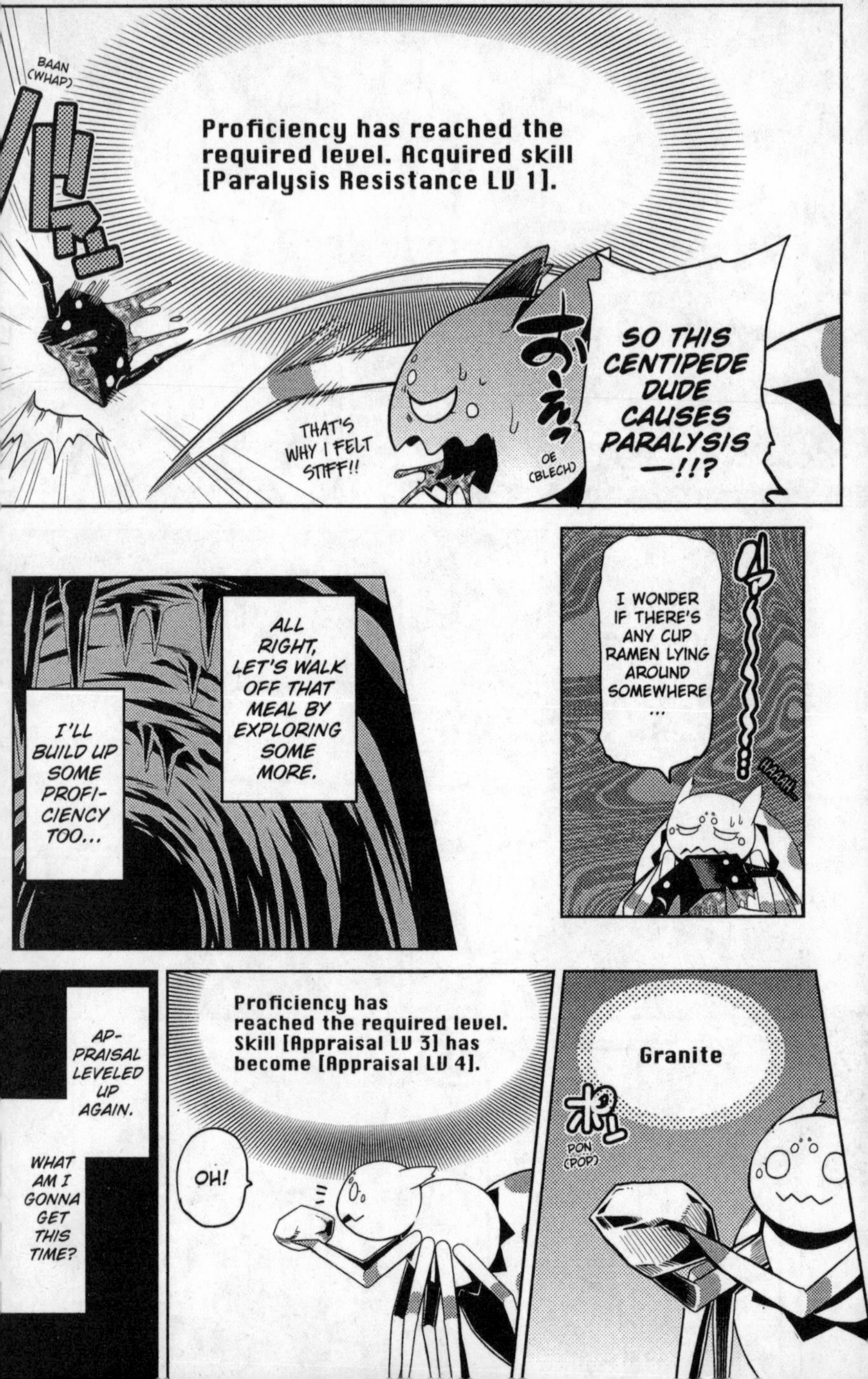
Proficiency has reached the required level. Acquired skill [Paralysis Resistance LV 1].
SO THIS CENTIPEDE DUDE CAUSES PARALYSIS—!!?
OE (BLECH)
THAT'S WHY I FELT STIFF!!
BAAN (WHAP)
I WONDER IF THERE'S ANY CUP RAMEN LYING AROUND SOMEWHERE...
ALL RIGHT, LET'S WALK OFF THAT MEAL BY EXPLORING SOME MORE.
I'LL BUILD UP SOME PROFI-CIENCY TOO...
Granite
PON (POP)
Proficiency has reached the required level. Skill [Appraisal LV 3] has become [Appraisal LV 4].
OH!
AP-PRAISAL LEVELED UP AGAIN.
WHAT AM I GONNA GET THIS TIME?

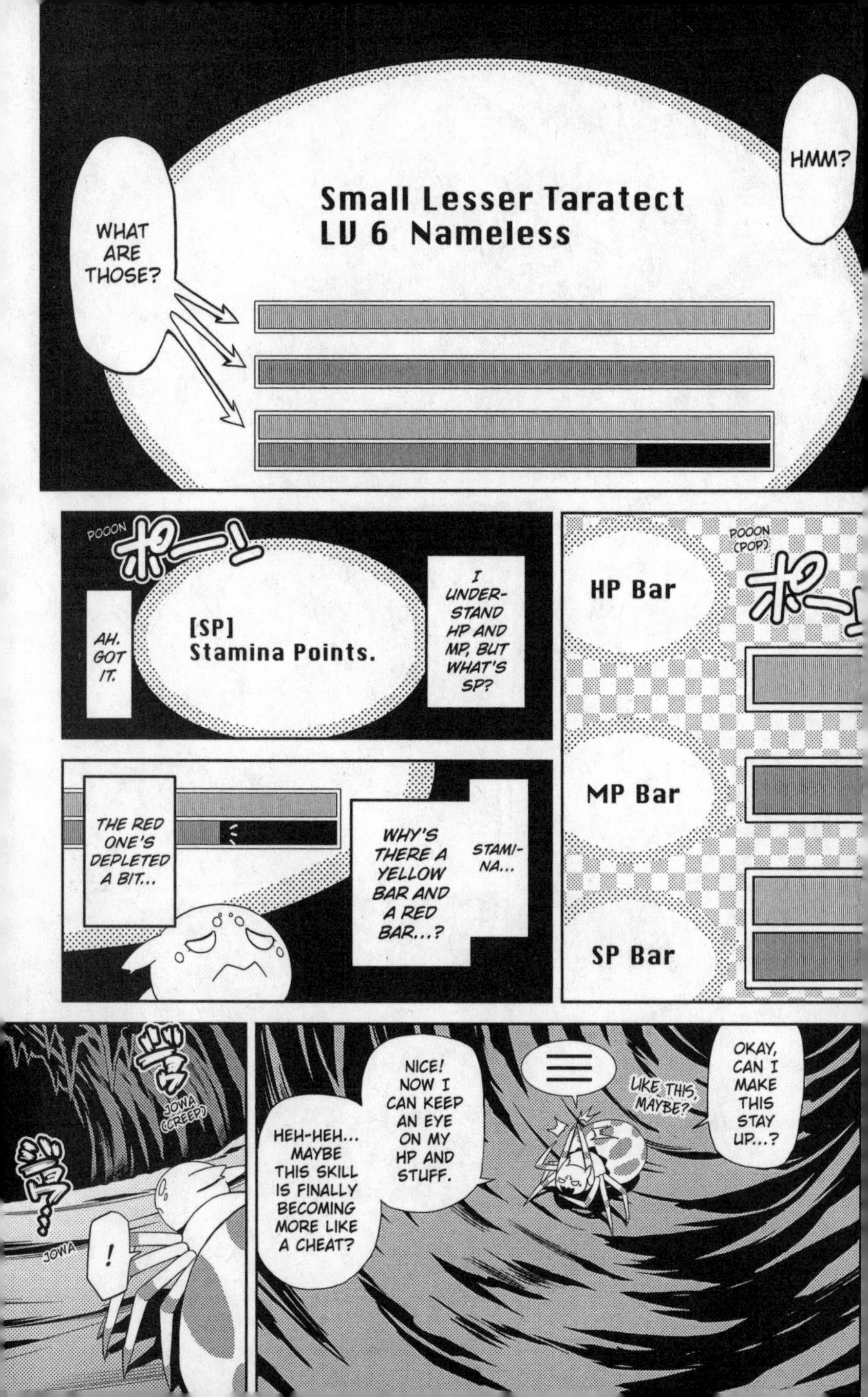
HMM?
Small Lesser Taratect
LV 6 Nameless
WHAT ARE THOSE?
POOON (POP)
HP Bar
MP Bar
SP Bar
I UNDERSTAND HP AND MP, BUT WHAT'S SP?
POOON
[SP]
Stamina Points.
AH. GOT IT.
STAMINA...
WHY'S THERE A YELLOW BAR AND A RED BAR...?
THE RED ONE'S DEPLETED A BIT...
OKAY, CAN I MAKE THIS STAY UP...?
LIKE THIS, MAYBE?
NICE! NOW I CAN KEEP AN EYE ON MY HP AND STUFF.
HEH-HEH... MAYBE THIS SKILL IS FINALLY BECOMING MORE LIKE A CHEAT?
JOWA (CREEP)
JOWA
!

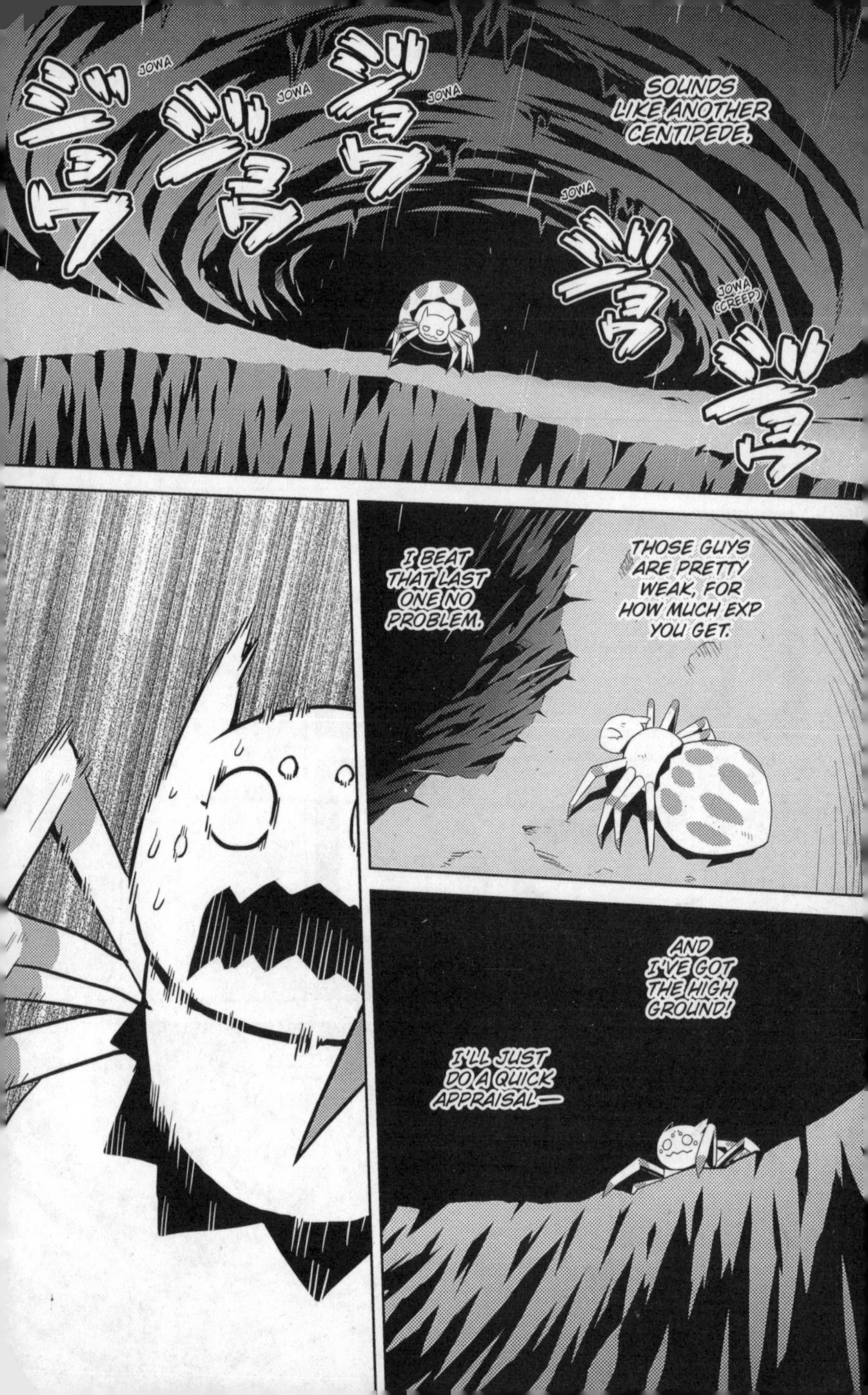
SOUNDS LIKE ANOTHER CENTIPEDE.
JOWA (CREEP)
JOWA
JOWA
JOWA
JOWA
THOSE GUYS ARE PRETTY WEAK, FOR HOW MUCH EXP YOU GET.
I BEAT THAT LAST ONE NO PROBLEM.
AND I'VE GOT THE HIGH GROUND!
I'LL JUST DO A QUICK APPRAISAL—

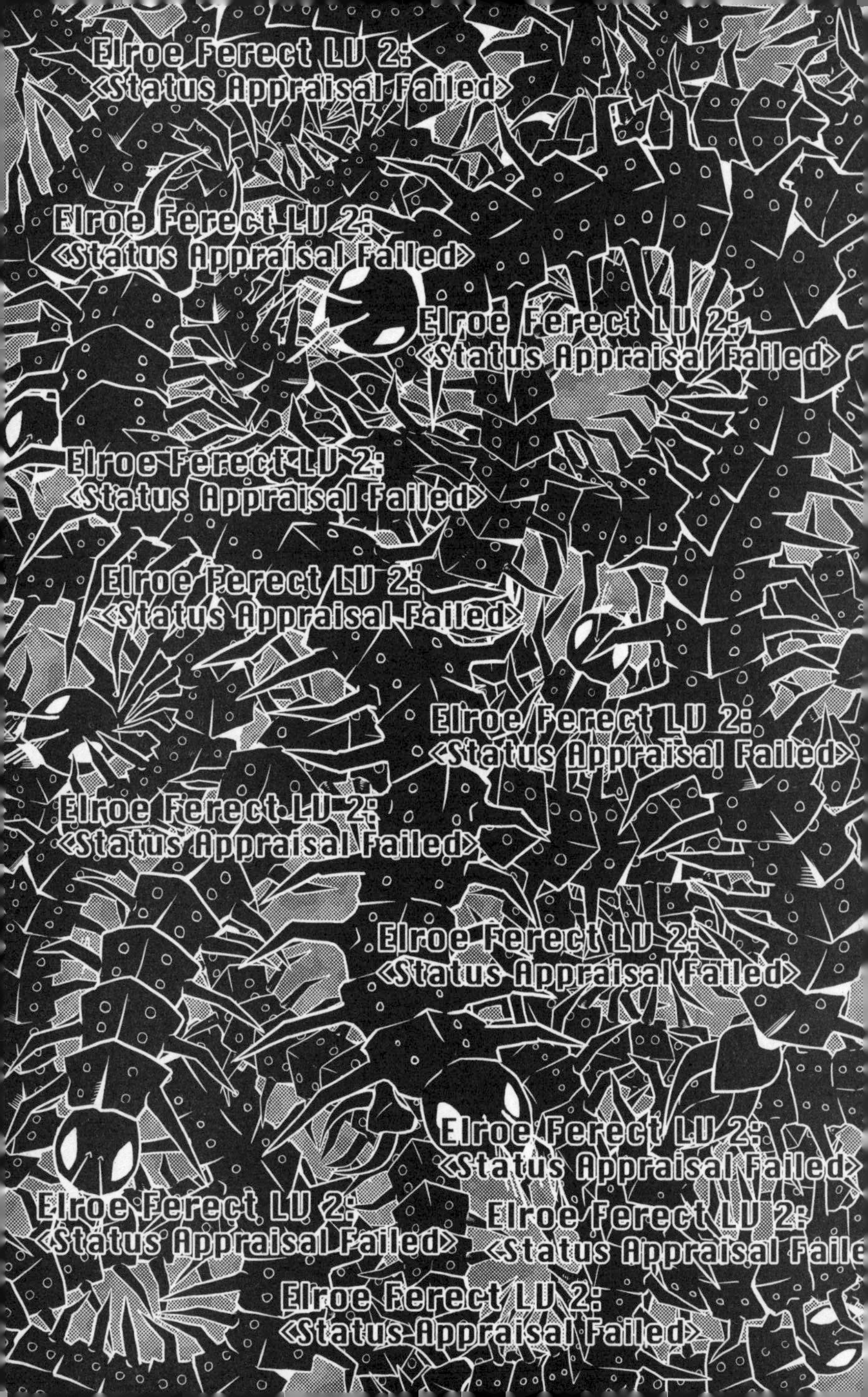
Elroe Ferect LV 2:
<Status Appraisal Failed>
Elroe Ferect LV 2:
<Status Appraisal Failed>
Elroe Ferect LV 2:
<Status Appraisal Failed>
Elroe Ferect LV 2:
<Status Appraisal Failed>
Elroe Ferect LV 2:
<Status Appraisal Failed>
Elroe Ferect LV 2:
<Status Appraisal Failed>
Elroe Ferect LV 2:
<Status Appraisal Failed>
Elroe Ferect LV 2:
<Status Appraisal Failed>
Elroe Ferect LV 2:
<Status Appraisal Failed>
Elroe Ferect LV 2:
<Status Appraisal Failed>
Elroe Ferect LV 2:
<Status Appraisal Faile
Elroe Ferect LV 2:
<Status Appraisal Failed>

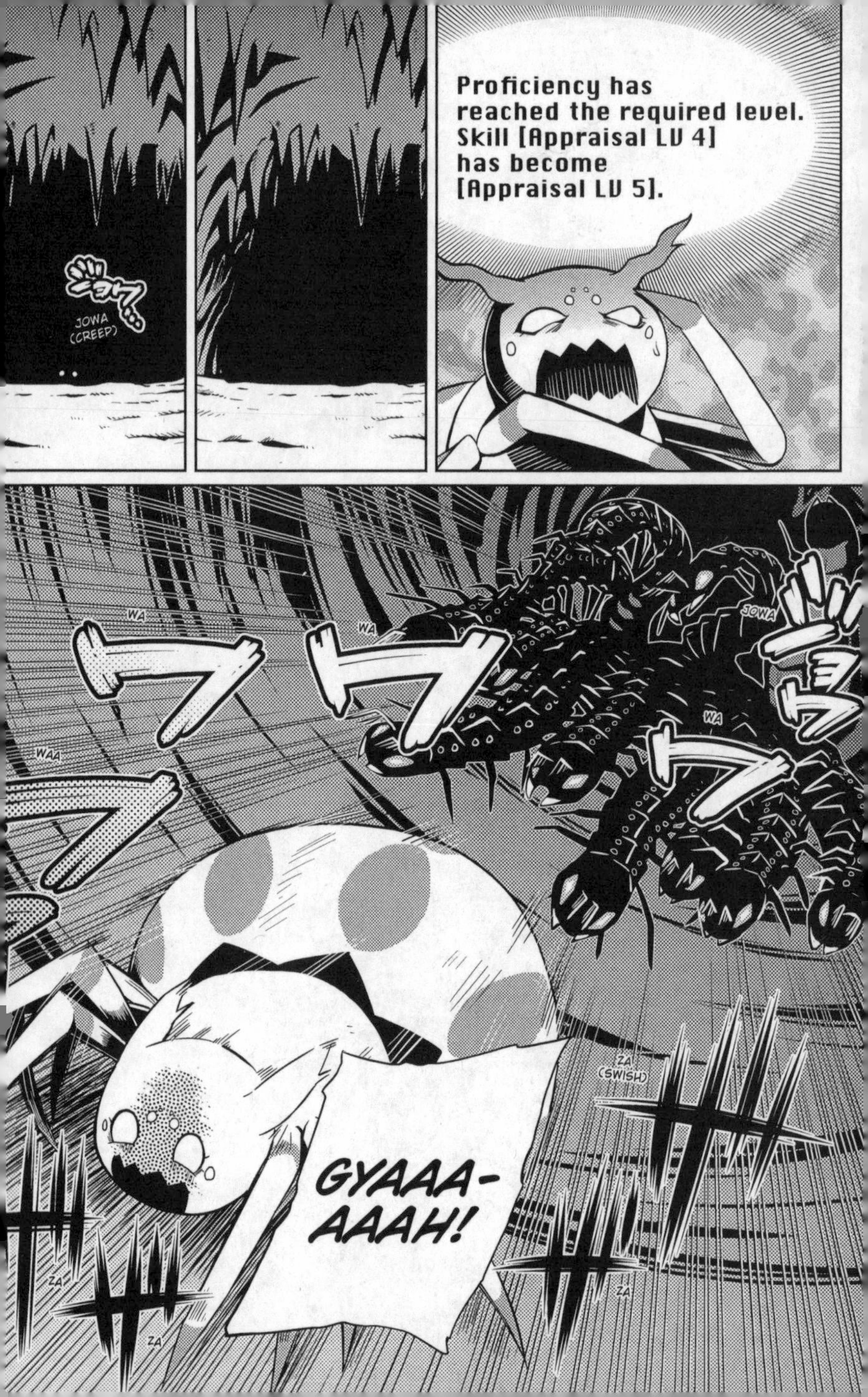
Proficiency has reached the required level. Skill [Appraisal LV 4] has become [Appraisal LV 5].
JOWA (CREEP)
JOWA
WA
WA
WA
WAA
ZA (SWISH)
GYAAA-AAAH!
ZA
ZA
ZA

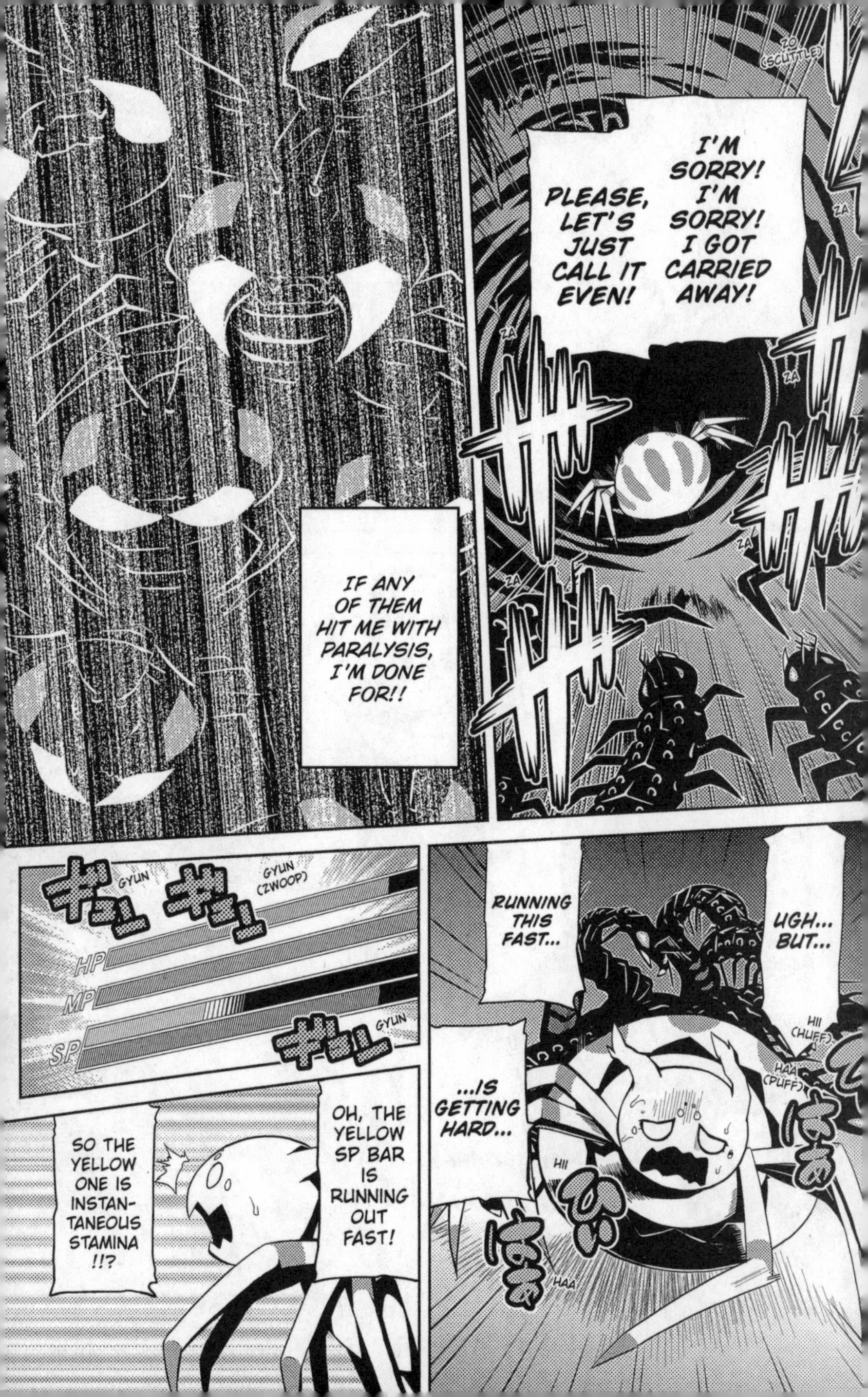
ZO (SCUTTLE)
I'M SORRY! I'M SORRY! I GOT CARRIED AWAY!
PLEASE, LET'S JUST CALL IT EVEN!
ZA
ZA
ZA
ZA
ZA
IF ANY OF THEM HIT ME WITH PARALYSIS, I'M DONE FOR!!
UGH... BUT...
RUNNING THIS FAST...
HII (CHUFF)
HAA (PUFF)
...IS GETTING HARD...
HII
HAA
GYUN (ZWOOP)
GYUN
HP
MP
SP
GYUN
OH, THE YELLOW SP BAR IS RUNNING OUT FAST!
SO THE YELLOW ONE IS INSTANTANEOUS STAMINA!!?

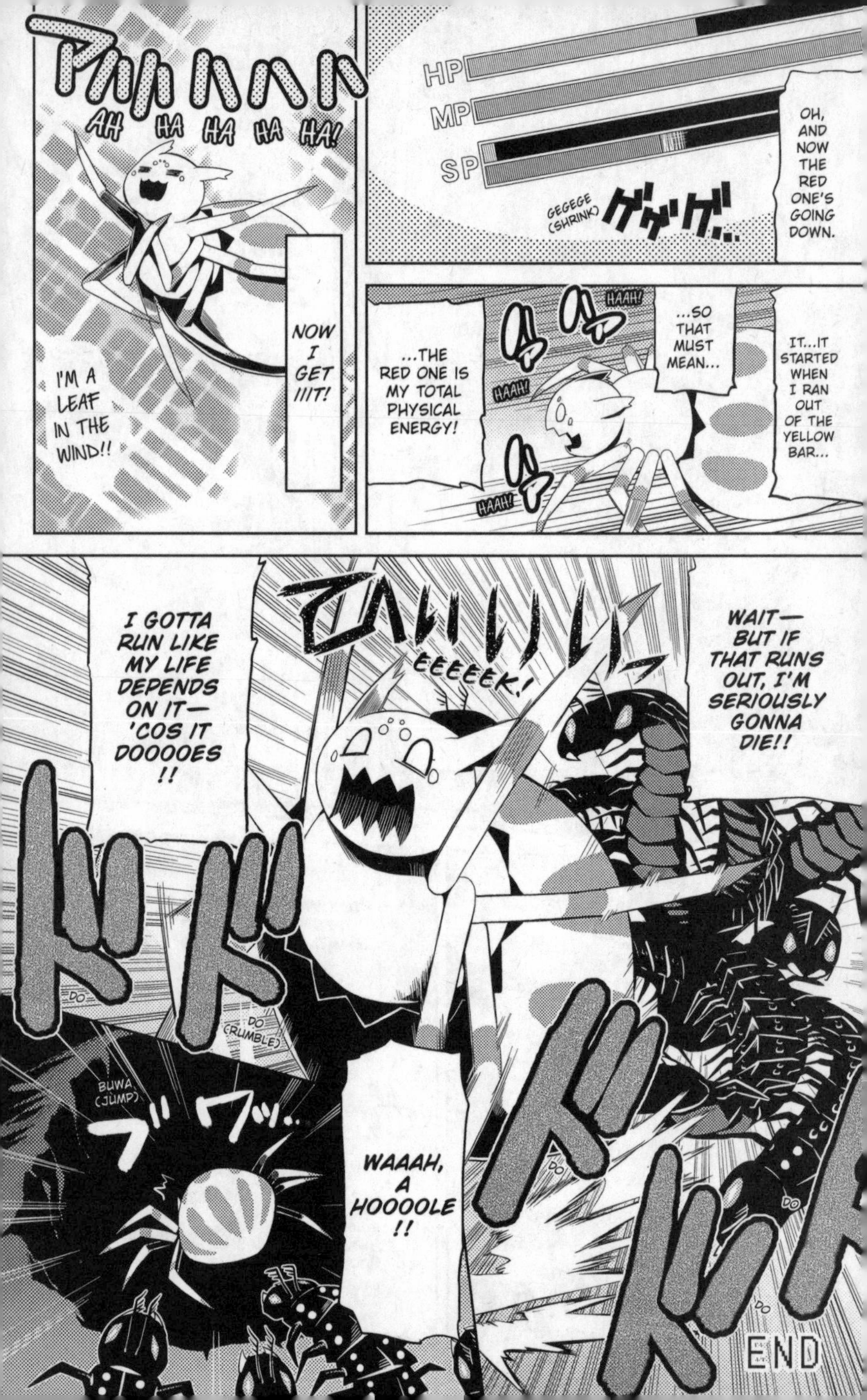
HP
MP
SP
OH, AND NOW THE RED ONE'S GOING DOWN.
GEGEGE (SHRINK)
ゲゲゲ…
IT…IT STARTED WHEN I RAN OUT OF THE YELLOW BAR…
HAAH!
…SO THAT MUST MEAN…
HAAH!
…THE RED ONE IS MY TOTAL PHYSICAL ENERGY!
HAAH!
アハハハハ
AH HA HA HA HA!
NOW I GET IIIT!
I'M A LEAF IN THE WIND!!
WAIT—BUT IF THAT RUNS OUT, I'M SERIOUSLY GONNA DIE!!
EEEEEEK!
I GOTTA RUN LIKE MY LIFE DEPENDS ON IT—'COS IT DOOOOES!!
DO
DO
DO (RUMBLE)
DO
WAAAH, A HOOOOLE!!
BUWA (JUMP)
END

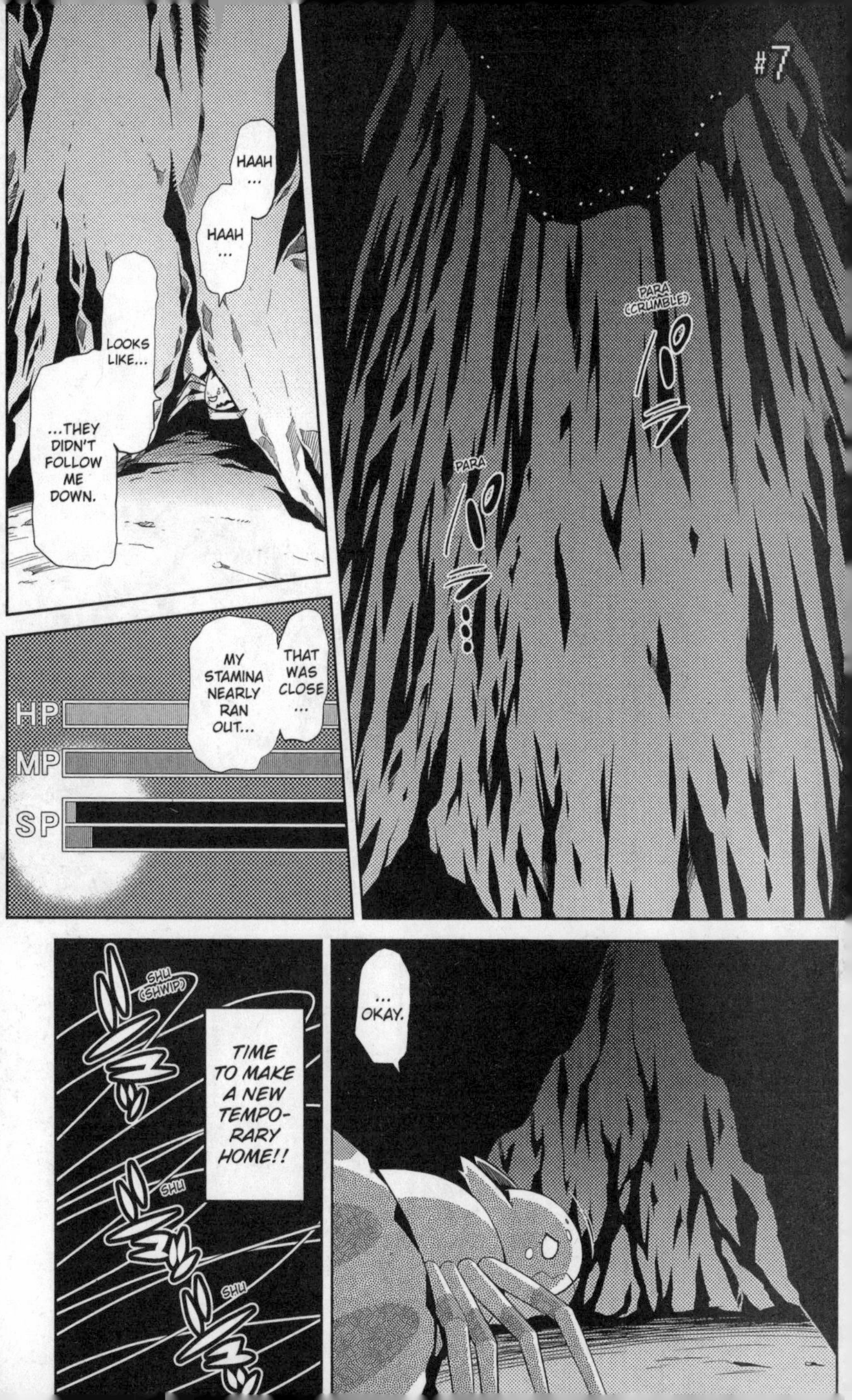
#7
PARA (CRUMBLE)
PARA
HAAH ...
HAAH ...
LOOKS LIKE...
...THEY DIDN'T FOLLOW ME DOWN.
THAT WAS CLOSE ...
MY STAMINA NEARLY RAN OUT...
HP
MP
SP
... OKAY.
SHU (SHWIP)
TIME TO MAKE A NEW TEMPO-RARY HOME!!
SHU
SHU

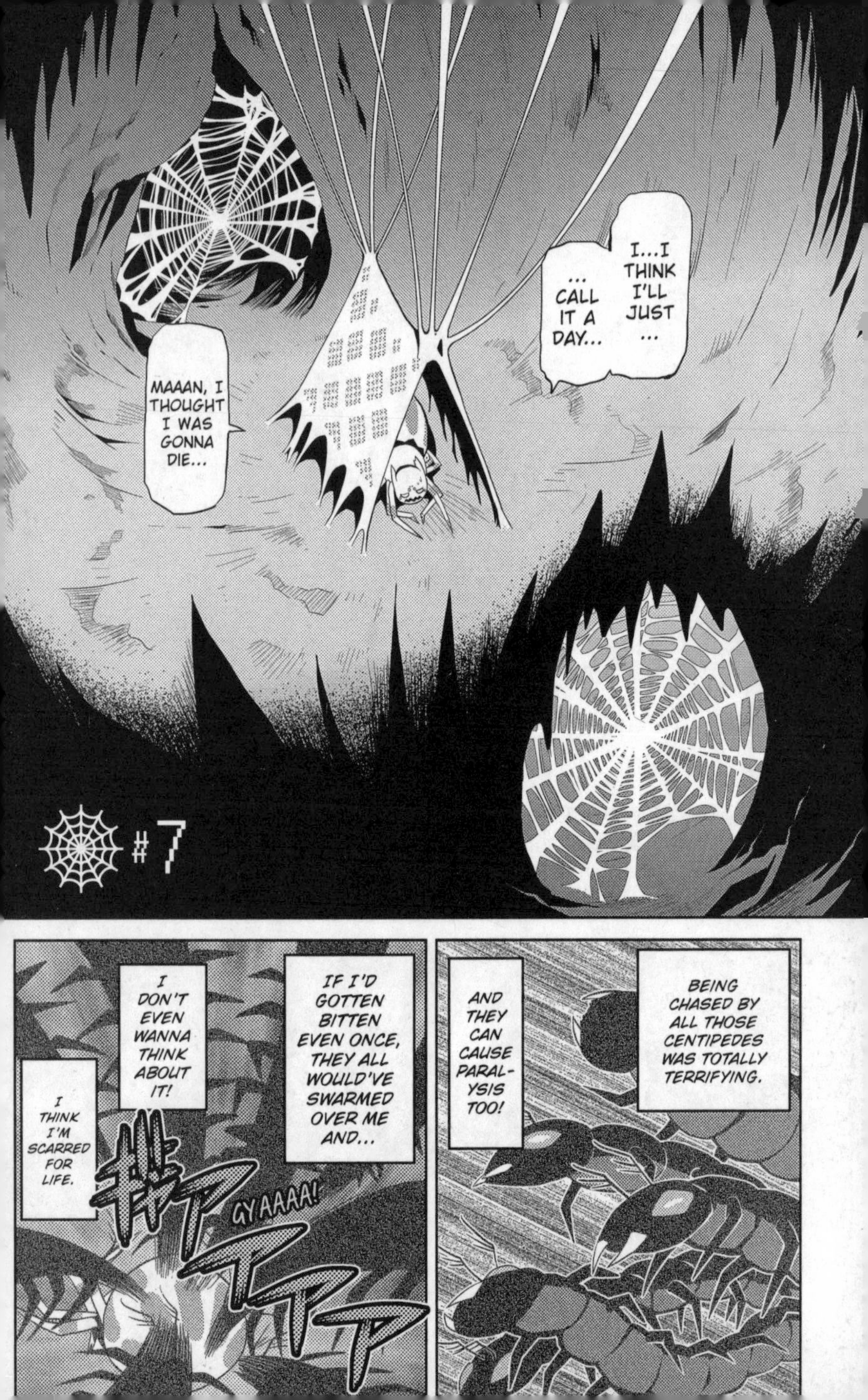
I...I THINK I'LL JUST ...
... CALL IT A DAY...
MAAAN, I THOUGHT I WAS GONNA DIE...
#7
BEING CHASED BY ALL THOSE CENTIPEDES WAS TOTALLY TERRIFYING.
AND THEY CAN CAUSE PARAL-YSIS TOO!
IF I'D GOTTEN BITTEN EVEN ONCE, THEY ALL WOULD'VE SWARMED OVER ME AND...
I DON'T EVEN WANNA THINK ABOUT IT!
I THINK I'M SCARRED FOR LIFE.
GYAAAA!

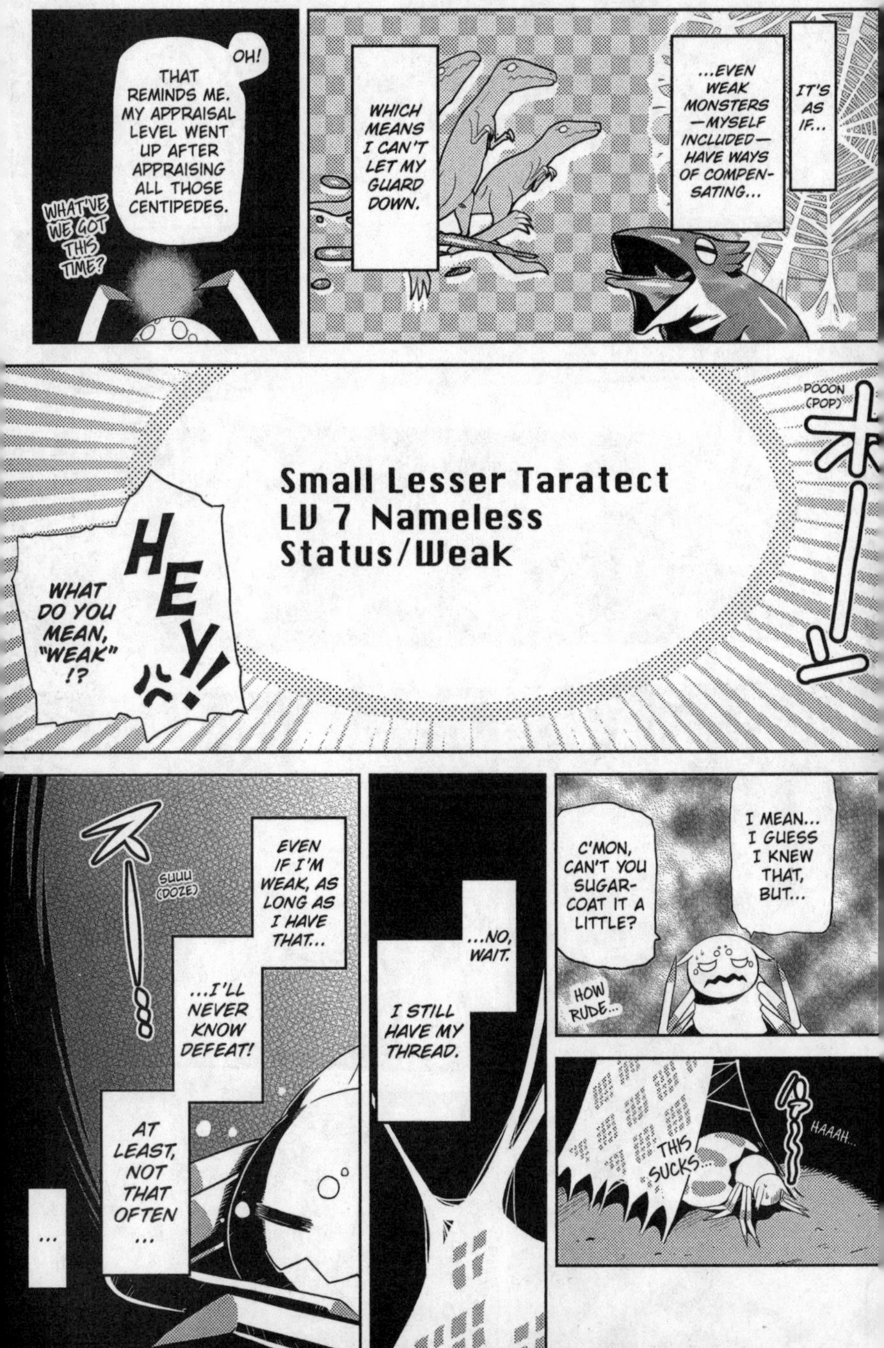
IT'S AS IF...
...EVEN WEAK MONSTERS—MYSELF INCLUDED—HAVE WAYS OF COMPENSATING...
WHICH MEANS I CAN'T LET MY GUARD DOWN.
OH!
THAT REMINDS ME. MY APPRAISAL LEVEL WENT UP AFTER APPRAISING ALL THOSE CENTIPEDES.
WHAT'VE WE GOT THIS TIME?
POOON (POP)
Small Lesser Taratect
LV 7 Nameless
Status/Weak
HEY!!
WHAT DO YOU MEAN, "WEAK"!?
I MEAN... I GUESS I KNEW THAT, BUT...
C'MON, CAN'T YOU SUGAR-COAT IT A LITTLE?
HOW RUDE...
HAAAH...
THIS SUCKS...
...NO, WAIT.
I STILL HAVE MY THREAD.
SUUU (DOZE)
EVEN IF I'M WEAK, AS LONG AS I HAVE THAT...
...I'LL NEVER KNOW DEFEAT!
AT LEAST, NOT THAT OFTEN...
...

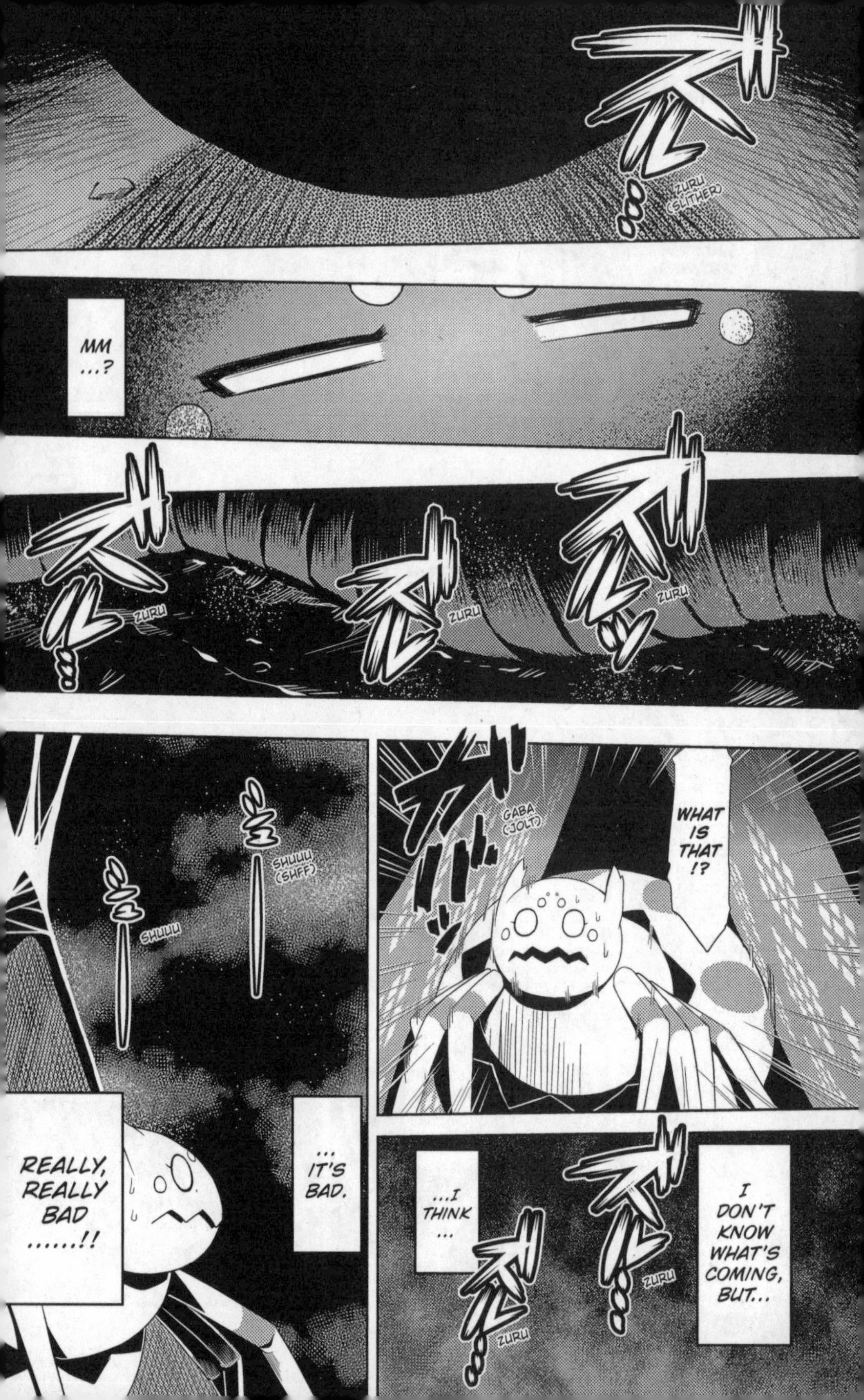
ZURU (SLITHER)
MM ...?
ZURU
ZURU
ZURU
WHAT IS THAT !?
GABA (JOLT)
I DON'T KNOW WHAT'S COMING, BUT...
ZURU
...I THINK ...
ZURU
SHUUU (SHFF)
SHUUU
... IT'S BAD.
REALLY, REALLY BAD ......!!

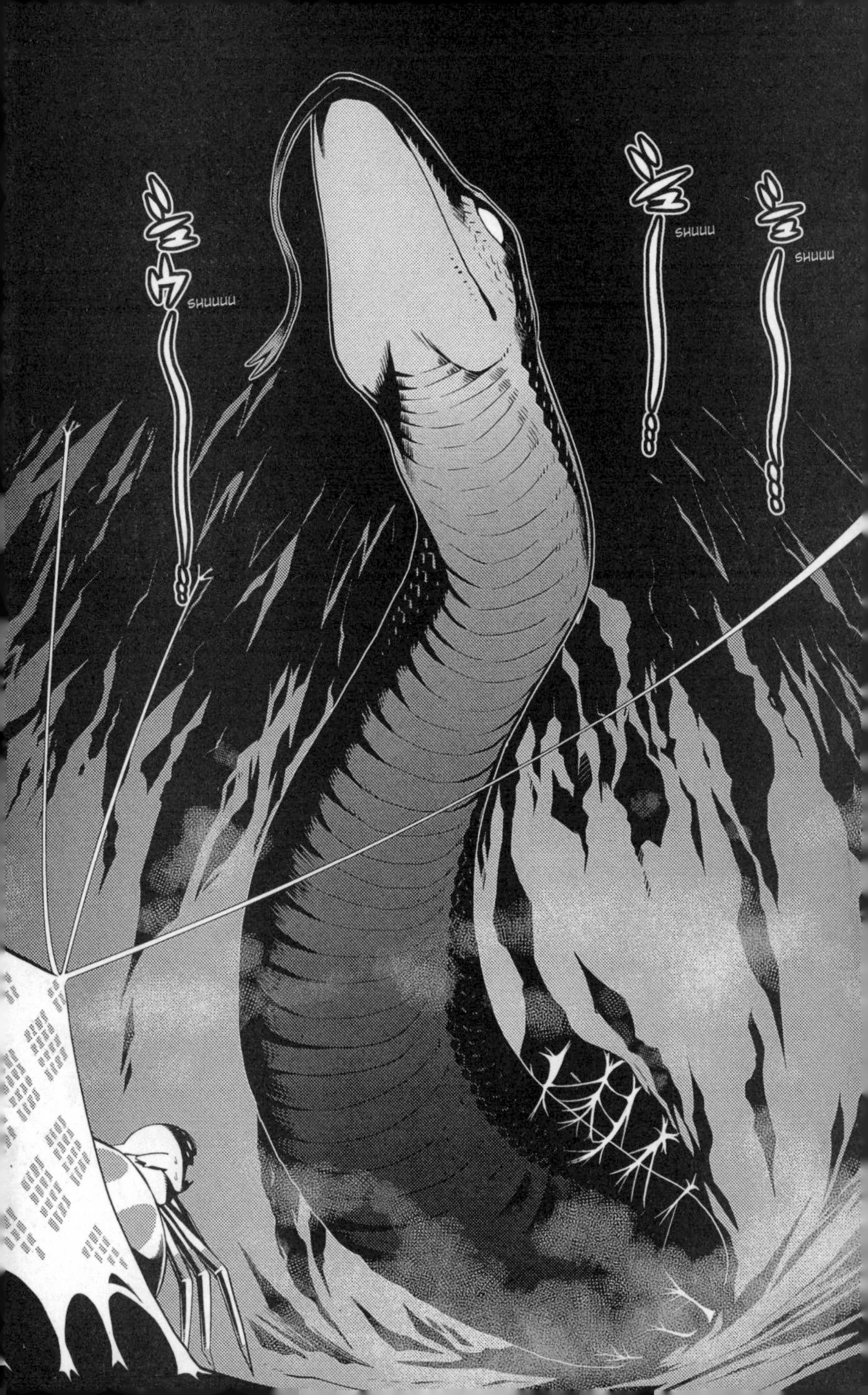
SHUUU
SHUUU
SHUUUU

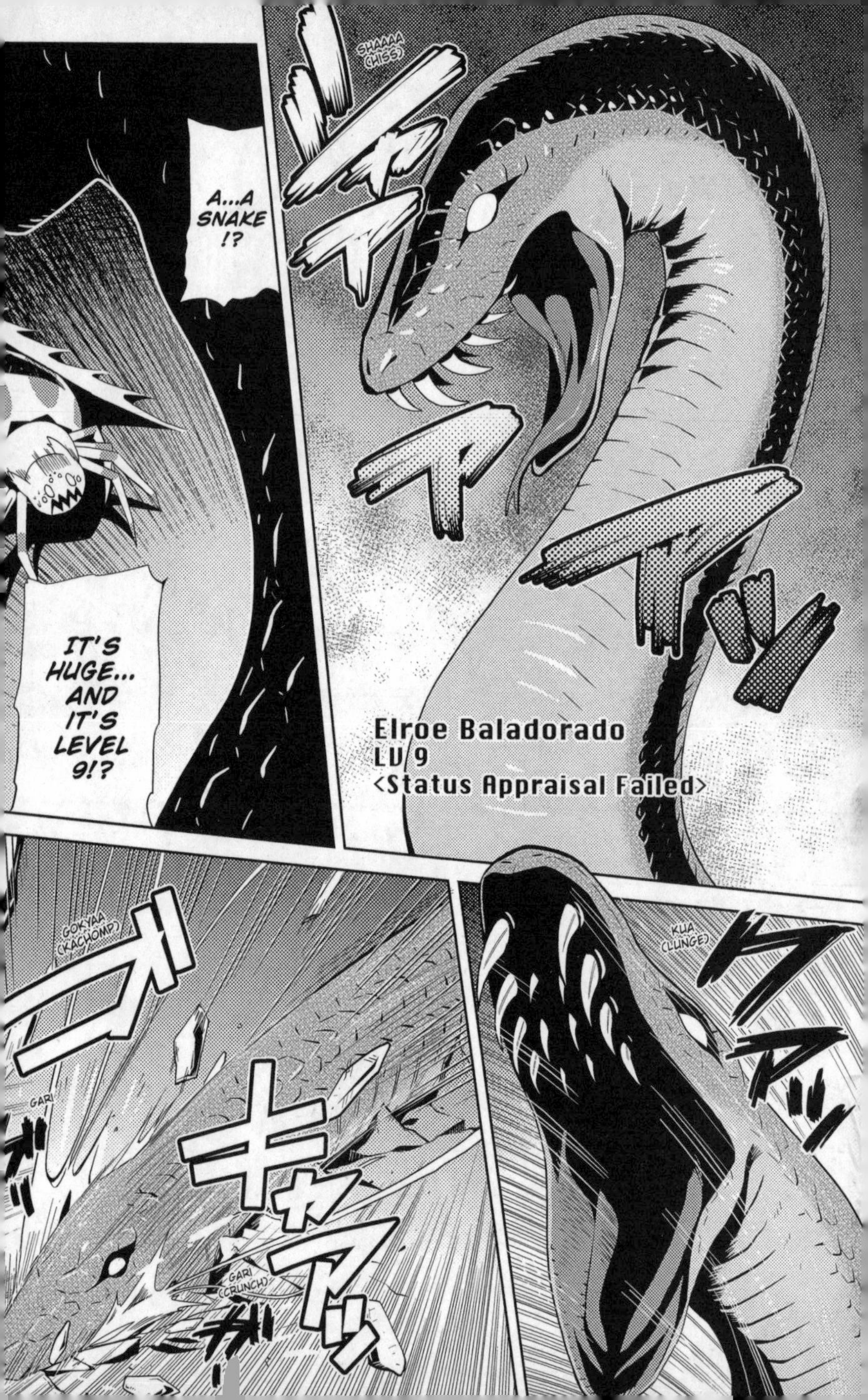
SHAAAA (HISS)
Elroe Baladorado
LV 9
<Status Appraisal Failed>
A...A SNAKE!?
IT'S HUGE... AND IT'S LEVEL 9!?
KUA (LUNGE)
GOKYAA (KACHOMP)
GARI
GARI (CRUNCH)

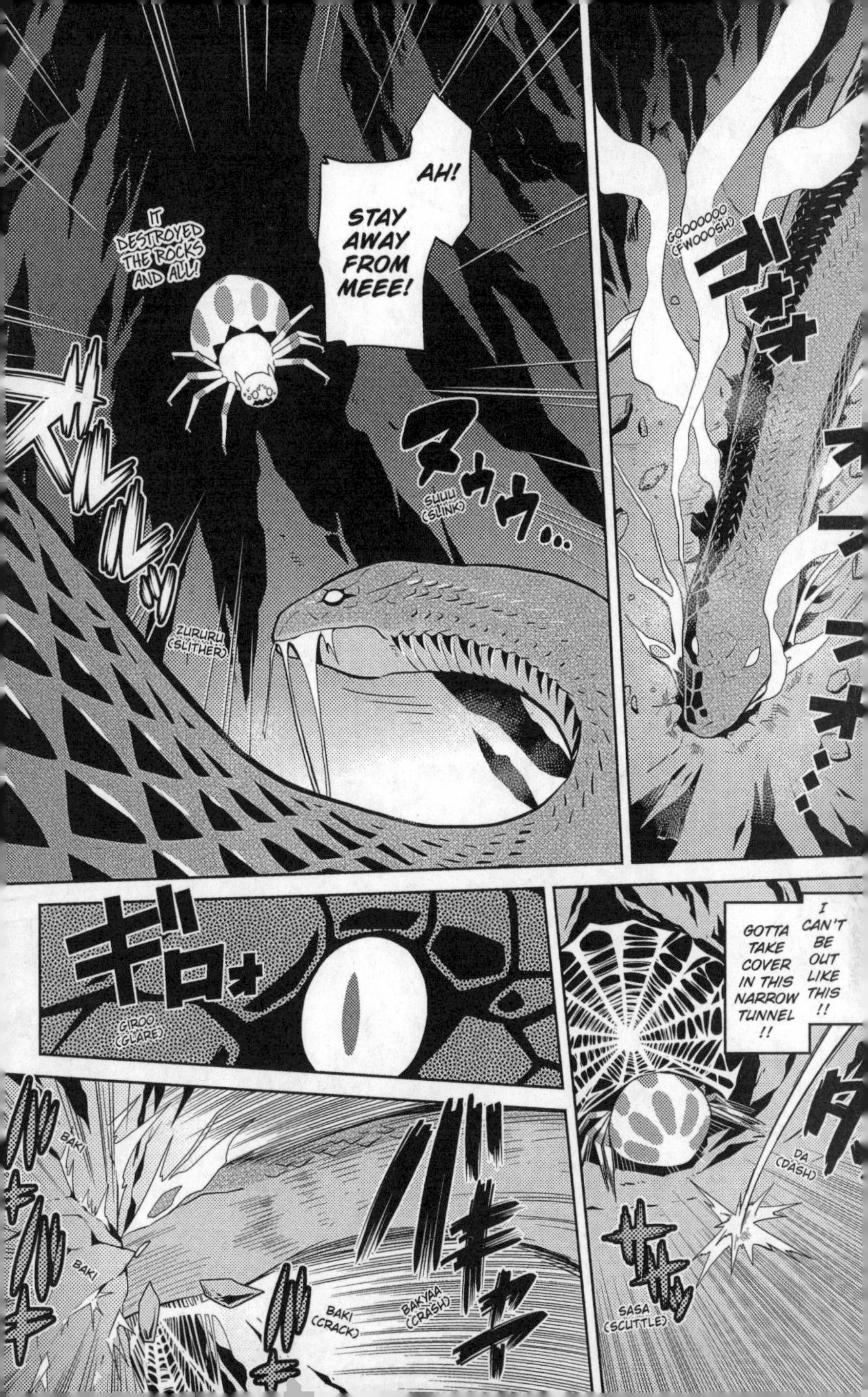
GOOOOOOO (FWOOOSH)
AH!
STAY AWAY FROM MEEE!
IT DESTROYED THE ROCKS AND ALL!
SUUU (SLINK)
ZURURU (SLITHER)
I CAN'T BE OUT LIKE THIS!!
GOTTA TAKE COVER IN THIS NARROW TUNNEL!!
DA (DASH)
SASA (SCUTTLE)
GIROO (GLARE)
BAKYAA (CRASH)
BAKI (CRACK)
BAKI
BAKI

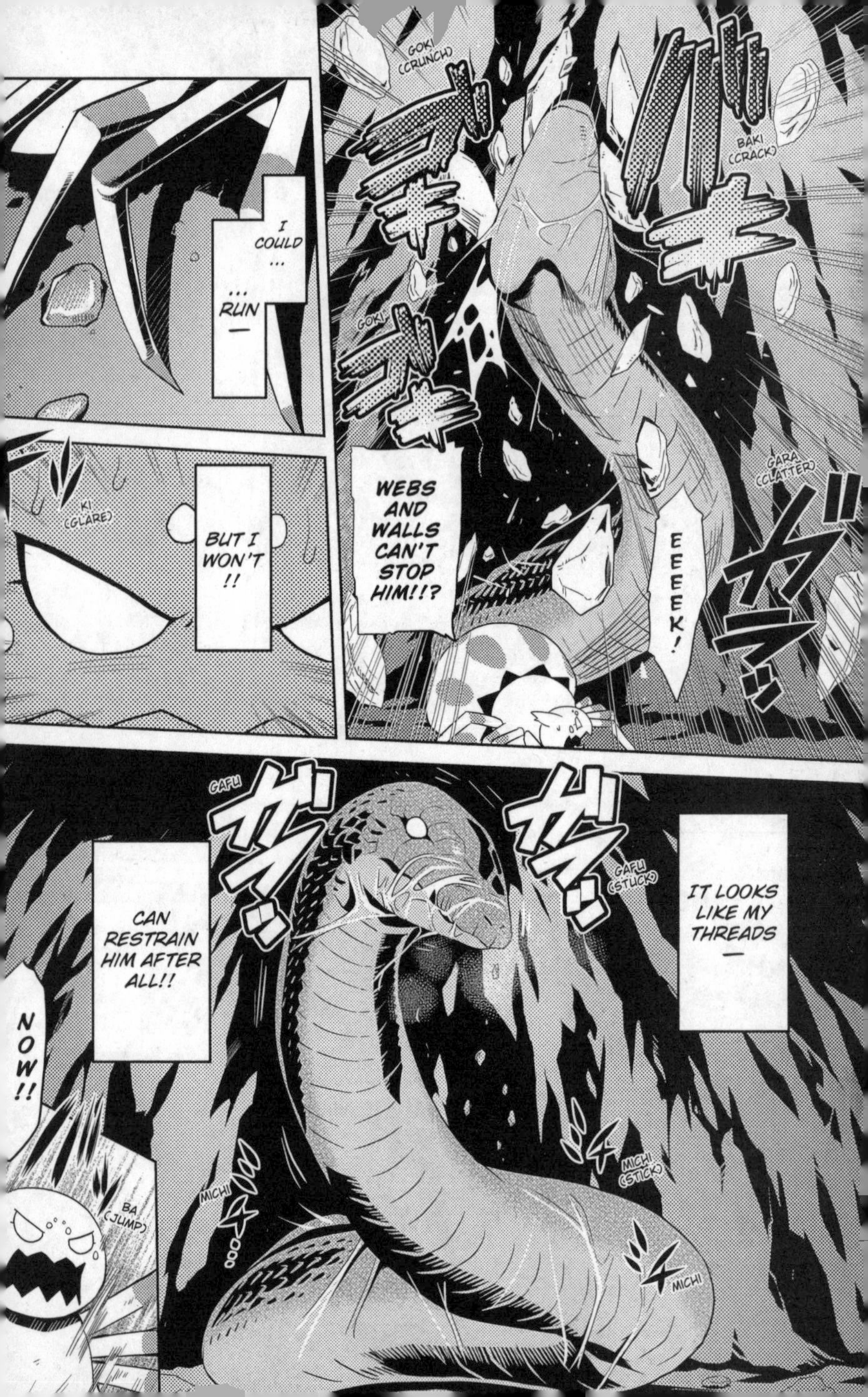
BAKI (CRACK)
GOKI (CRUNCH)
GOKI
GARA (CLATTER)
EEEEK!
WEBS AND WALLS CAN'T STOP HIM!!?
I COULD ...
... RUN —
KI (GLARE)
BUT I WON'T !!
IT LOOKS LIKE MY THREADS —
GAFU (STICK)
GAFU
CAN RESTRAIN HIM AFTER ALL!!
MICHI (STICK)
MICHI
MICHI
NOW!!
BA (JUMP)

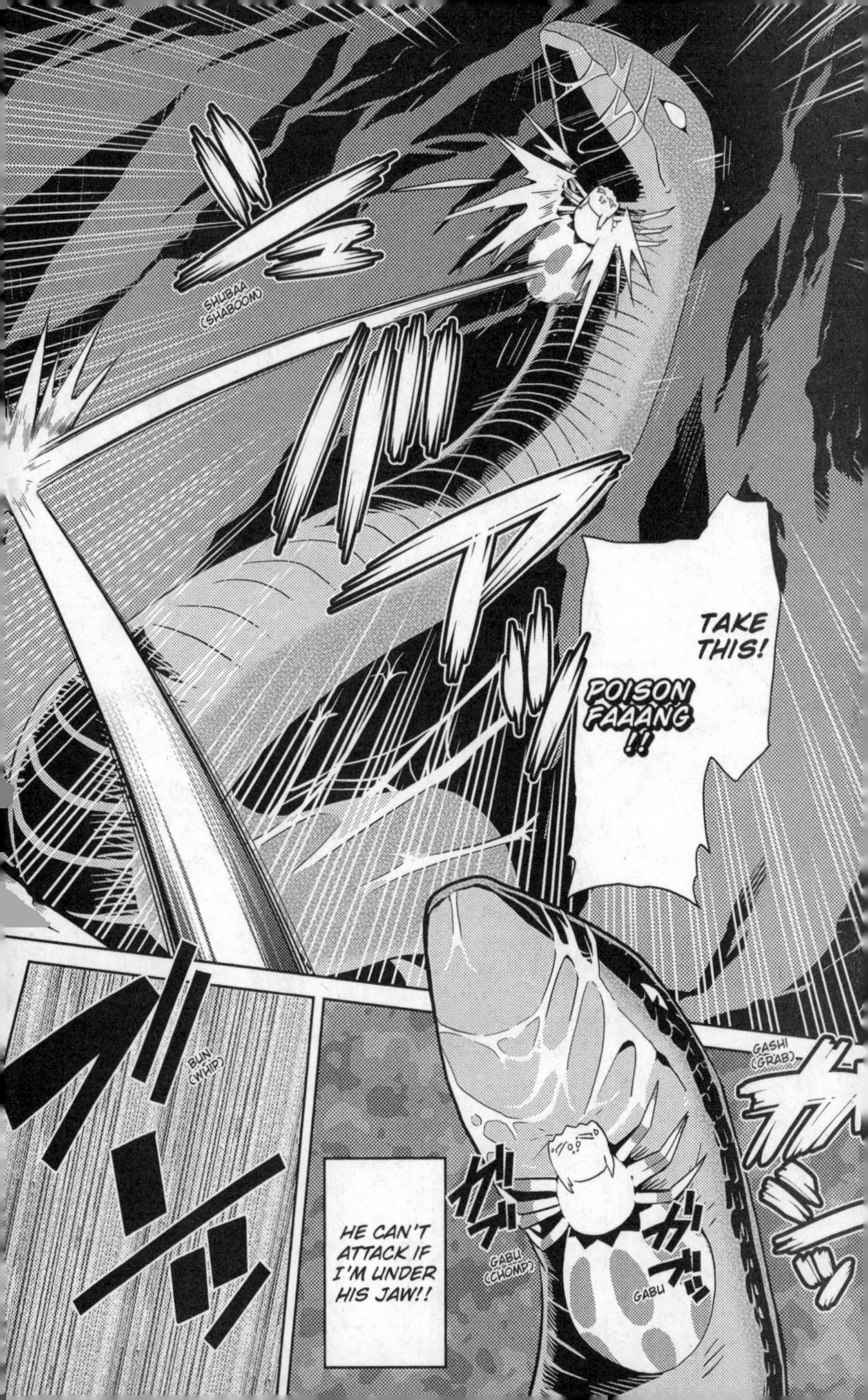
TAKE THIS!
POISON FAAANG!!
SHUBAA (SHABOOM)
GASHI (GRAB)
GABU (CHOMP)
GABU
HE CAN'T ATTACK IF I'M UNDER HIS JAW!!
BUN (WHIP)

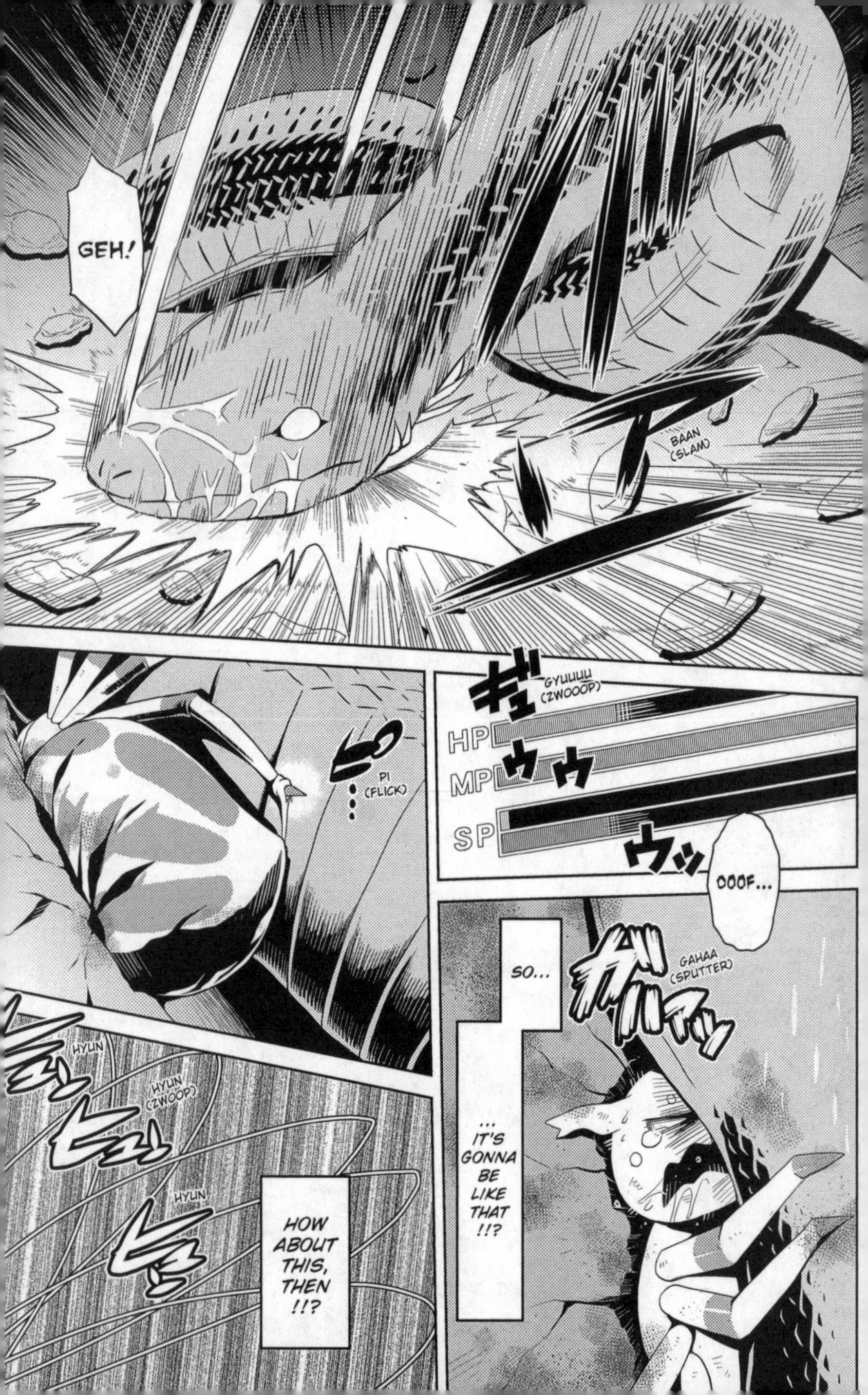
GEH!
BAAN
(SLAM)
GYUUUU
(ZWOOOP)
HP
MP
SP
PI
(FLICK)
...
OOOF...
SO...
GAHAA
(SPUTTER)
...IT'S GONNA BE LIKE THAT!!?
HYUN
HYUN
(ZWOOOP)
HYUN
HOW ABOUT THIS, THEN!!?

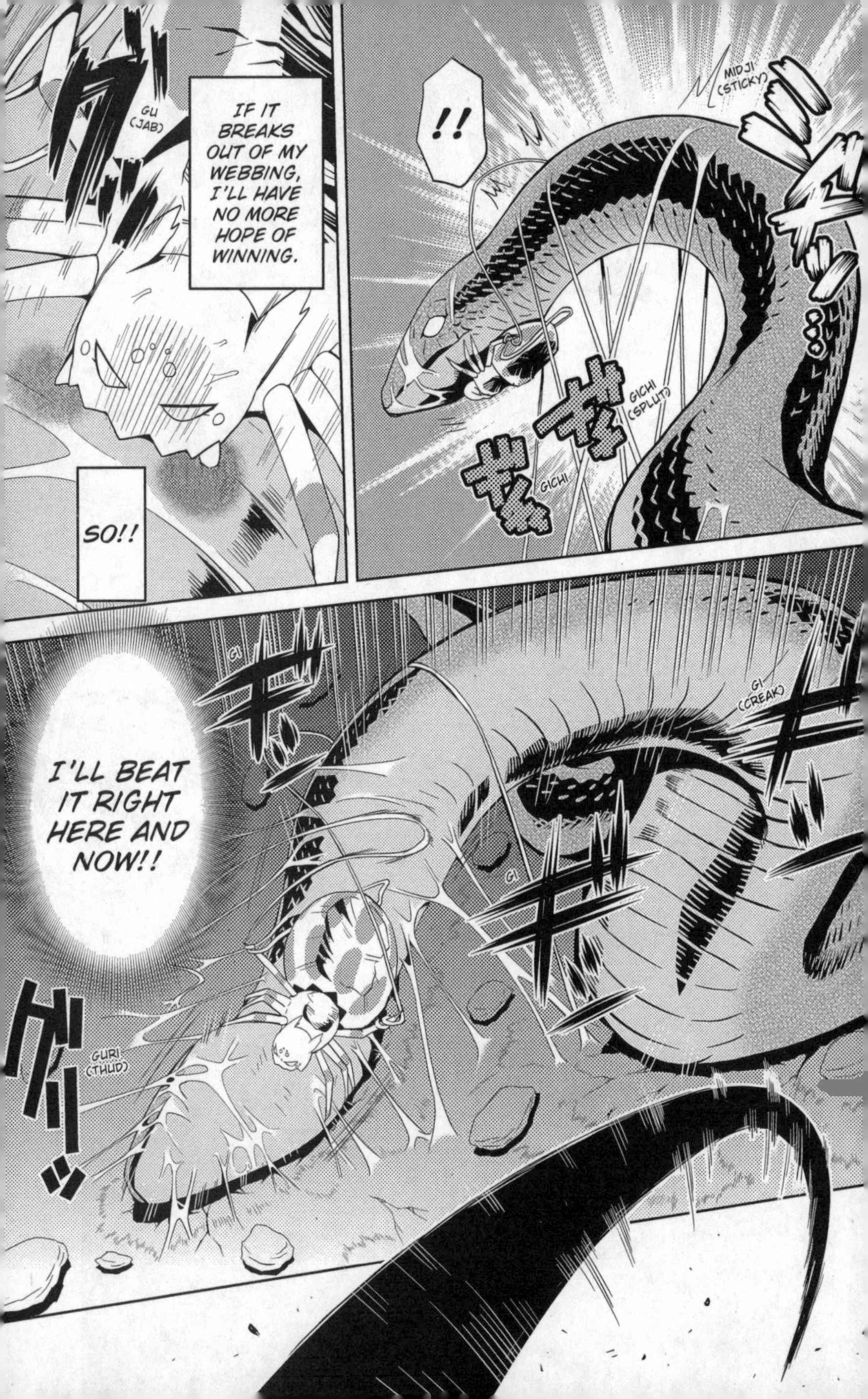
MIDJI (STICKY)
!!
GICHI (SPLUT)
GICHI
IF IT BREAKS OUT OF MY WEBBING, I'LL HAVE NO MORE HOPE OF WINNING.
GU (JAB)
SO!!
GI (CREAK)
GI
GI
I'LL BEAT IT RIGHT HERE AND NOW!!
GURI (THUD)

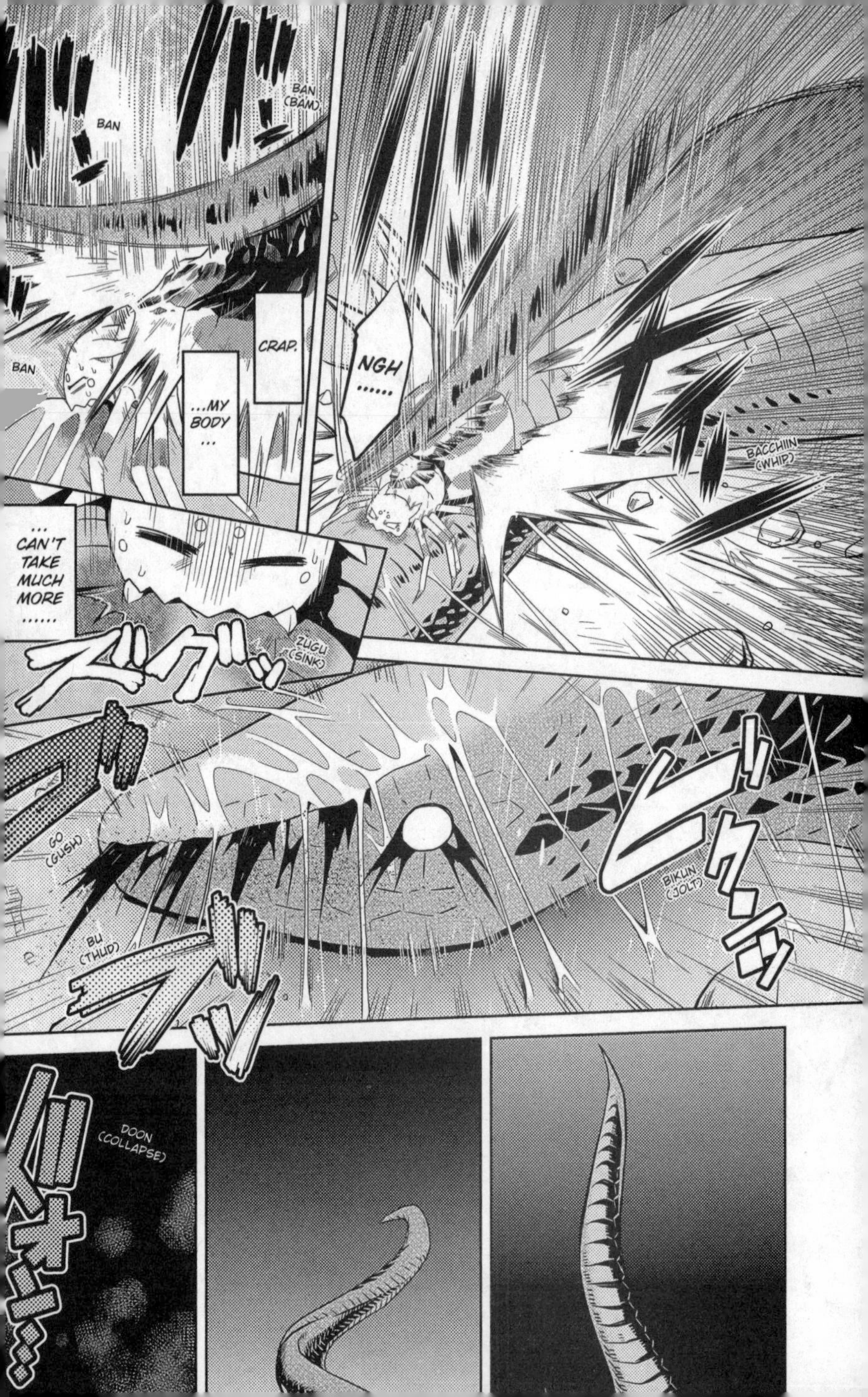
NGH ......
BACCHIIN (WHIP)
BAN (BAM)
BAN
CRAP.
...MY BODY ...
BAN
... CAN'T TAKE MUCH MORE ......
ZUGU (SINK)
BIKUN (JOLT)
GO (GUSH)
BU (THUD)
DOON (COLLAPSE)

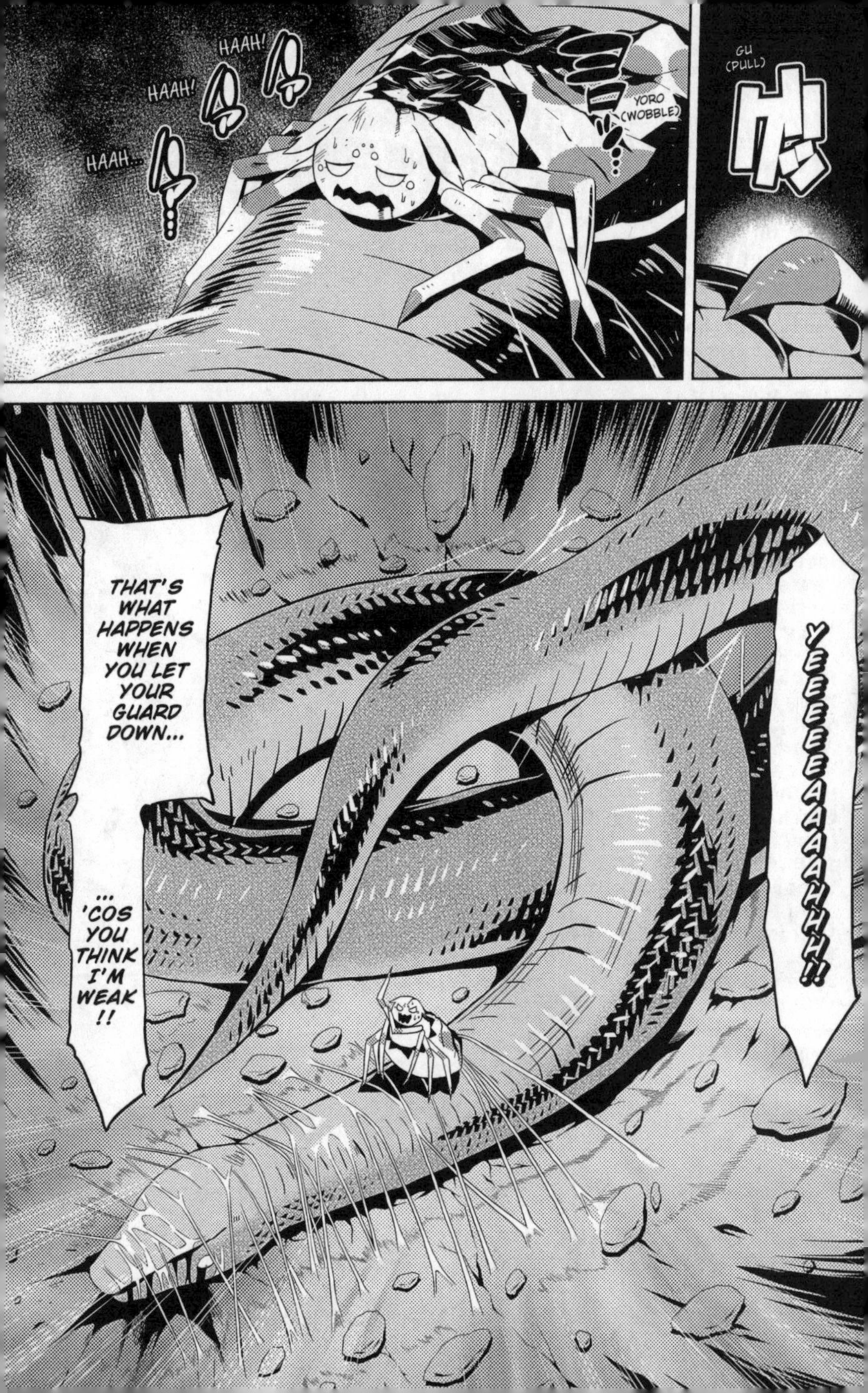
GU (PULL)
HAAH!
HAAH!
HAAH...
YORO (WOBBLE)
YEEEEEAAAAAHHH!!
THAT'S WHAT HAPPENS WHEN YOU LET YOUR GUARD DOWN...
...'COS YOU THINK I'M WEAK!!

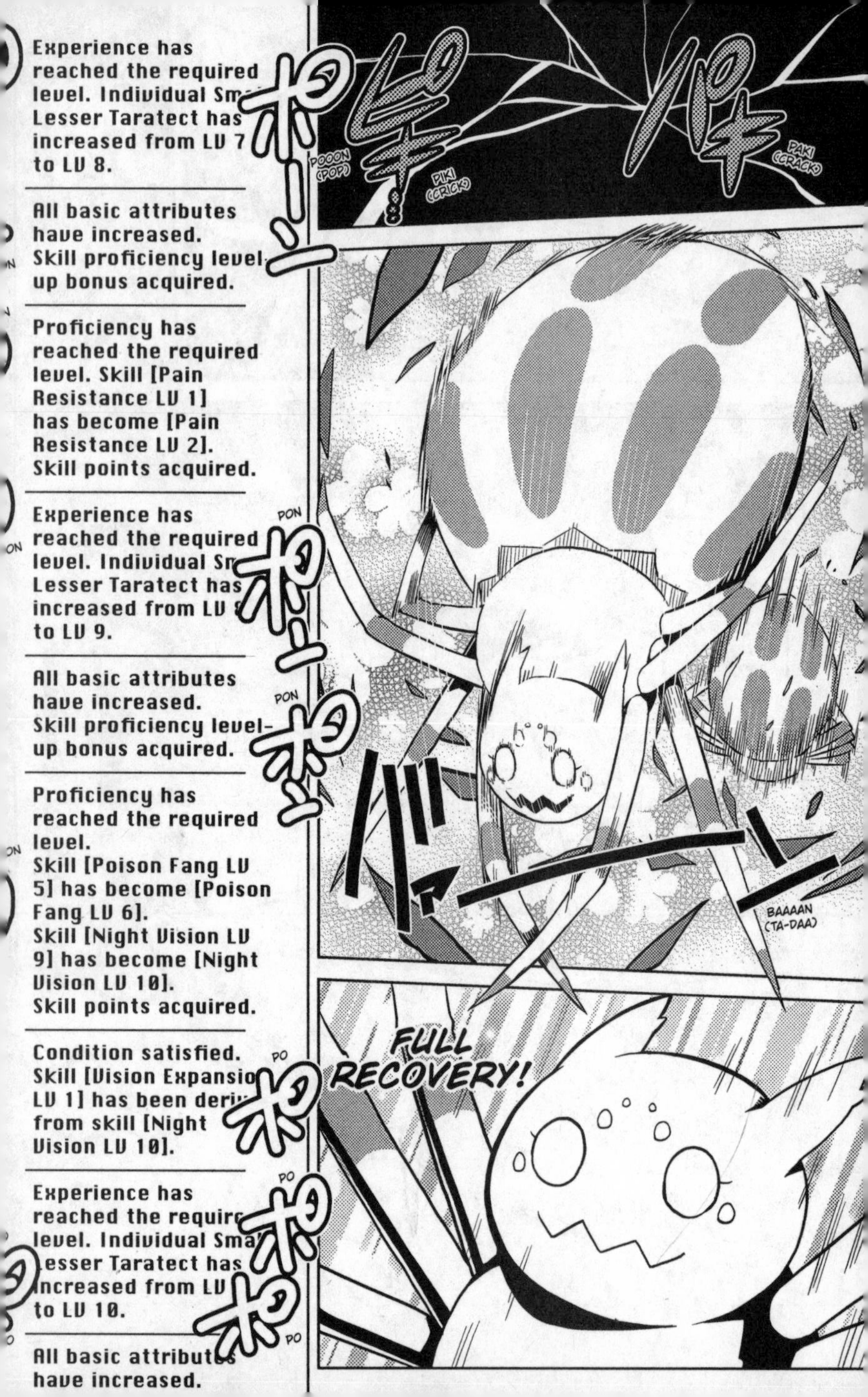
PAKI (CRACK)
PIKI (CRICK)
POOON (POP)
PON
PON
BAAAAN (TA-DAA)
FULL RECOVERY!
PO
PO
PO
Experience has reached the required level. Individual Sm Lesser Taratect has increased from LV 7 to LV 8.
All basic attributes have increased. Skill proficiency level-up bonus acquired.
Proficiency has reached the required level. Skill [Pain Resistance LV 1] has become [Pain Resistance LV 2]. Skill points acquired.
Experience has reached the required level. Individual Sm Lesser Taratect has increased from LV to LV 9.
All basic attributes have increased. Skill proficiency level-up bonus acquired.
Proficiency has reached the required level. Skill [Poison Fang LV 5] has become [Poison Fang LV 6]. Skill [Night Vision LV 9] has become [Night Vision LV 10]. Skill points acquired.
Condition satisfied. Skill [Vision Expansio LV 1] has been deri from skill [Night Vision LV 10].
Experience has reached the requir level. Individual Sma esser Taratect has ncreased from LV to LV 10.
All basic attribut have increased.

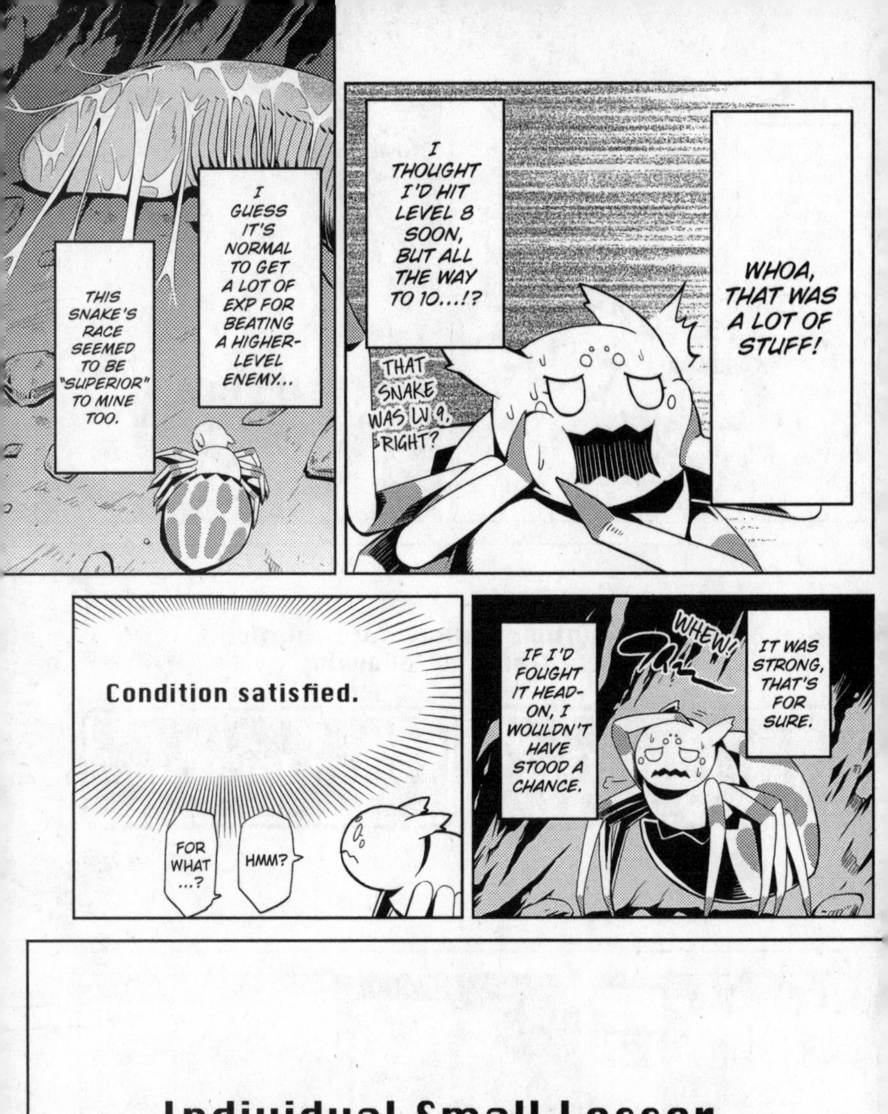
WHOA, THAT WAS A LOT OF STUFF!
I THOUGHT I'D HIT LEVEL 8 SOON, BUT ALL THE WAY TO 10...!?
THAT SNAKE WAS LV 9, RIGHT?
I GUESS IT'S NORMAL TO GET A LOT OF EXP FOR BEATING A HIGHER-LEVEL ENEMY...
THIS SNAKE'S RACE SEEMED TO BE "SUPERIOR" TO MINE TOO.
IT WAS STRONG, THAT'S FOR SURE.
WHEW!
IF I'D FOUGHT IT HEAD-ON, I WOULDN'T HAVE STOOD A CHANCE.
Condition satisfied.
HMM?
FOR WHAT ...?
Individual Small Lesser Taratect can now evolve.

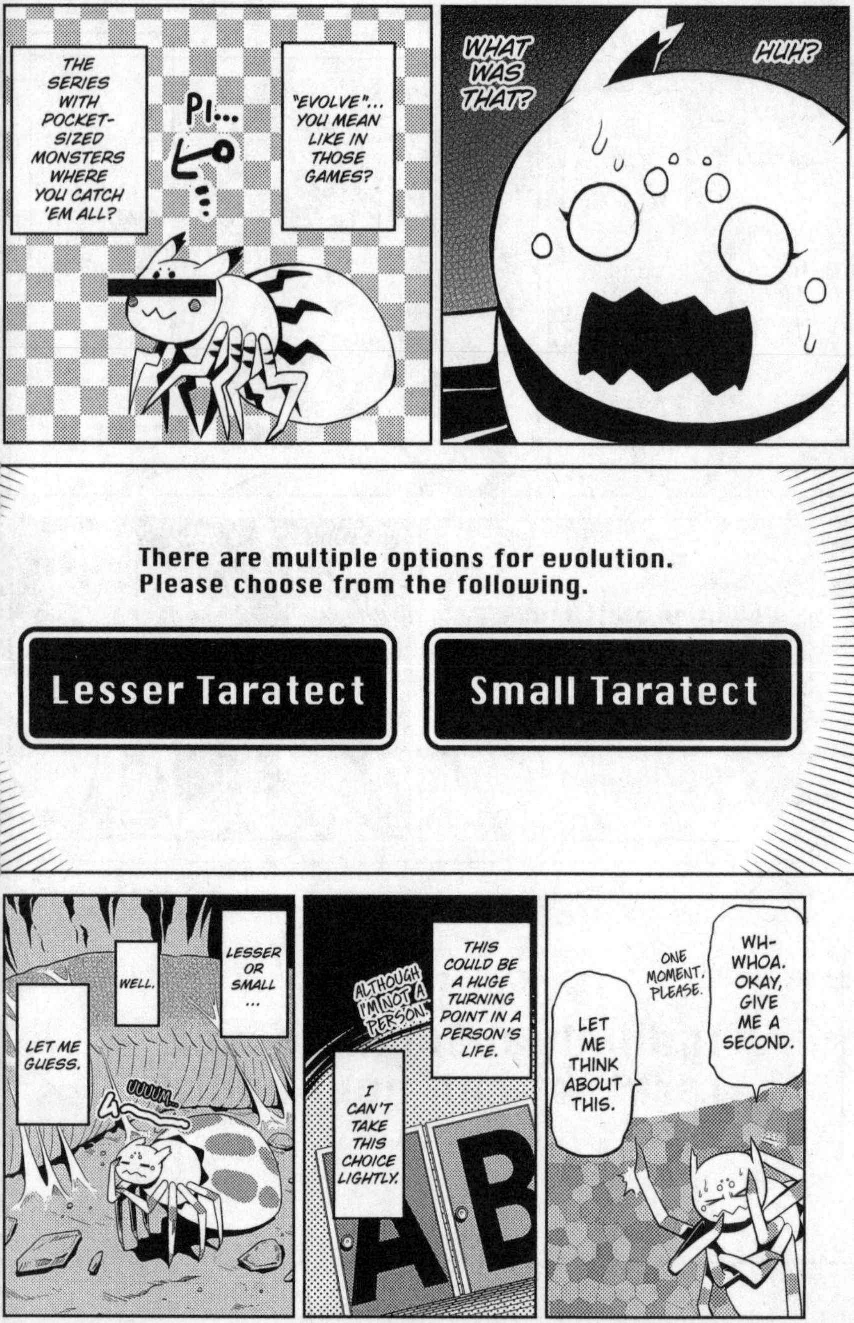
HUH?
WHAT WAS THAT?
"EVOLVE"... YOU MEAN LIKE IN THOSE GAMES?
PI...
THE SERIES WITH POCKET-SIZED MONSTERS WHERE YOU CATCH 'EM ALL?
There are multiple options for evolution.
Please choose from the following.
Lesser Taratect
Small Taratect
WH-WHOA. OKAY, GIVE ME A SECOND.
ONE MOMENT, PLEASE.
LET ME THINK ABOUT THIS.
THIS COULD BE A HUGE TURNING POINT IN A PERSON'S LIFE.
ALTHOUGH I'M NOT A PERSON.
I CAN'T TAKE THIS CHOICE LIGHTLY.
A
B
LESSER OR SMALL...
WELL.
LET ME GUESS.
UUUUM...

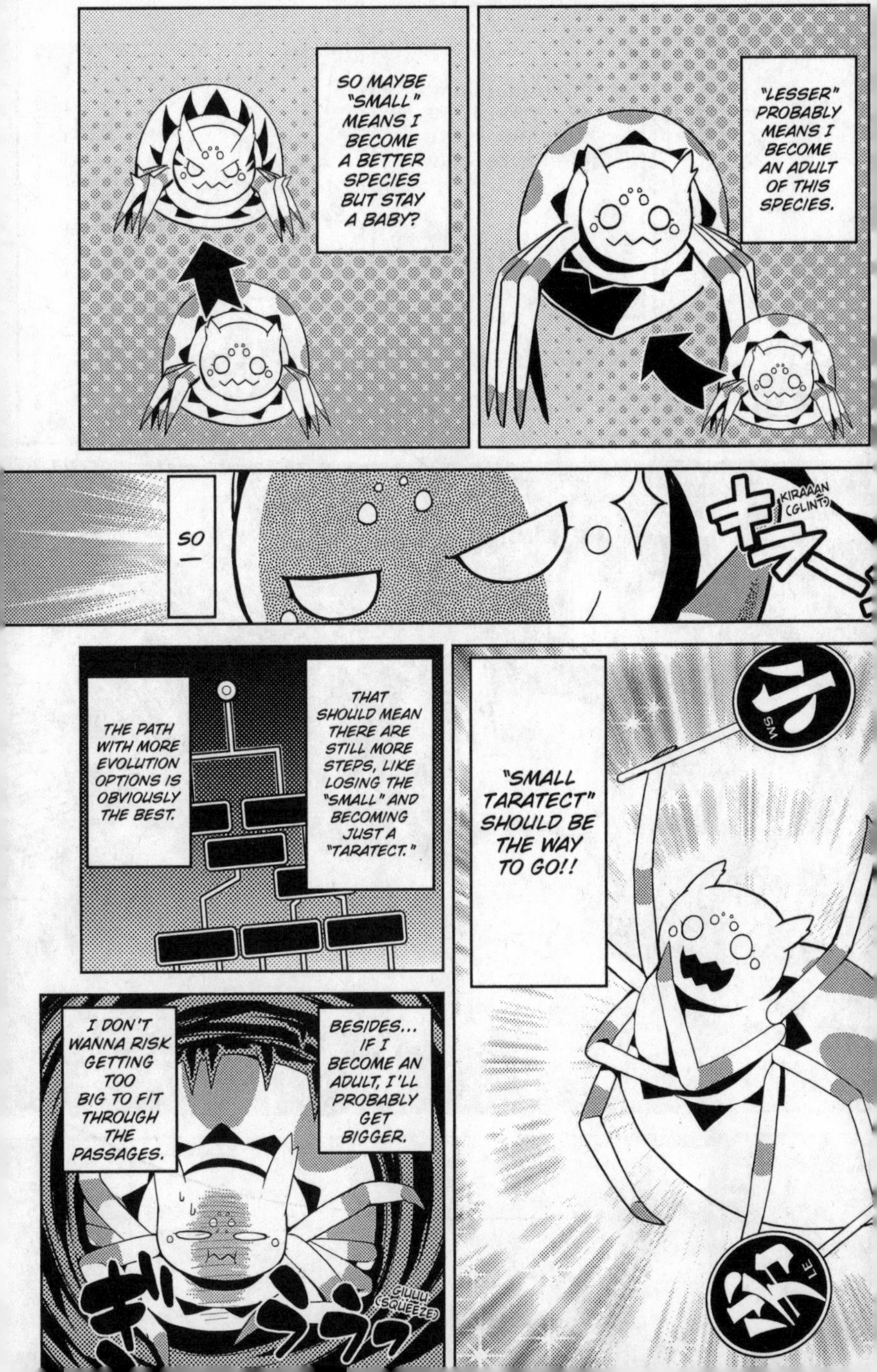
"LESSER" PROBABLY MEANS I BECOME AN ADULT OF THIS SPECIES.
SO MAYBE "SMALL" MEANS I BECOME A BETTER SPECIES BUT STAY A BABY?
KIRAAAN (GLINT)
SO —
"SMALL TARATECT" SHOULD BE THE WAY TO GO!!
THAT SHOULD MEAN THERE ARE STILL MORE STEPS, LIKE LOSING THE "SMALL" AND BECOMING JUST A "TARATECT."
THE PATH WITH MORE EVOLUTION OPTIONS IS OBVIOUSLY THE BEST.
BESIDES... IF I BECOME AN ADULT, I'LL PROBABLY GET BIGGER.
I DON'T WANNA RISK GETTING TOO BIG TO FIT THROUGH THE PASSAGES.
GIUUU (SQUEEZE)

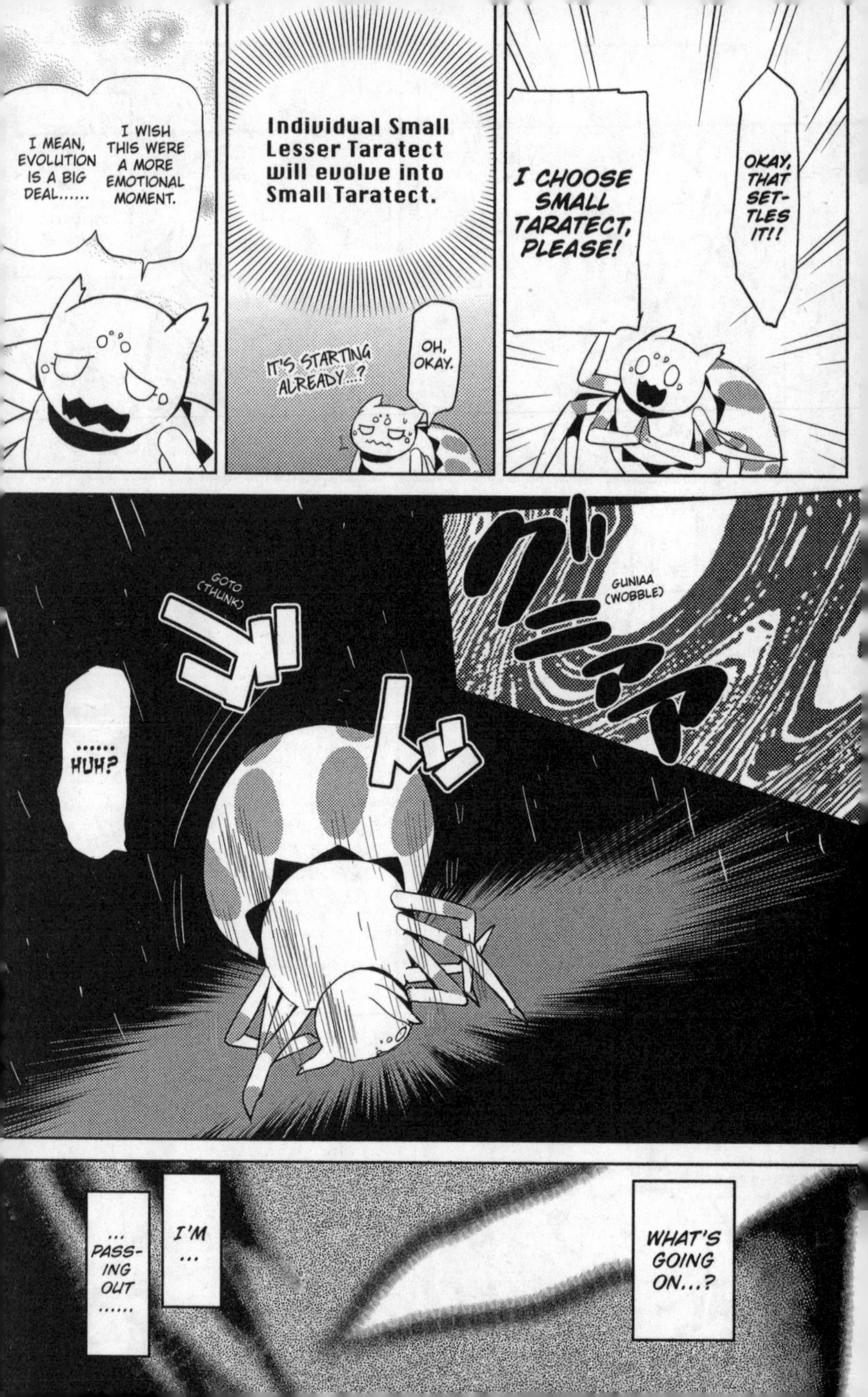
OKAY, THAT SETTLES IT!!
I CHOOSE SMALL TARATECT, PLEASE!
Individual Small Lesser Taratect will evolve into Small Taratect.
OH, OKAY.
IT'S STARTING ALREADY...?
I WISH THIS WERE A MORE EMOTIONAL MOMENT.
I MEAN, EVOLUTION IS A BIG DEAL......
GUNIAA (WOBBLE)
GOTO (THUNK)
......HUH?
WHAT'S GOING ON...?
I'M ...
... PASSING OUT ......

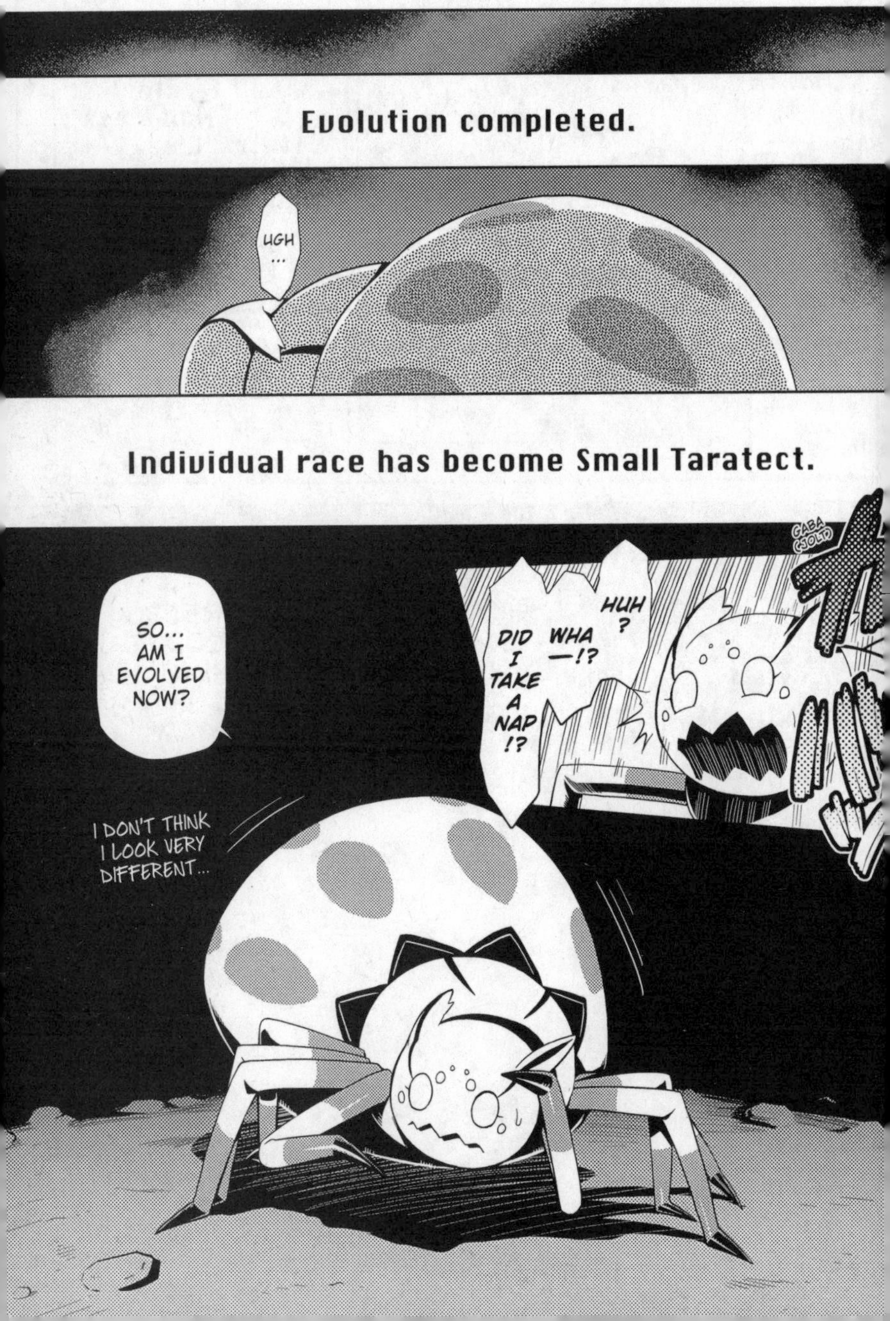
Evolution completed.
UGH...
Individual race has become Small Taratect.
GABA (JOLT)
HUH?
WHA—!?
DID I TAKE A NAP!?
SO... AM I EVOLVED NOW?
I DON'T THINK I LOOK VERY DIFFERENT...

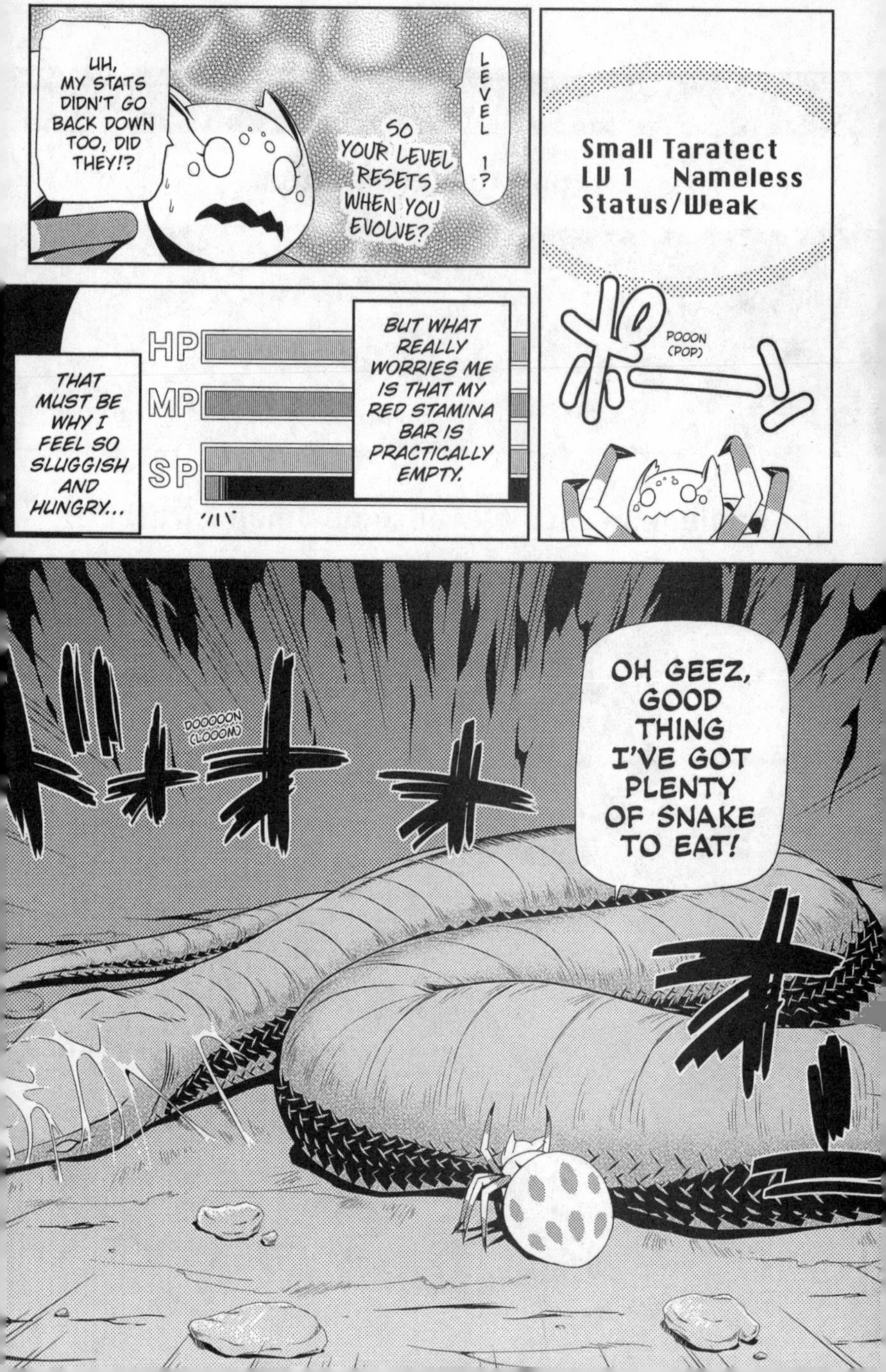
Small Taratect
LV 1 Nameless
Status/Weak
POOON (POP)
LEVEL 1?
SO YOUR LEVEL RESETS WHEN YOU EVOLVE?
UH, MY STATS DIDN'T GO BACK DOWN TOO, DID THEY!?
BUT WHAT REALLY WORRIES ME IS THAT MY RED STAMINA BAR IS PRACTICALLY EMPTY.
HP
MP
SP
THAT MUST BE WHY I FEEL SO SLUGGISH AND HUNGRY...
OH GEEZ, GOOD THING I'VE GOT PLENTY OF SNAKE TO EAT!
DOOOOON (LOOOM)

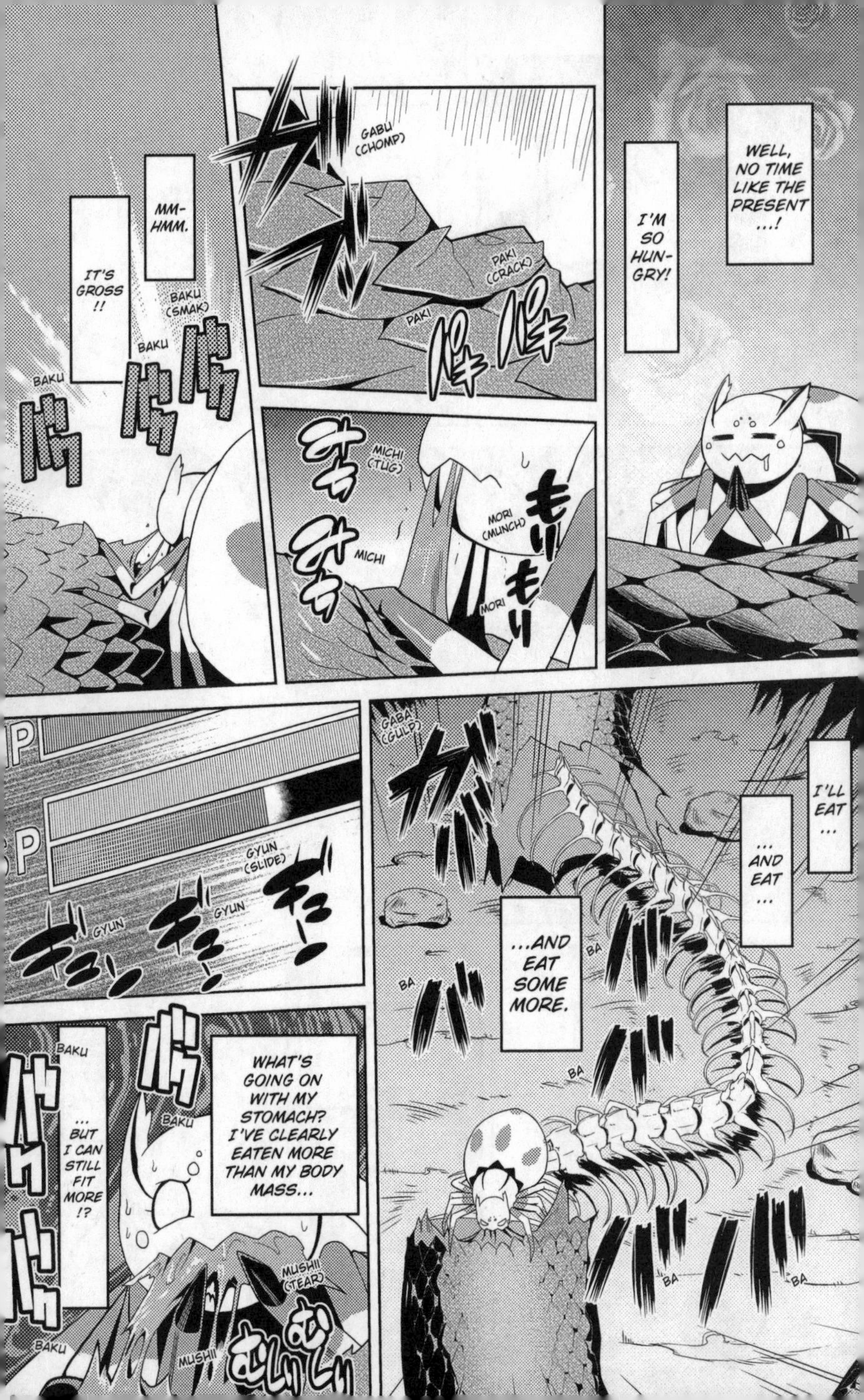
WELL, NO TIME LIKE THE PRESENT...!
I'M SO HUN-GRY!
GABU (CHOMP)
PAKI (CRACK)
PAKI
MICHI (TUG)
MICHI
MORI (MUNCH)
MORI
MM-HMM.
IT'S GROSS!!
BAKU (SMAK)
BAKU
BAKU
I'LL EAT...
...AND EAT...
...AND EAT SOME MORE.
GABA (GULP)
BA
BA
BA
BA
BA
P
P
GYUN (SLIDE)
GYUN
GYUN
WHAT'S GOING ON WITH MY STOMACH? I'VE CLEARLY EATEN MORE THAN MY BODY MASS...
...BUT I CAN STILL FIT MORE!?
BAKU
BAKU
MUSHI (TEAR)
MUSHI
BAKU

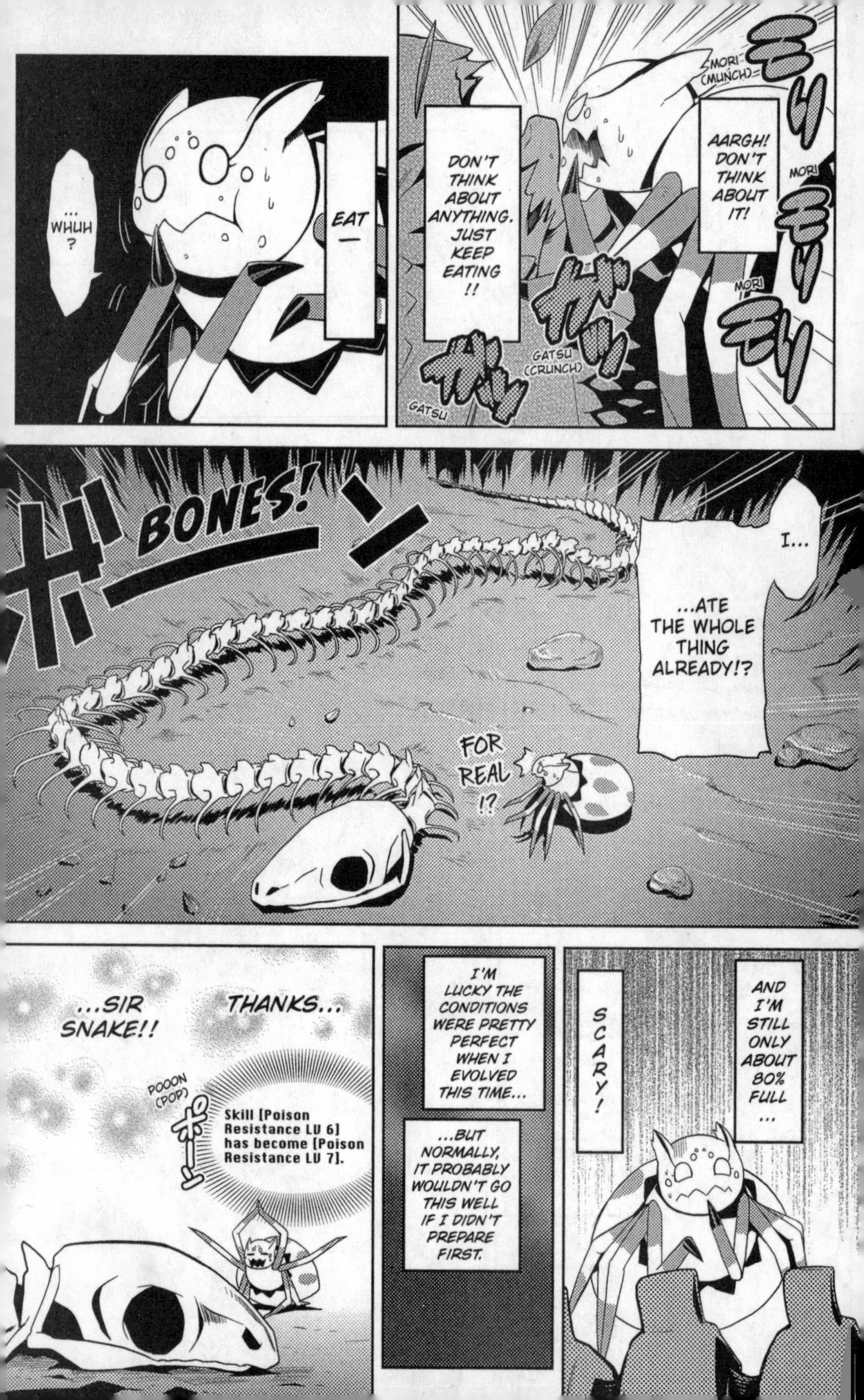

MORI (MUNCH)
AARGH! DON'T THINK ABOUT IT!
MORI
MORI
DON'T THINK ABOUT ANYTHING. JUST KEEP EATING!!
GATSU (CRUNCH)
GATSU
EAT—
...WHUH?
I...
...ATE THE WHOLE THING ALREADY!?
BONES!
FOR REAL!?
AND I'M STILL ONLY ABOUT 80% FULL...
SCARY!
I'M LUCKY THE CONDITIONS WERE PRETTY PERFECT WHEN I EVOLVED THIS TIME...
...BUT NORMALLY, IT PROBABLY WOULDN'T GO THIS WELL IF I DIDN'T PREPARE FIRST.
THANKS...
...SIR SNAKE!!
POOON (POP)
Skill [Poison Resistance LV 6] has become [Poison Resistance LV 7].

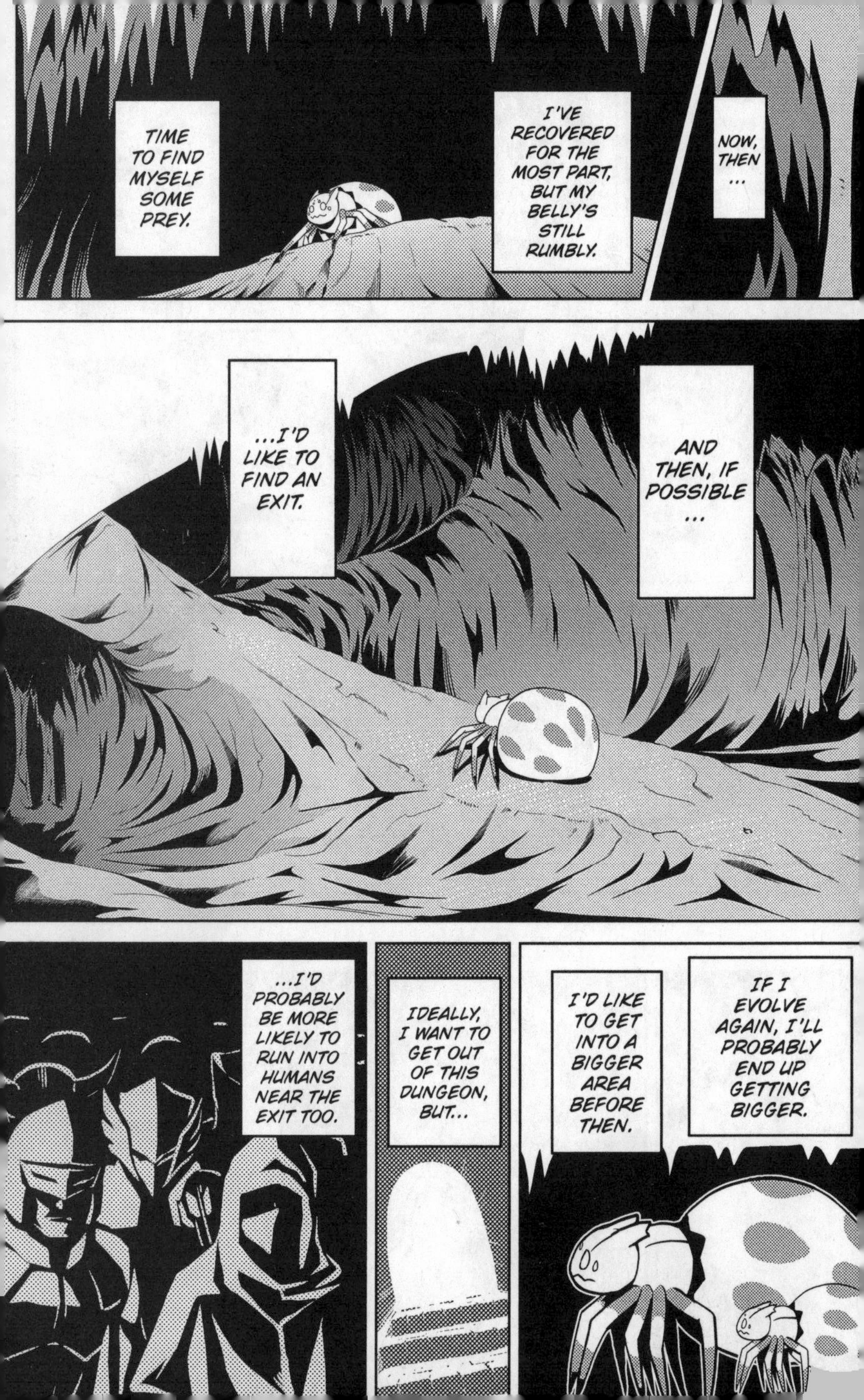
NOW, THEN ...
I'VE RECOVERED FOR THE MOST PART, BUT MY BELLY'S STILL RUMBLY.
TIME TO FIND MYSELF SOME PREY.
AND THEN, IF POSSIBLE ...
...I'D LIKE TO FIND AN EXIT.
IF I EVOLVE AGAIN, I'LL PROBABLY END UP GETTING BIGGER.
I'D LIKE TO GET INTO A BIGGER AREA BEFORE THEN.
IDEALLY, I WANT TO GET OUT OF THIS DUNGEON, BUT...
...I'D PROBABLY BE MORE LIKELY TO RUN INTO HUMANS NEAR THE EXIT TOO.

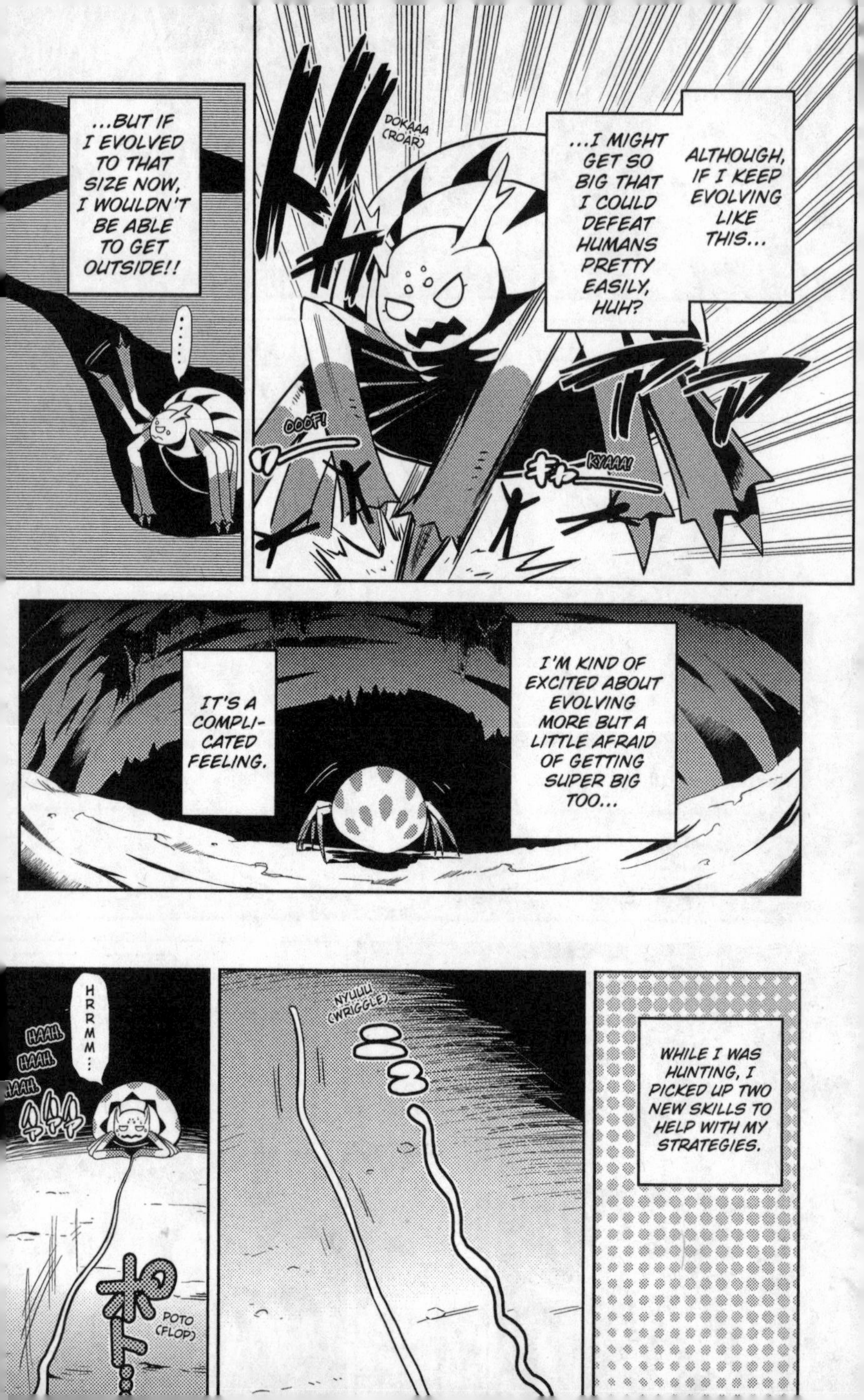
ALTHOUGH, IF I KEEP EVOLVING LIKE THIS...
...I MIGHT GET SO BIG THAT I COULD DEFEAT HUMANS PRETTY EASILY, HUH?
DOKAAA (ROAR)
KYAAA!
OOOF!
...BUT IF I EVOLVED TO THAT SIZE NOW, I WOULDN'T BE ABLE TO GET OUTSIDE!!
......
I'M KIND OF EXCITED ABOUT EVOLVING MORE BUT A LITTLE AFRAID OF GETTING SUPER BIG TOO...
IT'S A COMPLICATED FEELING.
WHILE I WAS HUNTING, I PICKED UP TWO NEW SKILLS TO HELP WITH MY STRATEGIES.
NYUUU (WRIGGLE)
HRRMM...
HAAH, HAAH, HAAH,
POTO (FLOP)

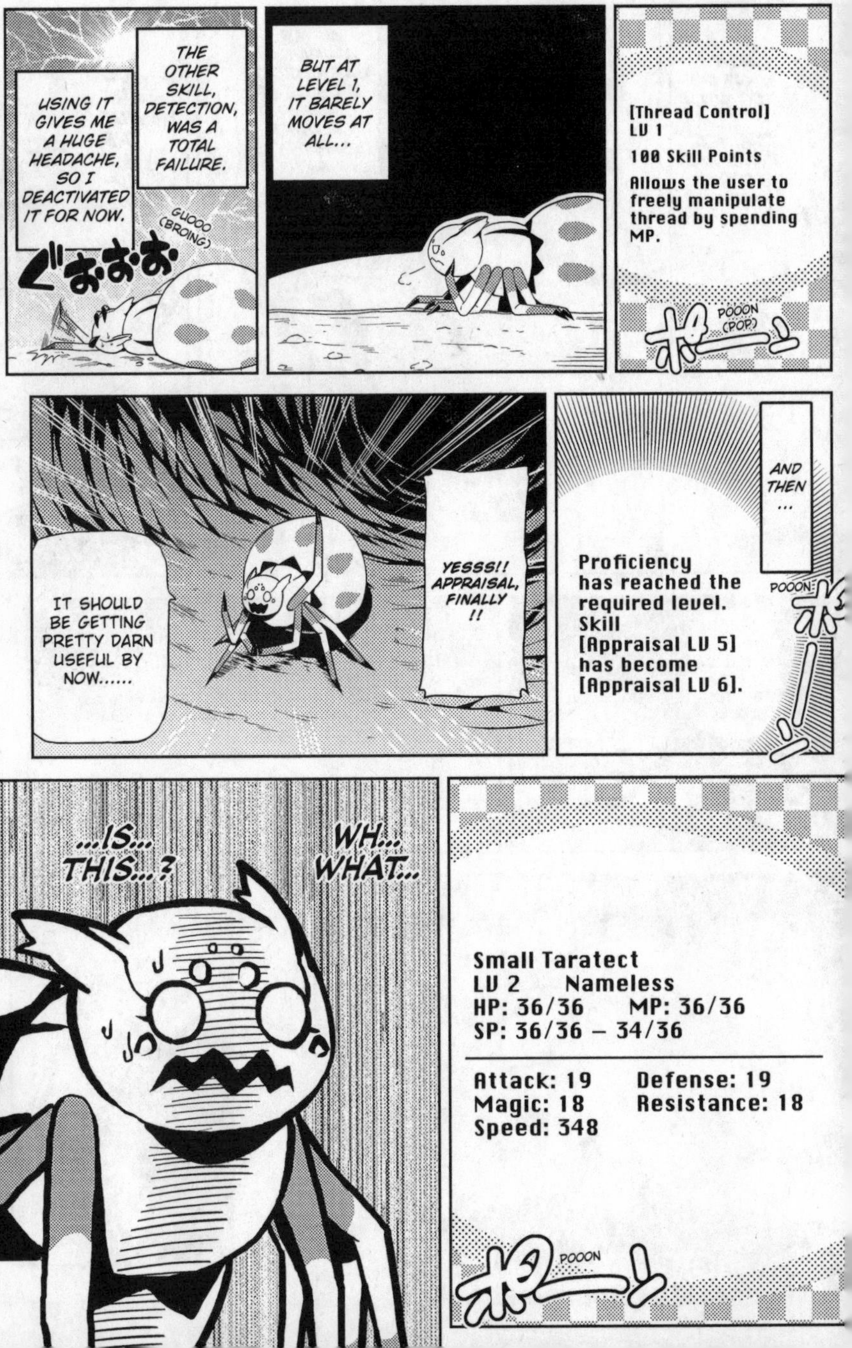
[Thread Control] LV 1
100 Skill Points
Allows the user to freely manipulate thread by spending MP.
POOON (POP)
BUT AT LEVEL 1, IT BARELY MOVES AT ALL...
THE OTHER SKILL, DETECTION, WAS A TOTAL FAILURE.
USING IT GIVES ME A HUGE HEADACHE, SO I DEACTIVATED IT FOR NOW.
GUOOO (BROING)
AND THEN...
Proficiency has reached the required level. Skill [Appraisal LV 5] has become [Appraisal LV 6].
POOON
YESSS!! APPRAISAL, FINALLY!!
IT SHOULD BE GETTING PRETTY DARN USEFUL BY NOW......
Small Taratect
LV 2 Nameless
HP: 36/36 MP: 36/36
SP: 36/36 – 34/36
Attack: 19 Defense: 19
Magic: 18 Resistance: 18
Speed: 348
POOON
WH... WHAT...
...IS... THIS...?

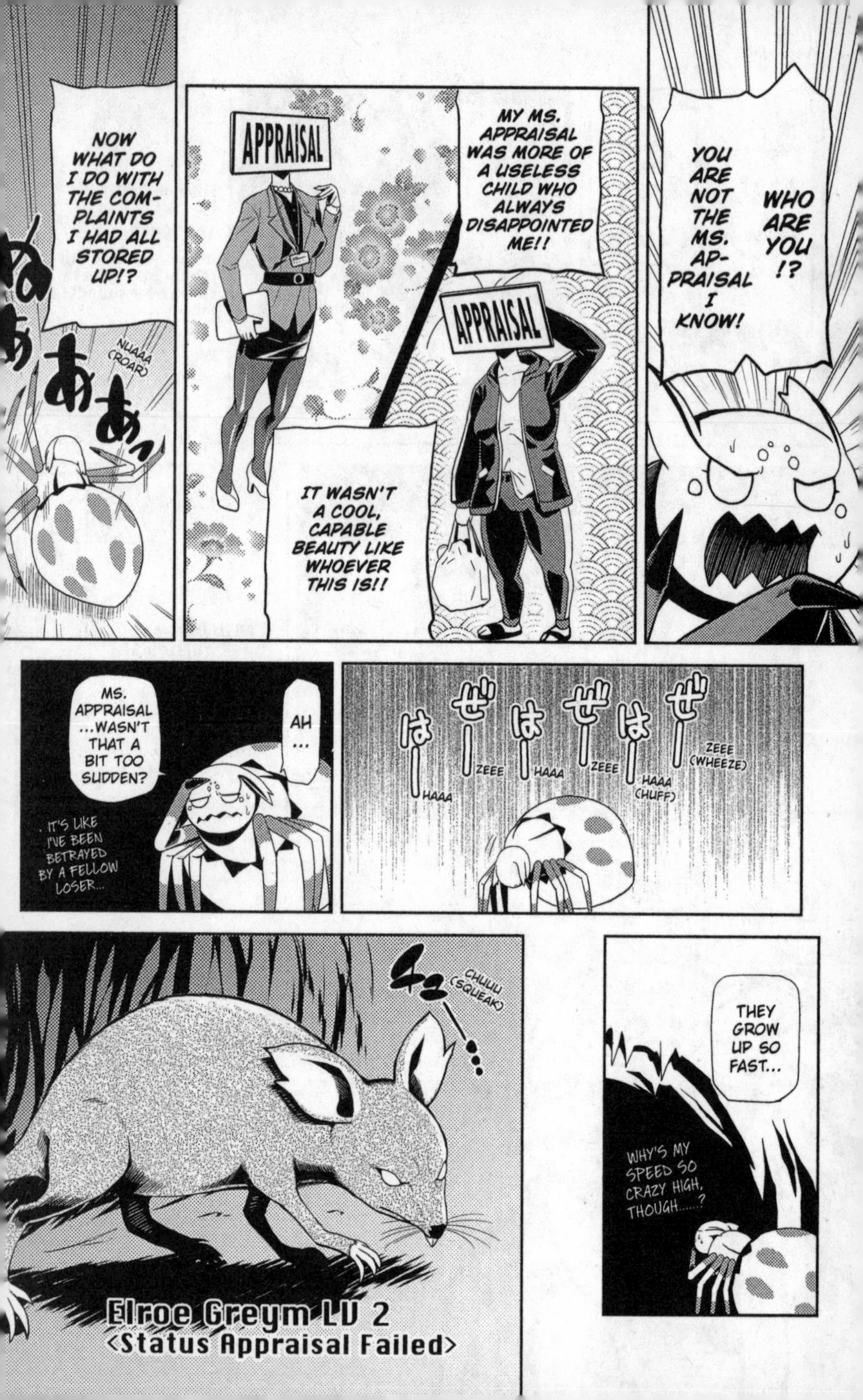
YOU ARE NOT THE MS. APPRAISAL I KNOW!
WHO ARE YOU!?
MY MS. APPRAISAL WAS MORE OF A USELESS CHILD WHO ALWAYS DISAPPOINTED ME!!
APPRAISAL
APPRAISAL
IT WASN'T A COOL, CAPABLE BEAUTY LIKE WHOEVER THIS IS!!
NOW WHAT DO I DO WITH THE COMPLAINTS I HAD ALL STORED UP!?
NUAAA (ROAR)
ZEEE (WHEEZE)
HAAA (CHUFF)
ZEEE
HAAA
ZEEE
HAAA
AH ...
MS. APPRAISAL ...WASN'T THAT A BIT TOO SUDDEN?
IT'S LIKE I'VE BEEN BETRAYED BY A FELLOW LOSER...
THEY GROW UP SO FAST...
WHY'S MY SPEED SO CRAZY HIGH, THOUGH......?
CHUUU (SQUEAK)
Elroe Greym LV 2
<Status Appraisal Failed>

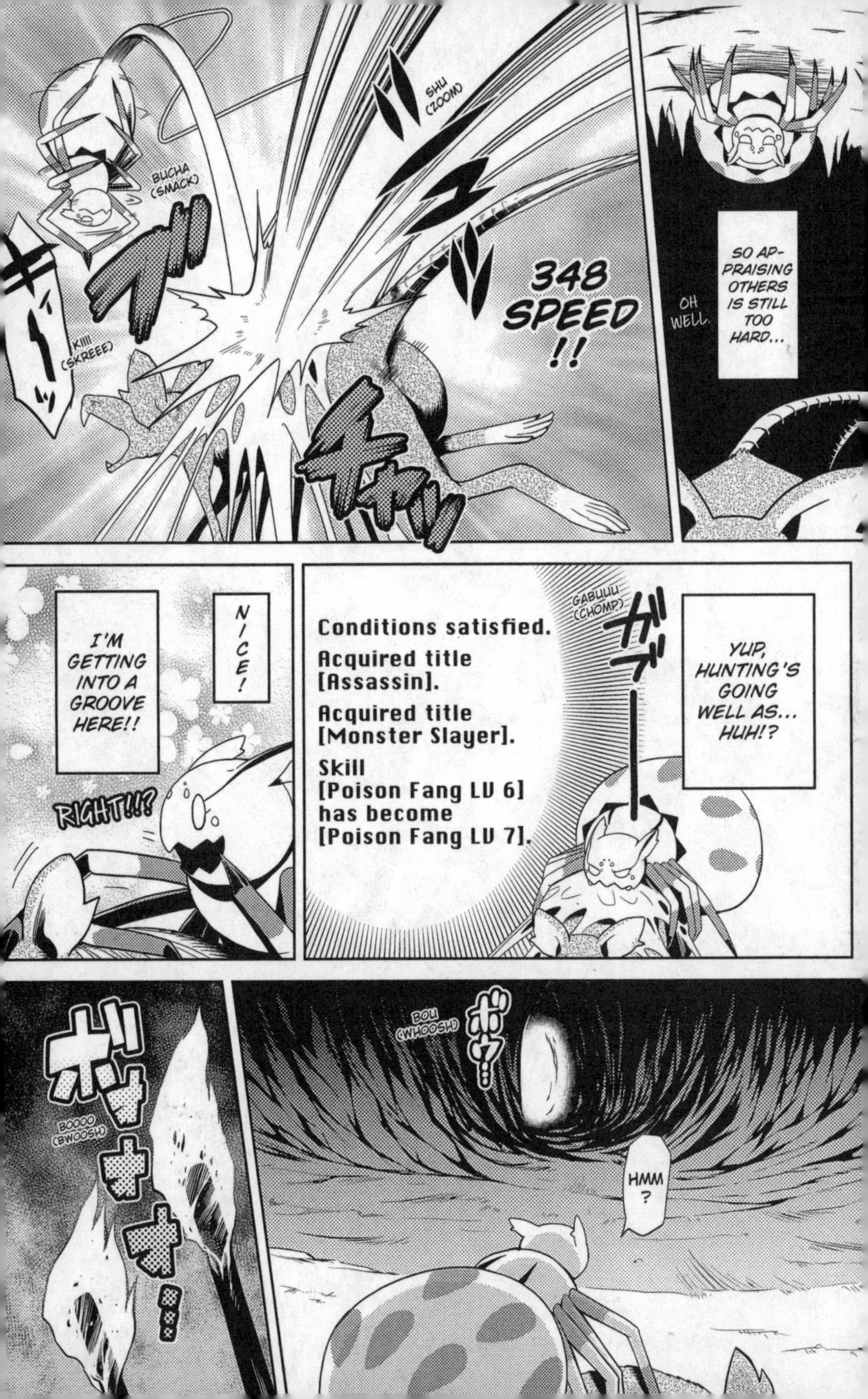
SO AP-PRAISING OTHERS IS STILL TOO HARD...
OH WELL.
SHU (ZOOM)
348 SPEED!!
BUCHA (SMACK)
KIIII (SKREEE)
GABUUU (CHOMP)
YUP, HUNTING'S GOING WELL AS... HUH!?
Conditions satisfied.
Acquired title [Assassin].
Acquired title [Monster Slayer].
Skill [Poison Fang LV 6] has become [Poison Fang LV 7].
NICE!
I'M GETTING INTO A GROOVE HERE!!
RIGHT!!?
BOU (WHOOSH)
HMM?
BOOOO (BWOOSH)

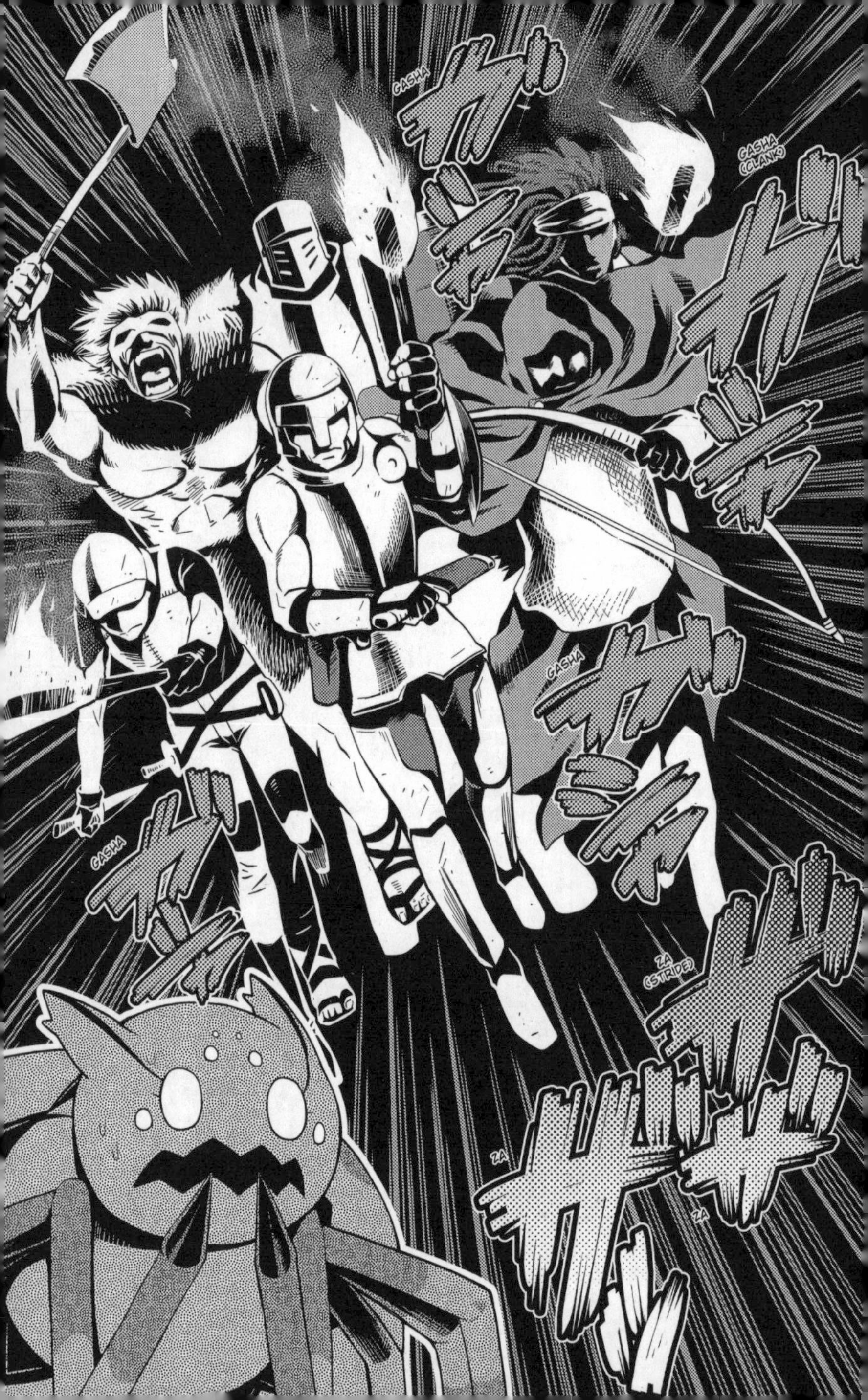
GASHA (CLANK)
GASHA
GASHA
GASHA
ZA (STRIDE)
ZA
ZA

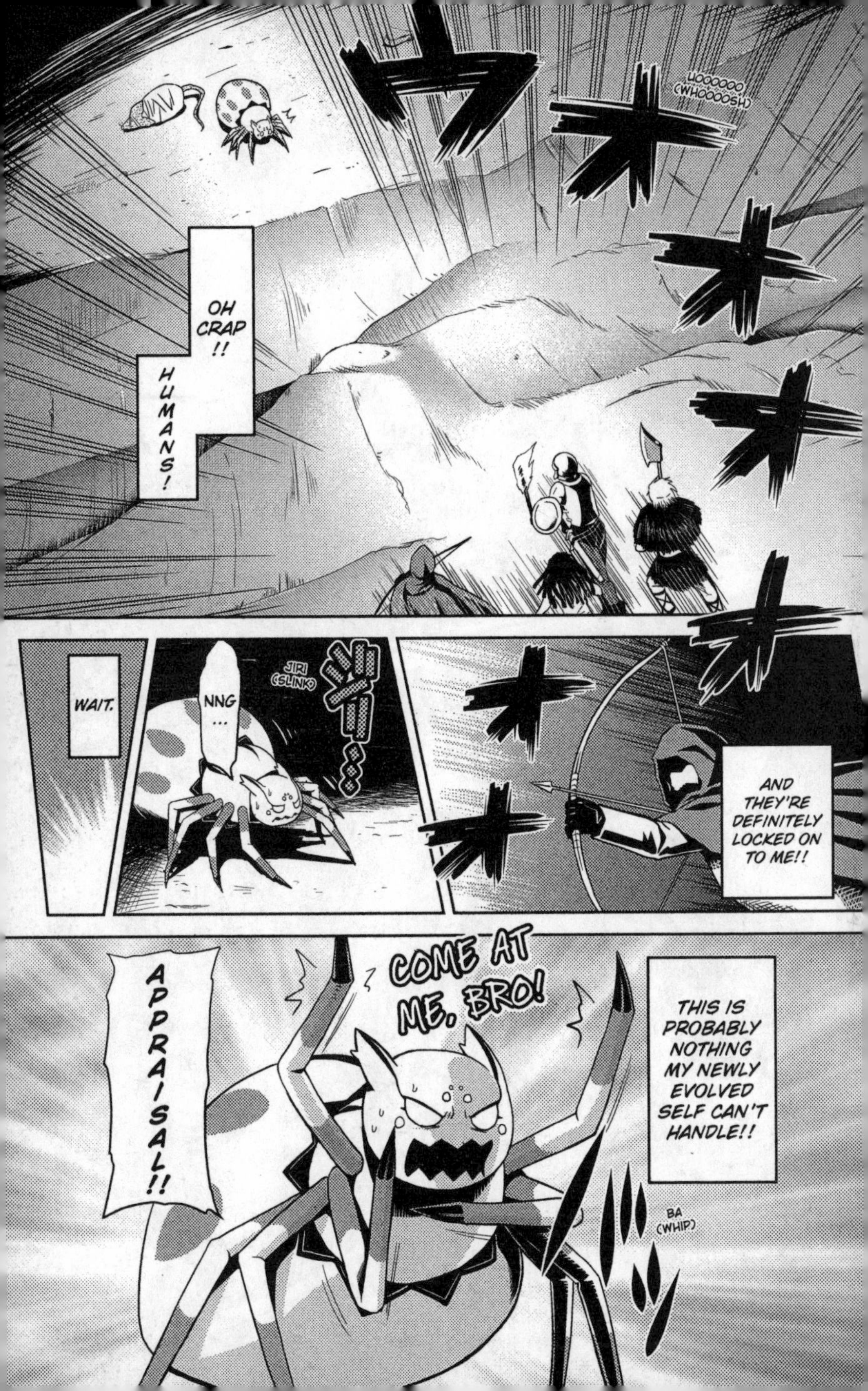
UOOOOOO
(WHOOOOSH)
OH CRAP!! HUMANS!
AND THEY'RE DEFINITELY LOCKED ON TO ME!!
JIRI
(SLINK)
NNG...
WAIT.
THIS IS PROBABLY NOTHING MY NEWLY EVOLVED SELF CAN'T HANDLE!!
BA
(WHIP)
COME AT ME, BRO!
APPRAISAL!!

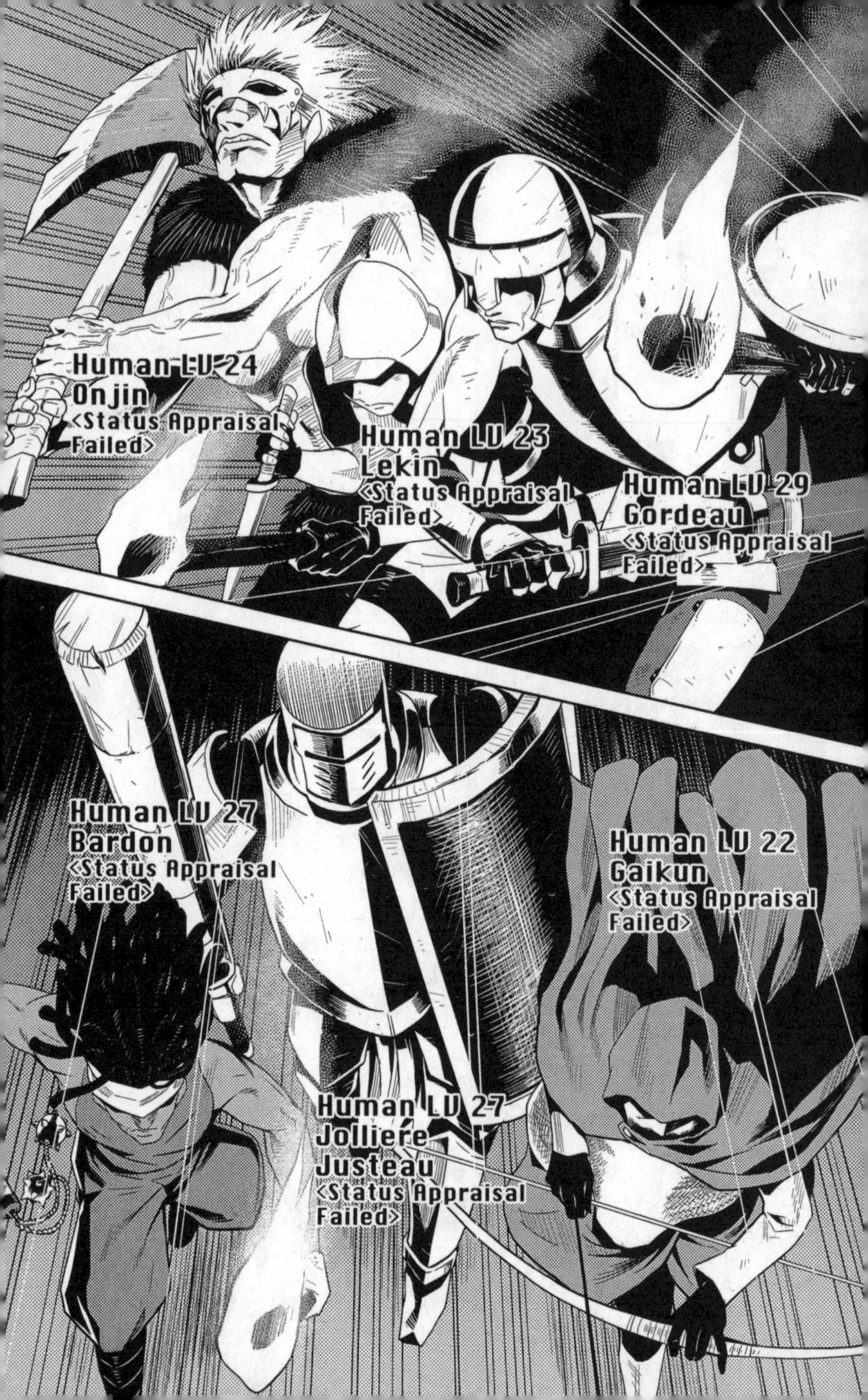
Human LV 29
Gordeau
<Status Appraisal
Failed>
Human LV 23
Lekin
<Status Appraisal
Failed>
Human LV 24
Onjin
<Status Appraisal
Failed>
Human LV 22
Gaikun
<Status Appraisal
Failed>
Human LV 27
Jolliere
Justeau
<Status Appraisal
Failed>
Human LV 27
Bardon
<Status Appraisal
Failed>

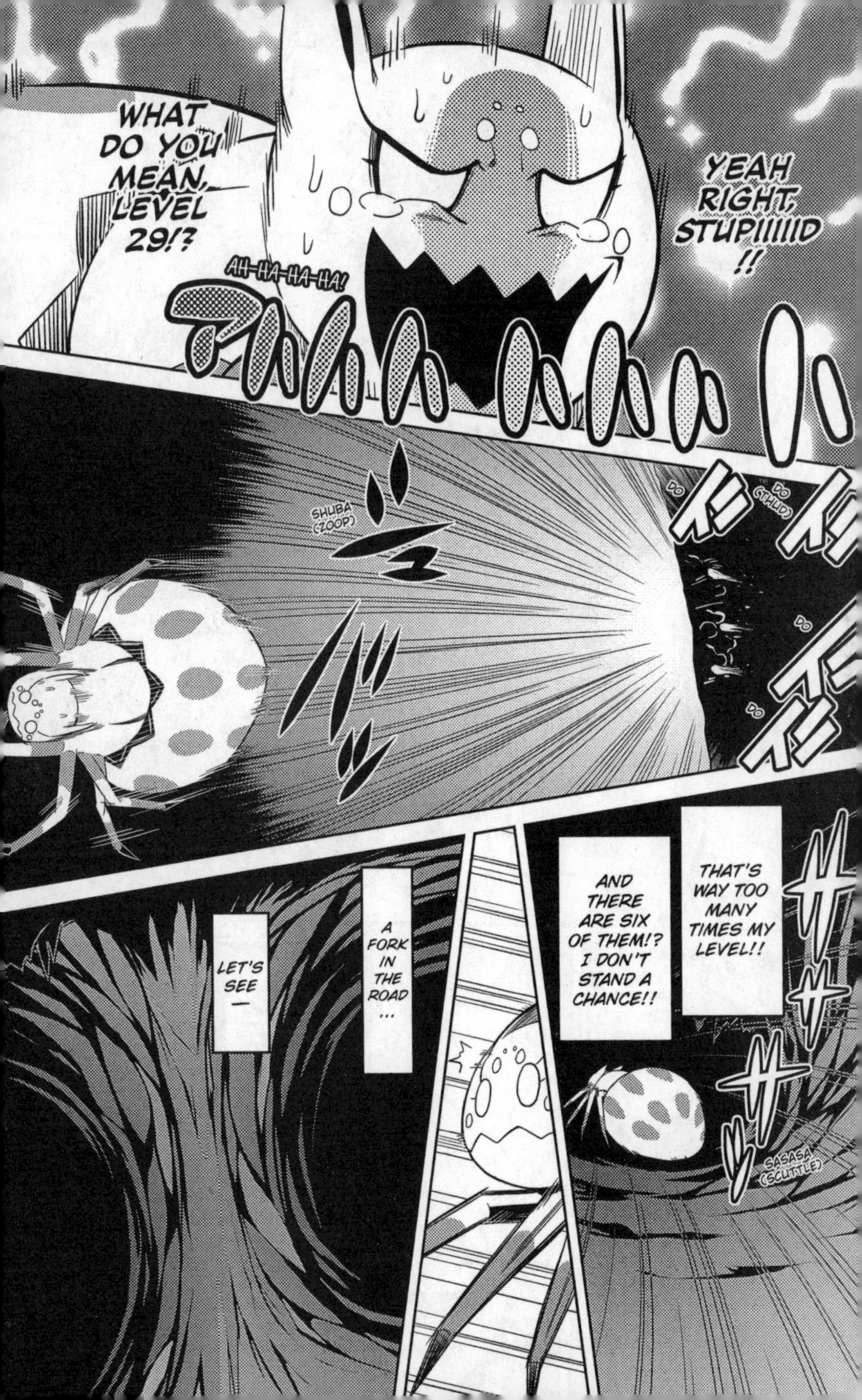
YEAH RIGHT, STUPIIIIIID!!
WHAT DO YOU MEAN, LEVEL 29!?
AH-HA-HA-HA!
DO DO (THUD)
DO DO
SHUBA (ZOOP)
THAT'S WAY TOO MANY TIMES MY LEVEL!!
AND THERE ARE SIX OF THEM!? I DON'T STAND A CHANCE!!
A FORK IN THE ROAD...
LET'S SEE—
SASASA (SCUTTLE)

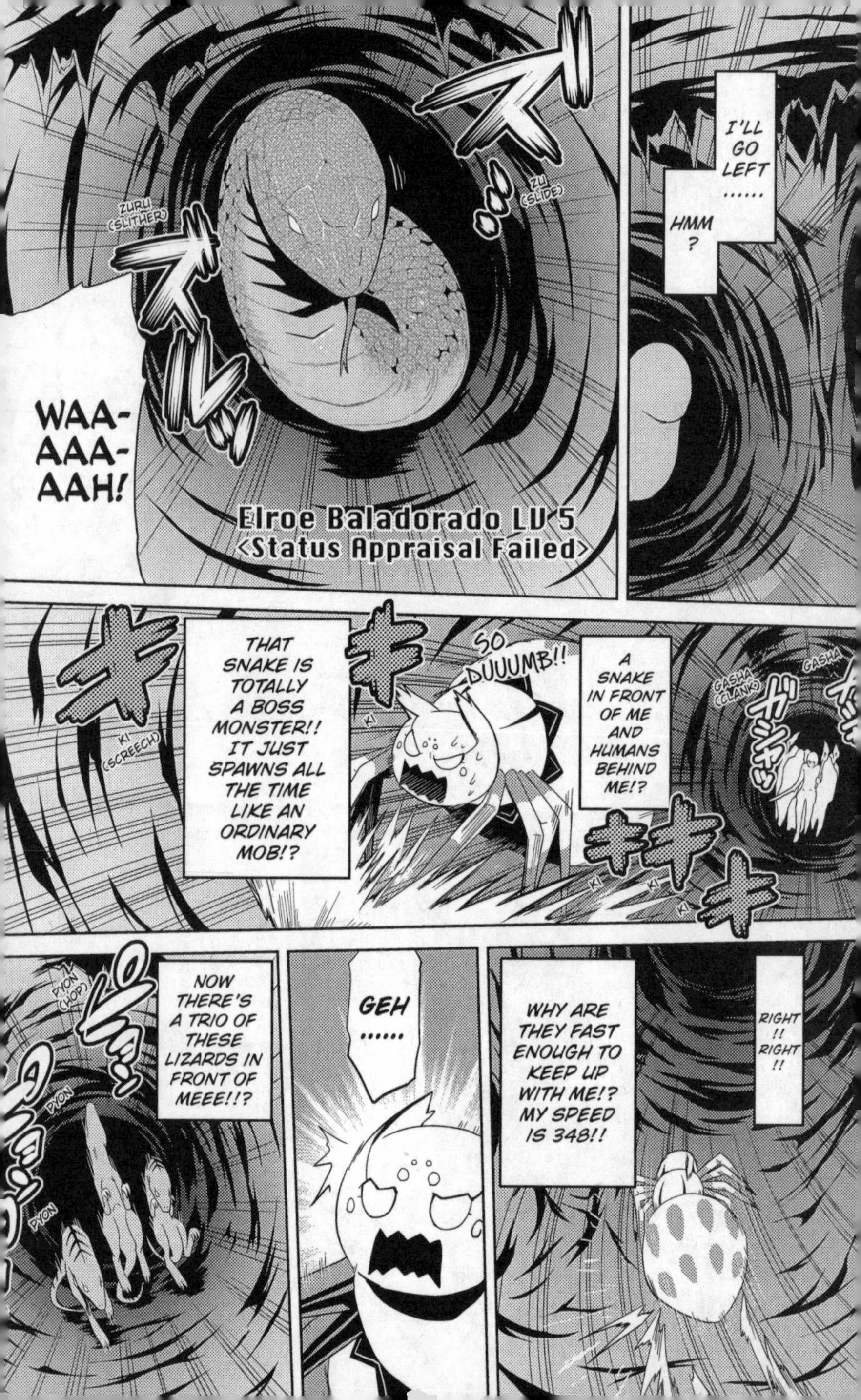
I'LL GO LEFT ......
HMM ?
ZU (SLIDE)
ZURU (SLITHER)
WAA-AAA-AAH!
Elroe Baladorado LV 5
<Status Appraisal Failed>
GASHA
GASHA (CLANK)
A SNAKE IN FRONT OF ME AND HUMANS BEHIND ME!?
SO DUUUMB!!
KI
KI
KI
KI
THAT SNAKE IS TOTALLY A BOSS MONSTER!! IT JUST SPAWNS ALL THE TIME LIKE AN ORDINARY MOB!?
KI (SCREECH)
RIGHT!! RIGHT!!
WHY ARE THEY FAST ENOUGH TO KEEP UP WITH ME!? MY SPEED IS 348!!
GEH ......
NOW THERE'S A TRIO OF THESE LIZARDS IN FRONT OF MEEE!!?
PYON (HOP)
PYON
PYON

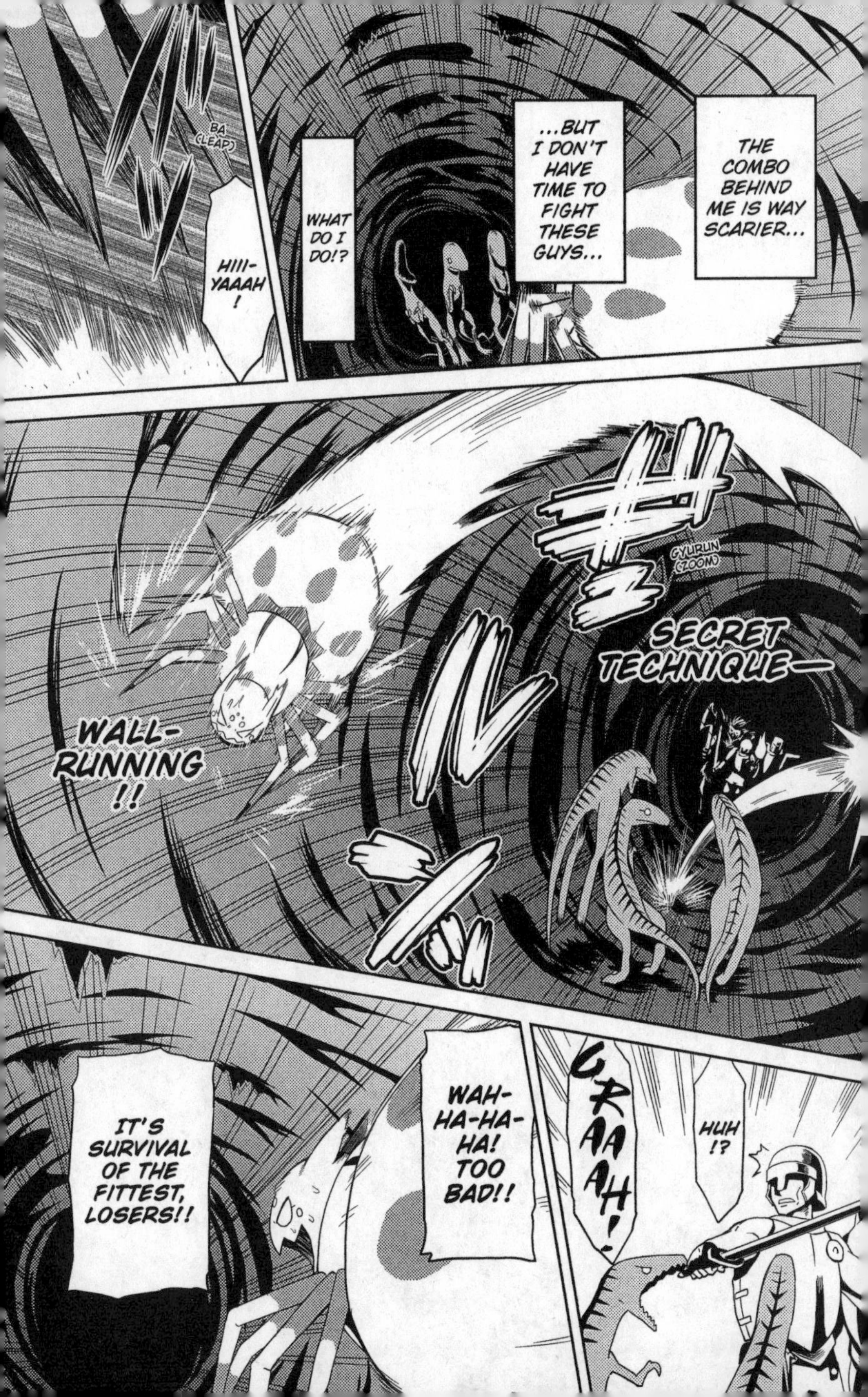
THE COMBO BEHIND ME IS WAY SCARIER...
...BUT I DON'T HAVE TIME TO FIGHT THESE GUYS...
WHAT DO I DO!?
BA (LEAP)
HIII-YAAAH!
GYURUN (ZOOM)
SECRET TECHNIQUE—
WALL-RUNNING!!
HUH!?
URAAAH!
WAH-HA-HA-HA! TOO BAD!!
IT'S SURVIVAL OF THE FITTEST, LOSERS!!

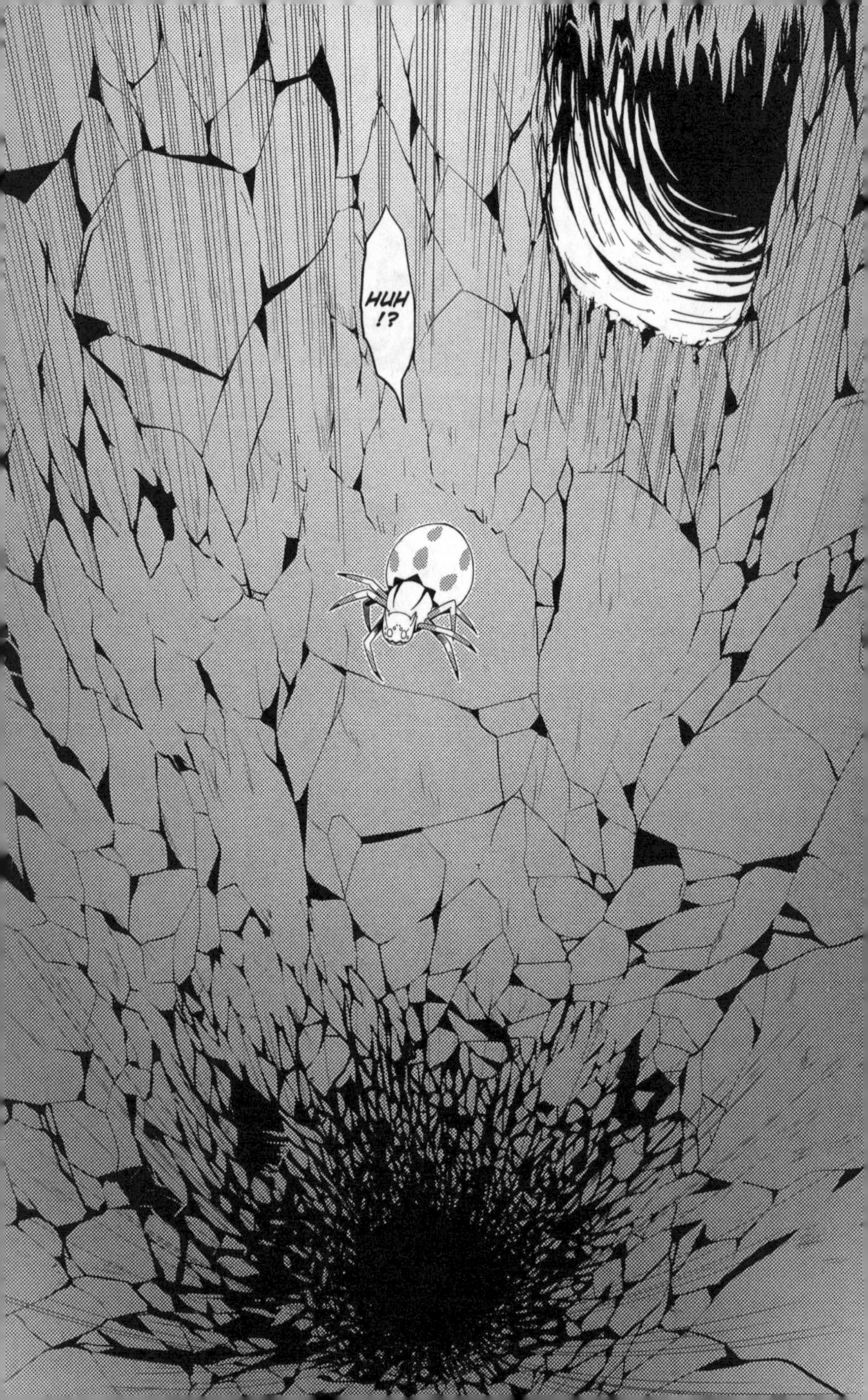
HUH!?

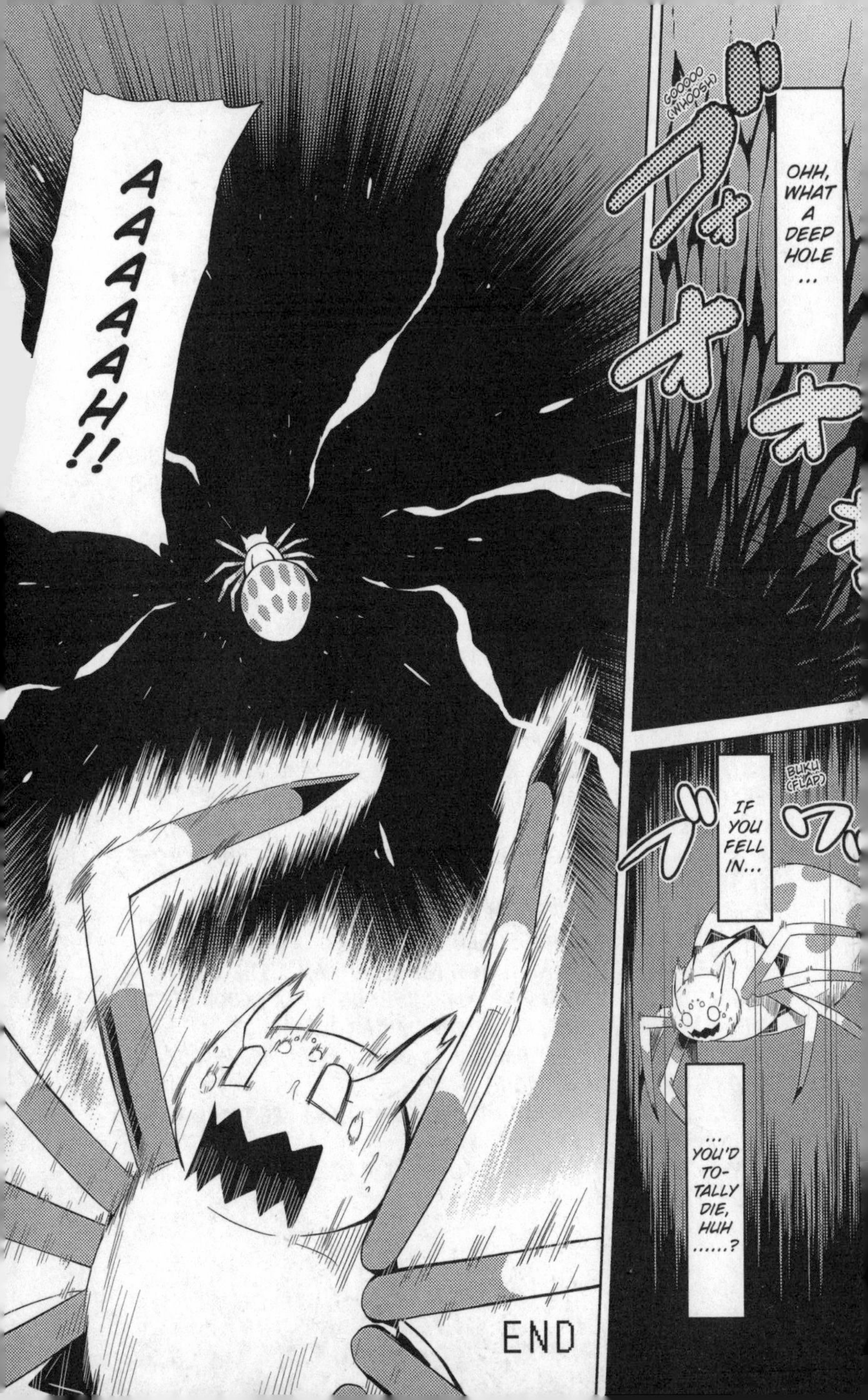
GOOOOO (WHOOSH)
OHH, WHAT A DEEP HOLE...
BUKU (FLAP)
IF YOU FELL IN...
...YOU'D TO-TALLY DIE, HUH......?
AAAAAAH!!
END

AFTERWORD

ORIGINAL CREATOR: OKINA BABA

HELLO. I'M OKINA BABA, AND I WROTE THE ORIGINAL STORY THIS MANGA IS BASED ON.

SINCE THE PROTAGONIST IS A SPIDER, WHICH SURELY NOBODY WOULD EVER BE INTERESTED IN, I NEVER EVEN DREAMED THE STORY MIGHT BECOME A MANGA SOMEDAY.

AND AS SOMEONE WHOSE ONLY SKILL IS WRITING, I COULD ONLY IMAGINE HOW DIFFICULT IT WOULD PROBABLY BE TO DRAW A MANGA OF MY STORY.

THE MAIN CHARACTER IS A SPIDER, AND EVERYTHING ELSE IS MONSTERS — THERE ARE HARDLY ANY HUMANS AT ALL.
MOST IMPORTANTLY, THERE AREN'T ANY CUTE GIRLS.

THE PROTAGONIST?

I DON'T KNOW IF YOU CAN REALLY COUNT HER...

SO I HAVE TO SALUTE KAKASHI-SENSEI, WHO MANAGED TO OVERCOME ALL THAT AND MAKE THIS ENTIRE FIRST VOLUME!

AS THE ORIGINAL CREATOR, I GOT TO CHECK OVER THE THUMBNAILS FOR APPROVAL, BUT I OKAYED THEM WITHOUT QUESTION ALMOST EVERY TIME.

YES, I DEFINITELY HAD FAITH THAT EVERYTHING WOULD BE FINE IF I LEFT IT UP TO KAKASHI-SENSEI!

BY THE WAY, NOT THAT IT MATTERS, BUT AM I THE ONLY ONE WHO CAN'T HELP IMAGINING A FARMHOUSE WHENEVER I LOOK AT THE NAMES KAKASHI (SCARECROW) AND OKINA (OLD MAN)?

I'M SURE BY NEXT VOLUME WE'LL BE PLOWING FIELDS FOR NO REASON AT ALL! (NO WE WON'T.)

ANYWAY, I HOPE THIS FARMHOUSE COMBO CAN KEEP TELLING AN EXCITING SPIDER STORY.

PLEASE CONTINUE TO SUPPORT BOTH THE MANGA AND THE ORIGINAL NOVELS. THANK YOU.

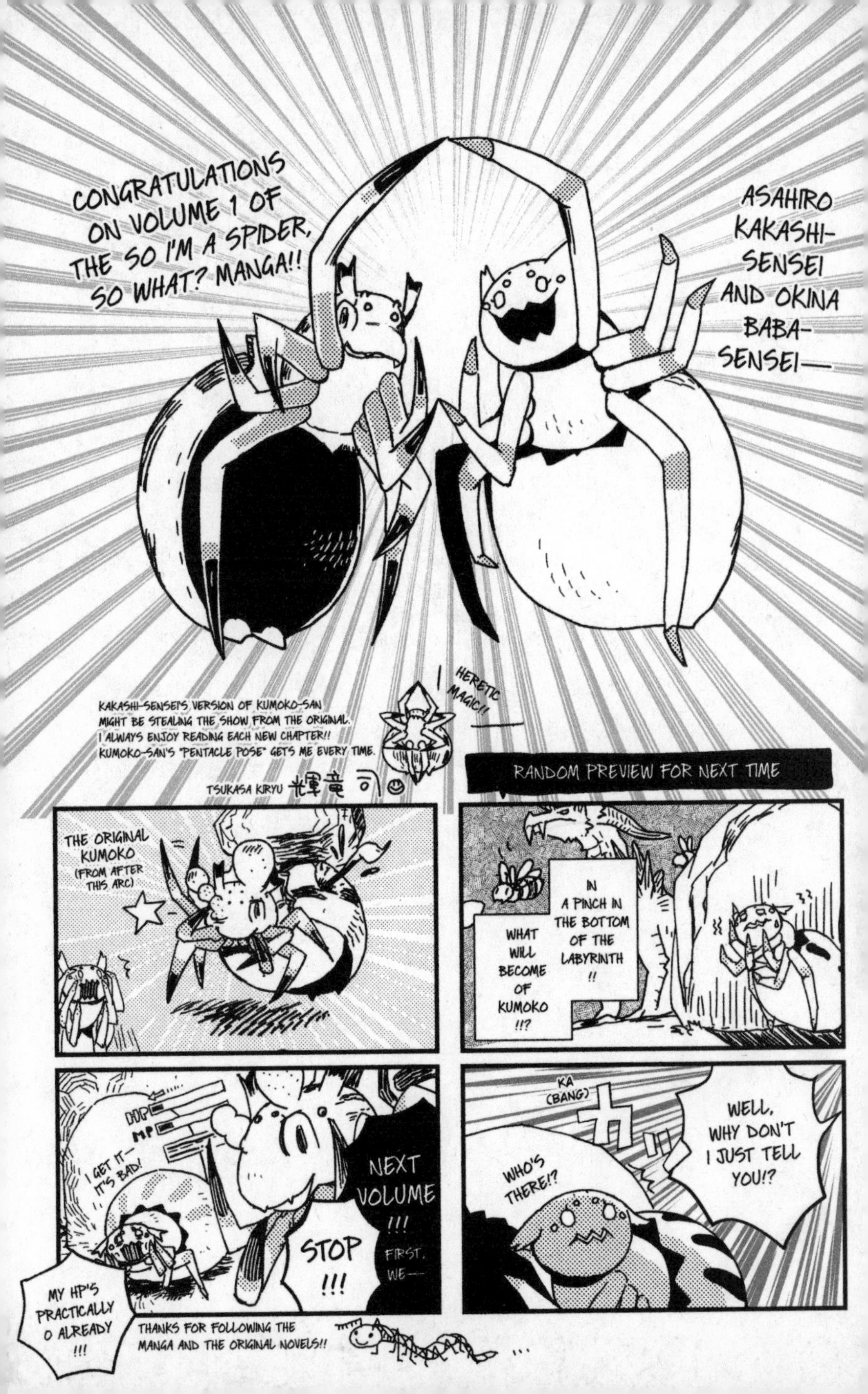
ASAHIRO KAKASHI-SENSEI AND OKINA BABA-SENSEI—
CONGRATULATIONS ON VOLUME 1 OF THE SO I'M A SPIDER, SO WHAT? MANGA!!
HERETIC MAGIC!!
KAKASHI-SENSEI'S VERSION OF KUMOKO-SAN MIGHT BE STEALING THE SHOW FROM THE ORIGINAL. I ALWAYS ENJOY READING EACH NEW CHAPTER!! KUMOKO-SAN'S "PENTACLE POSE" GETS ME EVERY TIME.
TSUKASA KIRYU 輝竜 司
RANDOM PREVIEW FOR NEXT TIME
IN A PINCH IN THE BOTTOM OF THE LABYRINTH!!
WHAT WILL BECOME OF KUMOKO!!?
THE ORIGINAL KUMOKO (FROM AFTER THIS ARC)
WELL, WHY DON'T I JUST TELL YOU!?
KA (BANG)
WHO'S THERE!?
NEXT VOLUME!!!
FIRST, WE—
STOP!!!
HP
MP
I GET IT— IT'S BAD!
MY HP'S PRACTICALLY 0 ALREADY!!!
THANKS FOR FOLLOWING THE MANGA AND THE ORIGINAL NOVELS!!
...

You're reading
the wrong way!
Turn the page to read
a bonus short story by
So I'm a Spider, So What?
original creator,
Okina Baba!

But while I'm having an inner conversation with myself, the frog suddenly spasms violently.

The movement surprises me so much that I twitch a bit myself.

But afterward, I start feeling afraid.

The frog convulses again and again.

I can't help but be a little fascinated by this strange development.

What's this? What's going on?

Right before my eyes, the frog starts shriveling up...almost like all the liquid is being drained out of its body.

Then, just like that, the flower pops out of its head.

The plant unfurls its roots, which look more like alien tentacles that nobody under eighteen should be allowed to see.

GYAAAAAAAAH!!

Gross! Creepy! Geez!

As I stand there trembling in fear, the flower casually sinks its roots into the ground.

With the tendrils hidden, it just looks like an ordinary flower.

Just a thin little flower, sprouting neatly out of the ground next to a dried-up frog.

You'll have to forgive me if I shamelessly flee for my life.

Nobody wants to see a "tentacle X spider" scenario, especially not me!

The next day, I saw more of these parasitic flowers growing throughout the labyrinth, as well as herbivorous monsters feeding on them, but I didn't dare get any closer.

<Elroe wiris: A plant-type monster that lives in the Great Elroe Labyrinth. The flower that grows on its upper half is camouflage, while the lower portion is its true form. When the flower portion is eaten, there is a small possibility it will become a parasite, and if the body of the host fails to resist its intrusion, the seed will sprout and consume the host from the inside out. Even so, the flower grows back quite quickly, so it is an important source of food for herbivorous monsters in the labyrinth.>

[The end]

Can you really eat that?

Does it taste any good?

I mean, I was shocked at seeing monsters taking a bite out of some rocks lying around or the wall or whatever.

I didn't try it myself, of course.

This stomachache is probably just my imagination. Yeah.

If you think about it logically, there's no way for me to digest minerals and stuff like that.

Well, I can't, but apparently, there are some monsters that can live off that just fine.

In which case, they never have to worry about starving to death.

I'm kinda jealous.

Not that I'm going to try it myself. Seriously, I mean it.

Anyway, one mineral-eating species is apparently called the small rock turtle.

As the name implies, their shells seem to be made of rock, and as long as nothing attacks them, they generally just sit around chewing on stone.

Also, it turns out the Elroe basilisk, which has petrification powers, and even those frogs I've gotten so used to can both eat minerals.

The basilisk makes sense, really. It turns its prey to rock anyway, so it has to be able to eat them.

And I guess since the frogs have acid abilities, they can eat the stuff if they absolutely need to, but they don't seem to enjoy it.

I've only ever seen a frog eat boulders once, so maybe they only do it if they've exhausted every other option?

I mean, I'm sure rocks don't taste very good.

That being said, poisonous monsters taste gross, too, so I couldn't tell you which is worse.

Anyway, on the subject of those frogs I've come to know so well, the one I'm looking at now has something I've never seen before.

A flower.

For some reason, this frog has a flower growing out of its head.

What's up with that?

Is this a new fashion trend?

I don't think you can blame me for forgetting to attack and just gaping at it instead.

Why is the first flower I've ever seen in this world growing out of a frog's face?

I mean, it's not just on its head. It's definitely growing out of it, yeah?

So I'm a Spider, So What?
The Labyrinth's Frightening Food Chain
Okina Baba

I'm pretty much constantly wondering what's going on with the food chain in this dungeon.

Like, seriously, all kinds of monsters live here, and it's not as though every last one can be 100-percent carnivore, right?

There are some deer-looking monsters that are probably herbivores, and I've seen some other things out and about that I seriously doubt are meat eaters.

My assumptions aren't totally based on appearances, either. It's more that I don't know how this ecosystem could realistically function if everything in it is a carnivore.

I mean, in that case, the strongest monsters would eat the less powerful ones, and those guys would eat stuff even weaker than them, etcetera, etcetera—but then, wouldn't the weakest species get wiped out right away?

And the next monster in the chain would go extinct, too, and so on down the line, but clearly, that's not the case.

I'm easy pickings myself, but there are tons of relatively powerless monsters who seem to survive all right.

Plus, humans come here and hunt even though they're not natural predators, so surely, this dungeon must have some kind of system that nurtures living things.

I know this world resembles video games with stats and skills galore, but I still hatched from an egg, so there must be other monsters here that were born normally, too.

They don't just randomly spawn into existence, or at least, I don't think they do.

In which case, I'd like to know what the noncarnivorous monsters in this labyrinth eat.

One answer turns out to actually be the labyrinth itself.

Much to my surprise, I've seen creatures just chewing away on rocks.

So I'm a Spider, So What?

Art: **Asahiro Kakashi**

Original Story: **Okina Baba**

Character Design: **Tsukasa Kiryu**

Translation: Jenny McKeon ✴ Lettering: Bianca Pistillo

This book is a work of fiction. Names, characters, places, and incidents are the product of the author's imagination or are used fictitiously. Any resemblance to actual events, locales, or persons, living or dead, is coincidental.

Kumo desuga, nanika? Volume 1
© Asahiro KAKASHI 2016
© Okina Baba, Tsukasa Kiryu 2016
First published in Japan in 2016 by KADOKAWA CORPORATION, Tokyo.
English translation rights arranged with KADOKAWA CORPORATION, Tokyo,
through TUTTLE-MORI AGENCY, INC.

English translation © 2017 by Yen Press, LLC

Yen Press
150 West 30th Street, 19th Floor
New York, NY 10001

Visit us at yenpress.com
facebook.com/yenpress
twitter.com/yenpress
yenpress.tumblr.com
instagram.com/yenpress

First Yen Press Edition: December 2017

Yen Press is an imprint of Yen Press, LLC.
The Yen Press name and logo are trademarks of Yen Press, LLC.

The publisher is not responsible for websites (or their content)
that are not owned by the publisher.

Library of Congress Control Number: 2017954138

ISBNs: 978-0-316-41419-7 (paperback)
978-0-316-52107-9 (ebook)

10 9 8 7 6 5 4

BVG

Printed in the United States of America